COGNITIVE SKILLS AND THEIR ACQUISITION

COGNITIVE SKILLS AND THEIR ACQUISITION

Edited by

JOHN R. ANDERSON

CARNEGIE-MELLON UNIVERSITY

LEA LAWRENCE ERLBAUM ASSOCIATES, PUBLISHERS
1981 Hillsdale, New Jersey

Lawrence Erlbaum Associates, Inc., Publishers
365 Broadway
Hillsdale, New Jersey 07642

Library of Congress Cataloging in Publication Data
Symposium on Cognition, 16th, Carnegie-Mellon Uni-
    versity, 1980.
    Cognitive skills and their acquisitions.
    Bibliography: p.
    Includes index.
    1. Cognition—Congresses.   2. Learning, Psychology
of—Congresses.   I. Anderson, John Robert, 1947–
II. Title.   [DNLM: 1. Cognition—Congresses.   2. Learning
—Congresses.   W3 C126B 16th 1980c / BF 311 C6785 1980]
BF311.S83 1980   153.4   80-28702
ISBN 0-89859-093-0

Printed in the United States of America

Contents

Preface

This book is a collection of the papers presented at the Sixteenth Annual Carnegie Symposium on Cognition, held in May 1980. A couple of years earlier Pat Langley and Bob Neches persuaded the psychology department about the need to have a symposium on the topic of learning, and I was recruited to organize the Symposium. I too was persuaded that the time was ripe for a new attack on issues of learning. In separating itself from behaviorism, cognitive psychology had abandoned interest in learning and for 20 years had focused on understanding the performance of established cognitive skills. As a consequence we have acquired a fair knowledge of cognitive mechanisms, but this knowledge of performance is both disjointed and hard to use in educational applications. Learning theory offers both the potential of achieving a new degree of generality in our understanding of human cognition and the possibility of opening the way for applications. Given our much more sophisticated understanding of cognition, we can hope that learning mechanisms can be developed that avoid the weaknesses of past learning theories. The need for a new learning theory and potential of such a learning theory is discussed at length in the Langley and Simon chapter.

In the past few years there has developed a number of exciting new endeavors at understanding learning. I invited what I thought were among the best practitioners of this new approach to learning, and they all accepted. The symposium promised to be exciting and it was. It turned out that our ideas about learning were more similar than I had expected, given what a broad domain of phenomena might fit under the topic. In particular, we were interested in cognitive skills and how they develop in complex environments over long periods of practice. Moreover, we found we were using similar manipulations, choosing similar types of skills for study, finding similar results, and proposing similar theoretical mechanisms.

I have simply ordered the papers into chapters as they were presented in the conference. It seems unwise to try to organize these chapters into subgroups concerned with various topics. The problem is that there are so many shared themes running through these chapters that there are multiple possible classification schemes. I leave it to the reader to decide what the most salient dimensions are. Perhaps, presented in this order the reader can get a sense for some of the excitement we felt at the Symposium presentations as we waited to hear what each presenter had to say.

Newell and Rosenbloom look at the ubiquitous power law that relates time to perform a task to amount of practice. They show how difficult it is to derive the power law but are able to show how it might be derived from a set of assumptions about chunking and variability in the environment. Neves and Anderson look at what we call knowledge compilation processes that are responsible for the specialization of procedures to particular tasks and for the creation of larger operators in a production system framework. This is related to the power law and to various behaviors associated with automaticity. Clayton Lewis presents an analysis of the differences (or lack of differences) between the algebraic skills of expert mathematicians and students of varying strengths. He also shows how various speedups in performance of algebraic operations cannot be explained by composition learning mechanisms assumed both by Newell and Rosenbloom and by Neves and Anderson.

Shiffrin and Dumais provide a review of their extensive research concerned with the development of automaticity and a theoretical discussion of the distinction between controlled and automatic processing. They also describe some experimental investigations of why consistency is critical to the development of automaticity. Chase and Ericsson provide a description of their marvelous subject who has trained his memory span to over 80 digits. They also provide a careful theoretical analysis of the memory skills underlying this feat, challenging some of the established notions about human memory.

Anderson, Greeno, Kline, and Neves provide an analysis of the development of the problem-solving skills that underlie proof generation in geometry. We try to identify the learning processes responsible for the initial understanding and encoding of the skill, its speedup, and the tuning of the proof search with practice. Hayes-Roth, Klahr, and Mostow analyze the kind of learning that is involved in taking advice. Typically, a considerable amount of analysis is required before advice can be converted into an executable procedure. Jeffries, Turner, Polson, and Atwood consider the differences between experts and novices at software design. They argue that experts have acquired a design schema that enables them successfully to decompose a design problem into subproblems.

De Kleer and Brown provide an analysis of the kinds of representations and

processes needed to reason about mechanisms. This analysis is critical to understanding how people can learn simply by running mental simulations of processes
and trying to troubleshoot problems that come up in the mental simulations.
Larkin provides an analysis of the mechanisms underlying solving physics problems and how one becomes more expert in this domain. Critical to her learning
analysis is the idea that working-forward productions are created that embellish a
problem representation with information that previously had to be obtained by
working backward. Rumelhart and Norman are concerned with how new
schemata can be created out of analogy to existing schemata. They provide both a
discussion of the mechanisms underlying the analogical process and an application of this process to explaining confusions students have in learning to use a
text editor.

Finally, we have the chapter by Simon and Langley. Theirs is not a symposium commentary, although the chapter does make comments on the Symposium papers. In their chapter they provide an analysis of why there is this
renewed interest in learning, why it is a central problem for cognitive psychology, and what the issues are that need to be addressed in this new work on
learning.

These chapters represent some of the best work in the area and contain ideas
that should prove to have growing importance in the 1980s. The chapters are
well-written, even though I put much pressure on the authors to get them out
quickly. So, read and enjoy.

ACKNOWLEDGMENTS

Lee Gregg was very helpful during the early stages of planning this Symposium,
and much of the credit for its success goes to him. His loss is profoundly felt in
the Department. We are grateful to the Alfred P. Sloan Foundation for a grant
that provided a substantial part of the support of this year's Symposium. Vickie
Silvis Wille has had a major hand in organizing the Symposium and preparing
material for the book. The success of the Symposium and the processing of the
book has depended critically on her efforts, and we all owe her our deepest
gratitude. She is supported by my NSF Grant BNS78-17463 and by my ONR
Contract N00014-77-C-0242.

John R. Anderson

1 Mechanisms of Skill Acquisition and the Law of Practice

Allen Newell and Paul S. Rosenbloom
Department of Computer Science
Carnegie-Mellon University

INTRODUCTION[1]

Practice makes perfect. Correcting the overstatement of a maxim: Almost always, practice brings improvement, and more practice brings more improvement. We all expect improvement with practice to be ubiquitous, though obviously limits exist both in scope and extent. Take only the experimental laboratory: We do not expect people to perform an experimental task correctly without at least some practice; and we design all our psychology experiments with one eye to the confounding influence of practice effects.

Practice used to be a basic topic. For instance, the first edition of Woodworth (1938) has a chapter entitled "Practice and Skill." But, as Woodworth [p. 156] says, "There is no essential difference between practice and learning except that the practice experiment takes longer." Thus, practice has not remained a topic by itself but has become simply a variant term for talking about learning skills through the repetition of their performance.

With the ascendence of verbal learning as the paradigm case of learning, and its transformation into the acquisition of knowledge in long-term memory, the study of skills took up a less central position in the basic study of human behavior. It did not remain entirely absent, of course. A good exemplar of its

[1]This chapter relies on the data of many other investigators. We are deeply grateful to those who made available original data: John Anderson, Stu Card, Paul Kolers, Tom Moran, David Neves, Patrick Rabbitt, and Robert Seibel. We are also grateful to John Anderson, Stu Card, Clayton Lewis, and Tom Moran for discussions on the fundamental issues and, especially, to Clayton Lewis for letting us read his paper, which helped to energize us to this effort.

1

continued presence can be seen in the work of Neisser, taking first the results in the mid-sixties on detecting the presence of ten targets as quickly as one in a visual display (Neisser, Novick, & Lazar, 1963), which requires extensive practice to occur; and then the recent work (Spelke, Hirst, & Neisser, 1976) showing that reading aloud and shadowing prose could be accomplished simultaneously, again after much practice. In these studies, practice plays an essential but supporting role; center stage is held by issues of preattentive processes, in the earlier work, and the possibility of doing multiple complex tasks simultaneously, in the latter.

Recently, especially with the articles by Shiffrin & Schneider (1977; Schneider & Shiffrin, 1977), but starting earlier (LaBerge, 1974; Posner & Snyder, 1975), emphasis on *automatic* processing has grown substantially from its level in the sixties. It now promises to take a prominent place in cognitive psychology. The development of automatic processing seems always to be tied to extended practice and so the notions of skill and practice are again becoming central.

There exists a ubiquitous quantitative law of practice: It appears to follow a power law; that is, plotting the logarithm of the time to perform a task against the logarithm of the trial number always yields a straight line, more or less. We shall refer to this law variously as the *log–log linear learning law* or the *power law of practice*.

This empirical law has been known for a long time; it apparently showed up first in Snoddy's (1926) study of mirror-tracing of visual mazes (see also Fitts, 1964), though it has been rediscovered independently on occasion (DeJong, 1957). Its ubiquity is widely recognized; for instance, it occupies a major position in books on human performance (Fitts & Posner, 1967; Welford, 1968). Despite this, it has captured little attention, especially theoretical attention, in basic cognitive or experimental psychology, though it is sometimes used as the form for displaying data (Kolers, 1975; Reisberg, Baron, & Kemler, 1980). Only a single model, that of Crossman (1959), appears to have been put forward to explain it.[2] It is hardly mentioned as an interesting or important regularity in any of the modern cognitive psychology texts (Calfee, 1975; Crowder, 1976; Kintsch, 1977; Lindsay & Norman, 1977). Likewise, it is not a part of the long history of work on the *learning curve* (Guilliksen, 1934; Restle & Greeno, 1970; Thurstone, 1919), which considers only exponential, hyperbolic, and logistic functions. Indeed, a recent extensive paper on the learning curve (Mazur & Hastie, 1978) simply dismisses the log–log form as unworthy of consideration and clearly dominated by the other forms.

---

[2]But see Suppes, Fletcher, and Zanotti (1976), who do develop a model yielding a power law for instructional learning, though their effort appears independent of a concern with the general regularity. Unfortunately, their description is too fragmentary and faulty to permit it to be considered further.

The aim of this chapter is to investigate this law. How widespread is its occurrence? What could it signify? What theories might explain it? Our motivation for this investigation is threefold. First, an interest in applying modern cognitive psychology to user–computer interaction (Card, Moran, & Newell, 1980a; Robertson, McCracken, & Newell, in press) led us to the literature on human performance, where this law was prominently displayed. Its general quantitative form marked it as interesting, an interest only heightened by the apparent general neglect of the law in modern cognitive psychology. Second, a theoretical interest in the nature of the architecture for human cognition (Newell, 1980) has led us to search for experimental facts that might yield some useful constraints. A general regularity such as the log–log law might say something interesting about the basic mechanisms of turning knowledge into action. Third, an incomplete manuscript by Clayton Lewis (no date) took up this same problem; this served to convince us that an attack on the problem would be useful. Thus, we welcomed the excuse of this conference to take a deeper look at this law and what might lay behind it.

In the next section we provide many examples of the log–log law and characterize its universality. In the following section we perform some basic finger exercises about the nature of power laws. Then we investigate questions of curve fitting. In the next section we address the possible types of explanations for the law; and we develop one approach, which we call the *chunking theory of learning*. In the final section, we sum up our results.

THE UBIQUITOUS LAW OF PRACTICE

We have two objectives for this section. First, we simply wish to show enough examples of the regularity to lend conviction of its empirical reality. Second, the law is generally viewed as associated with *skill*, in particular, with perceptual-motor skills. We wish to replace this with a view that the law holds for practice learning of all kinds. In this section we present data. We leave to the next section issues about alternative ways to describe the regularity and to yet subsequent sections ways to explain the regularity.

We organize the presentation of the data by the subsystem that seems to be engaged in the task. In Table 1.1 we tabulate several parameters of each of the curves. Their definitions are given at the points in the chapter where the parameters are first used.

Perceptual-Motor Skills

Let us start with the historical case of Snoddy (1926). As remarked earlier, the task was mirror-tracing, a skill that involves intimate and continuous coordination of the motor and perceptual systems. Figure 1.1 plots the log of performance on the vertical axis against the log of the trial number for a single subject.

TABLE 1.1
Power Law Parameters for the (Log-Log) Linear Data Segments

Data Set	Power Law $T = BN^{-\alpha}$		
	B	α	r^2
Snoddy (1926)	79.20	.26	.981
Crossman (1959)	170.1	.21	.979
Kolers (1975) - Subject HA	14.85	.44	.931
Neisser et al. (1963)			
Ten targets	1.61	.81	.973
One target	.68	.51	.944
Card, English & Burr (1978)			
Stepping keys - Subj. 14	4.95	.08	.335
Mouse - Subj. 14	3.02	.13	.398
Seibel (1963) - Subject JK	12.33	.32	.991
Anderson (1980) - Fan 1	2.358	.19	.927
Moran (1980)			
Total time	30.27	.08	.839
Method time	19.59	.06	.882
Neves & Anderson (in press)			
Total time - Subject D	991.2	.51	.780
The Game of Stair			
Won games	1763	.21	.849
Lost games	980	.18	.842
Hirsch (1952)	10.01	.32	.932

The first important point is:

• The law holds for performance measured as the *time* to achieve a fixed task.

Analyses of learning and practice are free a priori to use any index of performance (e.g., errors or performance time, which decrease with practice; or amount or quality attained, which increase with practice). However, we focus exclusively on measures of performance time, with quality measures (errors, amount, judged quality) taken to be essentially constant. Given that humans can often engage in tradeoffs between speed and accuracy, speed curves are not definable without a specification of accuracy, implicit or otherwise.[3] As we illustrate later, the log–log law also appears to hold for learning curves defined

---

[3]Snoddy used an indicator, 1/(time+errors), and we have replotted the figure using time+errors. This strikes the modern eye as incongruous, adding together apples and oranges. In fact, the measure is almost purely performance time. Snoddy was endeavoring to cope with the speed/accuracy tradeoff. He fixed the error rate to be equal to the performance time (in seconds) and had the subject work faster or slower in order to hold the error rate at that level. Thus the error rate bore a fixed average relationship to time; and adding the actual value of the errors to the performance time was a way of compensating for momentary shifts in the speed/accuracy tradeoff.

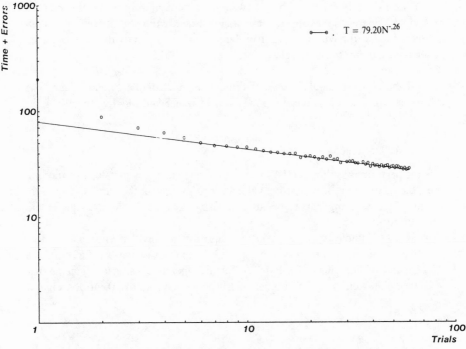

FIG. 1.1.   Learning in a mirror tracing task (log–log coordinates). Replotted from Snoddy (1926).

on other performance criteria. Though significant for understanding the cause of the power law, we only note the existence of these other curves.

Several other things can be noted in Fig. 1.1, which show up generally in the other curves.

• The points are sparse at the left and become denser to the right. This arises from taking the log of the trial number. Even when trials are aggregated into blocks, this is usually done uniformly in linear space. Thus, this is just an artifact of the display.

• There is systematic deviation at one end. Here it is the beginning. Snoddy made a lot of this initial deviation, though we need not follow him in this. As we shall see, systematic deviation can occur at either end.

• There is little doubt that the bulk of the curve lies along a line in log–log space. This arises in part because of the relatively large number of points available.[4] The curves are for an individual, not for grouped data. This is not a condition of the law, but it shows that the law holds for individual data.

---

[4]Obvious deviations at the ends of the empirical curves were eliminated before the fits in Table 1.1 were computed. The equations therefore primarily represent this linear portion of the curve. The solid line in Fig. 1.1 (and in the following figures) reflects this fit.

• Data are rarely presented on many subjects, though in some cases such data exists and (apparently) is robust. For instance, Snoddy took his curve as diagnostic and appears to have gathered it on large numbers of individuals, though he never reported any mass of data.

In Table 1.1 we tabulate several critical features of the Snoddy data. The following equations describe the power law in linear and log–log spaces:

$$T = BN^{-\alpha} \tag{1}$$

$$\log(T) = \log(B) - \alpha \log(N) \tag{2}$$

B is the performance time on the first trial ($N = 1$) and α is the slope of the line (i.e., the learning rate). A positive value of α (e.g., .26 for the curve of Fig. 1.1) indicates a decreasing curve, because we have located the minus sign in the equation itself.

Another example from a task that appears to involve intimate motor-perceptual coordination is shown in Fig. 1.2. This is Crossman's (1959) famous data on the manufacture of cigars by female operators using a cigar-making machine. Noteworthy is the number of trials, namely, up to 20 million cigars.

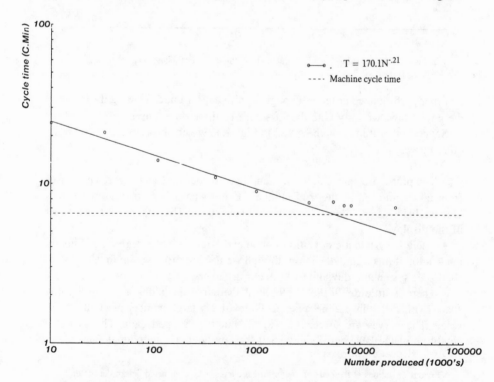

FIG. 1.2.   Cross-sectional study of learning in cigar manufacturing (log–log coordinates). Replotted from Crossman (1959).

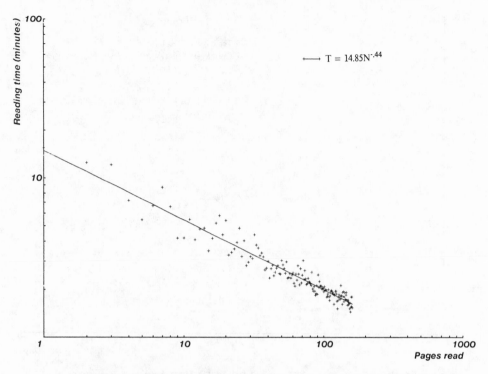

FIG. 1.3.   Learning to read inverted text (log–log coordinates). Plotted from the original data for Subject HA (Kolers, 1975).

Also, there is a known lower bound for the performance time, namely, the cycle time of the machine. The curve eventually deviates from the log–log line, flattening out in submission to physical necessity. Still, practice followed the law for almost 3 million trials (and 2 years). Furthermore, additional small improvements continued; and it would be foolish indeed to predict that no further improvements would occur. Crossman's data differs from all other data in being cross-sectional (i.e., different individuals make up each point).

Perception

Figure 1.3 shows the data from one subject (of eight) in Kolers's well known studies on reading graphically transformed text (Kolers, 1975). Here, the transformation is inversion of each line around its horizontal axis. The task of the subject is to read many pages of such text for comprehension. Reading in general is a complex task, but the difficulties here are clearly strongly perceptual, being caused primarily by the perceptual transformation. Without inversion, reading is much faster and improves hardly at all (though we don't show Kolers's control data on this). In any event, as the figure shows, learning is log–log linear.

Figure 1.4 shows some data replotted from a paper by Neisser, Novick, & Lazar (1963). The task consisted of finding any of multiple targets in pages of

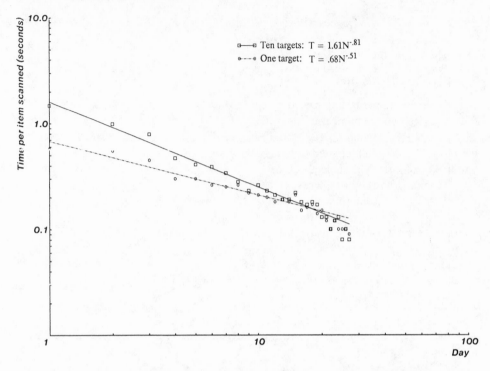

FIG. 1.4.   Learning to scan for visual targets (log-log coordinates). Replotted from Neisser, Novick, & Lazar (1963).

letters. The result was that, with practice, identification time becomes essentially independent of the size of the target set. As Fig. 1.4 shows, this data also follows the log–log law, though there seems to be a slight drop at the end. These two curves (scanning for one target and for ten targets) represent the two bounding conditions of the five used in the experiment. Each curve is the average of six subjects. One of the reasons for exhibiting these particular curves is to point out that much learning data in the literature fits the log–log law, even though it has not been plotted that way.

Motor Behavior

Figure 1.5 is from a task where a subject sees a target mark appear on a video terminal and has to position the cursor at that mark (Card, English, & Burr, 1978). Four different pointing devices were used: a mouse, which permits a smooth pointing motion isomorphic to the motion of the cursor; a joystick; a set of stepping keys; and a set of text keys, which allow movement by paragraph, word, etc. Some of these devices are well described by Fitts's law (Fitts, 1954); some have a different structure. The two curves in Fig. 1.5 show the mouse and stepping key data for one subject, averaged over blocks of 20 trials (excluding errors). For all of the devices, the total performance time follows the law, though the degree of variability increases as one moves from the Fitts's law devices (the mouse) toward the other ones.

Elementary Decisions

Figure 1.6 is from a task designed by Seibel (1963) to probe the dependence of reaction time on the number of alternatives. It followed in the wake of the work by Hick (1952), Hyman (1953), and others showing that choice RT was linear in the information (bits) required to select the response, at least for small ensembles (up to 3 or 4 bits). The subject's 10 fingers rested on 10 response keys (shaped to fit the natural position of the resting hand) and looked at 10 stimulus lights that were configured isomorphically to the keys. A subset of the lights would turn on, and the subject was to strike the corresponding keys. There are 1023 ($2^{10} - 1$) different subsets of the lights; hence, the arrangement achieves a choice RT task of 10 bits. For our purposes what is interesting is that the learning over a large number of trials (40,000) was log–log linear, though at the end the curve flattens out. This is data for a single subject, averaged over blocks of 1023 trials; approximately the same behavior was shown by each of three subjects.

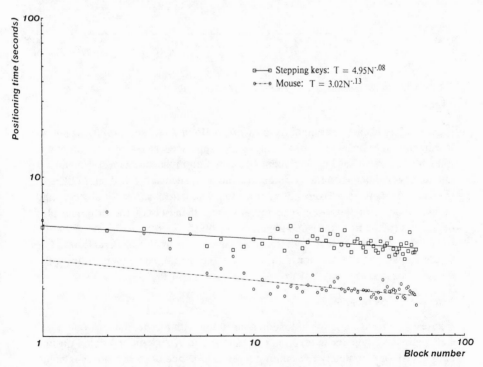

FIG. 1.5. Learning to use cursor positioning devices (log–log coordinates). Plotted from the original data for Subject 14 (Card, English, & Burr, 1978).

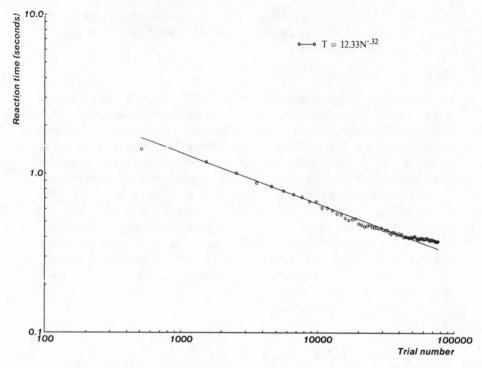

FIG. 1.6.   Learning in a ten finger, 1023 choice task (log–log coordinates).
Plotted from the original data for Subject JK (Seibel, 1963).

Memory

Figure 1.7 is from some unpublished work of John Anderson (1980). It shows
learning performance in a task that would appear to stress mostly memory,
though of course it has both a perceptual and a motor response aspect. The task is
an old–new judgment on a set of simple sentences, such as "The doctor talked to
the lady." There is a fixed population of grammatical subjects, objects, and
verbs; a subset of these are seen initially, and then sets of the originals plus
distractors (made from the same populations) are shown repeatedly. After awhile
of course a subject has seen both the targets and the distractors several times. The
figure shows that the reaction time to make the memory judgment follows the
log–log linear law.

Complex Routines

Figure 1.8 is from some work done in connection with a general attack on understanding user–computer interaction (Moran, 1980). A specific, complex on-line
editing task of completely rearranging a given sentence of three clauses is being
performed repeatedly. The task is absolutely identical each time (i.e., the same
sentence). Thus we are seeing a subject simply follow an internally familiar,
complex plan. The top curve is the total time to perform the task. The lower

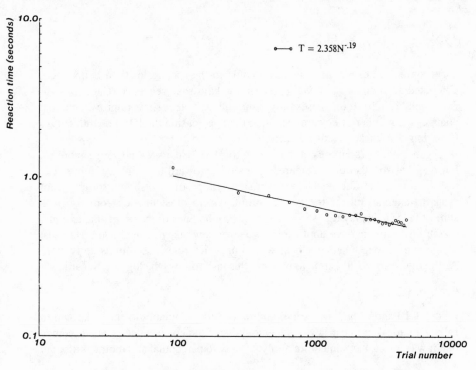

FIG. 1.7. Learning in a sentence recognition task (log–log coordinates). Plotted from the fan 1 data of Anderson (1980).

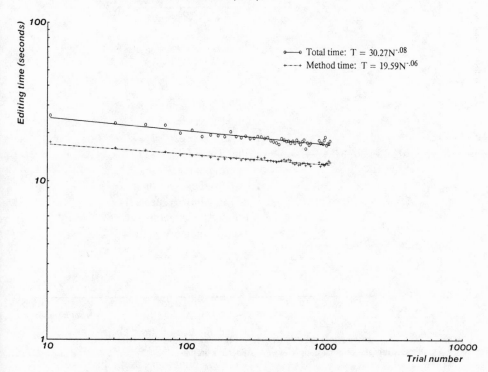

FIG. 1.8. Learning of a complex on-line editing routine (log–log coordinates). Plotted from the original data of Moran (1980).

curve shows the execution time attributable to the specific method being used, computed according to a model based on the keystroke sequence (Card, Moran, & Newell, 1980b). It decreases only if the subject makes some improvement that changes the number of keystrokes rather than decreasing think time. Both curves show log–log linear practice effects.

Figure 1.9 shows a more complex cognitive task (Neves & Anderson, in press), but one that still can be considered as evolving toward a complex routine. The task is to find the rule justifying each step in a proof in a simple formal proof system, taken to mirror the typical proof system of synthetic geometry. The subject faces a display that shows (on request) the lines of the proof, the axioms, or the theorems that are applicable to derive new steps in the proof. He must assign to each step whether it is an axiom or which rule is used in its derivation. As the figure shows, the time to perform this task follows the log–log linear law.

Problem Solving

Figure 1.10 shows our own small addition to the population of tasks known to follow the log–log linear law. As the ubiquity of the law became clear, it seemed that it was miscast as something applying only to perceptual and motor skills, but

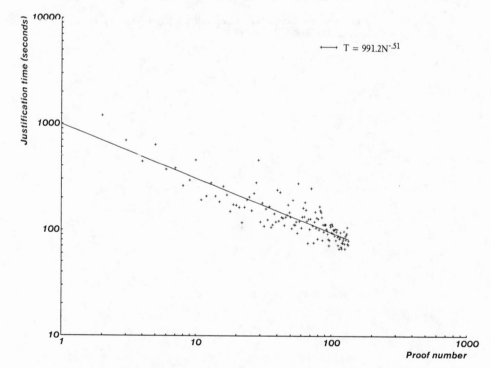

FIG. 1.9.   Learning in a geometry proof justification task (log–log coordinates). Plotted from the original data (Neves & Anderson, in press).

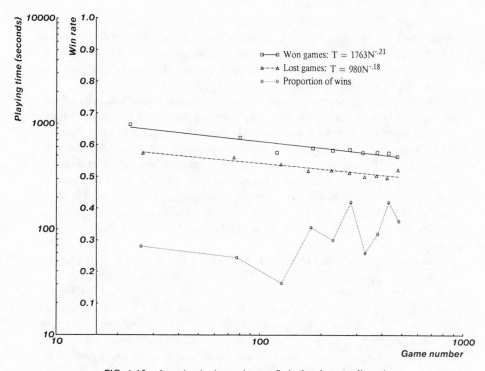

FIG. 1.10.   Learning in the card game Stair (log–log coordinates).

rather it applied to all forms of mental behavior. To test whether the law applied to problem solving tasks, we had a single subject play 500 hands of a game of solitaire called *Stair*.

> Stair involves laying out all 52 cards face up from a shuffled deck, in 8 *columns* (four with 7 rows, four with 6 rows). There are also four *spots* (initially empty), each of which can hold only a single card. The aim is to build four *stacks*, ace to king, one for each suit, by moving cards around under typical solitaire constraints. A card in a spot or at the bottom of a column may be moved: (1) to a spot, if it is empty; (2) to a stack, if the card is the next in order building up; or (3) to the bottom of another column, if the card is the next lower in the same suit (e.g., the six of spades appended to the seven of spades).

The game can be seen to be one of perfect information—all cards are faceup. The shuffled deck simply picks out one of the possible initial conditions at random. From that point no further chance element enters. Whether the game can be won or not, or how many cards can be moved to the stacks, is derivable from the initial configuration. The subject, whose ability to calculate ahead is of course limited, may create a partial plan and then proceed to execute it; in doing so, he may make irrevocable moves that lose him the possibility of winning. But such failures all arise, as in chess or checkers, because of his limited problem-solving ability. Although this task certainly has a strong perceptual component (and a weak motor component), it is to be classed as fundamentally an intellectual task, in the same way as games such as chess and checkers or problems such as the *traveling salesman problem*.

Turning to the figure, the top curve shows the time for games that the subject won; the lower curve shows the time for games that the subject lost; at the bottom the proportion of games won is shown. The points are averaged over 50 games. There is of course only one series of trials, since all games, won or lost, contribute to practice. Each group of 50 games is therefore split between the two curves before being averaged. Both curves essentially follow the log–log linear law. In general it takes longer to win than to lose, since losing involves becoming stuck after a relatively small number of cards has been played to the stack, whereas winning always involves working through all 52 cards (though the tail end goes rapidly).

The issue of the speed–accuracy tradeoff reveals itself in this data. Clearly, the subject is applying various criteria of certainty to his play. He could conceivably, as a strategy choice, study each initial layout for 5 hours before making his first move or play impulsively with no contemplation at all. In fact, the subject felt he had little genuine control of the speed–accuracy tradeoff, partly because the complexity of the initial position made it unclear whether an apparently lost game was just a bad layout or was due to a failure to spend enough time analyzing. Note that the most deviant point from the log–log line (at 150–200 trials) corresponds to the lowest win frequency.

Other Tasks and Measures

The story does not quite end at this point. Learning in other tasks and measured on other criteria seems to follow the log–log law. We give here a couple of examples.

Figure 1.11 is reproduced from Stevens and Savin (1962). It plots eight tasks with various response measures in log–log space. The criteria are all oriented to increase with practice. The plot is actually of the *cumulated* responses (i.e., the integral of the usual curve). This is just the same as the usual power law, because the integral of a power law is a power law (though integration tends to smooth the curve, helping to account for the lovely appearance of the curves, in addition to the relatively large numbers of subjects).

$$\int_{1}^{N} Bx^{-\alpha}\, dx = B(1 - \alpha)^{-1}(N^{1-\alpha} - 1) \tag{3}$$

Some of these curves are time curves (actually, amount accomplished per unit time, to make them positive curves); but several are not (e.g., 1 is the number of correct anticipations in learning nonsense syllables, 2 is the time on target in a pursuit tracking task; 3 is the number of balls thrown into a target area; 4 is the num-

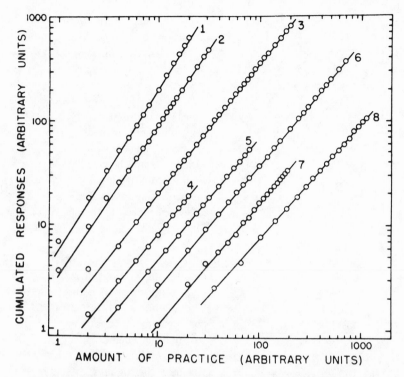

FIG. 1.11.   Eight cumulated response practice curves (log–log coordinates). Figure from Stevens & Savin (1962). Copyright 1962 by the Society for the Experimental Analysis of Behavior, Inc.

ber of correct responses in an animal experiment in learning a maze, and so on.)

As a second type of example, it has long been known in industrial engineering that the so-called learning curve for production of manufactured projects was log–log linear. In part this comes of various simple rules of thumb (e.g., "... each time the quantity of [air]planes is doubled, the cumulative average man-hours per plane will be [reduced by] 80%" [Rigon, 1944]). However, Fig. 1.12 shows an empirical curve from machine tool manufacture (Hirsch, 1952). Notice that the index of performance is not time but cost.

Summary

We have shown some 12 diverse examples of the log–log linear law of practice for trials versus time. From Table 1.1 we can make one more particular point:

- The learning rates, α, are all less than 1.

Our main point is that the law is ubiquitous when one measures the log of performance time against the log of trial number. Where the general impression

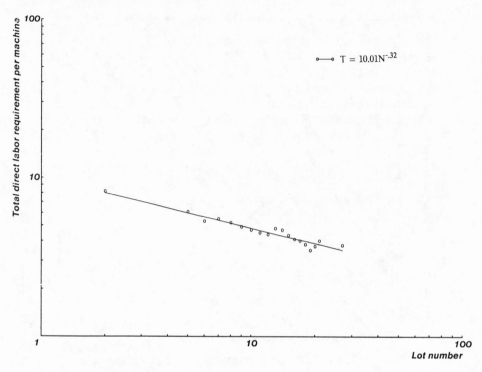

FIG. 1.12. The effect of practice on direct labor requirement in machine production (log–log coordinates). Replotted from Hirsch (1952).

seems to have been that the law showed up in perceptual-motor behavior, we
think it is clear that it shows up everywhere in psychological behavior—at least it
cannot easily be restricted to some part of the human operation.

Our proposition on ubiquity is extended, perhaps beyond our druthers, to
learning curves involving other measures of performance and even to tasks
possibly (but not certainly) beyond the pale of individual human behavior. We do
not however claim that all learning is log–log linear. Nor do we claim that
practice always leads to learning.

We do not wish to assert that such an effect stems from a single cause or
mechanism. Indeed, its ubiquity might seem to indicate multiple explanations.
We do wish to make one general comment about the regularity and what might be
expected from understanding it. Its widespread occurrence implies that it depends on quite general features of the learning situation or of the system that
learns. If we develop a theory that depends on detailed perceptual or motor
mechanisms, we shall just create trouble for the more cognitive instances or vice
versa.

One is immediately reminded of other examples of ubiquitous regularities and
their explanation. The *normal distribution,* which arises out of the independent
additive combination of many small increments, is the most well known.

Another, usually known as *Zipf's law*, gives the distribution for items according to their rank order, which is common to word frequencies, city sizes, incomes, and many other ordered phenomena (Simon, 1955). Consistently, highly general stochastic models underly these various phenomena. They explain the regularity but leave open the detailed mechanisms that produce the stochastic processes.

Thus, in searching for an explanation for this regularity, we should expect at best to find some such general considerations. Though it will not tell us in detail about the learning mechanism, it may still tell us something worth having.

BASICS ABOUT POWER LAWS

In this section we present some general perspectives on power laws and what they mean.

Differential Forms and Rates of Change

We start with the power law and its equivalent log–log form:

$$T = BN^{-\alpha} \tag{4}$$

$$\log(T) = \log(B) - \alpha\log(N) \tag{5}$$

It is instructive to see this in terms of the local rate of learning, dT/dN.[5]

$$\frac{dT}{dN} = -\alpha BN^{-\alpha-1} \tag{6}$$

$$= -\frac{\alpha T}{N} = -\left(\frac{\alpha}{N}\right)T \tag{7}$$

$$= -\alpha B^{-1/\alpha}T^{1+1/\alpha} \tag{8}$$

Now, one baseline form for learning is exponential. It can arise, for instance, from any mechanism that is completely local. If there is something that learns on each local part of a performance, independent of any other part, then the change in T (the sum of the changes to each part of T) is proportional to T:

$$\frac{dT}{dN} = -\alpha T \tag{9}$$

$$T = Be^{-\alpha N} \tag{10}$$

Comparing this differential form to that of the power law, shows that power-law learning is like exponential learning in which the instantaneous rate α' decreases with N, that is,

$$dT/dN = -\alpha'T \tag{11}$$

where $\alpha' = \alpha/N$

---

[5]For ease of exposition we treat the trial number N as a continuous variable. In fact, nothing material depends on it; we could work with finite differences throughout, at the cost of added complexity.

Both the exponential and the power function are monotonically decreasing functions that asymptote at 0. The decreasing rate of learning in the power function leads to its approaching asymptote much more slowly. Figure 1.13 shows these two curves in linear coordinates, with identical initial values ($B = 1$). This corresponds to $N = 0$ for the exponential, and $N = 1$ for the power. Thus, one way to think of power law learning is that it is a learning process in which some mechanism is slowing down the rate of learning.

Not every scheme of slowed-down learning leads to the power law. For instance, if we generalize the differential equation above we obtain a different law:

$$\frac{dT}{dN} = \left(\frac{\alpha}{N^\beta} \right) T, \tag{12}$$

where $\beta \neq 1$.

$$T = Be^{-\alpha N^{1-\beta}} \tag{13}$$

A representative curve for β less than 1 is also shown in Fig. 1.13, which produces asymptoting between the exponential and the power law.

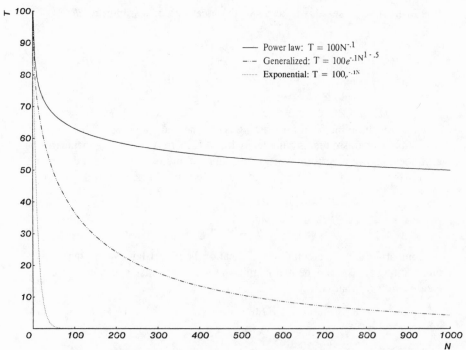

FIG. 1.13.   Basic learning curves: power law, exponential, and a generalized curve.

The form of the power law can be appreciated in terms of a simple global rule, as well as in differential form:

Power Law Decay: If T decreases by a factor δ in the first N trials, it will take another $N(N - 1)$ trials to decrease by a factor of δ again.

Comparison with the corresponding global rule for the exponential, shows again how much more slowly the power law drops off:

Exponential Law Decay: If T decreases by a factor of δ in the first N trials, it will take another N trials to decrease by a factor of δ again.

Asymptotes and Prior Experience

As given in Equation 4, the law assumes: (1) the asymptote of the learning is 0 (i.e., the task can be performed in arbitrarily small time after enough learning); and (2) the initial trial of the learning occurs at the first trial of the measured series. Neither of these assumptions need be true.

The more general form of the law is

$$T = A + B(N + E)^{-\alpha} \tag{14}$$

A (≥ 0) is the *asymptote* of learning as N increases indefinitely. E (≥ 0) is the number of trials of learning that occurred prior to the first trial as measured (i.e., prior *experience*); it thus identifies the true *starting point* of learning. (Neither $A < 0$ or $E < 0$ make immediate sense, given these interpretations; $A = 0$, $E = 0$ reproduces the basic form of Equation 4.)

Plotting $\log(T - A)$ against $\log(N + E)$ still yields a straight line whose slope is $-\alpha$. The difficulty of course is that A and E are not known in advance, so the curve cannot be plotted as an initial exploratory step in an investigation.

One alternative is just to plot in $\log(T) - \log(N)$ space and understand the deviations:

$$\log(T - A) = \log(B) - \alpha\log(N + E) \tag{15}$$

$$\log(T) = \log(B) - \log(1 - A/T) - \alpha\log(N) - \alpha\log(1 + E/N) \tag{16}$$

There is an error term for each parameter. If T is large with respect to the asymptote, A, then $\log(1 - A/T)$ is close to $\log(1)$, which is 0. This occurs at early values of N. If N is large with respect to E, then $\log(1 + E/N)$ is close to $\log(1)$, which is 0. Thus, the two deviations affect the curve at opposite parts: Non-zero values of E distort the straight line for low N, non-zero values of A distort it for high N.

Figure 1.14 shows a power law with a starting point ($-E$) of -25 and a time asymptote (A) of 5. Figure 1.15 shows the same curve in log–log space. Characteristically, the starting point pulls the initial segment of the curve down toward the horizontal and the finite asymptote pulls the high N tail of the curve up toward the horizontal. A central region of the curve appears as a straight line. It is however less than the true slope ($-\alpha$), as the line shows.

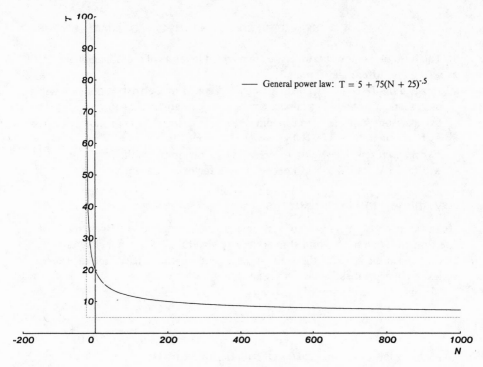

FIG. 1.14.   A general power law curve.

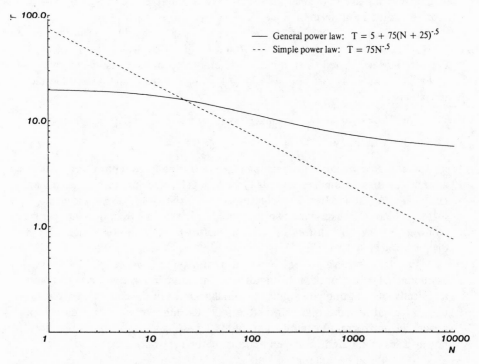

FIG. 1.15.   A general power law in log–log coordinates. The simple power law
with the same α and B is also shown.

20

The derivative of the general power function in log–log space is given by

$$\frac{d[\log(T)]}{d[\log(N)]} = -\alpha \left(1 - \frac{A}{T} \right) \Big/ \left(1 + \frac{E}{N} \right) \tag{17}$$

It can be seen that the slope is everywhere smaller than α and becomes increasingly so as either A or E increases. A reasonable estimate of the apparent slope as viewed on the graph, α^*, is at the inflection point. It is easy to obtain by setting the derivative of Equation 17 to zero:

$$\frac{d}{dN} \left[\frac{d[\log(T)]}{d[\log(N)]} \right] = - \left(\frac{\alpha}{N} \right) \left(\frac{E}{N} - \frac{\alpha A}{T} \right) \left(1 - \frac{A}{T} \right) \left(1 + \frac{E}{N} \right)^{-2} = 0 \tag{18}$$

$$\alpha^* = \frac{(\alpha N^* - E)}{(N^* + E)} \tag{19}$$

N^* is the point at which the inflection occurs. The exact value of N^* is not expressible in simple terms, but a reasonable approximation is

$$N^* = \left[\frac{BE}{\alpha A} \right]^{1/(1+\alpha)} \tag{20}$$

where $E/N^* < < \alpha < 1$.

The structure of Fig. 1.15 suggests that many of the deviations in the empirical curves could be due simply to starting point or asymptote effects. Because the effect of these two phenomena is to bend toward the horizontal at separate ends, it is possible to tell from the curve in log–log space what effect might be operating. The original Snoddy data in Fig. 1.1 provides an example of a clear initial deviation. It cannot possibly be due to an earlier starting point, because the initial curve rises toward the vertical. However, it could be due to the asymptote, because raising the asymptote parameter (A) will pull the right-hand part of the curve down and make its slope steeper. The Seibel data in Fig. 1.6 provides an example where there are deviations from linearity at both ends. Use of a nonzero value for E (previous experience) will steepen the initial portion of the curve, whereas doing likewise for A will steepen the high N portion of the curve. (The results of such a manipulation are seen in Fig. 1.21.)

Trials or Time?

The form of the law of practice is performance time (T) as a function of trials (N). But trials is simply a way of marking the temporal continuum (t) into intervals, each one performance-time long. Since the performance time is itself a monotone decreasing function of trial number, trials (N) becomes a nonlinear compression of time (t). It is important to understand the effect on the law of practice of viewing it in terms of time or in terms of trials.

The fundamental relationship between time and trials is

$$t(N) = T_0 + \sum_{i=1}^{N} T_i = T_0 + \sum_{i=1}^{N} Bi^{-\alpha} = T_0 + B \sum_{i=1}^{N} i^{-\alpha} \qquad (21)$$

T_0 is the time from the arbitrary time origin to the start of the first trial. This equation cannot be inverted explicitly to obtain an expression for $N(t)$ that would permit the basic law (Equation 4) to be transformed to yield $T(t)$. Instead, we proceed indirectly by means of the differential forms. From Equation 21 we obtain

$$\frac{dt}{dN} = T \qquad (22)$$

Think of the corresponding integral formulation,

$$\frac{d}{dz} \int_{a}^{z} f(x)\, dx = f(z)$$

Now, starting with the power law in terms of trials we find:

$$\frac{dT}{dt} = \frac{dT/dN}{dt/dN} = \frac{-\alpha T/N}{T} = \frac{-\alpha}{N} \qquad (23)$$

But from the basic Equation (4):

$$N = \left(\frac{T}{B} \right)^{-1/\alpha} \qquad (24)$$

Thus, we obtain the trials power law reexpressed in terms of time:

$$\frac{dT}{dt} = -\alpha B^{-1/\alpha} T^{1/\alpha} \qquad (25)$$

For $\alpha \neq 1$ this integrates to yield

$$T^{-(1-\alpha)/\alpha} = (1 - \alpha)B^{-1/\alpha}t + C \qquad \text{for } \alpha \neq 1 \qquad (26)$$

But C is an arbitrary constant of integration and if the origin and scale of t is adjusted appropriately, we find:

$$T = B't^{-\alpha/(1-\alpha)} \qquad \text{for } \alpha \neq 1 \qquad (27)$$

Thus, a power law in terms of trials is a power law in terms of time, though with a different exponent, reflecting the expansion of time over trials. The results are significantly altered when $\alpha = 1$ (the hyperbolic) however. Equation 25 becomes

$$\frac{dT}{dt} = -B^{-1}T \qquad (28)$$

This is no longer the differential form of a power law. Instead it is that of an exponential:

$$T = Ce^{-B^{-1}t} \qquad (29)$$

It is left as an exercise for the reader to confirm that an exponential function in trials transforms to a *linear* function in time (hence, Zeno-like, an infinite set of trials can be accomplished in a finite amount of time).

FITTING THE DATA TO A FAMILY OF CURVES

Given empirical curves, such as occur in abundance in the second section, it is important to understand how well they are described by curves of a given family (e.g., power laws) and whether there are alternative general forms that fit them just as well (as noted in the introduction, exponential, hyperbolic, and logistic curves have enjoyed much more favor than power functions). Curve fitting without benefit of a model is notoriously a black art. Nonetheless, we have deliberately chosen not to be model driven initially, because we want to have empirical generalizations as the starting point in the search for theory, not just the raw data.

The basic issue of curve fitting can be introduced from Seibel's own treatment of his data (Fig. 1.6), which appears to be an extremely good fit to the log–log law over an extensive range (40,000 trials). Seibel (1963) fit his points to three curves by least squares: (1) a power law with asymptote only (i.e., E fixed at 0); (2) an exponential with asymptote; and (3) a general power law with both asymptote and starting point.[6] He obtained an r^2 of .991 for the power function with asymptote only. But he also obtained an r^2 of .971 for the exponential with asymptote. His general power law fit was .997. (His parameters for asymptotes and starting points are mostly reasonable but not entirely.) Thus, all the curves give good fits by normal standards. If only differences in the least-squared residual are used, there can hardly be much to choose from. This is an annoying result, in any case; but it is also somewhat unexpected, for the plots that we have shown, though they surely contain noise, are still impressively linear by intuitive standards and involve lots of data.

It is important to recognize that two basic kinds of failure occur in fitting data to a family of smooth curves: (1) failure of the shape of the data curve to fit to the shapes available within the family; and (2) noise in the data, which will not be fit by any of the families under consideration or even noticeably changed by parametric variation within a family. These distinctions are precisely analogous to the frequency spectrum of the noise in the data. However, the analogy proba-bly should not be exploited too literally, because an attempt to filter out the high-frequency noise prior to data fitting simply adds another family of empirical curves (the filters) to confound the issues. What does seem sensible is to attempt to distinguish fits of shape without worrying too much about the jitter.

A simple example of this point of view is the (sensible) rejection of the family of logistic curves from consideration for our data. The logistic provides a sig-

---

[6]The exponential is translation invariant, so a special starting point is not distinguishable for it; that is, $Be^{N+E} = (Be^E)e^N = B'e^N$.

moid curve (i.e., a slow but accelerating start with a point of inflection and then asymptoting). No trace of an S-shape appears in any of our data, though it would not be lost to view by any of the various monotone transformations (logs, powers, and exponentials) that we are considering. Hence, independent of how competing the measure of error, the logistic is not to be considered.

The size of the jitter (i.e., the high-frequency noise) will limit the precision of the shape that can be detected and the confidence of the statements that can be made about it. It provides a band through which smooth curves can be threaded, and if that band is wide enough—and it may not have to be very wide—then it may be possible to get suitable members of conceptually distinct curves through it. In all cases, the main contribution to any error measure will be provided by the jitter, so that only relatively small differences will distinguish the different families.

The Data Analysis Procedure

With the elimination of the logistic from consideration, we have focused our efforts on three families of curves: *exponential, hyperbolic,* and *power law.* The analysis procedure that we have ended up using is primarily graphical in nature. We look at what types of deviations remain, once an empirical curve has been fit optimally by a family of theoretical curves. The analysis consists of judgments as to whether the deviations represent actual distortions of shape, or merely jitter. The procedure has the following components:

1. Find spaces where the family of curves should plot as straight lines. Judgments of shape deviation are most easily made and described when the norm is a line. These are the *transformation spaces* of the given family. There may be more than one such space.

2. For each family of curves, find the best linear approximation to the data in the transformation spaces of the family. This will generally involve a combination of search and linear regression.

3. Accept a curve for a family, if the best fit plots as a straight line in the space of that family. Reject it, if it has significant shape distortion.

4. Understand the shape distortion of family X when plotted in the space of family Y. Expect curves of family X to show the characteristic distortion when plotted in the spaces of alternative families.

5. Compute an estimate of fit (r^2) for the best approximation in each transformation space. Expect these values to support the judgments made on the basis of shape distortion.

These criteria contain elements both of acceptance and rejection and provide a mixture of absolute judgments about whether data belong to a given family and relative judgments about the discrimination between families. The parameters for the best fits as well as the estimates of fit (r^2) can be found in Table 1.2.

TABLE 1.2
The General Learning Curves: Parameters from Optimal Fits in the *Log Transformation* Spaces

Data Set	Exponential $T = A + Be^{-\alpha N}$				Hyperbolic $T = A + B/(N + E)$				Power Law $T = A + B(N + E)^{-\alpha}$				
	A	B	α	r^2	A	B	E	r^2	A	B	E	α	r^2
Snoddy (1926)	27.01	38.80	.061	.916	24.49	243.6	1.3	.962	21.74	119.2	0.0	.71	.975
Crossman (1959)	7.19	4.59	1×10^{-7}	.842	7.10	2.4×10^6	151000	.983	6.91	20481	31000	.66	.990
Kolers (1975) - Subject HA	1.36	3.82	.018	.849	1.10	94.02	9.8	.915	.18	15.25	0.0	.46	.931
Neisser et al. (1963)													
Ten targets	.06	.83	.13	.905	.00	2.74	.9	.965	.00	2.35	.6	.95	.965
One target	.06	.44	.094	.938	.00	3.16	4.6	.951	.00	2.57	3.9	.94	.951
Card, English & Burr (1978)													
Stepping keys - Subj. 14	2.35	1.99	.011	.335	2.14	171.4	75.2	.338	.02	6.36	9.3	.14	.340
Mouse - Subj. 14	1.46	1.28	.028	.452	1.46	16.70	5.0	.603	.59	4.28	0.0	.33	.729
Seibel (1963) - Subject JK	.371	.461	.000055	.956	.328	3888.1	3042	.993	.324	2439.9	2690	.95	.993
Anderson (1980) - Fan 1	.487	.283	.00055	.774	.466	231.6	319.7	.902	.353	4.322	0.0	.39	.947
Moran (1980)													
Total time	13.80	6.66	.00073	.546	14.77	3335.9	474.6	.637	.03	30.24	0.0	.08	.839
Method time	11.61	3.11	.0010	.652	11.75	1381.8	360.0	.737	.26	19.35	0.0	.06	.882
Neves & Anderson (in press)													
Total time - Subject D	57.5	240.2	.019	.660	45.6	5000.2	7.3	.728	0.0	991.2	0.0	.51	.780
The Game of Stair													
Won games	476	319	.0052	.689	449	29800	40.1	.783	120	1763	0.0	.25	.849
Lost games	152	326	.0016	.634	247	41270	124.1	.751	1	1009	2.5	.19	.841
Hirsch (1952)	2.76	4.35	.070	.819	2.34	37.05	4.9	.897	.00	10.01	0.0	.32	.932
General Power Law $T = 5 + 75(N + 25)^{-0.5}$	7.21	6.78	.0037	.983	6.41	1069.6	91.2	.997	5.00	74.85	24.9	.50	1.000
40 Term Additive Mixture	1.60	45.37	.0065	.904	.58	1231.2	10.2	.997	.19	753.1	7.2	.89	.998
Chunking Model													
Combinatorial TE	4.61	4.71	.0046	.957	4.35	365.7	55.3	.992	2.86	17.40	6.6	.33	1.000

The remainder of this section shows how we applied this data analysis procedure. We start by looking at the transformation spaces. This is followed by an examination of the distortions that occur when a theoretical curve is plotted in a space belonging to a different family. We are then in a position to analyze a couple of the empirical curves that appeared in the second section.

The Transformation Spaces

The curves that we are interested in belong to multiparameter families (3 for the exponential and hyperbolic; 4 for the power law). Regression can be used to fit a line to an empirical curve plotted in a multidimensional space. Unfortunately, for the three families that we are interested in, there is no space in which all the parameters (three or four) can be determined by linear regression. The most that we can obtain is two parameters. The remainder must be determined by some other means, such as search. The choice of which parameters are to drop out of the analysis determines the transformation space. We have primarily worked in two different types of transformation spaces. The first type consists of the *log* spaces. These are the most commonly used linearizing spaces for functions with powers. The log transformations that we use are the following:

Exponential: $T' = \log(B) - \alpha N$ for $T' = \log(T - A)$ (30)
Hyperbolic: $T' = \log(B) - N'$ for $T' = \log(T - A)$ and $N' = \log(N + E)$ (31)
Power Law: $T' = \log(B) - \alpha N'$ for $T' = \log(T - A)$ and $N' = \log(N + E)$ (32)

The log spaces for the hyperbolic and the power law turn out to be the standard log–log space, whereas the exponential is in semilog space. Determining fits in these spaces requires a combination of search (over $0 \le A \le T_{min}$ and $0 \le E$) and regression (for B and α). Because the exponential and hyperbolic families are each missing one of these parameters, the process becomes simpler for them. The exponential only requires a one-dimensional search (over $0 \le A \le T_{min}$), whereas the hyperbolic can replace the regression (for B and α) with the computation of the average for B.

The log spaces have been used exclusively for the data analyses that are described in the following section (Table 1.2 was computed in the log spaces). It is important to realize though that they are not the only transformation spaces that can be used. We have explored what we call the T–X spaces, though space precludes presenting the analysis. Transforming a curve into its T–X space involves pushing all the nonlinearities into the definition of X as follows:

Exponential: $T = A + BX$ for $X = e^{-\alpha N}$ (33)

Hyperbolic: $T = A + BX$ for $X = \dfrac{1}{(N + E)}$ (34)

Power Law: $T + A + BX$ for $X = (N + E)^{-\alpha}$ (35)

In the T–X spaces, searches are over $\alpha \ge 0$ and $E \ge 0$, with A and B determined by regression. Only single-dimensional searches are needed for the two three-parameter families. The T–X spaces prove especially useful for estimating the asymptote (A), because it maps into the intercept of the transformed curve.

The Theoretical Curves

When a curve is optimally fit in a space corresponding to its family, it plots as a straight line (by definition). This is not true though when the curve is fit in a space corresponding to some other family. There will be distortions that show up as nonlinearities in the plot. By understanding these characteristic shape distortions, we are able to interpret the deviations that we find when we plot the data in these spaces. This will help us to distinguish between random jitter and distortions that signal a bad fit by the family of curves. Data that plot with the same deviations as one of the theoretical curves have a good chance of belonging to that curve's family.

Figure 1.16 shows the best that a power law can be fit in exponential log space. The power law curve is

$$T = 5 + 75(N + 25)^{-0.5} \qquad\qquad (36)$$

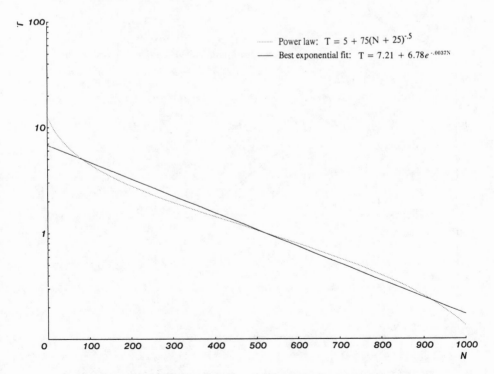

FIG. 1.16. Optimal fit of a power law in the exponential transformation space (semi-log coordinates).

This is the same curve that is plotted in Figs. 1.14 and 1.15. The parameters for the optimal exponential fit can be found in Table 1.2. The r^2 value of .983 is deceptively high, as an examination of Fig. 1.16 shows. There are strong deviations in all portions of the curve. The curve starts out high, goes low, then high again, and finally tails off downward. If we see deviations of this type when a set of data has been optimally fit by an exponential, we can conclude that the exponential family is not a good model for the data and that the power law might be.

Figure 1.17 shows the same curve optimally fit in hyperbolic log space. We see the same sorts of deviations that were found in the exponential case, but they are much attenuated. It will be hard to rule out the hyperbolic family in such a case because the variability of the data is likely to swamp out much of the distortion. At most we can hope to see the slight upturn at low N and the slight downturn for high N.

It is not necessary to look at the theoretical plots for the hyperbolic, as it is a special case of the power law. It will plot with no distortion in the power law log space, and it will have the same type of distortion in the exponential log space as did the power law. This leaves only exponential curves to be examined. We cannot present a plot of the optimal fit of an exponential in the power law log space. All attempts to find such optimal fits have led to at least one of the

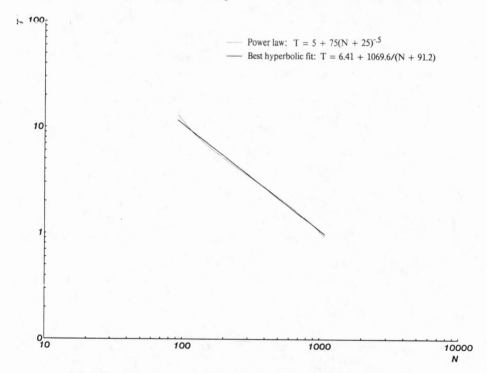

FIG. 1.17. Optimal fit of a power law in the hyperbolic transformation space (log–log coordinates).

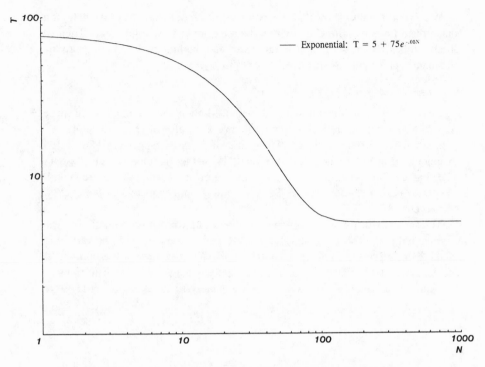

FIG. 1.18.   A general exponential function in log–log coordinates.

parameters requiring a value that is too large to be represented in our computer. Though this makes the generation of a plot impossible, this information can be used in lieu of a plot. If analysis in the power law log space leads to immense parameter values, then that is evidence against a power law and for an exponential.

   In addition to this information, it is useful to see what an exponential function looks like in log–log space. Figure 1.18 is characteristic of such plots. In log–log space, exponentials tend to have a flat portion followed by a rapid drop to asymptote. The central portion is considerably steeper ($\alpha > 1$) than the equivalent portion of the empirical curves that we have seen, and the asymptote is approached more suddenly.

The Analysis of a Data Set

We can now use the machinery that we have generated to analyze the data from some of the tasks in the second section. There is no space to provide a detailed examination of the data analysis techniques or of their results over the entire data set. But we do need to illustrate them enough to support the conclusions. To do this we look closely at two curves: Kolers's subject 3 (Fig. 1.3) and Seibel's subject JK (Fig. 1.6).

We first attempt to show that the exponential is not a good fit to the data, that shape distortions remain, even though the measure of fit is impressive. Then we attempt to show that both the general power and the hyperbolic families provide adequate representations of the empirical curves.

The Exponential Family

Figure 1.19 shows the optimal fit of Seibel's data in the exponential log space. As was true of the theoretical power-law curve, the value of r^2 and the plot of the optimal fit tell different stories. The value of r^2 is a respectable .956, so the exponential family can account for over 95% of the variance of Seibel's data. The characteristic power-law distortions can be clearly seen in the figure though. The value of r^2 notwithstanding, Seibel's data is not adequately fit by an exponential curve.

The same distortions can be seen in Kolers's data when it is optimally fit by an exponential (Fig. 1.20). Though they are somewhat obscured by the variability of the data, there are significant nonlinearities. With respect to the optimal fit, the data is high, then low, then high, and finally low again. These distortions are the signal that Kolers's data is also not adequately fit by an exponential curve.

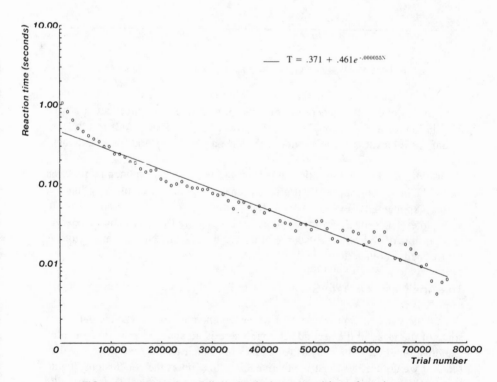

FIG. 1.19.   Optimal fit to Seibel's data in the exponential transformation space (semi-log coordinates).

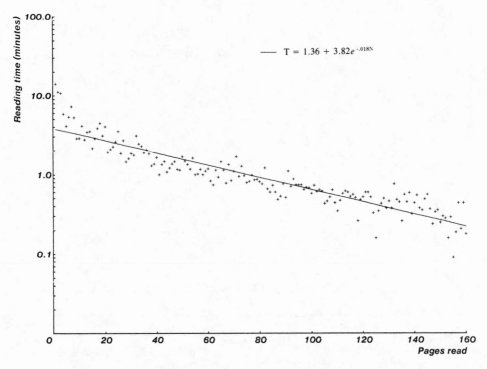

FIG. 1.20.   Optimal fit to Kolers's data in the exponential transformation space
(semi-log coordinates).

The Power-Law Family

In contrast to the exponential plots, the power-law plots are highly linear.
Figures 1.21 and 1.22 show the optimal power-law transformations for the two
data sets. Very little needed to be done to Kolers's data to achieve the optimal fit
(the asymptote was assigned the value of .18). There was not much to straighten
out in Kolers's data to begin with. Figure 1.3 shows that even the raw log–log
plot of the data is quite linear. Seibel's data is a different matter though. In the
raw log–log plot it has deviations at both ends of the curve. By giving non-zero
values to the asymptote (.324) and to the prior experience (2690), the data gets
straightened. This straightening yields a sharply higher α. It rises from .32 to .95
during this process. Though seemingly large, the initial experience of 2690 trials
is not excessive, given the full trial range of 70,000.

The linearity of the optimal power-law plots is strong evidence for the power
law as a model of learning curves. This is bolstered even further by the r^2 values
that are considerably higher than those for the equivalent exponential fits (.993
versus .956 for Seibel and .931 versus .849 for Kolers). An examination of Table
1.2 reveals that the value of r^2 for a power law fit is higher than for an exponential fit for all of the practice curves that we have examined.

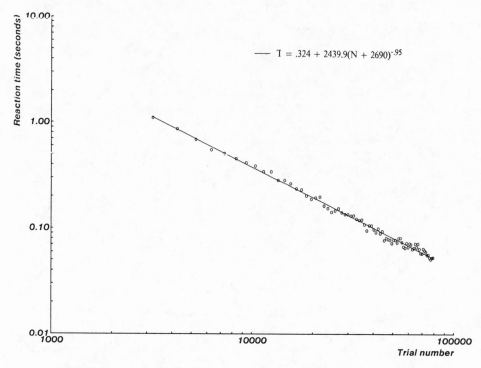

FIG. 1.21. Optimal fit to Seibel's data in the power law transformation space (log–log coordinates).

The Hyperbolic Family

It is not surprising that Seibel's data is well fit by a hyperbolic as the optimal power (α) turned out to be .95. The r^2 value remains unchanged in a shift of α to 1, and the plot remains highly linear (Fig. 1.23). What is more surprising (considering the amount of data involved) is that Kolers's data (with an optimal α of .46) is also adequately fit by a hyperbolic (Fig. 1.24). By assuming larger values for A and E, the whole curve is tilted to be steeper. There is a small loss in r^2, from .931 for the power law to .915 for the hyperbolic, but it is nowhere near as large a drop as to the exponential (.849). There does appear to be a small upturn at the beginning of the curve, and a similar downturn at the end, but the overall deviation from linearity is not large. This small inferiority of the hyperbolic (with respect to the power law) must be traded off against the fact that it has one less parameter.

Summary

Table 1.2 shows the results of this analysis for all the data sets shown in the second section. We believe that it establishes the reasonableness of excluding the possibility that practice learning is exponential and the reasonableness of describ-

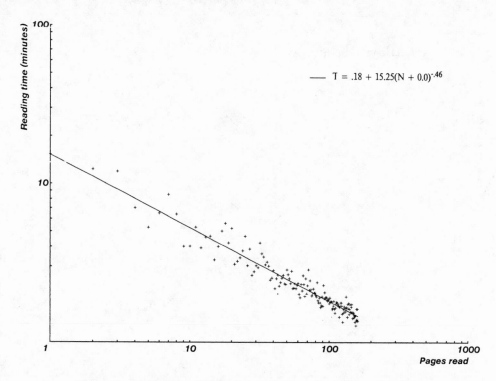

FIG. 1.22. Optimal fit to Kolers's data in the power law transformation space (log–log coordinates).

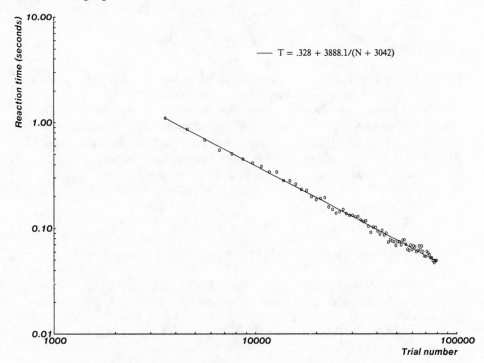

FIG. 1.23. Optimal fit to Seibel's data in the hyperbolic transformation space (log–log coordinates).

33

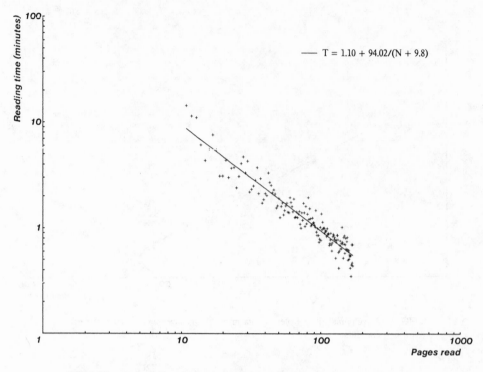

FIG. 1.24.   Optimal fit to Kolers's data in the hyperbolic transformation space (log–log coordinates).

ing the data by power laws. The hyperbolic family is somewhere in the middle. From Table 1.2 it is apparent that most of the data sets can be adequately modeled as hyperbolics. There are cases though, such as the data from Moran (1980), that do seem to suffer by the loss of the extra parameter. It would be nice to be more precise about the appropriateness of the hyperbolic, but the data we have considered do not allow it. These conclusions agree with those of Mazur and Hastie (1978) in rejecting exponentials but not in rejecting general power laws.

POSSIBLE EXPLANATIONS

For the purposes of this paper, we have come to accept two propositions:

- Practice learning is described by performance-time as a power function of the number of trials since the start of learning (the hyperbolic is included as a special case).
- The same law is ubiquitous over all types of mental behavior (possibly even more widely).

What are the possible explanations for such a regularity? In this section we try to enumerate the major alternatives and to concentrate on one.

There seem to be three major divisions of explanation. The first reaches for the most general characteristics of the learning situation, in accord with the end of the second section that such a widespread phenomenon can only result from some equally widespread structural feature. One of the assumptions underlying much of cognitive psychology is the *decomposability* of thought processes. A task can be broken down into independent subtasks. *Mixture* models attempt to derive the power law from the aggregate behavior of such a collection of independent learners. The second division is some sort of improving statistical selection, in the manner of mathematical learning theory or evolution. No specific orientation exists to obtain the power law. Rather, simple or natural selective schemes are simply posited and examined. The third division takes the exponential as somehow the *natural* form of learning. Observing that the power law is much slower, it seeks for what slows down learning. What could be *exhausted* that keeps the learning from remaining exponential?

We shall concentrate on an explanation of the exhaustion type. However, we do not consider it the exclusive source of the power law of practice. So we first wish to lay out the wider context before narrowing to one.

General Mixtures

The following qualitative argument has a certain appeal.

> *The Mixtures Argument:* Performance depends on a collection of mechanisms in some monotone way [i.e., an increase in the time taken for any mechanism increases (possibly leaves unchanged) the total performance time]. The learning mechanisms that improve these performance mechanisms will have a distribution of rates of improvement—some faster, some slower. At any moment total system learning will be dominated by the fast learners, since a fortiori they are the fast ones. However, the fast learners will soon make little contribution to changes in total performance, precisely because their learning will have been effective (and rapidly so, to boot), so the components they affect cannot continue to contribute substantially to total performance. This will leave only slow learners to yield improvement. Hence the rate of improvement later will be slower than the rate of improvement initially. This is the essential feature of the log–log law—the slowing down of the learning rate. Hence learning in complex systems will tend to be approximately linear in log–log space.

The great virtue of this argument, or some refinement of it, is that it would explain the ubiquity, even unto the industrial production functions.

We do not know how to examine this law in full generality. However, restriction to a subclass of learning functions, if the subclass is rich enough, can shed some useful light on the issue, for the argument should hold for the subclass as well.

The complete definition of a mixture model requires both the specification of a class of learning functions and a scheme by which they are aggregated. A natural class of learning functions is the exponential functions. They form a rich enough class (a three-parameter family of α, A, and B). They also are as good a candidate as any for primitive learning functions. We can place sufficient restriction on the means of aggregation if we assume that performance consists of the *serial* execution of subtasks. This places us within the class of additive systems, that is, where each component adds its contribution to the total performance.[7] The result is that T is a weighted sum of exponentials:

$$T = \sum_i W_i e^{-\mu_i N} \tag{37}$$

Figure 1.25 shows a plot in log–log space of a 40-term sum with weights (the W's) and rates (the μ's) selected at random ($0 < W_i < 5$ and $0 < \mu_i < .1$). One achieves a reasonable approximation to a straight line over much of the range, though it is a little wavy.

Mixtures of this type have one primary source of variation: the set of weights $\{W_i\}$. The plausibility of mixture models as a source for power laws can best be evaluated by determining the classes of functions that are generated under reasonable assumptions for $\{W_i\}$. If the result is always a power law, then mixture models are strongly implicated. On the other hand, if any function can be generated with equal facility, mixtures would be of little use as an explanation for the ubiquity of power laws.

Sums of exponentials do provide a sufficient ensemble of functions to compose (essentially) any function desired. A convenient way to see this is to go over to the continuous case:

$$T(N) = \int_0^\infty W(\mu) e^{-\mu N} \, d\mu \tag{38}$$

On the one hand, this simply expresses the continuous analog of a sum of exponentials: the exponential for every μ is represented, each with its own weight, $W(\mu)$. On the other hand, this will instantly be recognized (at least by engineers and mathematicians) as the Laplace transform of the function W (Churchill, 1972). The significance of this is that we know that for any function $T(N)$ there is a function $W(\mu)$ that produces it.[8] Thus, by choosing appropriate weights, any total learning function whatsoever can be obtained.

---

[7]Simple additive combination is not the only way to put learning mechanisms together. Clayton Lewis (no date) explored the notion of series–parallel combinations of exponential learning mechanisms. The results were unclear, sometimes looking log–log, sometimes looking more like an exponential, sometimes wandering. He arrived (1980) at the position that another source of constraint or uniformity is needed.

[8]T must be mathematically well behaved in certain ways to be so represented, but this is of no consequence in the present context.

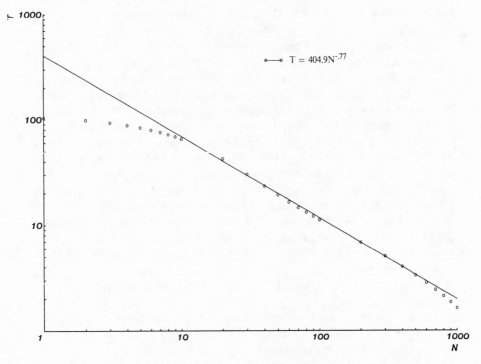

FIG. 1.25.   A forty term additive exponential mixture (log–log coordinates). The weights ($0 < W_i < 5$) and exponents ($0 < \mu_i < .1$) were selected at random.

We can of course choose weights to make T a power law, as in Equation 4, with α and B. Consulting any standard table of Laplace transforms shows

$$W(\mu) = \left[\frac{B}{\Gamma(\alpha)} \right] \mu^{-(1-\alpha)} \qquad (39)$$

That is,

$$T(N) = BN^{-\alpha} = \int_0^\infty \left[\frac{B}{\Gamma(\alpha)} \right] \mu^{-(1-\alpha)} e^{-\mu N} d\mu \qquad (40)$$

The component exponentials correspond to learning at all rates, indefinitely fast (large μ) to indefinitely slow (small μ). Because $(1 - \alpha) \geq 0$, the weight W becomes very small for fast learning and very large for slow learning. Without a justification for this particular distribution of weights, it would seem implausible that mixtures of learning components would always lead to power laws.

However, we can turn the argument around and obtain a positive result. One distribution of weights for which there is a natural justification is the rectangular (i.e., all component processes have the same weight, at least stochastically). This is especially true in the present approximation, where a random distribution of weights would be taken to be rectangular. As seen from Equations 39 and 40, this corresponds to $(1 - \alpha) = 0$, which yields $\alpha = 1$. The resulting law is the hyperbolic.

It is beyond the bounds of this chapter to inquire how closely random weighting functions can be approximated by the mean. Within our limits, it appears that a mixture of exponentials yields a special case of the power law, namely, the hyperbolic. Put together with the results of the data–fit analysis, which showed that hyperbolics were a reasonable candidate descriptive curve, this adds up to a significant observation (it can hardly be distinguished as a "result").

Real mixtures can only strive to approximate the distribution of exponentials that the use of rectangular weights implies. They must fall short because there can only be a finite number of components. The initial portion of Fig. 1.25 is flattened because of the lack of terms in the mixture that decay quickly enough to affect that portion. We restricted the fastest term to have a μ less than .1, but there must always be a maximum μ. Regions of the curve that are affected by only a few terms will look highly exponential, leading to a roller coaster effect where two such regions meet [e.g., for N in the region (10,200) in Fig. 1.25]. In regions where only one term is relevant, the curve is an exponential. This must always occur at least in the tail of the curve, where only the slowest term in the mixture is still active.

The amount of deviation within a region of the curve is thus determined by the number of terms affecting that region. Linearity over a wide range requires a large number of terms in the mixture.

Stochastic Selection

The work in stochastic modeling generated a large range of models, well beyond what we can review. However, a few of the models are particularly relevant to this work.

Crossman's Model

Twenty years ago, Crossman (1959), in an effort similar in spirit to the present one, wrote a paper reviewing much data on practice. He proposed a general model based on an improving process of selecting methods from a fixed population of methods with fixed durations, $\{t_i\}$. Improvement occurs, because each method is selected according to a probability and these probabilities are adjusted on the basis of experience. Namely, the change in probability is proportional to the difference between the mean time, $T(N)$, and the actual time of the selected method, t_i:

$$\delta p_i = -k[t_i - T(N)] \tag{41}$$

By assuming that the entire probability vector shifts at each trial according to its expected adjustment (i.e., as if all methods were tried each trial, each with frequency p_i), the expected shift for the mean time can be expressed as

$$T(N + 1) = T(N) - k\text{Var}(N) \tag{42}$$

where $\text{Var}(N)$ is the variance of the $\{t\}$ on cycle N.

In general, the time course cannot be calculated without knowing the actual distribution of the t_i, for the following relationships hold for this model [$M_j(N)$ is the jth moment of the $\{t_i\}$ on cycle N]:

$$T(N) = M_1(N) \tag{43}$$

$$\text{Var}(N) = M_2(N) - [M_1(N)]^2 \tag{44}$$

$$M_j(N + 1) = [1 + kM_1(N)]M_j(N) - kM_{j+1}(N) \tag{45}$$

Thus, as N increases, higher moments of the initial distribution are needed to compute $\text{Var}(N)$. Crossman assumed an (somewhat arbitrary) example distribution and examined the resulting curve numerically. In log–log space it plotted as a sigmoid with a large straight section, somewhat in the manner of Fig. 1.15. He concluded that it was a satisfactory form of model, though clearly needing more development.

Unfortunately, the model rests very heavily on the way it uses its expected value assumptions. As seen from Equation 41, nothing prevents p_i from moving outside the [0, 1] interval, thereby violating the basic property of being a probability. Indeed, if the ith method is selected often enough, it must move outside. Crossman avoids the unavoidable by making the change really be $p_i\delta p_i$, the expected change. Even this modification is not sufficient to guarantee that p_i remains in the range of [0, 1]. If k is greater than $1/(t_{\max} - t_{\min})$, then it is possible for $\delta p_{\min}$ to be less than -1. An additional assumption about the legal values of k could of course be added to handle this problem.

We have expounded Crossman's model at some length, because not only is it the one existing attempt to deal with the power-law data, but it is often referred to as a viable explanation of this law.

The Accumulator and Replacement Models

Among the basic stochastic learning models two broad classes are often distinguished, depending on whether correct responses replace incorrect ones— called *replacement* models—or whether correct responses are simply added to the total pool, thus gradually swamping out the incorrect ones—called *accumulator* models. A presentation of these two models is given in Restle and Greeno (1970).

The replacement models yield exponential functions (when expressed in terms of rate of generation of correct responses). It is worth taking a look at an accumulator model, as it will provide another model that yields the hyperbolic. Restle and Greeno show that the proportion of correct responses in the pool at trial N (P_N) is given by (the interpretations of the other parameters are not important for our purposes)

$$P_N = \frac{b + \theta a(N - 1)}{1 + \theta(N - 1)} \tag{46}$$

To get this in terms of time, we can assume that the time to generate a response is inversely proportional to the rate of generation of correct responses. Thus $T(N)$ would be the inverse of Equation 46:

$$T(N) = \frac{1 + \theta(N - 1)}{b + \theta a(N - 1)} \tag{47}$$

With a little rearrangement, this becomes:

$$T(N) = \frac{1}{a} + \frac{(a - b)/\theta a^2}{N + [b/\theta a - 1]} \tag{48}$$

This is the equation for a general hyperbolic function, with $A = 1/a$, $B = (a - b)/\theta a^2$, and $E = b/\theta a - 1$.

Exhaustion of Exponential Learning

The notion of exhaustion comes from examining Equation 11. A power law is like an exponential in which the exponent (α) does not remain constant over trials. In fact, α decreases as $1/N$. An exhaustion model would postulate that this decrease stems from the diminishment of some necessary portion of the learning process. Many different exhaustion models can be developed according to what is being diminished. We have concentrated our efforts on one variety of exhaustion model; what we call the *chunking model of learning*. Before we examine it in detail, it is useful to look briefly at the range of possible exhaustion models. In the descriptions that follow it is assumed that the learner uses some *method* for the performance of the task on which he is working. Learning consists of finding and incorporating *improvements* to the current method.

• *Improvements harder to find (search exhaustion):* Improvements may not always be right at hand. It would then be necessary to search for improvements that can be made in the method being used. Each time one is found, it would result in the time (T) decreasing by some constant factor (α), just as in exponential learning. As improvements are found and applied, the space of unused improvements becomes sparser, decreasing the rate at which new improvements can be found. The effective rate of learning would thus be slowed.

• *Less time for improvement (time exhaustion):* If learning is exponential in time (rather than in trials), then as the trials get shorter, there is less time for improvement on each trial. We saw earlier that an exponential in time yields a hyperbolic in trials.

One long standing view is that learning consists of transforming a deliberate, conscious and resource limited process into an automatic, unconscious and resource independent one. One image of this in mechanism is that learning consists of a transformation from a serial to a parallel processing structure. The amount of processing required remains constant. Only the elapsed time until completion decreases. Exhaustion occurs if it is assumed that learning is proportional to the amount of time available (T)—the usual exponential assumption. As the amount of process that is packed into a fixed time slice increases, the amount of learning per unit of process would have to decrease. A simple version of this model that we have developed yields the hyperbolic.

• *Improvements less effective (effectiveness exhaustion):* Improvements used later in learning, may prove to be less effective than the same improvements used earlier.

• *Improvements less applicable (applicability exhaustion):* Improvements may vary from being general purpose to being highly specialized. General-purpose improvements are always applicable, while special purpose ones may only be applicable under highly constrained conditions. In order to specify a model of this type fully, an assumption must be made as to the order in which the improvements are incorporated into the method. If they are used in order of decreasing applicability, then learning would slow down even if the improvements are equal in effectiveness (when they are applicable). The theory we present now is a version of this case.

The Chunking Theory of Learning

We take as central to our model a theme that has been a mainstay of information-processing psychology since Miller's famous 1956 paper.

> *The Chunking Hypothesis:* A human acquires and organizes knowledge of the environment by forming and storing expressions, called *chunks*, which are structured collections of the chunks existing at the time of learning.

This brief statement glosses over things not central to our purpose, for example: (1) the nature of the primitive chunks; (2) the internal representation of chunks as collections of symbols for chunks, rather than the chunks themselves; and (3) distinctions, if any, between perceptual chunks, internal-processing chunks, and motor chunks. Other aspects, such as the size and composition of chunks, require further specification.

Consider Seibel's task (Seibel, 1963), to make matters concrete. There are ten lights $L_1, \ldots , L_{10}$, which define perceptual events of a light being off ($-$) or on ($+$). Originally, the only chunks available are the individual lights and the states of *off* and *on*. If we define the notion of the *span* of a chunk as the number of primitive elements that it contains, then these are chunks with a span of one. Clearly they are built up from still more primitive features, relations, etc., but they can be taken as the primitives from the point of view of Seibel's task. Gradually, with learning, chunks will form: first chunks such as ($L_1\ +$), which we might also write as L_1^+; then chunks such as ($L_3^+ L_4^+$) or ($L_1^- L_{10}^-$); then still higher chunks such as $(L_2^+(L_3^- L_4^-))$, and so on. The chunks need not just be of perceived lights; they could be of responses $(R_5^+ R_6^+)$ (the + meaning to press the button) or even of mixed character, $(L_3^+ R_3^+)$ or $((L_7^+ L_8^-)(R_7^+ R_8^-))$. These chunks are of increasing span; for example, the span of the last mentioned chunk, $((L_7^+ L_8^-) (R_7^+ R_8^-))$, is eight of the primitive chunks such as L_7, +, L_8. Chunks thus hold information about the *patterns* in the environment and in the subject's relation to the environment.

The chunking assumption only defines a unit of structure and declares it central. To create a learning system, we must tie down how this structure couples to: (1) the performance of the task; (2) the structure of the task environment; and (3) the process of learning new information about the task environment. These lead to three corresponding general assumptions:

• *Performance assumption:* The performance program of the system is coded in terms of high-level chunks, with the time to process a chunk being less than the time to process its constituent chunks.

• *Task structure assumption:* The probability of recurrence of an environmental pattern decreases as the pattern size increases.

• *Learning assumption:* Chunks are learned at a constant time rate on average from the relevant patterns of stimuli and responses that occur in the specific environments experienced.

On Performance.   If having chunks does not permit the system to perform more quickly, then one major reason for their existence vanishes (though there might be other reasons). How high-level aggregate chunks enter into performance programs is actually somewhat problematical. For instance, computers gain no performance advantage from the subroutine hierarchy (an example of multilevel chunking); it is completely unwound down to the lowest level machine operations on every execution.

In Seibel's task the performance program can be related directly to the chunks that exist. If only the lowest chunks are available, then it might take the processing of five chunks for each light:

$$((L_x\ +)(R_y\ +))$$
$$L_1\ +\ R_1\ +$$

The top chunk is the rule derived from the instructions for general lights (L_x) and responses (R_y); it is used to interpret each of the four primitive chunks of information about the task, one after the other. If, on the other hand, more complete chunks are available, such as $(L_1\ +)$, then this part can be done in a single step, and so on for more aggregate chunks. Aggregation, of course, takes place not just within a light, but across lights. Thus, a lowest-level performance program would take something like 5 steps per light times 10 lights = 50 steps. At the other extreme, the highest-level program would take only a single step, using many mammoth chunks, such as the one below of span 40, to cover all the cases.

$$(((((L_1^+R_1^+)(L_2^-R_2^-))(L_3^+R_3^+))\ ((L_4^+R_4^+)(L_5^+R_5^+))\ ((L_6^+R_6^+)((L_7^-R_7^-)(L_8^-R_8^-))$$

$$((L_9^-R_9^-)(L_{10}^+R_{10}^+)))) \tag{49}$$

Most programs would be composed of chunks of some intermediate span. Our example chunks have used stimulus adjacency and stimulus–response connection as the principles on which to chunk. Lots of others are possible (e.g., symmetry of position). Likewise, wrong connections are possible as well as correct ones.

On the Structure of the Task Environment.   Task environments can be thought of as being composed from a set of elements that can vary with respect to attributes, locations, relations to other elements, etc. Seibel's task is a good example of such a task environment once chunking has reached beyond the most primitive level (the lights, on, off, etc.). Observe that (thinking only about the lights) there is a set of elements (the 10 lights) each of which has an attribute for the state of the light (*on* or *off*). On each trial the subject is exposed to a single *concrete environment* out of the *ensemble* of concrete environments that make up the *task environment*. A subject in Seibel's experiment would see the 10 lights in one particular state on each trial. The trial sequence provides the sample of concrete environments actually experienced.

Figure 1.26 shows a four-light version of Seibel's task environment. At the left are the primitive chunks, the lights, which can be either on or off. Proceeding toward the right yields higher level chunks made by combining lower-level ones. At the far right are the top-level chunks. Each top-level chunk spans one concrete environment (consisting of each light in one particular state). The bold lines outline one concrete environment out of the ensemble that makes up the task environment. One important point to notice is that the branchiness of the task environment (increasing toward the right) is in the opposite direction from that of the tree for a single concrete environment (increasing toward the left). As the chunks increase in span, there are more of them in the task environment but fewer in any one concrete environment.

Task environments such as Seibel's present the learner with a combinatorial number of possible patterns. There are only 2 patterns of 1 light (on and off), but 4 patterns of 2 lights, 8 patterns of 3 lights, and so on, up to 1024 patterns of 10 lights. Inherently, many more possibilities for patterns of elements exist than for the elements themselves. Correspondingly, there are many more possibilities for chunks that encode larger patterns than smaller ones. If each of the elements can take on any of b different values (the *branchiness* of the task environment), then for every set of s elements there would be b^s possible patterns. Different task environments will have constraints that limit what new combinations can in fact occur; not all elements are or can be chunked with each other. The basic combinatorial nature of most task environments, combined with these constraints, will determine what can be called the *cardinality* of the task environment,

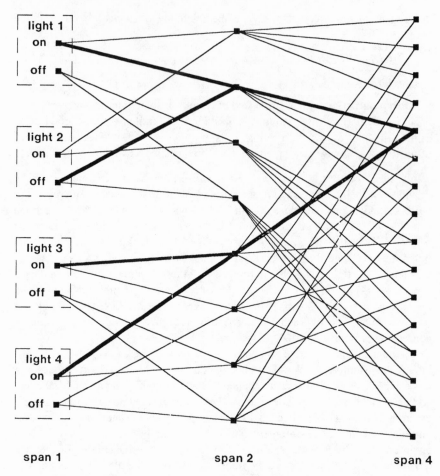

span 1   span 2   span 4

FIG. 1.26.   Seibel's task environment for four lights. At the left are the two
primitive chunks for each light (for the *on* and *off* states) and at the right are the
top-level chunks.

namely, the number of patterns that can actually occur of each different span.
This cardinality (whether exponential, power law, etc.) will have a great deal to
do with the form of the final learning curve.

The *task structure assumption* follows directly from this structure of the task
environment. There are more of the larger patterns, but each one appears in fewer
concrete environments. Indeed, at the topmost level, the entire concrete environment at a trial can be encoded in a single chunk, as in Example 49. Chunks of
this type appear in only one concrete environment each, whereas a chunk that
only contains a single light and its state would appear in many concrete environments. The multiplicity of patterns (chunks) depends on there being an entire
ensemble of possible concrete environments. In any particular concrete environment only a small number of the possible chunks occur.

On Learning by Experience.   This assumption starts from the view that the human is a time-independent processing mechanism. It processes information the same way one hour as the next, one day as the next—as a function of stored knowledge and learned procedures but not of time per se. In short, there is no built-in historical clock. Thus, there exists a basic constant rate of chunk acquisition (with respect to time, not trials). This same view underlies the appeal of the *total time hypothesis* of verbal learning (Cooper & Pantle, 1967).

Not all chunks learned need be relevant to the task at hand. The assumption that learning is by experience says the subject is picking up relevant chunks while performing in a concrete environment. This is consonant with theories that have learning occurring automatically from the chunks that are built in *working memory* (involving both the stimuli and the subject's own responses). When the subject is attending to the task, working memory is full of task-related chunks, and relevant learning occurs.

In our example, given L_1 and $+$ perceived by the subject, the chunk $(L_1 +)$ could be built, but not the chunk $(L_1 -)$. Also, it would take the same length of time to build the first-level chunk as to build $(((L_1 +) (R_1 +)) ((L_2 -) (R_2 -)))$ given that the constituent chunks, $((L_1 +) (R_1 +))$ and $((L_2 -) (R_2 -))$, were available in the subject (i.e., had already been learned) and were being perceived in the environment.

These three assumptions, though still general, provide a basis on which specific learning models can be built. In this chapter we only present the simplest form of this model so that the basic mechanisms can be clearly seen. Various limiting conditions and the like may appear a little strained in this simple version.

A Simple Version

For the theory to be specific, we need to determine T as a function of N. One way to do this is to define the differential learning law, dT/dN. Corresponding to the previous assumptions, we introduce the following variables:

C = the total number of chunks learned at any time.

s = the span to which the subject has chunked.

In terms of these variables, we can compose dT/dN as follows:

$$\frac{dT}{dN} = \left(\frac{dT}{ds} \right) \left(\frac{ds}{dC} \right) \left(\frac{dC}{dN} \right) \tag{50}$$

The first term, dT/ds, expresses how performance time (T) changes with the chunk span. In a simple form of our performance assumption, the time to perform the task will simply be proportional to the number of high-level chunks it takes to describe the task (at the time of the performance). Let P be the number of chunks involved in the performance initially (and take the unit of time to be the time to process one chunk, so as to avoid an arbitrary constant). Then, if chunking has proceeded to a span of s, each top-level chunk spans s initial chunks.

Thus, the number of top-level chunks that are required to span the performance is P/s and we find for the performance time,

$$T = \frac{P}{s} \tag{51}$$

$$\frac{dT}{ds} = \frac{-P}{s^2} = \frac{-T^2}{P} \tag{52}$$

If this holds for unlimited values of s, it implies that P is infinitely divisible and that T can be driven to zero. We just accept such simplifications for the purposes of this model. Given this simplification, however, we cannot expect to find an asymptote parameter (A) in this version.

The second term of Equation 50, ds/dC, expresses how fast the span of the chunks increases as the subject accumulates more chunks. It depends on how many chunks of each span are needed to describe the task environment. According to the assumption about the structure of the task environment, new chunks will be formed to encompass larger patterns in the environment. If a chunk covers a pattern of some set of elements, then it will be relevant to connect it with a certain number of additional elements in the environment to form the next higher level of chunk. We postpone until later the quantification of this process. For now we can just talk in terms of $C_{te}(s)$, the number of chunks needed to cover all patterns of s elements or less in the task environment.

We need to relate $C_{te}(s)$ to $C(N)$, the number of chunks that the subject has at a given trial. By the nature of how chunks are learned, low-level chunks must be acquired before higher-level chunks; that is, chunks are learned from the bottom up. If C chunks have been learned, they will constitute a pyramid up from the bottom. By making the further simplifying assumption that the pyramid is acquired layer by layer (i.e., if the subject has learned C chunks, these will consist of all the chunks provided by the environment from the elementary chunks up to some span), we can equate C and C_{te}.[9] Hence we find

$$C = C_{te} \tag{53}$$

$$\frac{dC}{ds} = C'_{te}(s), \text{ writing } C'_{te}(s) \text{ for } \frac{dC_{te}(s)}{ds} \text{ for clarity} \tag{54}$$

$$\frac{ds}{dC} = \frac{1}{C'_{te}(s)} \tag{55}$$

The final term of Equation 50 follows directly from the assumptions on learning: that the number of chunks learned per unit time is a constant, say λ chunks:

---

[9]We are glossing over three complications to this picture: (1) M elements can be covered by chunks of span s in a number of ways, depending on how the M elements are partitioned into groups of size s; (2) M elements can be covered by a number of different chunks of span M that vary in internal structure; and (3) many patterns in the environment are totally irrelevant to performance on the task.

$$\frac{dC}{dt} = \lambda \tag{56}$$

Therefore by Equation 22, which relates time to trials,

$$\frac{dC}{dN} = \left(\frac{dC}{dt} \right) \left(\frac{dt}{dN} \right) = \lambda T \tag{57}$$

We now have assembled all the components of Equation 50:

$$\frac{dT}{dN} = \left(\frac{-T^2}{P} \right) \left[\frac{1}{C'_{te}(s)} \right] (\lambda T) \tag{58}$$

$$= \frac{-\lambda}{P} \left[\frac{T^3}{C'_{te}(s)} \right] \tag{59}$$

We can see in what sense this is an exhaustion model. The subject continues to learn at a constant rate and chunks remain equally potent in terms of what they do to the performance programs in which they occur. However, the chance that a chunk will be used becomes increasingly rare. It becomes rarer, actually, because of the increased span of the chunk, which makes it ever more specialized, thus occurring in ever fewer environments. However, this turns out to be correlated with time, because general (i.e., low level) chunks are learned first and specialized chunks are learned later.

A Combinatorial Task Environment

To complete the definition of the chunking model it will be necessary to be more specific about $C_{te}(s)$, the cardinality of the task environment, which expresses how fast the number of patterns increase as their span increases. One possibility is to start from the basic combinatorial structure described under the task structure assumption. Suppose there are M elements in the task environment, each with b possible values. We need to know how many chunks of span s it takes to cover the task environment. One way to do this is to partition the task environment into M/s groups of s elements. It will take b^s chunks of span s to cover each group and so $(M/s)b^s$ chunks to cover the whole task environment. We thus find

$$C_{te}(s) = \sum_{i=1}^{s} \left(\frac{M}{i} \right) b^i \tag{60}$$

This summation does not have a closed form solution. We can however derive $C'_{te}(s)$ directly from the summation in the same manner that dt/dN is obtained in Equation 22.

$$C'_{te}(s) = \left(\frac{M}{s} \right) b^s = \left(\frac{M}{s} \right) e^{\beta s} \tag{61}$$

where $\beta = \log(b)$.

Substituting $C'_{te}(s)$ into Equation 59, we find:

$$\frac{dT}{dN} = - \left(\frac{\lambda}{PM} \right) T^3 s e^{-\beta s} \tag{62}$$

We can eliminate s by noticing that $s = P/T$ (from Equation 51):

$$\frac{dT}{dN} = - \left(\frac{\lambda}{M} \right) T^2 e^{-\beta P/T} \tag{63}$$

By suitable rearrangement and integration, the final form of the learning curve is obtained:

$$T^{-2} e^{\beta P/T} \, dT = - \left(\frac{\lambda}{M} \right) dN \tag{64}$$

$$\int T^{-2} e^{\beta P/T} \, dT = - \left(\frac{\lambda}{M} \right) \int dN \tag{65}$$

$$(\beta P)^{-1} e^{\beta P/T} = \left(\frac{\lambda}{M} \right) (N + E) \tag{66}$$

where E comes from the integration constant.

$$T = \frac{\beta P}{\log(\lambda \beta P/M) + \log(N + E)} \tag{67}$$

Though this is not a power law, it does resemble one when plotted in log–log coordinates. Figure 1.27 shows such a learning curve with parameters of $b = 2$, $P = 50$, $\lambda = 1$, $M = 20$, and $E = 10$. The reason for this linearity can best be seen by looking at dT/dN. Substituting for $1/T$ in the exponent of Equation 63 yields

$$\frac{dT}{dN} = - \left[\frac{(\beta P)^{-1}}{N + E} \right] T^2 \tag{68}$$

$$= - \left[\frac{\alpha}{N + E} \right] T \tag{69}$$

where $\alpha = T/\beta P$.

The function thus behaves like a power law with a slowly decreasing α. In log–log space the decreasing α is difficult to distinguish from the presence of an asymptote.

The Power Law Chunking Model

Instantiations of the chunking model can be generated for various types of task environment that a learner may have to deal with. There is no space here to examine possible task environments systematically. An alternative is to determine what type of task environment leads the chunking model to predict power-

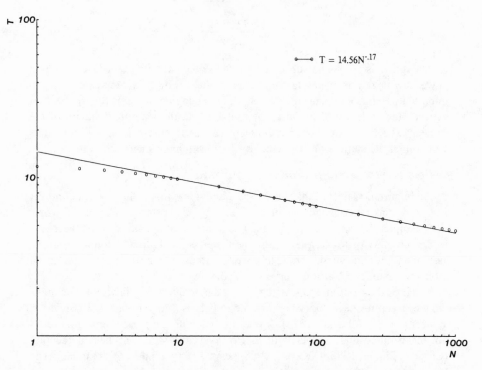

FIG. 1.27. The learning curve for the *chunking model* in a combinatorial task environment (log-log coordinates). The parameter values are: $b = 2$, $P = 50$, $\lambda = 1$, $M = 20$, and $E = 10$.

law learning. From Equation 8 we know that one form for the differential of a power law is

$$\frac{dT}{dN} = -\alpha B^{-1/\alpha} T^{1+1/\alpha} \tag{70}$$

Combining this with Equation 59 yields

$$-\alpha B^{-1/\alpha} T^{1+1/\alpha} = -\left(\frac{\lambda}{P}\right)\left[\frac{T^3}{C'_{te}(s)}\right] \tag{71}$$

We want $C_{te}(s)$, so first solving for $C'_{te}(s)$

$$C'_{te}(s) = \left(\frac{\lambda B^{1/\alpha}}{P\alpha}\right) T^{2-1/\alpha} \tag{72}$$

$$= \left(\frac{\lambda B^{1/\alpha}}{P\alpha}\right)\left(\frac{P}{s}\right)^{2-1/\alpha} \tag{73}$$

$$= \left(\frac{\lambda B^{1/\alpha} P^{1-1/\alpha}}{\alpha}\right) s^{1/\alpha-2} \tag{74}$$

Now we can find $C_{te}(s)$ by integrating $C'_{te}(s)$ with respect to s.

$$C_{te}(s) = \left[\frac{\lambda B^{1/\alpha} P^{1-1/\alpha}}{1 - \alpha} \right] s^{1/\alpha - 1} \tag{75}$$

Though it is somewhat obscured by the complex initial constant, this is a power law in s. Power-law learning thus implies a power-law environment. An important, and indeed pleasing, feature of the chunking model is this connection between the structure of the task environment and the learning behavior of the subject. The richer the task environment (i.e., the ensemble of environments with which the subject must potentially cope) the more difficult his learning.

Relation to Existing Work on Chunking

An important aspect of the chunking model of learning is the amount of power it gets by making connection with a wide body of existing psychological work. For example, the pervasiveness of the phenomenon of chunking amply accounts for the ubiquity of log–log learning. We have been able to develop the primary assumptions of the model from this work without the necessity of pulling an arbitrary "natural" learning curve out of the air.

Much of the existing work on chunking has focused on showing that chunks are the structures of memory and operate in behavior in various ways (Bower & Winzenz, 1969; Johnson, 1972). It is consonant with the present model but does not make interesting contact with it. However, the work on chess perception (Chase & Simon, 1973; DeGroot, 1965) bears directly on the present model. The basic phenomenon investigated there was the differential short-term memory for meaningful chess positions with expertness. Novices are able to recall only a few pieces of a complex middle-game position after a 5-second exposure, whereas masters can recall most of the pieces.

A well-articulated theory has evolved to explain this striking phenomenon. The theory is an elaboration of the basic assumptions about chunking. The master has acquired an immense memory for chess positions, organized as a collection of chunks. His ability for immediate perception and short-term memory of chess positions depends directly on how many chunks are used to encode a position. Estimates of the number of chunks available to the master are of the order of 50,000, based on extrapolation of a simulation program (Simon & Gilmartin, 1973) that fits novice- and expert-level players. By implication, master players must spend an immense amount of time with the game, in order to acquire the large number of chunks; this seems to be well supported by historical data.

The chunking model of learning presented here for the power law is essentially the same as the chess perception model. The present model has been elaborated quantitatively for learning data, whereas the chess perception data had the products of learning to work with. The explanation for why the number of perceptual chess chunks is so large lies in the combinatorial complexity of chess positions. High-level chess chunks encode large subpatterns of pieces on the board; they are the necessary means for rapid perception. But the actual configurations to which they apply do not show up often. Thus to gain coverage of the population of chess positions requires acquisition of immense numbers of high-level chunks. This is precisely the notion of environmental exhaustion that is the key mechanism of the present model.

One would expect from this that the time course of chess skill would also follow the power law, if one would take the trouble to measure it. Indeed, the data on the *Stair* game of solitaire in Fig. 1.10 can be taken as a reasonable analog of the chess game.

CONCLUSION

If we may, let us start this conclusion by recounting our personal odyssey in this research. We started out, simply enough, intrigued by a great quantitative regularity that seemed to be of immense importance (and of consequence for an applied quantitative psychology), well known, yet seemingly ignored in cognitive psychology. We saw the law as tied to skill and hence relevant to the modern work in automatization. The commitment to write this chapter was the goad to serious research. When we started, our theoretical stance was neutral—we just wanted to find out what the law could tell us. Through the fall of 1979, in searching for explanations, we became convinced that plausible substantive theories of power laws were hard to find, though it seemed relatively easy to obtain an exponent of -1 (i.e., hyperbolics). In November, discovering the chunking model (by looking for forms of exhaustion, in fact), we became convinced that it was the right theory (at least A. N. did) and that lack of good alternative theories helped to make the case. The chunking model also implied that the power law was not restricted to perceptual-motor skills but should apply much more generally. This led to our demonstration experiment on *Stair*, which showed a genuine problem-solving task to be log–log linear. At the same time, in conversations with John Anderson, additional data emerged from the work of his group (Figs. 1.7 and 1.9) that bolstered this.

This picture seemed reasonably satisfactory, though the existence of log–log linear industrial learning curves (Fig. 1.12) nagged a bit, as did the persistence of some of our colleagues in believing in the argument of mixtures. However, as we proceeded to write the chapter, additional work kept emerging from the literature, including especially the work by Mazur and Hastie (1978), that raised substantial doubts that the power law was the right empirical description of the data. The resulting investigation has brought us to the present chapter.

The picture that emerges is somewhat complex, though we believe at the moment that this complexity is in the phenomena, and not just in our heads as a reflection of only a momentary understanding. We summarize this picture below, starting with the data and progressing through theoretical considerations.

1. The empirical curves do not fit the exponential family. Their tails are genuinely slower than exponential learning and this shape deviation does not disappear with variation of asymptote.

2. The data do satisfactorily fit the family of generalized power functions (which includes the hyperbolic subfamily). There is little shape variance remaining in the existing data to justify looking for other empirical families.

In particular, there is no reason to treat apparent systematic deviations, such as occur in Snoddy's or Seibel's data in log–log space (Figs. 1.1, 1.6), as due to special causes, distinct from their description as a generalized power function.

3. The data do not fit the simple power law (i.e., without asymptote or variable starting point). There are systematic shape deviations in log–log space (the space that linearizes the simple power law), which disappear completely under the general power law.

4. We were unable to confirm either whether the data fit within the hyperbolic subfamily or actually requires the general power family. This is so despite the multitude of existing data sets, some with extremely lengthy data series (some of it as extensive as any data in psychology).

5. The major phenomenon is the ubiquity of the learning data (i.e., its common description by a single family of empirical curves). We extended the scope to all types of cognitive behavior, not just perceptual-motor skill.

However, we restricted our view to performance time as the measure of performance, though learning curves measured on other criterion also yield similar curves. Also, we restricted our view to clear situations of individual learning, though some social (i.e., industrial) situations yield similar curves. Our restriction was dictated purely by the momentary need to bound the research effort.

6. Psychological models that yield the power law with arbitrary rate (α) are difficult to find. (Positive asymptotes and arbitrary starting points are, of course, immediately plausible, indeed, unavoidable.)

7. Models that yield the hyperbolic law arise easily and naturally from many sources—simple accumulation assumptions, parallelism, mixtures of exponentials, etc.

8. The various models are not mutually exclusive but provide an array of sources of the power law. Several hyperbolic mechanisms could coexist in the same learner. Independent of these, if the humans learn by creating and storing chunks, as there is evidence they do, then the environmental-exhaustion effect would also operate to produce power-law learning, independent of whether there were other effects such as mixing to produce hyperbolic learning curves.

9. A maintainable option is that the entire phenomenon is due to exponential component learning yielding an effective hyperbolic law through mixing.

This would cover not only the data dealt with here but probably also the data with other criteria and the data from industrial processes.

However, the exponential learning of the component learners remains unaccounted for.

10. The chunking model provides a theory of the phenomena that offers qualitatively satisfactory explanations for the major phenomena.

However, some of the phenomena, such as the industrial processes, probably need to be assigned to mixing. Parsimony freaks probably will not like this.

The theory is pleasantly consistent with the existing general theory of information processing and avoids making any a priori assumptions.

Though power laws are not predicted for all task environments, the learning curves do closely approximate power laws.

ACKNOWLEDGMENTS

This research was sponsored in part by the Office of Naval Research under contract N00014-76-0874 and in part by the Defense Advanced Research Projects Agency (DOD), ARPA Order No. 3597, monitored by the Air Force Avionics Laboratory under contract F33615-78-C-1551.

The views and conclusions in this document are those of the authors and should not be interpreted as representing the official policies, either expressed or implied, of the Office of Naval Research, the Defense Advanced Research Projects Agency, or the U.S. Government.

REFERENCES

Anderson, J. Private communication, 1980.

Bower, G. H., & Winzenz, D. Group structure, coding, and memory for digit series. *Experimental Psychology Monograph*, 1969, *80*, 1–17 (May, Pt. 2).

Calfee, R. C. *Human experimental psychology*. New York: Holt, Rinehart & Winston, 1975.

Card, S. K., English, W. K., & Burr, B. Evaluation of mouse, rate controlled isometric joystick, step keys, and text keys for text selection on a CRT. *Ergonomics*, 1978, *21*, 601–613.

Card, S. K., Moran, T. P., & Newell, A. Computer text editing: An information-processing analysis of a routine cognitive skill. *Cognitive Psychology*, 1980, *12*(1), 32–74. (a)

Card, S. K., Moran, T. P., & Newell, A. The keystroke model for user performance time with interactive systems. *Communications of the ACM*, 1980, *23*. (In press; available as SSL-79-1, Xerox PARC). (b)

Chase, W. G., & Simon, H. A. Perception in chess. *Cognitive Psychology*, 1973, *4*, 55–81.

Churchill, R. V. *Operational mathematics*. New York: McGraw-Hill, 1972.

Cooper, E. H., & Pantle, A. J. The total-time hypothesis in verbal learning. *Psychological Bulletin*, 1967, *68*, 221–234.

Crossman, E. R. F. W. A theory of the acquisition of speed-skill. *Ergonomics*, 1959, *2*, 153–166.

Crowder, R. G. *Principles of learning and memory*. Hillsdale, N.J.: Lawrence Erlbaum Associates, 1976.

deGroot, A. D. *Thought and choice in chess*. The Hague: Mouton, 1965.

DeJong, R. J. The effects of increasing skill on cycle-time and its consequences for time-standards. *Ergonomics*, 1957, *1*, 51–60.

Fitts, P. M. The information capacity of the human motor system in controlling amplitude of movement. *Journal of Experimental Psychology*, 1954, *47*, 381–391.

Fitts, P. M. Perceptual-motor skill learning. In A. W. Melton (Ed.), *Categories of human learning*. New York: Academic Press, 1964.

Fitts, P. M., & Posner, M. I. *Human performance*. Belmont, Calif.: Brooks/Cole, 1967.

Guilliksen, H. A rational equation of the learning curve based on Thorndike's law of effect. *Journal of General Psychology*, 1934, *11*, 395–434.

Hick, W. E. On the rate of gain of information. *Quarterly Journal of Experimental Psychology*, 1952, *4*, 11–26.

Hirsch, W. Z. Manufacturing progress functions. *Review of Economics and Statistics*, 1952, *34*, 143–155.

Hyman, R. Stimulus information as a determinent of reaction time. *Journal of Experimental Psychology*, 1953, *45*, 188–196.

Johnson, N. F. Organization and the concept of a memory code. In A. W. Melton & E. Martin (Eds.), *Coding processes in human memory*, Washington, D.C.: Winston, 1972.

Kintsch, W. *Memory and cognition*. New York: Wiley, 1977.

Kolers, P. A. Memorial consequences of automatized encoding. *Journal of Experimental Psychology: Human Learning and Memory*, 1975, *1*(6), 689–701.

LaBerge, D. Acquisition of automatic processing in perceptual and associative learning. In P. A. M. Rabbitt & S. Dornic (Eds.), *Attention and performance V*, New York: Academic, 1974.

Lewis, C. Speed and practice, undated.

Lewis, C. Private communication, 1980.

Lindsay, P., & Norman, D. *Human information processing: An introduction to psychology* (2nd ed.). New York: Academic, 1977.

Mazur, J., & Hastie, R. Learning as accumulation: A reexamination of the learning curve. *Psychological Bulletin*, 1978, *85*(6), 1256–1274.

Miller, G. A. The magic number seven plus or minus two: Some limits on our capacity for processing information. *Psychological Review*, 1956, *63*, 81–97.

Moran, T. P. Compiling cognitive skill, 1980 (AIP Memo 150, Xerox PARC).

Neisser, U., Novick, R., & Lazar, R. Searching for ten targets simultaneously. *Perceptual and Motor Skills*, 1963, *17*, 955–961.

Neves, D. M., & Anderson, J. R. Knowledge compilation: Mechanisms for the automatization of cognitive skills. In J. R. Anderson (Ed.), *Cognitive skills and their acquisition*, Hillsdale, N.J.: Lawrence Erlbaum Associates (in press).

Newell, A. Harpy, production systems and human cognition. In R. Cole (Ed.), *Perception and production of fluent speech*, Hillsdale, N.J.: Lawrence Erlbaum Associates, 1980.

Posner, M. I., & Snyder, C. R. R. Attention and cognitive control. In R. L. Solso (Ed.), *Information processing and cognition*, Hillsdale, N.J.: Lawrence Erlbaum Associates, 1975.

Reisberg, D., Baron, J., & Kemler, D. G. Overcoming Stroop interference: The effects of practice on distractor potency. *Journal of Experimental Psychology: Human Perception and Performance*, 1980, *6*, 140–150.

Restle, F., & Greeno, J. *Introduction to mathematical psychology*. Reading, Mass.: Addison-Wesley, 1970 (chap. 1).

Rigon, C. J. Analysis of progress trends in aircraft production. *Aero Digest*, May 1944, 132–138.

Robertson, G., McCracken, D., & Newell, A. The ZOG approach to man-machine communication. *International Journal of Man-Machine Studies* (in press).

Schneider, W., & Shiffrin, R. M. Controlled and automatic human information processing: I. Detection, search and attention. *Psychological Review*, 1977, *84*, 1–66.

Seibel, R. Discrimination reaction time for a 1,023 alternative task. *Journal of Experimental Psychology*, 1963, *66*, 215–226.

Shiffrin, R. M., & Schneider, W. Controlled and automatic human information processing: II. Perceptual learning, automatic attending, and a general theory. *Psychological Review*, 1977, *84*, 127–190.

Simon, H. A. On a class of skew distribution functions. *Biometrika,* 1955, *42,* 425–440.

Simon, H. A., & Gilmartin, K. A simulation of memory for chess positions. *Cognitive Psychology,* 1973, *5,* 29–46.

Snoddy, G. S. Learning and stability. *Journal of Applied Psychology,* 1926, *10,* 1–36.

Spelke, E., Hirst, W., & Neisser, U. Skills of divided attention. *Cognition,* 1976, *4,* 215–230.

Stevens, J. C., & Savin, H. B. On the form of learning curves. *Journal of the Experimental Analysis of Behavior,* 1962, *5*(1), 15–18.

Suppes, P., Fletcher, J. D., & Zanotti, M. Models of individual trajectories in computer-assisted instruction for deaf students. *Journal of Educational Psychology,* 1976, *68,* 117–127.

Thurstone, L. L. The learning curve equation. *Psychological Monographs,* 1919, *26*(114), 51.

Welford, A. T. *Fundamentals of skill.* London: Methuen, 1968.

Woodworth, R. S. *Experimental psychology.* New York: Holt, 1938.

Knowledge Compilation: Mechanisms for the Automatization of Cognitive Skills

David M. Neves and John R. Anderson
Carnegie-Mellon University

INTRODUCTION

People get better on a task with practice. In this chapter we take this noncontroversial statement, elaborate what it means to "get better," and propose two mechanisms that account for some of the ways people get better. We trace the development of a skill from the point when it is initially being memorized and applied in a slow and halting fashion to the point where it has become fast and automatic through practice.

We are interested in how students learn to use postulates and theorems in geometry tasks like that illustrated in Fig. 2.1. A scenario of how a student (based on two students we have looked at in detail in geometry and three subjects working on an artificial proof system) learns postulates is as follows: The student reads each of several postulates in a section of a textbook. After a brief inspection of the postulates the student goes on to the problems at the end of the section that require the student to use the postulates. In the student's initial attempts with the postulates there is much looking back to them in the textbook because they have not yet been committed to memory. These applications are slow and there are mutterings that show low-level matching of the postulates like "If A is RO and B is NY, then I can assert that. . . ." After some practice the student has committed the postulates to memory. After much practice their selection and application is very fast.

In this chapter we consider how postulates are initially encoded, how procedures are created out of these encoded postulates, and lastly how procedures speed up with practice. The processes we describe have been implemented and tested as mechanisms on the computer.

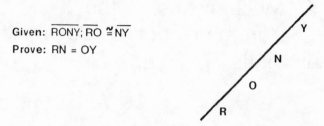

Given: $\overline{RONY}$; $\overline{RO} \cong \overline{NY}$
Prove: RN = OY

Proof:

Statements	Reasons
1. $\overline{RO} \cong \overline{NY}$	1. ?
2. RO = NY	2. ?
3. ON = ON	3. ?
4. RO + ON = ON + NY	4. ?
5. $\overline{RONY}$	5. ?
6. RO + ON = RN	6. ?
7. ON + NY = OY	7. ?
8. RN = OY	8. ?

FIG. 2.1.   A proof to be completed by writing reasons.

In our work we have focused on a particular task within geometry. That task is providing reasons to an already worked-out proof. We have been working mainly with the geometry textbook of Jurgensen, Donnelly, Maier, and Rising (1975). In this textbook, before being asked to generate proofs the student is shown an example or two of a proof. Then the student is shown a proof lacking reasons, or justifications, for each of the lines (see Fig. 2.1). The student's task with these nearly whole proofs is to provide the justifications for each of the lines. A justification can be that the line was a given or that it was the result of the application of a definition, theorem, or postulate. Besides showing how a proof works, these problems give practice with the postulates.

Figure 2.2 shows a simple flow chart of our production system program that provides justifications for lines in a proof. When it comes to a line, it first checks to see whether the line is a given. If so, it puts down *given* and goes to the next line. If it is not a given, the program matches the consequent of a postulate to the current line. If there is a match, it then tries to match the antecedent of the postulate to previous lines. If failure occurs, it tries another postulate; and so on. When it verifies that a postulate can apply, it writes the name of the postulate and goes to justify the next line in the proof.

At this high level of analysis, the flow chart in Fig. 2.2 provided a good model for the behavior of all subjects at all levels of skill. However, there is a lot of information-processing detail being hidden in Fig. 2.2 in the two boxes (e and f) where the consequent and antecedents are being matched. Much of the learning we observed, particularly concerning the postulates, took place with respect to the matching processes. Our discussion focuses on how these matching skills evolve. Our analysis of this matching skill identifies three stages similar to the general analysis of skill acquisition by Fitts (1964). The first is encoding, where a set of facts required by the skill are committed to memory. The second is proceduralization, where facts are turned into procedures. The third is composition by which the procedures are made faster with practice. We talk about each stage in turn in subsequent sections. First we describe the encoding stage.

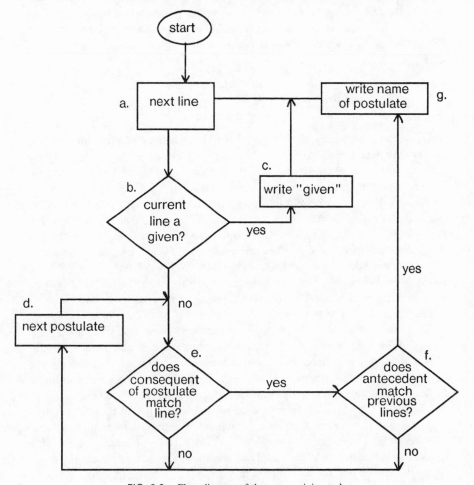

FIG. 2.2.   Flow diagram of the reason giving task.

ENCODING

We propose that all incoming knowledge is encoded declaratively; specifically, the information is encoded as a set of facts in a semantic network. To explain what this assumption implies we should describe the consequences of storing knowledge declaratively versus procedurally. (See also Winograd, 1975, for a discussion of procedural versus declarative encodings for knowledge).

Declarative Encodings

In a declarative encoding, the knowledge required to perform a skill is represented as a set of facts. In our scheme these facts are represented in a semantic network. These facts are used by general interpretive procedures to guide behavior. To take a nongeometry example, suppose we learn in a French class the fact that *chien* means *dog*. Then this factual knowledge can be used to generate a French phrase by a general interpretive procedure of the form:

> P1:   *If*   the goal is to describe an object
> and a word means the object
> and the word is masculine
> *Then*   say "le" followed by the word.

This rule can apply to any piece of vocabulary knowledge we have—for instance, that *garcon* means *boy*—to generate the correct phrase (e.g., le garcon). (By the way, the previous general procedure P1 is represented in production form; we shall be using production representations extensively.)

Perhaps the greatest benefit in representing the knowledge underlying procedures declaratively comes from the flexibility in using that knowledge. For example, suppose the system has learned the transitive rule of equality, "If $A = B$ and $B = C$, then $A = C$." This rule could then be used by one procedure to make a forward deduction. That is, if statements $RO = NY$ and $NY = WZ$ were stated, then $RO = WZ$ could be asserted. The same knowledge could also be used by a different general interpretive procedure to reason back from the consequent, "$A = C$", to test whether "$A = B$ and $B = C$" are true.

Two other benefits of declarative representations are ease of analysis and change. With the knowledge underlying procedures represented as data one can reason about the procedures and use that reasoning to plan action or to change the procedures to make them more efficient. Changing the procedure is simply a matter of adding or deleting links in the semantic network.

The major drawback of a declarative representation is that its interpretative application is slow. Each fact must be separately retrieved from memory and interpreted. The interpretive procedures, to achieve their generality, are unable to take any shortcuts available in applying the knowledge in a particular situation. Many unnecessary or redundant tests and actions may be performed.

Procedural Encodings

A second way of representing knowledge about procedures is as something that can be directly executed and so needs no costly interpretation phase. One way of representing procedures is production systems (Anderson, 1976; Newell & Simon, 1972). The ACT production system (Anderson, 1976) is a collection of If–Then rules that operate on the active part of a semantic network. When an *If* part matches some part of active memory, then the *Then* part of the rule is executed. The *Then* part either activates existing memory structure or builds new memory structure.

One of the advantages of a procedual representation such as a production system is that it handles variables in a natural and easy manner. For instance, in reason giving, variable handling can become quite difficult when matching a postulate to a line to see if it applies. When the consequent is matched to a line, the variables in that consequent are given values. Those values or bindings of the variables are used when the antecedent is matched to previous lines. This variable handling is accomplished much more felicitously if the postulate is encoded as a production than if it is encoded as a set of semantic network structures. An example of a postulate is the addition property of equality that is stated in the text as:

If $a = b$ and $c = d$, then $a + c = b + d$.

To build a production to encode this postulate for reason giving, one builds into the *If* side of the production the consequent of the postulate as a test of the current goal and the antecedent part of the postulate as a test of previous lines. So, the postulate would become:

P2:　*If*　the goal is to give reasons for $a + c = b + d$
　　　　and a previous line contains $a = b$
　　　　and a previous line contains $c = d$
　　Then　write "Addition property of equality".

This production combines boxes e, f, and g from Fig. 2.2. In the first line (the goal is to prove $a + c = b + d$) the production binds the variables $a,b,c,$ and d to elements in the current to-be-justified line. In the other two lines of the *If* side it checks that these bindings are consistent with elements in previous lines.

Procedural knowledge represented in this way is fast because the *If* side of the production is matched as one step. Although time to execute a procedure is largely independent of the number of productions in memory, execution time does depend on the number of productions that are applied in performing the procedure. So one can achieve even more speedup of a procedure by making its component productions bigger so that there are fewer selections of productions. We talk about this possibility later when we talk about the composition mechanism.

On the other hand, there are several disadvantages to such a procedural representation. In this form the knowledge cannot be inspected. However, some understanding of a production's content is available by noting what it does. Changes cannot be made to the productions, although there are schemes for creating new productions that will effectively delete or restrict the range of applicability of "bad" productions (Anderson, Kline, & Beasley, 1980). Also, when a rule gets put into production form, it can only be used in that form. For instance, the production P2 does not capture the use of the postulate for forward inferencing. For that, we would need another quite different production:

P3: *If* it is known that $a = b$
and it is known that $c = d$
Then assert that it is known that $a + c = b + d$.

Getting the Best of Both Encodings

We clearly would like to have the advantages of both representations. One way of achieving this, of course, is to keep knowledge in both representations. When speed is needed, the procedural encoding is used. When analysis or change is needed, the declarative encoding is used.

There is little problem in creating a declarative description of a rule because creating new structure in semantic nets from external input is relatively simple. On the other hand it is much more difficult to encode that knowledge procedurally. We have seen that a procedural encoding is a highly specific interpretation of a rule. If there are many procedural encodings possible, which one should we pick? In present production systems the answer to this question changes with every task and is built in by the programmer.

From a psychological point of view a system that can directly encode rules as productions has a number of undesirable features. First, learning is faster than what we observe in people. People become proficient at a skill gradually rather than in an all-or-none manner. Second, by encoding the rule as a production you obtain an exact and specific match every time. There are no errors, and no other ways to make the match. One might want more flexibility in the match. For example, suppose P2 were to apply to the following situation (which occurs in Fig. 2.1):

Current statement: $RO + ON = ON + NY$
Previous statements: $RO = NY$
$ON = ON$

The first line of production P2 would apply with the following binding of variables: $a = RO$, $c = ON$, $b = ON$, and $d = NY$. This means that it must match for its second and third lines:

$a = b$ (i.e., $RO = ON$)
$c = d$ (i.e., $ON = NY$)

Of course these attempts will fail. The problem is that the production does not appreciate the commutative nature of the plus operator and this increases the number of possible rules that should be built for the postulate. Rather than try to anticipate all the possible procedural interpretations of a postulate, we suggest that the postulate be represented declaratively and it be interpreted by a general evaluator that could deal with commutativity.

Therefore, when such rules initially enter the ACT system, they are stored as facts in a semantic net. Through mechanisms to be discussed later the rule will automatically turn into one or more productions through its use. So with the initial encoding we have the benefits of a declarative representation. That knowledge can be turned into faster production form as a consequence of being used interpretively. To illustrate how declarative knowledge can be used interpretively, we next describe the general matching productions that interpret postulates stored in semantic net form.

Interpretive Matching Productions

To match a declarative representation of a rule to a statement, we use a general interpretive matcher written as productions. These matcher productions do more deliberately and in a piecemeal fashion what is done automatically by a production system when postulates are represented as productions. They try to put two structures into correspondence and bind variables along the way.

Table 2.1 lists the seven productions that do the match. They are stated in a more understandable English-like syntax than their actual implementation. The matcher goes through both the rule and the line comparing corresponding nodes. If a constant, like $=$, is pointed to in the rule, then a test for equality is made to see that the rule and the line contain the same constants. If a variable in the rule, as noted by the "isa variable" tag on the element, is pointed to, then a binding of that variable is checked or made.

Variable bindings are kept as temporary network structure. For a variable to be bound means that a proposition describing what it is bound to is resident in memory. If a variable has no binding, as seen by the failure to retrieve a binding from memory, then the binding is made with the node being pointed to in the statement as the value. If there is already a binding, then the equality of that binding to the statement node is checked. Because the bindings are held in memory, they are reportable unlike variable bindings in a production.

We now show how the matcher productions would match the consequent of the reflexive postulate, $A = A$, to $ON = ON$. First the A on the left is compared to ON on the left.

$$A = A \qquad ON = ON$$

$$\uparrow \qquad\qquad \uparrow$$

Production P6 fires in the matcher. It notes that A is an unbound variable so it

TABLE 2.1
Some General Interpretive Productions for Matching Postulates to
Lines of a Proof

P4:	*If*	the current element of the rule pattern is a constant
		and the same element occurs in the line
	Then	move to the next elements in the rule and the line.
P5:	*If*	the current element of the rule pattern is a constant
		and the same element does not occur in the line
	Then	the attempt to match has failed.
P6:	*If*	the current element of the rule is a variable
		and this variable does not have a binding stored with it
	Then	store the current element of the line as the binding of the variable
		and move to the next elements in the rule and the line.
P7:	*If*	the current element of the rule is a variable
		and the current element of the line is stored as the value of the variable
	Then	move to the next elements in the rule and the line.
P8:	*If*	the current element of the rule is a variable
		and the value stored with the variable is different than the current element of the line
	Then	the attempt to match has failed.
P9:	*If*	there are no more elements in either the rule or the line
	Then	the attempt to match has succeeded.
P10:	*If*	there are no more elements in the rule
		but there are in the line (or vice versa)
	Then	the attempt to match has failed.

deposits "*A* is bound to *ON*" into memory. It also switches attention to the next elements in the expressions. Next the two equals signs are compared.

$$A \ = \ A \qquad ON \ = \ ON$$
$$\uparrow \qquad\qquad \uparrow$$

Production P4 fires because it finds equal constants and increments the two pointers to *A* on the right and *ON* on the right.

$$A \ = \ A \qquad ON \ = \ ON$$
$$\qquad \uparrow \qquad\qquad\quad \uparrow$$

Production P7 fires here because it finds an already bound variable, *A*. It compares the binding for *A*, which is *ON*, with the element currently pointed to in the line, which is *ON*, and because they are equal, it succeeds. Now there are no more elements in either the rule or the line and production P9 fires and states that the match has succeeded. At this point the matcher has just completed a successful match and as a by-product has created a list of variables and their bindings.

The subject at this point is applying his or her knowledge in a slow interpretive fashion processing symbol by symbol. The procedural representations of the knowledge, for example, production P2, are much more efficient and apply the knowledge directly. Based on an analogy to a process in computer science, we use the term *knowledge compilation* to refer to the process by which subjects go from interpretive application of knowledge to direct application. This process translates declarative facts into productions. There are two subprocesses: proceduralization, which translates parts of declarative rules into small productions, and composition, which combines productions into larger productions.

PROCEDURALIZATION

With both a semantic net and productions to represent knowledge there is the problem of how to transfer knowledge smoothly from one store to the other. Production system models (Anderson, Kline, & Beasley, 1980; Waterman, 1975) have accomplished this transfer in the past by building productions with a special "build" operator in the *Then* side of a production. This special operator in ACT takes a network description of the knowledge underlying a production as an argument and adds the production to production memory. This implies that people can transfer their factual knowledge into procedures by abstractly ruminating upon the knowledge. However, this conflicts with our observation of students and with general wisdom about skill acquisition that skills only develop by exercising them.

Therefore, we have developed a different means of converting declarative knowledge into procedural knowledge—a mechanism that constitutes a major augmentation to existing production system architecture. Every time a production matches some long-term memory network structure that has to be retrieved into working memory, the proceduralization mechanism creates a new production that has that network structure incorporated into it and that avoids the need for the long-term memory retrieval. This simple mechanism merges semantic net knowledge into the production that uses it. In order for this mechanism to be selective in what memory it merges, we make a distinction between two kinds of declarative memory: a permanent memory and a transient, temporary memory. In ACT this permanent memory is the activated part of its semantic network (long-term memory) and the temporary memory is network structure that has just been created. Postulates, once committed to memory, are part of permanent memory. The representation of the current problem is part of temporary memory.

When the *If* side of a production matches memory, it matches some activated permanent memory and some temporary memory that has just been created by information entering from the environment. At this point a new production is created that has incorporated the permanent memory matched. As an example, we show how this process of proceduralization applies to production P6 of the matcher productions in Table 2.1. This production matches an unbound variable of a postulate to a corresponding part of a statement. To explain the operation of proceduralization we have to display more of the actual structure of P6 than was given in our informal statement of P6 in Table 2.1.

P6':   *If*   the goal is to match
and the rule pointer is pointing to an element in the rule
and the element is a variable
and the element is not bound
and the line pointer is pointing to an element in the line
and the rule pointer is before an element
and the line pointer is before an element
Then   bind the variable in the rule to the current element in the line
and move the rule pointer to its next element
and move the line pointer to its next element.

Now suppose the symmetric postulate "If $A = B$ then $B = A$" is a semantic network. Also, the statement "$RO = NY$" is in temporary memory because it is what ACT is currently attending to. Suppose P6' applied to this situation when an attempt was being made to create a match between B, of the consequent ($B = A$) of the rule, and RO, of the statement. The third and fifth lines of P6' would match to long-term memory elements as follows:

the element is a variable   <- -> B is a variable
the rule pointer is before an element <- -> B is before =

What is accomplished by these long-term memory retrievals is that the rule elements are identified as B (currently pointed to) and = (next in the rule). These are permanent facts that are known about the postulate. We can create a production that is equivalent to P6' in this situation by deleting the reference to these two clauses and, wherever else the rule elements are mentioned, replace them by B and =. This specialized version of the general production is given here:

P11:   *If*   the goal is to match
and the rule pointer is pointing to B in the rule
and B is not bound
and the line pointer is pointing to an element in the line
and the line pointer is before an element
Then   bind B to the current element in the line
and move the rule pointer to =
and move the line pointer to its next element.

In creating this production ACT has effectively proceduralized a bit of the knowledge that is contained in the symmetric postulate—namely, that the consequent consists of a variable B before =. It is now no longer necessary to retrieve this knowledge from memory. Rather, the knowledge is now implicit in the production. Note that, in this step of proceduralization, we have reduced the demand on working memory in terms of the amount of information that needs to be kept active from long-term memory.

Of course, production P11 by itself is far from being a proceduralized version of the postulate. To accomplish this, every step in the application of the postulate needs to be proceduralized. When this is accomplished, we shall have a procedural version of the postulate that embodies one possible use of the knowledge. Note that the knowledge at this state is still being applied in a piecemeal fashion. To get a unitary procedural representation of the postulate, we need the process of composition that is occurring concurrently with proceduralization.

COMPOSITION

In our development of composition we have been strongly influenced by the work of Lewis (1978). Composition occurs concurrently with proceduralization but we think it continues after proceduralization is complete. It is for this reason that we designate it the third stage in skill development. The basic idea of composition is that pairs of productions that are executed in sequence are combined into single productions. It is assumed that the time to execute a production system task is roughly proportional to the number of productions that were fired. Therefore one effect of combining productions into larger productions is to decrease the amount of time for a procedure to apply.

The easiest way of combining two productions into a third is to add together their *If* sides and their *Then* sides. So suppose the following two productions fired consecutively.

P12:   *If*   you see a red light
        Then   assert danger.

P13:   *If*   there is danger and another person is near you
        Then   warn that person.

The simple composite is:

P14:   *If*   you see a red light
                and there is danger
                and another person is near you
        Then   assert danger
                and warn that person.

There is a problem with this composite. There is a test for "danger" in the *If* side that will not be satisfied. That is because the danger that is being tested for in P14 was added by P12 in the original sentence. Because the *If* side of the composite, P14, is made of P12 and P13, the parts of P13 that are dependent on action taken by P12 must be changed in P14. The change needed in the algorithm that gave rise to P14 is that clauses in the *If* side of the composite are deleted if they were asserted in the *Then* side of the first production and tested in the *If* side of the second production. Lewis' algorithm for composition is as follows: Suppose two productions fire, one right after the other. The first *If A Then B* has *If* side clauses represented by *A* and *Then* side clauses represented by *B*. The second, *If C Then D,* has *If* side *C* and *Then* side *D*. Then, a new production can be constructed that will do the work of both.

$$If\ A\ Then\ B$$
$$If\ C\ Then\ D$$
- - - - - - - - - - - - - - - - -
$$If\ A\ \&\ (C\ -\ B)\ Then\ B\ \&\ D$$

This new production will have as an *If* side all the *If* clauses in *A* and all the *If* clauses in *C*, except the clauses that were asserted in *B*. As a *Then* side this new production has the union of the *Then* sides in *B* and *D*.

In this case the composite of productions P12 and P13 would be:

> P15:   *If*   you see a red light
> and another person is near you
> *Then*   assert danger
> and warn that person.

The *If* side of the new production contains all the *If* parts in the first production and the test of the presence of another person in the second production. The test for "danger" in the second production is not in the new production because it is asserted in the *Then* part of the first production. The *Then* part of the composite production contains all the assertions from the first two.

We made several modifications to the Lewis algorithm. The major change came because of the use of variables in the production system. A *join* process is applied that checks to see if the same element occurs in the two productions even if it is referred to differently. A variable may be bound to an element in one production but in another production the element may be bound to a different variable or be directly referenced (i.e., is a constant). If the element is directly referenced in one production, it is directly referenced in the composite rather than being referred to by a variable.

Suppose the following two productions fired.

> P16:   *If*   the length of segment *A* is equal to the length of segment *B*
> *Then*   the result is that segment *A* is congruent to segment *B*.

> P17:   *If*   the result is something
> *Then*   write the result.

As the composite production is being created, the *Then* side of P16 is *join*ed with the *If* side of P17. The reference to "the result" in P17 is replaced by the more specific "segment *A* is congruent to segment *B*". The composite production is:

> P18:   *If*   the length of segment *A* is equal to the length of segment *B*
> *Then*   the result is that segment *A* is congruent to segment *B*
> and write segment *A* is congruent to segment *B*.

This join process also takes place when the same clause occurs in the *If* sides of both productions. One of the clauses must be deleted so that the actual composition rule looks more like

$$If\ A\ Then\ B$$
$$If\ C\ Then\ D$$

- - - - - - - - - - - - - - - - -

$$If\ (A - C)\ \&\ (C - B)\ Then\ B\ \&\ D$$

where $(A - C)$ means all clauses in A excepting ones also in C. Other parts of the composition process are more specific to the production system language we are using and we do not discuss them here.

We have described two processes. The first process is proceduralization: the instantiation of variables bound to long-term memory structure. This process deletes *If* clauses in the specific production that match long-term memory propositions and instantiates variables that are bound to long-term memory. Proceduralization makes small and specific productions. The second process is composition. It combines two productions that fire after each other into a single production.

These two processes automatically bring about the transformation of declarative knowledge into procedural knowledge discussed earlier. When a rule is in semantic net form, they will, after much practice with it, create a production that embodies one procedural interpretation of that rule. To illustrate this process, let us look at how the consequent of the symmetric rule, "If $(A = B)$ then $(B = A)$", was turned gradually into a single production.

We used general matcher productions (that were somewhat more elaborate than the general productions showed in Table 2.1) to match the consequent, $B = A$, to several lines, such as $RO = NY$. It took 16 firings of these general matcher productions to accomplish the match the first time. During this pass the proceduralization process created 16 productions that were specific versions (specific to the consequent of the symmetric rule) of the matcher productions. There are 15 pairs of successive productions in the sequence of 16 general productions that fired. Composition of the general matcher productions was attempted and created 15 general composites with each composite able to do the work of two of the original matcher productions. However these general composites never applied later because the system favored the more specific productions created by the proceduralization process.

The consequent was then matched a second time and the 16 specific production created by the proceduralization process during the first pass fired. Because these productions were already specific, the proceduralization process could not produce any new productions. The composition process did produce 15 specific composites (i.e., 1 & 2, 2 & 3, . . . 15 & 16) from those 16 specific productions.

In the third pass the composites created during the second pass fired. Matching the consequent only took 16/2, or 8, production firings. After five sessions where the consequent of the symmetric rule was matched, a production was created that was able to match the consequent of the symmetric rule to a line in a single step. This production is:

> P19: *If* the goal is to match the line to the consequent
> of the symmetric rule
> and there are three elements in the line
> and the second element in the line is =
> *Then* bind *B* to the first element in the line
> and bind *A* to the third element in the line.

Although this production exists, all previously created productions are also around because proceduralization and composition do not destroy the productions they build from. At this point of practice there exists the original semantic net representation of the consequent, the general matcher productions, and the 15 general composites of those matcher productions that never executed. Also there are 16 specific productions created by proceduralization plus (15 + 7 + 3 + 1) 26 composites. Thus, in total, 57 new productions were created.

In this part of the chapter we described the mechanisms that enable one to become faster at a skill. In the second half we talk about some psychological phenomena that are accounted for by these mechanisms. But first we travel off the path of the discussion a bit and consider whether proceduralization might not be seen as a special case of composition.

Creating Specific Productions without Proceduralization

We have shown how knowledge is smoothly transferred from a declarative semantic net to production form. The proceduralization process that does this has the effect of deleting from the *If* side of composite productions clauses that match long-term memory. Proceduralization also makes specific productions. What would happen if there was no semantic net and declarative knowledge was stored as productions instead? This is the case with the OPS production system language (Forgy, 1979; Forgy & McDermott, 1977) whose only permanent memory is production memory. We show here that the effects of proceduralization can be duplicated with the composition process.

First, we must state how a semantic net can be functionally represented as productions. In a semantic net there are nodes, links leading from those nodes, and values attached to those links. One way of mapping this to productions is to have a node as the *If* part of a production and all facts known about it as the *Then* part. To retrieve facts about the node the node is asserted into memory. The production for that node then fires and deposits all facts about that node into working memory.

We now show how a production specific to matching part of the symmetric postulate can be created by composing memory retrieval productions with general matching productions. P20 is a production that deposits all links out of B (of the consequent $B = A$) when it executes. It mimics the retrieval from a semantic net of all facts about B.

> P20:   *If* B
>   *Then* B is a variable
>   and B is before $=$.

P21 is a production in the matcher that is identical to production P6′ given earlier. It matches a variable in a postulate to a piece of a statement.

> P21:   *If*   the goal is to match
>   and the rule pointer is pointing to an element in the rule
>   and the element is a variable
>   and the element is not bound
>   and the line pointer is pointing to an element in the line
>   and the rule pointer is before an element
>   and the line pointer is before an element
>   *Then*   bind the variable in the rule to the current element in the line
>   and move the rule pointer to its next element
>   and move the line pointer to its next element.

When the two productions P20 and P21 fire, then their composite is created as the production P22. This new production has fewer clauses in the *If* side because the composition algorithm causes "B is a variable" and "B is before $=$" to be deleted. These two clauses were asserted in P20 and matched to in P21. Also the reference to the current element in the rule has been replaced by its instantiation, B, because of the application of composition's join process.

> P22:   *If* B
>   and the goal is to match
>   and the rule pointer is pointing to B
>   and B is not bound
>   and the line pointer is pointing to an element in the line
>   and the line pointer is before an element
>   *Then*   bind B to the current element in the line
>   and move the rule pointer to $=$
>   and move the line pointer to its next element.

With P22 we have a production that is identical, except for the additional B, with the production P11 that was created by the proceduralization process from the application of a production to a piece of semantic network. Thus by representing all knowledge as productions the single mechanism of composition can also accomplish proceduralization.

EFFECTS OF PRACTICE

So far we have presented a proposal to explain how an information-processing system can have both the flexibility of a declarative semantic network representation and the speed of a procedural representation for rules. Our explanation of how a system automatically develops fast productions by practice rested on the combination of proceduralization and composition. In the following subsection we show how these mechanisms account for practice effects.

Einstellung

The speedup from composition seems too good to be true. Seemingly the only price is the storage space required to store all the new rules, and in the human organism this is a plentiful resource. However, there is another price to be paid. That price is a growing inflexibility and a lack of ability to adapt to change. This phenomenon associated with composition seems to correspond closely in the problem-solving literature to a phenomenon called *Einstellung*.

The Einstellung effect was extensively studied by Luchins (1945). He observed the effect using several tasks, but the most well-known task is the water jugs task. In this task the subject sees three different sized jugs with stated capacities. The problem is to measure out an amount of water using some or all of the jugs but using no measuring instrument other than the jugs. Subjects are shown two methods, a long and general method that takes four steps and uses three jugs, and a shorter method that takes two steps and uses two jugs.

After being shown both methods, one group is given practice problems in which they can use only the long method. Then they are given a problem that can be solved by either the short or long method. Most subjects solve it using the long method. In contrast, another group of subjects is shown both methods but does not receive practice on the long method. When they are presented with the problem that can be solved with either method, most use the short method. Luchins showed this effect with other tasks, like maze tracing, proofs in geometry, and extracting words from letter strings.

Lewis (1978) demonstrated Einstellung using a symbol replacement task. He gave subjects practice with rules in a symbol replacement task. At some later point he presented a new rule that would offer a shortcut in some cases. He showed that the more practice subjects had with the original set of rules, the less chance they would use the shortcut rule.

Lewis then showed how composition would predict the same results. His explanation relies on an interpretation of how the *If* part and *Then* part of a production are processed. The *If* part is processed at the beginning of a cycle with the selection of a production to fire. Every production in the system has an opportunity to match at this time. However, once a production is selected, each clause in the *Then* side is unconditionally executed. No other production can apply at this time.

The result of composition is to turn an open, conditional procedure into a closed, unconditional one. For example, when a production is created from the composition of five other productions, it does the job of those five productions as one uninterruptible step. If there was another production that might have applied in the middle of that five-step sequence, it cannot apply now because it is bypassed.

So we see composition can cause problems. In its early life, a procedure consists mostly of propositions in a semantic net. This gives the organism great flexibility in interpreting and even changing rules. However, once composition starts, there is less of a chance that a small (new) addition will be able to compete with the larger composite rules. This is because in most versions of production systems larger rules are given a preference in application over smaller rules. There are ways to get around the Einstellung effect, but some of them involve going back to the original semantic net representation of the procedure and reinitializing the slow interpretation of that procedure.

Speedup

People speed up at a task as they practice it, often without trying to speed up. Composition predicts this kind of automatic speedup. In our implementation of composition, on every cycle of the production system the current production is composed with the previously executed production. If 120 productions fire in the performance of a task, then the next time the exact same task is performed 60 productions will fire, then 30 productions, 15, 8, and so on. This is an exponential speedup, $t = a * (\frac{1}{2})^p$, where a is initial time to perform the task and p is the trial number. By assuming that pairs of productions are composed only with a certain probability we can obtain functions that are slower than halving. Even with such assumptions, composition by itself, with no further considerations, would predict an exponential practice function (i.e., $t = ab^p$).

It has consistently been shown that human speedup is not exponential but, rather, follows a power-law function (Crossman, 1959; Lewis, 1979; Snoddy, 1926), $t = a * p^b$, where a is initial time, p is trial number, and b is rate of speedup. When time versus trials (of practice) is plotted on log–log paper, the result approximates a straight line $[t = a * p^b => \log(t) = a' + b * \log(p)]$ where the intercept is the parameter a' and the slope is the parameter b. One explanation of this discrepancy between predicted and actual speedup that Lewis (1979) offers is based on the premise that power-law speedup is not produced by one mechanism but instead comes from the combination of speedup of many subprocesses. He notes that a power law can be approximated by the sum of many exponentially decreasing functions. Thus, there could be processes of a task that would be at various stages of exponential speedup (as composition would predict) but the measurable outcome of the task would be their sum. This summed result would follow the slower power-law function.

There are a number of other complicating factors that predict a slower-than-exponential speedup. Composed productions tend to have larger *If* sides and *Then* sides than the productions that gave rise to them. The analysis shown assumes that time to apply a production is independent of its size. However, this is not true in any known implementation and may not be true in the human head. For instance, it is reasonable to suppose that time to match the *If* side of a production, even assuming parallel machinery, would be a logarithmic function of complexity (Meyer & Shamos, 1977). Thus, part of the benefit of composition may be lost to increasing production size.

Another complexity has to do with strategy shifts that do occur in many complex tasks such as reason giving. Strategy shifts involve changing to an algorithm that requires fewer steps. It is unclear whether strategy shifts would produce immediate speedup. Although there are fewer logical steps in a better algorithm, the time to perform it may be longer because the processes underlying the steps have not been composed.

Still another complexity is pointed out by Newell and Rosenbloom (this volume) in their analyses of the power law. There is a variability in the problem situation and many production sequences will be needed to deal with different situations. This contrasts with the previous implicit assumption that there is just one sequence to be learned. Although short subsequences of productions may occur frequently, longer subsequences will occur less frequently. This means that few compositions of short sequences will be needed to cover all possible situations, but many compositions of long sequences may be needed. Thus it will take longer before enough compositions occur to cover all longer subsequences. Although we do not agree with the Newell and Rosenbloom assumptions that the number of sequences increases as a power or exponential function of length, any increase in the number of possible sequences with length will slow down the speedup.

So, to summarize: A pure application of composition leads to the prediction of exponential speedup. However, complications true of a realistic situation would tend to slow the speedup to less than exponential. This point has also been argued by Lewis (1979). True, it would be remarkable if these complications served to yield a pure power function. However, it is not possible to discriminate a pure power function from something that is close. Moreover, data do exist with systematic deviations from a power law. We discuss some of our own.

An Experiment Looking at Effects of Practice

We were interested in seeing how these various complications combined in the task we were most interested in (i.e., reason giving in a proof system). Three subjects were run for 10 one-hour sessions. These sessions were held on consecutive days except for weekends. All subjects were graduate students. We developed an artificial postulate set to minimize the effects of previous knowledge. A set of 8 postulates was used to construct 150 proofs. Each proof was 10 statements long and was made up of 4 givens and the application of 2 single antecedent rules and 4 double antecedent rules. No proof duplicated any other.

Proofs were displayed by computer on a terminal screen. Because we were interested in what subjects were looking at, only part of the proof was displayed at any time. The subject had to call explicitly for a part of the proof that was to be viewed next. In this way we could record both what the subject looked at and how much time was spent at that location. The screen had labeled columns for givens, statements, reasons, and antecedents and consequents of the postulates. At all times the statement to be justified was displayed on the screen. The subject pressed keys to view anything else.

Various commands were developed to facilitate movement through the proof. The basic command consisted of two keys, the first denoting the column to move to (i.e. g for given) and the second a digit for the row number. Shortcuts were also allowed. <Digit> would send the subject to row <digit> in the same column. <Period> would go to the previous line in the column, and <space> would go to the next line. Hitting the column key twice displayed an element in the same row but in the selected column. This was useful for the back and forth scanning of antecedents and consequents. Data collection consisted of the computer recording the location moved to and the time spent there. A location consisted of a given, statement, antecedent, or consequent.

Figure 2.3 shows the average data for the three subjects, plotted on a log-log graph. Subjects generally took about 25 minutes to provide justifications to the first proof. After 10 hours of practice with the task they were able to do it in about 1 to 2 minutes. We have plotted total time per problem, number of steps per problem (i.e., commands executed), and time per step. We thought time per step would reflect speedup on the problem due to such automatic factors as composition. We thought number of steps per problem would reflect other factors in addition to composition, such as strategy modifications. We were interested in how these two factors combined to yield an overall power law.

It is interesting to note that two power laws appear to underlie the overall power law for total time. This is seen by the relatively good approximations to straight line functions on the log-log plot. If the number of steps is decreasing at the rate $N = A_n P^{b_n}$ where N is the number of steps, A_n is the intercept in the log-log plot, P is the number of problems (practice), and b_n is the slope of the log-log function; and if the time per step is decreasing at the rate $T = A_t P^{b_t}$ where T is the time per step, A_t is the intercept, P is the number of problems (practice), and b_t is the slope, then the total time (TT) will obey the following power law:

$$TT = (A_n A_t)P^{b_n + b_t}$$

Subjects' search steps could be classified according to whether they were scanning givens, statements, consequents of postulates, or antecedents of postulates. Figure 2.4 shows log time plotted against log practice for each component

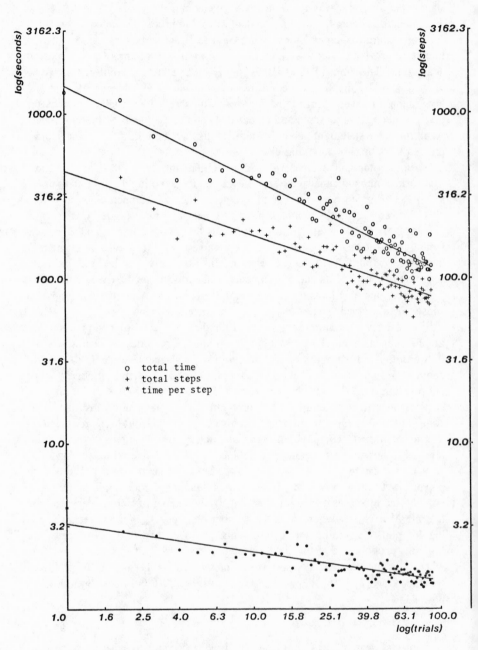

FIG. 2.3.   Log time versus log practice averages for three subjects.

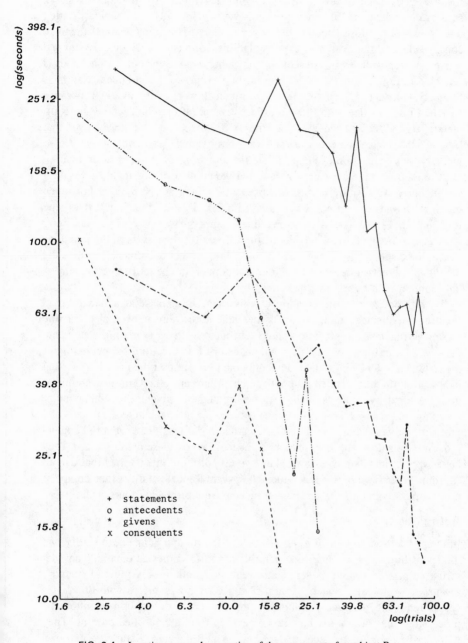

FIG. 2.4. Log time versus log practice of the components for subject R.

for subject R. The differing slopes in Fig. 2.4 reflect some major trends in subject improvement. Like the algorithms we developed earlier, subjects started out indexing the postulates by their consequents. They first learned the nine consequents and their order in the postulate list. Subjects fairly quickly stopped scanning the postulates by consequent and rather went to the correct one. This is reflected in Fig. 2.4 by the rapid drop-off on the curve for consequent scanning. Subjects' learning of the antecedents was much slower, partly no doubt, because they had less practice with these. Subject R came to the point where she completely learned the antecedents. The other two subjects never quite achieved that state. To the degree subjects were able to commit antecedents and consequents to memory, any inspection of the postulate list just dropped out of their protocols.

Although both the number of givens and the number of statements in Fig. 2.4 are fit fairly well by linear functions on the log–log scale, there is not much drop-off in these functions until after trial 20. Despite the fact that all the functions in Fig. 2.4 show a strong linear component, there is also a strong quadratic component in the deviations from linearity. Basically, all the functions appear to be speeding up faster than a power law. In fact for subject R, unlike the other two subjects, three out of the four components are better fit by an exponential function than by a power law.

To summarize our presentation of this data, it seems that a rather broad spectrum of changes underlie the systematic improvement of subjects at the reason giving task. There are strategy changes, such as searching statements backward from the to-be-justified line instead of forward from the beginning of the statements. One major development is memorization of the postulates so that they can be directly applied without search. There are other kinds of optimizations detected by subjects such as not searching the givens. The other major speedup occurs with respect to the time subjects spend in the individual steps of a problem. However our main point here is that in our task there seem to be many processes speeding up faster than a power law. When these are combined. they better approximate a power law. Thus, we do not think that the fact that overall speedup better fits a power law refutes the psychological validity of the composition process as one of the underlying mechanisms producing the speedup.

Automaticity

In their 1977 *Psychological Review* articles Shiffrin and Schneider identify two modes of human processing: one controlled and the other automatic. They describe controlled search as serial and requiring both processing and memory resources. Automatic search is parallel and does not interfere with other processes requiring resources. Although they provide a description of automatic processing, they do not say how it can develop from a controlled process. They do describe the circumstances under which it will develop. Parallel search of a list develops when a search procedure is applied over and over to the same list (their consistent mapping condition) and does not occur when a search procedure is applied over and over to varying lists (their varied mapping condition). In this section we show how composition and proceduralization turn a controlled, serial process into an automatic parallel process. But first we are more specific about some of the psychological data we want to explain.

The Neisser, Novick, and Lazar (1963) visual search task is one that showed a transition from serial to parallel search. Subjects scanned a matrix of letters for characters in either a 1-, 5-, or 10-character list. These lists were embedded, so that the 10-item list contained characters in the 5- and 1-character list. After about 20 days of practice, on the same lists, subjects were able to search a matrix for any one of 10 characters as fast as they searched for a single character.

Gibson and Yonas (1966) ran a visual search experiment with several age groups. After practice their subjects could search a matrix for two characters as fast as for one. Briggs and Blaha (1969) used a memory scanning task in which several characters are kept in memory and the subject responds whether a stimulus character is in that set. They found that subjects were as fast to respond with two characters in memory as with one character. Mowbray and Rhodes (1959) found that after 15 days of practice a subject responded as fast in a four-alternative forced-choice task as he did in a two-choice task.

In general, though, the data do not overwhelmingly point to the development of a completely parallel search. There are other data that, although they show a substantial reduction in search rate with practice, still show some residual effect of number of memory elements on search rate. It may be difficult to find evidence for complete, unlimited-capacity parallel search because any other serial process, like double-checking the answer, will hide it. Even if a serial subprocess is only occasionally added to an unlimited-capacity parallel one, the average data will look serial (i.e., show an effect of list length).

Searching memory sets that change from trial to trial does not show the same pattern of results as searching fixed memory sets. Kristofferson (1972) showed no change in the search rate per item for one- and four-item lists with practice in a memory scanning task. Nickerson (1966) showed only a slight reduction in search rate.

In summary, then, a motivated individual searching a never-changing list will, after much practice, search it in parallel (i.e., where reaction time is largely independent of the number of elements). However, if the list changes from trial to trial, the individual will have to search it serially and the rate of search will either not decrease or decrease very little with practice. We now show how composition and proceduralization predict these results.

It was shown earlier that composition can turn a several-step process into a single step. This can also be looked at as turning a serial process into a parallel one. We show how this occurs with a memory scan task with a fixed list, $A\ Q\ R\ T$. Two general productions follow that will compare a probe with a list in memory. These productions scan a list from left to right until an element in the list matches the probe.

P23: *If*   considering an element in the list
             and the probe equals that element
      Then say yes.

P24: *If*   considering an element in the list
             and it is not equal to the probe
             and the element is before another element
      Then consider the next element.

After some practice searching the list for T the following specific productions are created by the proceduralization process. Proceduralization causes the memory set elements, which are in long-term memory, to become incorporated into productions.

P25: *If*   considering A
             and Probe is not A
      Then consider Q.

P26: *If*   considering Q
             and Probe is not Q
      Then consider R.

P27: *If*   considering R
             and Probe is not R
      Then consider T.

P28: *If*   considering T
             and Probe is T
      Then say yes.

Then with more practice searching for T composition will combine these specific productions into a production that will recognize that the probe is equal to T in a single step. (Note that this production along with all the others produced by composition are shown with smaller *Then* sides than they actually have.) That production is:

P29: *If*   the probe is T
             and not A or Q or R
      Then say yes.

After practice searching for the other members of the memory set, composition also creates the following productions that will recognize when a probe is equal to a member of the list. These three productions are:

P30: *If*   the probe is A
      Then say yes.

P31:   *If*   the probe is Q
             and not A
       Then   say yes.

P32:   *If*   the probe is R
             and not A or Q
       Then   say yes.

Once these productions are created, then any of the elements in the memory set can be recognized with the application of a single production. If we assume that time to execute these productions is the same, then we have parallel search. So, with a fixed list, composition predicts parallel search. According to Schneider and Shiffrin (1977) another effect of automaticity is to make processing time independent of the number of alternatives in the display. This would be a result of composing together the productions that searched through the display. Then there would be specific productions that recognized each element in each possible position of the array.

The data for searching varying lists show little or no reduction of search rate with practice. In these cases the composition algorithm will only be combining general productions. Proceduralization will not occur because the memory sets are only kept in temporary memory. This is unlike the case when fixed lists are used and specific productions are also created. Here we show a general composite production that would be created after matching probes to the fourth item in lists with different elements.

P33:   *If*   pointing to the first element in the list
             and it is not equal to the probe item
             and the first element is before a second
             which is not equal to the probe item
             and the second is before a third element
             which is not equal to the probe item
             and the third is before a fourth
             which *is* equal to the probe item
       Then   say yes.

Unlike the specific production that searches for T this general production has more clauses in the *If* side. These extra elements are needed to match the structure of the memory set. The cost of generality is an increase in the size of the *If* side of a production. If we assume that working memory is limited in size, then we will not be able to keep all the memory set in working memory and so the large general production will never apply. Thus, in a search task with lists that vary we predict little or no improvement in search rate for subjects relatively experienced in searching lists because their general search productions are already as large as possible.

It is important to recognize that under our analysis two things are happening in the automaticity paradigm. For one thing, composition is collapsing a series of productions into one, producing a loss of the set size effect. In addition, proceduralization is relieving working memory of the need to maintain a representation of the memory set. This second factor we think is responsible for the loss of interference with concurrent tasks that Shiffrin and Dumais (this volume) report occurs with practice; that is, performance of one task does not suffer interference from a concurrent automatic task. This result is predicted because working memory no longer needs to maintain in active state long-term memory facts for performance of the automatic process.

Losing Track of Intermediate Results

There is some evidence that suggests that people lose conscious track of intermediate results with practice on a problem (Ericsson & Simon, 1980). Composition can predict this effect. We have seen that when two productions are composed, the resulting production will likely have fewer *If* side clauses than the sum of the number of *If* side clauses in each of the two productions. However, the *Then* side of the resulting production is precisely the sum of the *Then* sides of both productions. So, these *Then* sides can grow quite large. Intermediate results are deposited into working memory by means of the actions in *Then* sides. If the number of clauses in the *Then* side exceeds the capacity of working memory, the information conveyed by these clauses (i.e., intermediate results) will be lost.

CONCLUSION

We have described an automatic learning system based on proceduralization and composition. These mechanisms allow us to maintain the flexibility of representing knowledge in a semantic net and also to build production rules that will embody directly certain uses of the knowledge. The knowledge underlying procedures starts out as propositions in a network. Knowledge in this form can be changed and analyzed by the cognitive system. As one applies knowledge, the proceduralization process turns it into faster production rules automatically. Then composition forms larger units out of the individual proceduralized productions, in a gradual manner. These processes help explain some effects in the practice literature such as automatic speedup, development of parallel search, and inability to introspect on the application of well-learned procedures.

Composition speeds up procedures, but it does not change them. This is unlike other mechanisms of learning such as analogy, strategy modification, generalization, and discrimination (see Anderson, Greeno, Kline, & Neves, this volume) that may actually change procedures. Still we believe that composition does produce an effect that will change behavior. Problem solving by students is always under some time constraint, whether it be 30 minutes given for an exam or a few minutes allocated for homework. If we assume that a relatively constant amount of time will be spent on problems, then in the initial stages of practice some good solutions will not be discovered because they involve too much search time. As the search process with a problem becomes faster, more and more of the search tree can be explored and so new solutions will be discovered.

We observed this kind of development of competence in one of the students to whom we taught geometry. His early problem-solving behavior showed much linear search through the textbook for concepts he had read previously but had forgotten. Usually this search took much time and after several minutes he would give up even though eventually he would have found what he was looking for. Then we showed him a more efficient way of searching the textbook by checking the glossary. At this point he was able to find information much faster and so solved more problems successfully.

Similarly, proceduralization does not change the procedures. It only makes them specific to the knowledge used. However, it too can change the behavior the system is capable of by reducing the demand on working memory to maintain long-term memory facts. Thus, more different kinds of information can be kept in working memory and so new relationships can be seen between active information. Also proceduralization releases working memory for concurrent tasks that might facilitate the problem solving.

So we see that behavior will be changed by these simple automatic learning mechanisms. The interesting thing about them is that expertise comes about through the use of knowledge and not by analysis of knowledge. There is no intelligent homunculus deciding whether incoming knowledge should be stored declaratively or procedurally or how it should be made more efficient.

ACKNOWLEDGMENTS

We would like to thank David Klahr and especially Jola Jakimik for comments on an earlier draft. We also thank Bill Chase for helping our search through the memory scanning literature. The research described was supported by ONR Contract N00014-78-C-0725.

REFERENCES

Anderson, J. R. *Language, memory, and thought.* Hillsdale, N.J.: Lawrence Erlbaum Associates, 1976.

Anderson, J. R., Kline, P. J., & Beasley, C. M. Complex learning processes. In R. E. Snow, P. A. Federico, & W. E. Montague (Eds.), *Aptitude, learning, and instruction: Cognitive process analyses.* Hillsdale, N.J.: Lawrence Erlbaum Associates, 1980.

Briggs, G. E., & Blaha, J. Memory retrieval and central comparison times in information processing. *Journal of Experimental Psychology,* 1969, *79,* 395–402.

Crossman, E. R. F. W. A theory of the acquisition of speed-skill. *Ergonomics,* 1959, *2,* 153–166.

Ericsson, K. A., & Simon, H. A. Verbal reports as data. *Psychological Review*, 1980, *87*, 215–251.

Fitts, P. M. Perceptual-motor skill learning. In A. W. Melton (Ed.), *Categories of human learning*. New York: Academic, 1964.

Forgy, C. *The OPS4 reference manual*. Department of Computer Science, Carnegie-Mellon University, 1979.

Forgy, C., & McDermott, J. OPS, a domain-independent production system. *Proceedings of the Fifth International Joint Conference on Artificial Intelligence*, 1977, 933–939.

Gibson, E. J., & Yonas, A. A developmental study of visual search behavior. *Perception & Psychophysics*, 1966, *1*, 169–171.

Jurgensen, R., Donnelly, A., Maier, J., & Rising, G. *Geometry*. Boston: Houghton Mifflin, 1975.

Kristofferson, M. W. Effects of practice on character-classification performance. *Canadian Journal of Psychology*, 1972, *26*, 540–560.

Lewis, C. H. *Production system models of practice effects*. Unpublished dissertation, University of Michigan, Ann Arbor, 1978.

Lewis, C. H. *Speed and practice*. Unpublished manuscript, 1979.

Luchins, A. S. Mechanization in problem solving. *Psychological Monographs*, 1945, *58*, No. 270.

Meyer, A. R., & Shamos, M. I. Time and space. In A. K. Jones (Ed.), *Perspectives on Computer Science*. New York: Academic, 1977.

Mowbray, G. H., & Rhodes, M. V. On the reduction of choice reaction times with practice. *Quarterly Journal of Experimental Psychology*, 1959, *11*, 16–23.

Neisser, U., Novick, R., & Lazar, R. Searching for ten targets simultaneously. *Perceptual and Motor Skills*, 1963, *17*, 955–961.

Newell, A., & Simon, H. A. *Human problem solving*. Englewood Cliffs, N.J.: Prentice-Hall, 1972.

Nickerson, R. S. Response times with a memory-dependent task. *Journal of Experimental Psychology*, 1966, *72*, 761–769.

Schneider, W., & Shiffrin, R. M. Controlled and automatic human information processing: I. Detection, search and attention. *Psychological Review*, 1977, *84*, 1–66.

Shiffrin, R. M., & Schneider, W. Controlled and automatic human information processing: II. Perceptual learning, automatic attending, and a general theory. *Psychological Review*, 1977, *84*, 127–190.

Snoddy, G. S. Learning and stability. *Journal of Applied Psychology*, 1926, *10*, 1–36.

Waterman, D. A. Adaptive production systems. *Proceedings of the Fourth International Joint Conference on Artificial Intelligence*. Tbilisi, USSR, 1975, 296–303.

Winograd, T. W. Frame representations and the declarative-procedural controversy. In D. G. Bobrow & A. Collins (Eds.), *Representation and understanding: Studies in cognitive science*. New York: Academic, 1975.

3 Skill in Algebra

Clayton Lewis
IBM Watson Research Center

ABSTRACT

Skilled professional mathematicians who work with elementary algebra solved a set of problems previously attempted by students of varying skill. The strategic choices, use of operators, and mistakes made by the experts are discussed. In general, the experts' performance was not sharply different from that of the students, and reasons for this are considered. It is proposed that some streamlined procedures used by experts and less skilled solvers may be developed using only general facts about procedures, without any specifically mathematical insight. It is also shown that composition of productions cannot account for some of the streamlining observed, which takes the form of conversion of multiple-pass to single-pass procedures.

INTRODUCTION

Picture a tennis professional in mid-game and, on the next court, a novice. Contrast the consistency of the professional with the erratic play of the novice. Picture a chess master at one board and a novice at the next. Notice the master's ability to exploit subtle differences between positions. Now, picture a professional mathematician at work on a routine problem in elementary algebra and at the next desk a struggling student. What differences in performance are evident? This chapter presents such a comparison. To foreshadow the results, the *lack* of differences may be surprising.

This study of skilled performance was undertaken for two reasons. First, the behavior of skilled solvers contributes to our knowledge of the *natural history* of behavior in algebra. To the extent that they respond to the task differently from other people, we obtain a wider perspective on the possibilities of the reasoning system we all share. Second, understanding skilled performance may lead to an understanding of the learning mechanisms by which skill is attained. A longitudinal study of the development of skill might be most informative in this respect, but even a comparison of skilled and unskilled performance in different groups, as presented here, may be useful in spying out the lay of the land.

FRAMEWORK

The discussion to follow is largely organized around a particular general view of how people solve equations, which must be outlined first. The view is strongly influenced by Bundy's (1975) scheme for an artificial equation solver, modified to be appropriate as a description of mental processes in people. In this view algebra is a symbol-manipulation task, in which the solver must transform a given string of symbols, an equation like those in Fig. 3.1, into another string of symbols, using certain permitted operations. The goal string must have the unknown to be solved for (specified in the statement of the problem) on one side by itself, and no occurrence of the unknown on the other side. Figure 3.2 shows an example of a problem and a solution and shows the sort of operations that are commonly employed.

$1A$ $A = p + prt$ *solve for p* $1B$ $2x = x^2$

$2A$ $\frac{1}{3} = \frac{1}{x} + \frac{1}{7}$ $2B$ $\frac{1}{R} = \frac{1}{x} + \frac{1}{y} + \frac{1}{z}$ *solve for x*

$3A$ $9(x + 40) = 5(x + 40)$ $3B$ $7(4x - 1) = 3(4x - 1) + 4$

$4A$ $xy + yz = 2y$ *solve for x* $4B$ $\frac{x+3+x}{x^2} = 1$

$5A$ $\frac{5}{10} = \frac{x-10}{x+5}$ $5B$ $\frac{1-x^2}{1-x} = 2$

$6A$ $x + 2(x + 1) = 4$ $6B$ $x + 2(x + 2(x + 2)) = x + 2$

$7A$ $x - 2(x + 1) = 14$ $7B$ $6(x - 2) - 3(4 - 2x) = x - 12$

FIG. 3.1.   Problems given to all solvers.

$$x + 2(x + 1) = 4$$

multiply out

$$x + 2x + 2 = 4$$

transpose 2

$$x + 2x = 4 - 2$$

collect

$$3x = 2$$

divide by 3

$$x = \frac{2}{3}$$

FIG. 3.2.   A solution to Problem 6A.

To solve a problem, two kinds of knowledge must be employed. First, the solver must know an adequate set of correct operations. Difficulty will result if a needed operator is not known or if an incorrect operator is used (Carry, Lewis, & Bernard, 1980). Second, the solver must know how to *select* an appropriate operator to use at a given juncture. This is difficult, as there are a large number of operators and literally an infinite number of ways they can be correctly applied. For example, it is always legal to add any quantity to both sides of an equation, but it is rarely advisable. The knowledge needed to make this selection can be called *strategic* knowledge. That strategic knowledge can be considered separate from knowledge of operators is shown by the fact that a solver may know *how* to apply either of two operators in a given situation but may still not know *which* to apply. A competent solver, then, knows an adequate set of operators and has adequate strategic knowledge.

HYPOTHESES ABOUT SKILLED PERFORMANCE

In this framework, what features would one expect to see in the performance of highly skilled solvers?

First, skilled solvers should have strategic knowledge that enables them to select operators forming an economical solution. Contrast the solutions to the same problem shown in Fig. 3.3. Sometimes, as in the example in Fig. 3.4,

$$\frac{1}{R} = \frac{1}{x} + \frac{1}{y} + \frac{1}{z} \quad solve\,for\,x$$

$$xyz = Ryz + xzR + xyR$$

$$x(yz - zR - yR) = Ryz$$

$$x = \frac{Ryz}{yz - zR - yR}$$

$$\frac{1}{R} = \frac{1}{x} + \frac{1}{y} + \frac{1}{z} \quad solve\,for\,x$$

$$\frac{1}{x} = \frac{1}{R} - \frac{1}{y} - \frac{1}{z}$$

$$x = \frac{1}{\dfrac{1}{R} - \dfrac{1}{y} - \dfrac{1}{z}}$$

FIG. 3.3. Two solutions to Problem 2B.

$$3(x + (a + b)) + 2(b + (x + a)) = 1$$

$$5(x + a + b) = 1$$

$$x + a + b = \frac{1}{5}$$

$$x = \frac{1}{5} - a - b$$

FIG. 3.4. Using a hidden repeated subexpression.

Separate:

$$6x - 12 - 12 + 6x = x - 12$$

$$12x - 24 = x - 12$$

$$11x = 12$$

Combined:

$$6x - 12 - 12 + 6x = x - 12$$

$$11x = 12$$

FIG. 3.5.   Combining transposition and collection.

finding an economical solution depends on detecting a special structural feature of a problem. Skilled solvers should be good at this.

Second, the operators used might be more powerful than those used by poorer solvers, in that fewer of them would be required to solve a problem. For example, as shown in Fig. 3.5, a skilled solver might have a single operator that performs the work of separate transposition and collection operators.

Last, but not least, skilled solvers would be expected to make few errors. Their operators should be correct and accurately applied.

SUBJECTS

To investigate these expectations, solutions produced by people of different levels of skill will be compared. The *experts* are five working mathematicians at the IBM Watson Research Center. All have extensive publications in mathematics. Each was recommended by colleagues as a person skilled in elementary algebra and as one whose work involves a good deal of elementary algebra.

Performance of the experts will be compared with the performance of a group of students with a wide range of competence. Data from these students are taken from a study carried out at the University of Texas at Austin, in collaboration with John Bernard and Ray Carry (Carry, Lewis, & Bernard, 1980). The group includes 19 students in Introductory Psychology and 15 mathematics education and engineering students who were screened for speed and accuracy on problems similar to those to be discussed. For purposes of comparison the students will be subdivided according to their performance on the 14 problems that all were given. The 10 subjects in the bottom group solved 1–9 problems; the 14 subjects in the middle group, 10–11; and 10 subjects in the top group, 12–14. The expert mathematicians correctly solved 13 or 14 of the problems.

THE PROBLEMS

All participants were given the 14 problems shown in Fig. 3.1. The experts and the selected engineering and math education students were then given the additional problems shown in Fig. 3.6. The psychology students were not given these problems but rather others that will not be discussed here.

PROCEDURE

One problem from each of the seven pairs in Fig. 3.1 was given to the subject, who was asked to solve the seven problems using the paper provided. The subject was asked to solve the problem as he or she ordinarily would, writing down as much or little as desired and making no effort to be unusually clear or careful. Simplification of answers was not required. The subject was asked to "think aloud" while solving the problems, putting into words any thoughts that could be readily verbalized. A video tape record with sound track was made of the subject's work so that the order of writing and the temporal relationship of writing and spoken comments was preserved.

A1

$$\frac{\frac{1}{x} + \frac{1}{x^2}}{\frac{1}{x} + 2x^2} = 3$$

A2

$$3x + 5(x - 3) = (5x + 3) - 3(x - 2)$$

B1

$$\frac{1}{x} = \frac{2}{4 - x}$$

B2

$$\frac{a}{x - b} = c + d$$

C1

$$2(4x + 2) - 3(1 + 2x) = 0$$

C2

$$3(x + (a + b)) + 2(b + (x + a)) = 1$$

D1

$$\frac{(r + y + z)x}{\frac{1}{p} + \frac{1}{q}} = d$$

D2

$$y + 2(\frac{3x}{x + 1}) - (4 + y)(\frac{3x}{x + 1}) = 1$$

FIG. 3.6.   Additional problems given to some solvers.

When the first seven problems had been attempted, the second seven were presented under the same instructions, except that the subject was asked to explain the method of solution as if to a student asking for help with homework. It was therefore permissable for the subject to modify his or her normal approach to these problems for clarity of exposition.

The pairs of problems shown in Fig. 3.6 were split up and presented in the same way, half being attempted under "think aloud" instructions and half under "explain" instructions.

LENGTH OF SOLUTIONS

Figure 3.7 shows the lengths of the written solutions obtained from the experts and the bottom and top students. Only solutions obtained under "think aloud" instructions are shown, to avoid any inflation caused by the "explain" instructions. The lengths shown are the number of written lines indicating a change in the form of the equation.

Marks such as slashes indicating operations on a written line were not counted, and a written line might in some cases be formed of two or more parts, each reflecting a different operation on a previous line, so these counts should be regarded as only crude indicators of the number of operations that subjects performed in solving the problems. Of course, operations done mentally are not reflected either.

Two observations may be made about the overall pattern in Fig. 3.7. First, there is a general tendency for the solutions of the experts to be among the shortest for a given problem. This is as expected, according to the hypotheses presented previously. Some of the specific factors contributing to the economy of these solutions are discussed in detail in the following. Second, and perhaps more surprisingly, the experts' solutions are rarely as short as possible (one step). These experts did not just look at the problems and write down the solution, except in a few cases.

STRATEGIC CHOICES

Problem 2B presents an interesting study in strategy. Figure 3.3 shows two solutions, one in which the operations concentrate on isolating the lone instance of x, by transposing and inverting, and one in which the fractions are cleared. Experts might be expected to favor the more economical first strategy, and they do. The choices made by subjects are shown in Table 3.1 ("explain" solutions, as well as "think aloud", are included). As can be seen, there is a strong tendency for the more skilled subjects to be more likely to choose the transpose-invert method.

This tabulation confounds *strategy* and knowledge of *operators,* however. A subject might not know the invert operator and hence be forced to take another tack. To try to separate out the strategic component in the choice of method, Table 3.2 shows the frequency of choice of transposing the x term as first step. There is still a strong relationship between this choice and skill.

So problem 2B seems to confirm the hypothesis that skilled solvers should be able to select economical solutions. But the apparently similar Problem 2A shows a different pattern; see Table 3.3. For this problem the experts did *not* use the isolate–invert strategy. This indicates that strategic choices are flexible. It

```
Problem 1A          Problem 5A          Problem 1B          Problem 5B

B                   B      1            B 1                 B    1 1
M    2 1            M     32            M     32            M   11211
T  1 5              T     31            T 1111              T    3 1
E  1 2              E     2             E 11                E   111
  |||||||             |||||||              |||||||             |||||||
  1234567             1234567              1234567              1234567

Problem 2A          Problem 6A          Problem 2B
                                                            Problem 6B
B      111          B    121            B
M     333           M   14              M    11             B    1
T   12              T    42             T    14             M    12
E   111             E   21              E    11             T    31
  |||||||             |||||||             |||||||           E   2
  1234567             1234567             1234567             |||||||

Problem 3A          Problem 7A          Problem 3B           1234567

B    42             B    2              B                   Problem 7B
M   132             M   131             M    51
T   9               T    3 1            T    1              B    31
E   2               E    21             E    12             M   2212
  |||||||             |||||||             |||||||           T   231
  1234567             1234567             1234567           E   2
                                                              |||||||
Problem 4A                              Problem 4B            1234567

B   4                                   B   1
M   5                                   M   2  2
T  15                                   T     1111
E   1                                   E     4
  |||||||                                 |||||||
  1234567                                 1234567
```

FIG. 3.7. Lengths of written solutions to problems in Fig. 3.1. For each problem a scale of length from 1 to 7 is shown, with digits above indicating the number of solutions of each length collected from each of the four groups of solvers. Only correct solutions collected under "think aloud" instructions are shown. B = bottom 10 students, M = middle 14 students, T = top 10 students, E = 5 experts.

TABLE 3.1
Choice of Strategy for Problem 2B

	transpose-invert	other	proportion choosing transpose-invert
Experts	4	1	.8
Top 10 students	4	6	.4
Middle 14 students	3	11	.2
Bottom 10 students	0	10	0

chi squared with 3 df = 11.6, p<.01

TABLE 3.2
Choice of First Step for Problem 2B

	transpose	other	proportion choosing transpose
Experts	5	0	1.0
Top 10 students	8	2	.8
Middle 14 students	9	5	.5
Bottom 10 students	3	7	.3

chi squared with 3 df = 8.9, p<.05

TABLE 3.3
Choice of Strategy for Problem 2A

	transpose-invert	other	proportion choosing transpose-invert
Experts	0	5	0
Top 10 students	2	8	.2
Middle 14 students	1	13	.1
Bottom 10 students	0	10	0

may be that the smaller number of terms in 2A makes clearing fractions seem less unattractive than in 2B.

Problems 3A, 3B, and 7B bring out another aspect of strategic choice. As Fig. 3.8 shows, these problems may be solved either by multiplying out the parenthesized quantities and then collecting terms or by collecting the parenthesized quantities directly. It might be expected that experts would use the second

Problem 3A

$9(x + 40) = 5(x + 40)$

$9x + 360 = 5x + 200$

$4x = -160$

$x = -40$

$9(x + 40) = 5(x + 40)$

$4(x + 40) = 0$

$x + 40 = 0$

$x = -40$

Problem 3B

$7(4x - 1) = 3(4x - 1) + 4$

$28x - 7 = 12x - 3 + 4$

$16x = 8$

$x = \dfrac{8}{16}$

$7(4x - 1) = 3(4x - 1) + 4$

$4(4x - 1) = 4$

$4x - 1 = 1$

$4x = 2$

$x = \dfrac{2}{4}$

Problem 7B

$6(x - 2) - 3(4 - 2x) = x - 12$

$6x - 12 - 12 + 6x = x - 12$

$11x = 12$

$x = \dfrac{12}{11}$

$6(x - 2) - 3(4 - 2x) = x - 12$

$6(x - 2) + 6(x - 2) = x - 12$

$12(x - 2) = x - 12$

$12x - 24 = x - 12$

$11x = 12$

$x = \dfrac{12}{11}$

FIG. 3.8. Alternate solutions to problems with repeated subexpressions.

TABLE 3.4
Handling of Repeated Subexpressions for Problems 3A, 3B, 7B

E = experts, T = top 10 students, M = middle 14 students, B = bottom 10 students.

		E	T	M	B
3A	multiply out	3	6	7	8
	collect repeated subexpression	2	0	3	0
	cancel repeated subexpression	0	4	4	2
3B	multiply out	3	7	10	9
	collect repeated subexpression	1	1	3	0
	cancel repeated subexpression	0	0	0	1
	other uses of repeated subexpression	1	2	1	0
7B	multiply out	5	10	13	10
	collect repeated subexpression	0	0	1	0

method that cuts down on the amount of arithmetic and bookkeeping that must be done. Especially for Problem 7B they might be more likely to detect the possibility of the shortcut than less skilled solvers. Table 3.4 shows the frequency of exploiting the repeated subexpression. As seen, the experts usually did *not* use the subexpressions but, rather, multiplied out. Only *one* subject used the hidden repeated subexpression in Problem 7B.

In Problem 3A, the commonest use of the subexpression was to cancel, leading to the idea that there is no solution. This cancellation is actually a division by zero, and so it is incorrect. Cautious solvers then re-solved the problem by multiplying out. Cancellation accounts for 11 of the 26 uses of the repeated subexpressions, including one erroneous cancellation in Problem 3B.

The other uses of the repeated subexpression for Problem 3B are of some interest. One expert solver apparently noticed directly that replacing the subexpressions by 1 gives an identity. Thus the necessity of collecting terms was entirely avoided. Two solvers introduced an auxiliary variable for the subexpression, and one divided through by the subexpression but then abandoned that approach.

Problems C1 and C2 also offer opportunity for exploiting a repeated subexpression. As for the earlier problems the experts usually did *not* use the economical method.

Why are the experts so pedestrian on these problems? Two explanations come to mind. First, the incidence of problems that offer the chance to use subexpressions in this way may be low, so that it is in general not worth looking for then. Second, if one is a skilled solver, the saving in effort that results from avoiding multiplying out may not be meaningful, so that complicating one's strategic decision making is not profitable. It may be that the solvers who could benefit from spotting the common subexpressions are just those less skilled solvers who would be least likely to be able to detect them.

POWERFUL OPERATORS

Some operators do the work of a series of others. Figure 3.9 gives an example, the *cross-multiply* operator, which can replace two *clear-fraction* operators. Problem 5A, as shown in the figure, is a good problem to examine for use of this operator. Table 3.5 shows that the experts are consistent in using cross-multiply, as would be expected. There is some indication that more skilled solvers are more likely to use it. But Table 3.5 also shows that cross-multiply is the dominant choice for subjects in all groups. Only two students in the bottom 10 used methods that could have been replaced by cross-multiply. So although the experts use cross-multiply, so do other solvers.

The common operations of *multiplying-out* products with parenthesized quantities and *collecting* terms can also be replaced by a single composite operation, as shown in Fig. 3.10. The operations of *transposing* and *collecting* are frequently combined as well, as in Fig. 3.11.

The use of these combined operations cannot always be unambiguously diagnosed. The lack of any written indication of separate operations is not decisive, because a solver might perform two operations mentally. Sometimes spoken comments point to a combined operation, especially when there is a convenient name for it (as for cross multiplication). Sometimes the complexity of the intermediate products of a sequence of steps makes it implausible that no written mark would be made. In general, however, the incidence of combined operations can

TABLE 3.5
Choice of Operation in Problem 5A

	cross-multiply	clear fractions	other
Experts	5	0	0
Top 10 students	6	4	0
Middle 14 students	11	2	1
Bottom 10 students	5	2	3

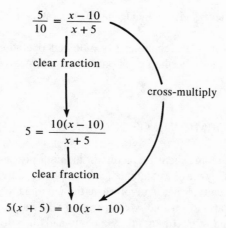

FIG. 3.9. Using cross multiplication to clear fractions.

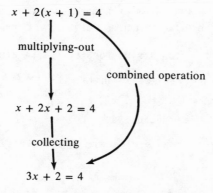

FIG. 3.10. Combining multiplying out with collecting.

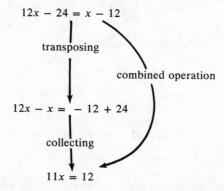

FIG. 3.11. Combining transposing and collecting.

easily be overcounted, and the incidence of separately performed operations undercounted.

Despite the potential overcounting of combined operations, experts by no means always used them. Further, even poor solvers sometimes combined operations.

THE FORMATION OF COMBINED OPERATIONS

Figure 3.12 gives a more schematic picture of the multiplying-out and collecting operators and how they may be combined. For simplicity, only collecting x terms is shown. Schematically, what is involved in the combination is the conversion of a *two-pass* operation to a *one-pass* operation. Instead of the symbol string being scanned twice, first for multiplying out and then for collecting, it is scanned once, and a composite of the multiplying out and collecting operators is applied to each term.

This replacement of a two-pass by a one-pass procedure is a commonly applicable simplification that often increases efficiency. Consider setting a table.

```
Multiplying out:      scan string for terms like a(bx+c)

                      replace by abx+ac


Collecting:           set RESULT to zero

                      scan string for terms like ax

                      delete

                      add or subtract a from RESULT,
                      according to sign

                      at end, RESULT is coefficient of x


Combination:          set RESULT to zero

                      scan string for terms like a(bx+c) or ax

                      if a(bx+c), add or subtract ab
                      from RESULT

                      if ax, add or subtract a from result

                      at end of string, RESULT is coefficient of x
```

FIG. 3.12.   Procedures for multiplying out, collecting, and performing both at once.

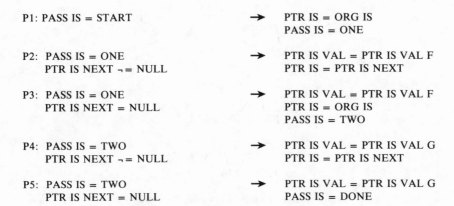

P1: PASS IS = START   →   PTR IS = ORG IS
                                            PASS IS = ONE

P2: PASS IS = ONE   →   PTR IS VAL = PTR IS VAL F
     PTR IS NEXT ¬= NULL   PTR IS = PTR IS NEXT

P3: PASS IS = ONE   →   PTR IS VAL = PTR IS VAL F
     PTR IS NEXT = NULL   PTR IS = ORG IS
                                            PASS IS = TWO

P4: PASS IS = TWO   →   PTR IS VAL = PTR IS VAL G
     PTR IS NEXT ¬= NULL   PTR IS = PTR IS NEXT

P5: PASS IS = TWO   →   PTR IS VAL = PTR IS VAL G
     PTR IS NEXT = NULL   PASS IS = DONE

FIG. 3.13.   Production system PS2P, which carries out a two-pass procedure.

One can circle the table twice, first laying out napkins and then flatware, or one can circle the table once, putting both napkin and flatware at one place before passing to the next.

Figure 3.13 shows a production system that abstracts the key features of a two-pass procedure that could represent either multiplying out and collecting or setting a table. The productions operate on the data structure shown in Fig. 3.14. The objects to be processed, which might be pieces of an equation or places at a table, are represented by A, B, and C. The objects FA, FB, FC represent the results of applying the first required operation to A, B, C. GFA, GFB, GFC represent the results of then applying the second operation. For example, if A is a place, FA is that place with a napkin, and GFA is the same place with flatware added. If A is a piece of an equation, FA is the piece after multiplying out, and GFA is what is left after collecting has removed the x terms, as shown in Fig. 3.15. Collecting also accumulates an x coefficient as it scans the pieces, but for simplicity that aspect of the operation will not be represented.

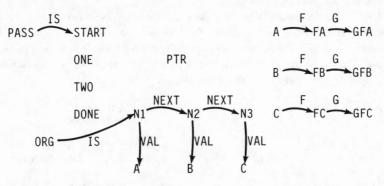

FIG. 3.14.   Initial data structure used by the production systems discussed in the text.

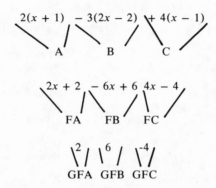

FIG. 3.15. Correspondence of structure processed by abstract procedures discussed in text with pieces of an equation.

The productions are written in the TRIPS language (Lewis, 1978). In TRIPS, an expression like ORG IS VAL is evaluated as follows: the node ORG is found. The link IS is followed from ORG. The link VAL is followed from that node. The node reached is the value of the expression. If any of the named links are not there, the value of the expression is a special node called NULL. A condition, like ORG IS VAL ¬= ORG IS NEXT VAL, is tested by evaluating the two expressions and comparing them as indicated to see if they are not equal (¬=). Given the structure in Fig. 3.14, ORG IS VAL has value A, and ORG IS NEXT VAL has value B, so the condition is true. An action like ORG IS VAL = ORG IS NEXT VAL is carried out as follows. The expression ORG IS is evaluated, yielding N1. ORG IS NEXT VAL is evaluated, yielding B. The VAL link from N1 is then deleted and replaced by a VAL link to B.

Figure 3.16 traces the execution of this production system. Productions P2 and P3 move the pointer PTR through the string of nodes, applying an operator F to each node's value. Then the productions P4 and P5 scan the string again, applying a different operator G.

A one-pass production system to do the same thing is shown in Fig. 3.17. It operates on the same data structure and obtains the same result as the first production system, but without the necessity to scan the symbol string twice. Figure 3.18 shows a state in the middle of the single scan. Note that G and F have been applied to A before anything has been done to B or C.

P1: PASS IS = START   →   PTR IS = ORG IS
                            PASS IS = ONE

P2: PASS IS = ONE   →   PTR IS VAL = PTR IS VAL F G
    PTR IS NEXT ¬= NULL   PTR IS = PTR IS NEXT

P3: PASS IS = ONE   →   PTR IS VAL = PTR IS VAL F G
    PTR IS NEXT = NULL   PASS IS = DONE

FIG. 3.17. Production system PS1P, which carries out a one-pass procedure.

(a) After applying P1, P2, P2

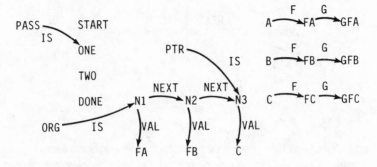

(b) P3,P4 then apply.

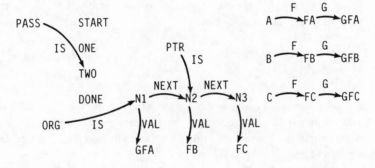

(c) P4 and finally P5 apply

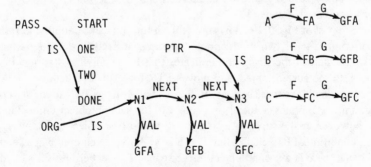

FIG. 3.16.   Trace of production system PS2P shown in Fig. 3.13.

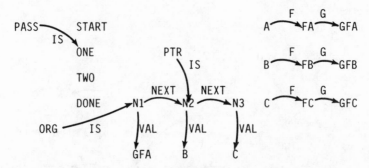

FIG. 3.18.   A state that PS1P passes through in processing the structure shown in Fig. 3.14.

What learning mechanism could develop the one-pass production system from the two-pass? Composition of productions (Lewis, 1978; Neves & Anderson, this volume) is worth investigating as a possibility. Under this scheme, if one production produces a result that is transformed by a second production. as shown here schematically, the two productions are combined to give a single production that does the work of both:

$$A \rightarrow B$$
$$+B \rightarrow C$$
$$\overline{A \rightarrow C}$$

It might appear that the key step in transforming the two-pass system PS2P into a one-pass system would be to combine the separate productions in PS2P that perform the operations F and G to form a single production that performs GF in the one-pass system.

The *perfect composite* of two productions P1 and P2 has as its action the functional composition of the actions of its ingredients. Its condition checks that P1 could apply, and if it did, P2 could then apply. A formal treatment of these notions is given in Lewis (1978).

The top part of Fig. 3.19 shows how this definition can be applied to form the perfect composite of two productions expressed in TRIPS. P1 sets the pointer PTR to the start of the string and indicates that PASS ONE is starting. P2 then applies F to the current object and moves PTR forward. The action of P12, the composite, combines these actions. It doesn't bother to set PTR to the start of the string, since P2 moves it ahead, but sets it to the second object immediately. It does, however, make sure that F is applied to the first object on the way.

The condition of P12 checks that PASS is START, as required by P1, and also checks that there is a second object in the string. This is because P2's condition could not be satisfied after P1 applied if the first object were the end of the string. P12 does not have to worry about PASS IS = ONE, the rest of P2's condition, because applying P1 would ensure that that be true.

Intuitively, it might appear that this composition mechanism could change a two-pass production system like PS2P to a one-pass system. It might seem that the productions that apply F could simply be composed with the productions that apply G. The lower part of Fig. 3.19 shows how a single production P12345 can be built up in this way from the productions in PS2P. When it applies, this one production does all the work of the two-pass system at one fell swoop—a zero-pass system.

This might look promising, but note that this production only works in case the symbol string has exactly two elements: the conditions ORG IS NEXT ¬= NULL and ORG IS NEXT NEXT = NULL boil down to this. It does *not* do what PS1P does, because PS1P will handle strings of any length. But there are other ways of composing the productions in PS2P. Might there be some way to find a system like PS1P? The answer is *no*.

Essentially, the problem is that a one-pass system does not really mimic a two-pass system, and composition produces faithful mimics. It is possible to prove (Lewis, 1978) that any set of composite productions that have mutually

P1: PASS IS = START   →   PTR IS = ORG IS
                            PASS IS = ONE

P2: PASS IS = ONE   →   PTR IS VAL = PTR IS VAL F
    PTR IS NEXT ¬= NULL   PTR IS = PTR IS NEXT

The composite of P1 and P2:

P12: PASS IS = START   →   PASS IS = ONE
     ORG IS NEXT ¬= NULL   PTR IS VAL = PTR IS VAL F
                                 PTR IS = ORG IS NEXT

Further composites:

P123: PASS IS = START   →   ORG IS VAL = ORG IS VAL F
      ORG IS NEXT ¬= NULL   ORG IS NEXT VAL =
                                   ORG IS NEXT VAL F
      ORG IS NEXT NEXT = NULL   PTR IS = ORG IS
                                 PASS IS = TWO

P1234: PASS IS = START   →   ORG IS NEXT VAL =
                                   ORG IS NEXT VAL F
       ORG IS NEXT ¬= NULL   PASS IS = TWO
       ORG IS NEXT NEXT = NULL   ORG IS VAL = ORG IS VAL F G
                                 PTR IS = ORG IS NEXT

P12345: PASS IS = START   →   ORG IS VAL = ORG IS VAL F G
        ORG IS NEXT ¬= NULL   PTR IS = ORG IS NEXT
        ORG IS NEXT NEXT = NULL ORG IS NEXT VAL =
                                   ORG IS NEXT VAL F G
                                 PASS IS = DONE

FIG. 3.19.   Compositions formed from the productions of PS2P.

exclusive conditions and are formed from a set of productions with mutually exclusive conditions cannot produce a state of the data structure on which they operate that could not have been produced by the original productions. But a one-pass system will under certain circumstances produce such states.

Consider an *infinite* string of objects. The two-pass system will pass through an unending sequence of states in which the operation F will have been applied to more and more of the string. It will *never* produce any state in which G has been applied, because it never reaches the end of its first pass. By contrast, the one-pass system will very soon produce states in which G has been applied to the first object in the string.

What do these arguments say about the manner in which combined operations might develop? They rule out composition. They also rule out *any* mechanism that produces only accurate mimics, unless the mechanism is privy to information that allows it to rule out unending object strings as inputs or to give them special treatment. It appears that the learning mechanism must take into account not just the nature of the process to be streamlined but also the range of possible inputs. Composition of productions does not do this.

COMBINING TRANSPOSING AND COLLECTING

Figure 3.20 shows how transposing and collecting can be combined, so that a single collection pass can be made across an entire equation without the necessity of first moving and negating x terms from the right-hand side. Arguments similar to those noted previously establish that this supercollection operator cannot be produced by composition from ordinary transposing and collecting. In fact, the same issue of two- and one-pass procedures is involved, where one pass negates and another collects.

One might feel that there might be other problems in converting ordinary collecting to supercollection, in that it might appear that a certain amount of knowledge of mathematics is needed to establish that the two procedures are equivalent. For example, it might seem important to know that negation distributes over addition or that negation is self-inverse. In fact, no mathematical knowledge at all is required to establish equivalence, and the transformation that relates the two procedures is of extremely general applicability.

To see this, consider the abstract representation of the fate of the pieces of an equation under transposing and collecting shown at the top of Fig. 3.21. For simplicity, only x terms are shown. As seen, each coefficient is ultimately added to or subtracted from the accumulating coefficient of x. The lower part of Fig. 3.21 shows the fates of the same coefficients under supercollection. As seen, each coefficient ends up the same way as before. Notice that none of the mathematical properties of signs or sign changes are relevant: The signs are treated simply as marks that indicate what is to be done with a coefficient. Note

Transposing:	Scan the right-hand side from the left
	For each x-term, move it to the left side and change its sign
Collecting:	Set RESULT to zero
	Scan the left-hand side for terms like ax or -ax
	If sign is plus add a to RESULT
	If sign is minus subtract a from RESULT
	At end RESULT is coefficient of x
Supercollection:	Proceed as in Collecting. Then:
	Scan right-hand side for terms like ax or -ax
	If sign is plus subtract a from RESULT
	If sign is minus add a to RESULT
	At end RESULT is coefficient of x

FIG. 3.20.   Procedures for transposing, collecting, and combining these to form supercollection.

also that when the equation is scanned from left to right, the *order* in which coefficients are added and subtracted is the same in the two processes. Thus it doesn't matter that addition is commutative or even associative for supercollection to work. There is no mathematics in supercollection that isn't already in transposing and collecting.

What *does* the validity of supercollection rest on? There are two insights about transposing and collecting that are involved. First, it has to be seen that *moving* the x terms is unnecessary. Second, one must see that it is unnecessary to change the signs of terms if the *interpretation* of the signs can be changed instead. Of course, these insights are not true of all procedures that are structurally like transposing and collecting. Some kinds of objects could be changed in an essential way by being moved, or the place to which they were moved might have an essential property like a high temperature. It must also be the case that the procedural equivalence that is desired extends only to the ultimate fate of the x terms and not, for example, to the number of sign changes carried out. This is not a trivial point. In the algebra domain, a student might well not appreciate that the object of the manipulations performed is strictly to obtain an answer and not

Separate transposing and collecting:

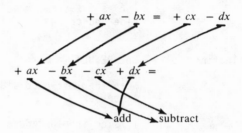

Supercollection:

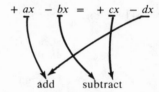

FIG. 3.21.   The fates of the coefficients of x in a sample problem under the procedures shown in Fig. 3.20.

to create particular marks on the page. A student who was confused on this point might be deterred from adopting a composite operator like supercollection.

To summarize, the combined operations discussed here do not require any mathematical insight to establish their validity but rather reflect generally valid rearrangements of procedures. The rearrangements, like the "strategy transformations" of Neches and Hayes (1978) might be used in a variety of tasks. This may explain why even relatively poor solvers may sometimes use these combined operations: Their use may depend on only general understanding of procedures rather than on specifics about algebra.

Why do experts often fail to use such operators? One expert explained that he was more likely to make errors when he skipped steps. This points up an important issue not considered in the present treatment of mechanisms: memory and processing load. Intuitively, the powerful composite operators have greater demands, and this is presumably important in determining when they are used and, perhaps, how they are learned or formed. The TRIPS productions used here are helpful for exploring composition but not for investigating this matter.

EXPERTS MAKE MISTAKES

The final aspect of the expert's performance to be considered here is its accuracy. Each of the five experts made at least one error on the 22 problems, perhaps correcting it later. Figure 3.22 shows all the errors collected. As seen, more than half the errors occur in the routine operations of multiplying out, collecting, and moving terms to the opposite side of an equation. Of course, because these are common operations, the frequency of errors may not reflect any special difficulty in performing them. Many errors occurred when these operations were being combined with others.

A few of the errors deserve special comment. Two are labeled "wishful" errors, because they make the problem so much nicer. If the errors are not made, the solver faces a quartic equation that does not factor. It is possible that some "top-down" processing is involved here, in which the solver identifies a desired form and then tries to transform the given string into it, being insufficiently strict about what operations are permissable in the process.

The error marked "confusion of one and zero" is interesting because zero and one share an important property: Both are identity elements, but for different operations. The solver may have noted that the term on the right was *an* identity but not which. This is reminiscent of Norman's (1979) "description" errors.

WHY DO THEY MAKE MISTAKES?

Why should skilled professionals make errors in this simple and familiar task? A number of reasons can be suggested. First, there is no external incentive for accurate performance. No one else cares if the mathematician makes a mistake—there is no Super Bowl of algebra where the most accurate solvers in the nation vie for handsome prizes. Accordingly, mathematicians are free to set their own tradeoffs among speed, effort, and accuracy. They may simply choose not to pay the price in time and effort for greater accuracy.

Second, careless errors, of the type the experts made, are easy to detect when work is reexamined. More than one of the experts remarked that he sometimes made careless mistakes in his work, but they were always caught in the course of preparing work for publication or further use. One expert noted that a problem could arise if a line of work were abandoned because of a careless error, because the error might not then be detected. He said that despite his concern for this problem he did not check any but the most important work.

To summarize, then, it may be that no one bothers to become a flawless equation solver.

REFLECTIONS

From a natural history standpoint, the experts are disappointing. They don't just look at problems and write down the answers. They occasionally have a flash of insight, but so do other solvers. They make mistakes. In short, on the routine problems considered here, they don't seem to be skilled in the way tennis profes-

$$3x + 5(x - 3) = (5x + 3) - 3(x - 2)$$
$$8x - 15 = 8x + 3 + 6$$

attempt to combine multiplying-out and collecting

$$x + 2(x + 2x + 4)$$
$$x + 3x + 8$$

ditto

$$\frac{1}{3} = \frac{1}{x} + \frac{1}{7}$$
$$\frac{1}{x} = \frac{1}{7} - \frac{1}{3}$$

attempt to switch sides and transpose in one step

$$2x + 3 = x^2$$
$$x^2 - 2x + 3 = 0$$

ditto

$$y + 2z - (4 + y)z = 2$$
$$(2 - y)z = 2 - y + 4$$

attempt to combine multiplying-out, transposing, and collecting

$$x + 2(x + 1) = 4$$
$$3x = 1$$

ditto

$$x[y + 6 - 12 - 3y - 2] = -y + 2$$
$$x[-2y + 4] = -y + 2$$

skipped -12 in collecting

$$\frac{(r + y + z)x}{\frac{1}{p} + \frac{1}{q}} = d$$
$$x = d(r + y + z)$$

confusion of numerator and denominator in moving across equals sign

FIG. 3.22.   Errors collected from the experts.

108

$$\frac{\frac{1}{x} + \frac{1}{x^2}}{\frac{1}{x} + 2x^2} = 3$$

$$\frac{1}{x} + \frac{1}{x^2} = 3\frac{1}{x} + \frac{2}{3}x^2$$

confusion of numerator and denominator in moving across equals sign

$$\frac{\frac{1}{x} + \frac{1}{x^2}}{\frac{1}{x} + 2x^2} = 3$$

$$\frac{1}{x} + \frac{1}{x^2} = \frac{3}{x} + \frac{6}{x^2}$$

ditto, wishful

$$\frac{\frac{1}{x} + \frac{1}{x^2}}{\frac{1}{x} + 2x^2} = 3$$

$$\frac{1}{x} + \frac{1}{x^2} = \frac{3}{x} + 6x^2$$

$$x + 1 = 3x + 6x^2$$

wishful

$$5x + 5(a + b) = 1$$

$$x = -(a + b)$$

confusion of 1 and 0

$$9(\cancel{x + 40}) = 5(\cancel{x + 40})$$

division by 0

$$6x^2 + 2x - 1 = 0$$

$$x = \frac{-2 \pm \sqrt{4+6}}{2(6)}$$

error in applying quadratic formula

FIG. 3.22. (*Continued*)

sionals or chess masters are. All this would have pleased Thorndike, who might have seen it as supporting his abandonment of the Law of Exercise: People don't necessarily get better just by doing something a lot.

The combined operations that experts (and other solvers) use are nevertheless interesting from a theoretical perspective. A consideration of them brought out an important limitation of production composition as a learning mechanism. It also led to the realization that some of the transformations of procedures involved in streamlining the operations of algebra really have nothing to do with algebra. So some of what counts as skill in algebra may really be skill in handling procedures in general.

ACKNOWLEDGMENTS

I would like to thank the five mathematicians who contributed their time and ideas to this study. I thank also John Bernard, Ray Carry, Cheryl White, and Karen Rowe for their contributions to the study of the student subjects discussed here, and NIE and NSF for their support of that study.

REFERENCES

Bundy, A. Analysing mathematical proofs. DAI Research Report No. 2, Department of Artificial Intelligence, University of Edinburgh, 1975.

Carry, L. R., Lewis, C. H., & Bernard, J. E. *Psychology of equation solving: An information processing study.* Department of Curriculum and Instruction, University of Texas at Austin, 1980.

Lewis, C. H. Production system models of practice effects. (Doctoral Dissertation, University of Michigan, 1978). *Dissertation Abstracts International,* 1979, *39,* 5105B. (University Microfilms No. 79-07,120)

Neches, R., & Hayes, J. R. Progress towards a taxonomy of strategy transformations. In A. M. Lesgold, J. W. Pellegrino, S. Fokkema, & R. Glaser (Eds.), Cognitive psychology and instruction. New York: Plenum Books, 1978.

Norman, D. A. *Slips of the mind and an outline for a theory of action.* CHIP 88, Center for Human Information Processing, University of California at San Diego, 1979.

4 The Development of Automatism

Richard M. Shiffrin
Indiana University

Susan T. Dumais
Bell Laboratories

INTRODUCTION

Many of the chapters in the present volume deal with the acquisition of cognitive skills. It is our intent to explore one fundamental component of skill development: automatization. We consider several interrelated questions: Does automatization exist? What is automatism? How are automatic processes and control processes distinguished? What is learned during automatization? What causes automatization to take place? What role does automatization play in skill acquisition?

The acquisition of skill is embodied in the adage "practice makes perfect." Consider the changes that occur, for example, when learning to play a musical instrument. At first, effort and attention must be devoted to each smallest movement and minor decision. Performance is slow and error prone. Eventually, long sequences of movements and decisions may be carried out with minor effort and little attention. Performance may be quite rapid and accurate. The changes are striking enough that a qualitative change appears to have occurred (James, 1890; Solomons & Stein, 1896). Schneider and Shiffrin (1977) and Shiffrin and Schneider (1977), among others, have made a strong experimental case for two qualitatively different forms of processing: controlled and automatic. Controlled processing requires attention and decreases the system capacity that is available for other processing. Automatic processing does not necessarily demand processing resources, freeing the system for higher-level processing and alternative control processing. This is not the only theoretical approach, however. One alternative model is put forth by Hirst, Spelke, Reaves, Caharack, and Neisser (1980), who view changes with practice as quantitative and continuous with level of skill.

Testing the validity of these alternative views is a delicate matter, because the two-process view assumes that virtually all complex and interesting processes of significant duration involve a mixture of automatic and control processes, often taking place in parallel, with each being able to initiate a process of the same type, or of the other type. At the least, a valid test should use an experimental task whose various components are well understood, whose control processes are highly circumscribed, and whose training conditions allow comparison of the most extreme forms of each type of processing. Although skill acquisition may be studied in many settings, relatively few paradigms come close to meeting these conditions. Because the search and detection paradigm of Schneider and Shiffrin (1977) meets these conditions, we take the space in this chapter to review some of that work, and to present a number of new results using the same paradigm.

AUTOMATISM AND CONTROL IN SEARCH–DETECTION TASKS

A *search–detection* paradigm involves the presentation of (one or more) stimuli that might or might not contain one (or more) of a set of (one or more) predefined stimuli termed the *memory set*. A presented memory set item is called a *target* and the other presented stimuli are termed *distractors*. The subject attempts to detect the presence of a target. Sometimes the task is so easy that accuracy is virtually perfect; in these cases, reaction time is the dependent measure. Such tasks are distinguished from *threshold-detection* tasks because the physical characteristics of presentation in search tasks are such that an error would never be made were only a single stimulus presented: an individual stimulus can be perceived clearly. When a single stimulus is presented (and reaction time is the measure), the task is known as *memory search* and has been investigated exten- sively by Sternberg (1966, 1969, 1975). When a single-item memory set is used, and several stimuli are simultaneously presented visually, the task is known as *visual search* (Atkinson, Holmgren, & Juola, 1969). When a sequence of stimuli are presented, the task is often termed *selective attention* or *divided attention* (Sperling, Budiansky, Spivak, & Johnson, 1971; Treisman, 1964, 1969).

Such tasks were explored extensively by Schneider and Shiffrin (1977) and Shiffrin and Schneider (1977). Their tasks always used visual presentation of alphanumeric characters. The main results (that are consistent with previous results in the literature, as discussed at length in the original papers) may be summarized as follows.

Varied mapping (denoted VM) conditions involve memory-set items and dis- tractors that are intermixed and change roles in random fashion across trials; that is, a target on one trial can be a distractor on another, and vice versa. In some VM conditions, a single visual display of up to four stimuli is presented, and the

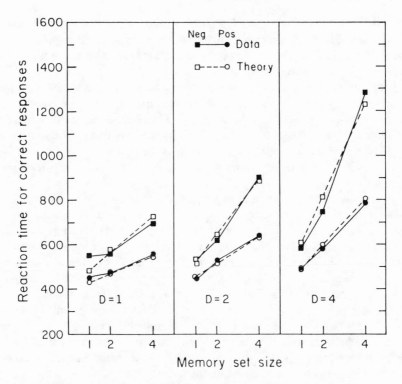

FIG. 4.1.   Mean reaction-time data from the varied mapping conditions from Schneider and Shiffrin (1977, Experiment 2). (D = display size.)

memory set consists of from one to four characters. In these conditions, accuracy is high, and reaction time is the dependent measure. The results are depicted in Fig. 4.1. Reaction time is a linear function of memory-set size (and display size). Target present responses have a slope about half that of target absent responses. The predictions shown are derived from a strictly serial comparison model in which each memory-set item is compared in turn to each display item, with termination occurring whenever a match is found. The slope of the lines depicted is determined by the mean comparison time per item, about 40 msec in this case. The overall reaction time decreases with practice in this task, but the slopes of the curves and the pattern of the results remain unchanged (except for the first session or two), even after months of practice (confirming results by Kristoffer-son, 1972).

An alternative version of this VM task involves rapid presentation of 20 successive displays, with detection accuracy (as a function of "frame time") the dependent measure. The results show that accuracy depends monotonically on load (defined as the product of memory-set size and display size), and monotonically on frame time. The high load conditions in this task are extremely difficult. Even at 800 msec per four item display, detection accuracy with a memory set of size 4 is only about 70%. The data can be fitted using the same model as that used for the reaction-time data in Fig. 4.1. These results are also stable over long periods of practice.

The subjects found these VM conditions to be arduous, demanding continuous attention and most or all of the available processing capacity. We think of the serial comparison process used in these VM conditions as an example of controlled processing (though there may well be some automatic components involved in the production of a response, such as the motor response process, or possibly even some automatic components contained within the comparison process itself).

An entirely different pattern of results occurs in the consistent mapping (i.e., CM) conditions. In these conditions, the memory-set items and distractors never change over trials, even across months of training. The results show that after consistent training, load no longer affects performance appreciably. Reaction time is fast in all conditions, and accuracy is high at all loads even at extremely rapid frame times. Schneider and Shiffrin (1977) proposed that detection became automatized during CM training. At the start of training, each stimulus, when presented, is processed independently and in parallel up to some central level of analysis, at which point the limited-capacity controlled processing system comes into play. With CM training, the targets gradually come to attract attention as part of the automatic parallel activation system. As a result, a controlled comparison process is not needed to locate the target.

Quite a few results testify to the accuracy of these conclusions. We mention a few of them here. First, the CM conditions are found by the subjects to be quite easy, requiring little attention or effort—they often would carry on conversations while performing the tasks. The hypothesis that automatic detection in these CM tasks does not require attention or utilize capacity has been verified by Schneider and Fisk (1980c). Subjects carried out two search tasks simultaneously, one automatic (CM) and one controlled (VM), each task being restricted to one diagonal of each display. When the subjects were instructed to give their main effort to the VM (controlled) task, their level of performance on that task was equal to the level attained when that task was carried out by itself. More important, the detection sensitivity for the simultaneous CM task was equal to that found when the CM task alone was carried out. However, instructions to give effort to the CM task decreased performance in the VM-controlled search task, suggesting that resources may be given to a task that does not require them, to the detriment of other tasks that do. Furthermore, a large performance decrement on at least one of the tasks is always found (compared with single-task conditions), when two VM tasks are carried out simultaneously. Thus, controlled search requires limited resources, but automatic detection may not.

If what has been learned in the CM conditions of Shiffrin and Schneider (1977) is truly automatic, then it should operate whether or not the subject desires

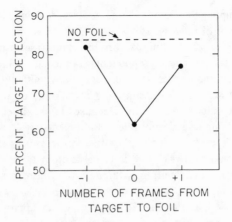

FIG. 4.2.   Data from a varied mapping multiple frame procedure from Shiffrin and Schneider (1977, Experiment 4d). Percentage of target detection is shown as a function of the spacing between the target item and a previously trained CM target that appeared in a to-be-ignored location.

and should be difficult to alter or unlearn. The evidence that attention to consistently trained targets is automatic is straightforward. After months of training with a set of items, A, always targets, a new task is introduced. On one diagonal of a display, subjects were asked to carry out a normal controlled search under VM conditions (with the previous VM stimuli). The other diagonal of each display is to be ignored entirely. It in fact contains VM stimuli also, but during one of the 20 frames, a CM item from the A set is presented in one position on that diagonal.

The results are shown in Fig. 4.2. When a to-be-ignored A item appears during the same frame as an actual target, detection of that target is reduced considerably. The implication is clear: a trained CM target attracts attention automatically, despite the subjects' attempts to ignore both it and its location; the attention given to the CM target distracts or delays the controlled search on the relevant diagonal, thereby reducing performance. These results assume extra importance, because they demonstrate that automatic processes can demand and/or utilize capacity, even if only temporarily.

A DEFINITION OF AND TEST FOR AUTOMATISM

How should an automatic process be distinguished from a controlled process? Several definitions of automatism seem possible. We choose one that appears to lead to a practical test and captures a few of the characteristics that are often deemed necessary for automatism.

It must be emphasized at the start that almost all processes complex enough, and of long enough duration, to be at all interesting will consist of both automatic and controlled components. Perhaps a momentary decision, in isolation, could approach a pure control process. However, a real decision, such as whether to turn right or left in order to minimize driving time to a desired location, will involve multiple processes and components, some automatic and some controlled. A purely automatic process is also quite rare, although certain types of motor actions and sensory processing (e.g., walking, or word identification during reading) may approach the ideal. Because almost all interesting processes consist of both automatic and controlled components, it does not make much sense to search for a test by which to classify all processes as either automatic or controlled. Still, a given process may be largely automatic or largely controlled, and it would be desirable to determine which. Furthermore, it may be possible to break down a process into subcomponents that can be shown to be primarily automatic or controlled. To do either of these things, an appropriate definition of automatism and control and a practical test are needed.

In light of the Schneider and Shiffrin (1977) and Schneider and Fisk (1980c) results, two factors seem most promising as a basis for a distinguishing definition: *limited capacity* and *control*. Limited capacity seems an important factor because controlled search did require resources, but the automatic detection process did not, judging by the effects of load and by the independence of simultaneous tasks. A lack of control over automatic processes is indicated by the attention study whose results are shown in Fig. 4.2: Automatic detection calls attention despite the best efforts the subject can make to prevent this disruption from occurring, even when the disrupting stimulus appears in a known-to-be irrelevant display location.

Let us begin by proposing a definition based on capacity usage, as follows:

Rule 1.   An automatic process does not use processing resources or decrease processing capacity.

One problem with this rule has to do with the concept of specific capacity. Any automatic process involves a sequence of neural–muscular events, the components of which surely are unavilable for system use while the automatic process is engaged. This is obvious in the motor domain. For example, playing a well-learned sequence on the piano may be automatized, but the fingers are not available during this time for other activities. The same sort of problem can arise in the domain of internal, neural processing. An "H" presented visually may be processed automatically in a series of stages, up to and beyond the "name" level. The visual pathways involved in this processing are not available at that time for independent processing of other visual stimuli presented in temporal and spatial contiguity to the "H".

This situation can be saved by modifying the rule as follows:

Rule 1.   Any process that does not use general, nonspecific processing resources and does not decrease the general, nonspecific processing capacity available for other processes is automatic. (It is understood in this definition that general, nonspecific processing refers to processing not directly involved in the automatic sequence.)

This rule does not characterize all automatic processes, because some automatic processes can engage the attention system itself. This is demonstrated by the results depicted in Fig. 4.2. A character trained to be detected automatically attracts attention thereafter. A simpler example is the presumably automatic startle response to a loud noise. In both cases, an automatic process engages the attention system, thereby reducing available capacity. One could attempt to distinguish an automatic process from its consequences. However, even if such a distinction were possible in theory, it would be unlikely to lead to a practical test for automatism.

One way to handle this situation, in part, is to modify the rule by taking the issue of *control* into account. The idea behind the modification is to include as automatic all processes whose initiation the subject cannot control, even though capacity is utilized in some fashion. This leads to the following definition:

Rule 2. Any process that always utilizes general resources and decreases general processing capacity whenever a given set of external initiating stimuli are presented, regardless of a subject's attempt to ignore or bypass the distraction, is automatic.

A process that satisfies either Rule 1 or Rule 2 is automatic, but some automatic processes may not satisfy either rule.

Mixed Processes

The utility of Rules 1 and 2 is open to question, because many processes will have pronounced automatic components along with some controlled components. For example, certain processes may be initiated by a control process and then proceed automatically thereafter. Stopping a car by depressing the clutch pedal and then the brake pedal may be an automatized sequence. It could be initiated by an external stimulus, such as a red light, or an internal decision, such as that following a recollection that luggage has been left behind.

It may be quite a difficult task to distinguish control processes from automatic processes that are initiated by control processes. There are two cases to consider. First, suppose an automatic process is initiated by a control process but then makes no further demands on attention or general (nonspecific) capacity. The initiating decision or control process will utilize at least some capacity and attention, but it may be possible by careful experimental design to demonstrate that no *further* capacity usage takes place. Second, suppose an automatic process is initiated by a control process and later engages attention. It would not be easy to demonstrate that attention engagement is a mandatory outcome of the process, because the initiation itself is under subject control. Cases like this could be dealt with when there is a substantial time period between the initiation and the attention engagement, so that the automatic phase could be tested separately. However, when the entire sequence is rapid, we do not presently see any simple method to decompose the process into controlled and automatic components (though some promising approaches have been developed by Logan, 1978, 1979).

Limitations of Capacity

The use of Rule 1 to identify automatic and controlled processes requires a definition of capacity limitation and methods of measuring or comparing capacity. Actually, we do not need to consider a complete model of capacity limitations; present needs require a consideration of changes in capacity usage that occur as processes are added. There are three models that deserve consideration, each incorporating a different version of the vague notion of limited capacity. Model 1 states that adding processes cannot increase capacity or total resources. Model 2 states that the resources available to a given set of processes must be reduced when new processes are added, if the new processes utilize any resources at all. Model 3 is a stronger form of Model 2, stating that the resources available to a given set of processes must be reduced when new processes are added, if the new processes utilize sufficiently large amounts of capacity. In effect, two controlled tasks together cannot both be accomplished as well as each alone.

Translating these models into practical tests is no easy matter, especially for Model 1. Model 1 requires us to make quantitative measurements of capacity utilization before a test of automatism can be made. Unfortunately, the present state of the art is not far enough advanced to allow such precise quantitative measurements. Models 2 and 3 may be tested qualitatively. To be precise, performance is evaluated at asymptote, after much training. Then a new candidate process is introduced by requiring an additional task to be carried out. If above-chance performance on the new task can be achieved without lowering performance on the original task, then automatism is implicated by Model 2. Model 3 makes the strongest assertions concerning automatism. A test is not difficult. Two tasks can be carried out in isolation, and jointly, until performance is at asymptote in all three cases. If neither task shows a decrement in the combined case, then at least one of the sets of processes associated with the two tasks must be automatic.

The Existence of Capacity Limitations

The preceding discussion is predicated upon the basic assumption that the information-processing system contains capacity limitations (in the form of one of Models 1, 2, or 3) that cannot be removed by training or practice. This is certainly the prevalent view among most researchers (Broadbent, 1958; Posner & Snyder, 1975; Shiffrin, 1976; Shiffrin & Schneider, 1977) but does not receive universal acceptance (Hirst et al. 1980).

The existence of unremovable limitations in the motor domain would probably not be questioned by anyone. Although practice can result in enormous improvements in speed and accuracy, physiological constraints on speed of neural conductance, muscular strength and response time, and skeletal stress resistance surely establish limits that no amount of practice can bypass. Similar unremovable limitations may be found in the information-processing domain. It suffices to mention just one clear-cut example: the rate of the comparison process in VM search. Kristofferson (1972) and Schneider and Shiffrin (1977) trained subjects for enormous numbers of trials in varied mapping search paradigms. The function relating reaction time to search load (the product of memory-set size and display size) remained linear, with no change in slope, virtually throughout the entire training period (small slope changes may occur in the first few sessions). The intercept of the function continued to drop toward an asymptotic level, reflecting improvement in automatic processes, such as sensory coding and motor-response movements. However, the presumably controlled part of the process, the comparison process, quickly attained a stable performance level and remained unchanged thereafter. Surely, this result reflects an information-processing limitation that is basic to the system. (It does not seem plausible to argue that the subjects could have come into the laboratory with this skill already trained to asymptote, because such tasks are seldom part of the pre-experimental environment.)

In light of such considerations, why would Hirst et al. (1980) claim "people can learn to do indefinitely many things indefinitely well [p. 114]," and that "the subjects' success was interpreted as evidence against the hypothesis of a fixed attentional capacity or limited cognitive resources . . . [p. 98]?" Actually, Hirst et al. do believe that automatization is occurring in part (pp. 115–116), and we suspect that their views are really not very different from ours, once a few sources of confusion are clarified.

A few of their subjects were given extensive training (say 100 hr or so) carrying out silent reading for comprehension while simultaneously taking dictation (writing of spoken words). As in Spelke, Hirst and Neisser (1976), the dictation could be accomplished even though reading speed and comprehension were about equal on trials requiring reading only (the control condition) and dual-task trials. Two subjects were found who could learn to copy three or five word sentences (or random groups of this length), while showing equal reading in the control and dual-task conditions. These subjects could be shown to have knowledge of the meaning of the sentences, to some extent. (There was even some evidence that implications drawn from several successive related sentences could be utilized at test.) Of course these subjects did not carry out the dictation as accurately, nor recall the dictation as well, as control subjects who did no reading.

In this chapter, we would use the data reported by Hirst et al. (1980) to draw rather different conclusions, probably because we use a different set of definitions of automatism, control, capacity, sharing, and so forth. Hirst et al. define automatism by simplicity (p. 106, line 16) and therefore rule out automatism if

meaning can be extracted during dictation (presumably because meaning extraction is "complex"). On the other hand, we define automatism by Rule 1.
Suppose it were true that dictation-plus-meaning-extraction did not harm simultaneous reading and did not harm any other simultaneous central processing task.
By Rule 1 (and Model 2), we would be led to the important and interesting
conclusion that meaning extraction could be automatized, at least to a small
degree.

We do not draw this conclusion, however, because the Hirst et al. data do not
satisfy the conditions of Rule 1. The problem is the interpretation of reading
speed in the conditions without simultaneous reading. The task setting and instructions induce subjects to attempt to match reading speeds and comprehension
in the control and dual-task conditions. Furthermore, the subjects are not trained
to maximize their reading speed and comprehension in the control condition. We
strongly suspect that with suitable training, encouragement, and 100 hours of
practice the subjects could have been trained to read faster (and perhaps with
increased comprehension) in the single-task condition. It may well be the case
that simultaneous dictation (with extracted meaning) cannot be carried out without lowering this (hypothetical) maximum performance level for reading. What
the Hirst et al. data do show is that some capacity limitations are present in the
weakest sense of Model 3. Although reading may be equal in the control and
experimental conditions, dictation was much poorer in the dual-task condition
than in the dictation-only control.

In summary, we think the remarkable dual-task performance of the Hirst et al.
subjects is possible because many of the components of dictation become automatized during training, thereby allowing limited capacity to be devoted
largely to reading. The fact that subjects can extract some meaning from their
dictated material (even when they report little "awareness") might result from an
automatic process that extracts meaning. Alternatively, the meaning extraction
might depend on the borrowing of some resources from the reading task; this
possibility cannot be tested unless the reading performance is trained to
maximum, a situation we doubt obtained in the Hirst et al. study.

Characteristics of Automatic and Controlled Processing

The experimental study of automatism and control is really in its infancy, at a point
when the definitions and characteristics, indeed confidence in the existence, of these
processes are still evolving. At this stage, different researchers mean very different things by the terms they use, and they focus upon very different characteristics as a basis for discrimination, depending on the tasks being studied. We
have proposed one definition, based on capacity and control, that may be used in
theory to classify certain "ideal" processes as automatic. In practice, most
processes are a mixture of (theoretically) automatic and controlled components.
It would be desirable to have a way to classify the degree of automatism of such

processes. One way to do this would be to establish a series of characteristics, each of which is typical of either automatism or control. A degree of automatism could be defined as some sort of average across these various characteristics, because one or another is sometimes put forward as an alternative definition of automatism.

How does one generate characteristics that might typify automatic and controlled processes? One can focus upon tasks in the normal environment that seem to typify what one means by these terms and then select the characteristics that appear to operate in those settings. Alternatively, one can attempt to produce in the laboratory states of processing that come as close to the extreme ideals as possible. This was the strategy of Schneider and Shiffrin (1977) and Shiffrin and Schneider (1977). The characteristics we discuss next arise from both types of approaches. However, we rely for evidence mainly upon experimental results in search tasks, because this paradigm is fairly well understood and explored. We turn now to a list of possible identifying characteristics.

1. *Capacity.*   The utilization of general processing capacity is a major component of the proposed criterion for distinguishing automatic and controlled processing (Rule 1). We do not repeat that discussion here.

2. *Control.*   The ability to control a process is used in Rule 2 to help define automatism; that is, some automatic processes may demand attention and thereby use capacity but do so in *mandatory* fashion, whenever an appropriate stimulus configuration is presented. Of course, automatized components of mixed processes may be initiated by controlled processes, but the process as a whole cannot be classified automatic.

The degree of automatism of mixed processes can be assessed on the dimension of control. For the most part, controlled processes are continuously monitored, attended to, and governed by the subject. One partial exception occurs when there exists an extremely rapid sequence of controlled processes. The speed apparently makes it difficult for the subject to learn the means of control. Consider the comparison process in VM search tasks; sometimes subjects terminate when a match is found, and sometimes exhaustive search occurs. The choice seems to be determined by the task requirements, rather than by the will of the subject. However, because subjects can use either mode, they could presumably be trained to use either at their discretion once the means of control had been identified.

When mixed sequences are largely automatized, the control is usually concentrated in the initiation phase; once started, such sequences tend to run to completion without further control. This leads to the next characteristic.

3. *Continuation.*   Automatic processes tend to run to completion, unless effort is expended to prevent such an occurrence or unless another automatic

process uses the same specific resources. Can a purely automatic process be halted before completion? Automatized motor sequences of some duration can surely be halted (e.g., a braking sequence can be switched to an acceleration sequence if an automobile driver judges an increase in speed is needed to prevent an accident). Similarly, an automatic process can be altered in progress by another automatic process demanding the same resources (e.g., throwing a baseball may be disturbed during the arm movement by a bee sting on the elbow). In fact, one way a control process could interfere with an ongoing automatic process is via initiation of another automatic process antagonistic to the first.

The question of interference is more difficult to test when all the processes in question are cognitive. If an automatic process does not result in attention demands or actions ("informational" in the terminology of Shiffrin & Schneider, 1977), then it is difficult to see why one would want to halt or change it prior to completion. It may also be difficult to test whether or not the process has been completed in such cases.

In general, controlled processes can be strung together in a sequence only through continuing effort. Even when a controlled sequence is quite rapid, as in VM search, it is clear that capacity and attention are required throughout the comparison process. The fact that a terminating strategy can be used, and the results from "signal-to-respond" studies (Reed, 1976) indicate that the VM search process can be interrupted prior to completion.

4. *Indivisibility.* Automatic processes tend to occur in units that begin and end at fixed points. Thus, it may be difficult to begin in the middle of an automatized sequence (e.g., it may be difficult to play a well-learned piano passage by beginning in the middle of a phrase). Controlled sequences may be started or ended at the subject's discretion.

5. *Practice.* Generally, controlled processes do not show much if any improvement with practice. Automatic processes often exhibit sustained and dramatic changes with increasing practice.

The lack of change with practice for a *given* controlled process must not be confused with the tremendous changes in *choice* of controlled process that occur as learning (or development) proceeds.

6. *Modification.* A controlled sequence is easily modified to fit new tasks, environments, or instructions. An automatic sequence will tend to reoccur in response to the previously trained initiating stimuli. Retraining of a new automatic sequence can be arduous and more difficult than the initial learning. In sports, it is an adage that a skill is best learned correctly the first time, because of the difficulty of retraining later. Evidence in the search domain includes the difficulties of reversing targets and distractors in CM conditions (as compared with the ease of changing stimuli in the VM conditions).

7. *Serial versus Parallel Processing.* The difficulties in distinguishing general serial from general parallel processes is well known (Townsend, 1971, 1972). Nevertheless, control processes tend to operate sequentially (due to capacity demands, very possibly), whereas automatic processes can operate in parallel, and often independently (if pathways and resources do not overlap, see Schneider & Fisk, 1980c).

8. *Learning and Storage.* Available evidence seems to indicate that long-term storage is produced largely by controlled processing of some sort. "Incidental" learning can occur, but often through the use of "incidental" control processing. Some storage may occur through the use of automatic processing, but the amount seems to be less than when controlled processing is used. This issue is one that has attracted much research and deserves a careful literature review, but space restrictions prevent any such consideration here.

9. *Performance Level.* A complex task can often be accomplished at higher accuracy and faster speed once automatization has occurred. However, this is not the case before learning has occurred and may not be the case for very simple tasks that require very little controlled resources. For example, in the search paradigm, CM search is generally superior to VM search, except in some cases when the load is only one (only a single comparison is required); in this simple case, we have reason to believe that controlled search can sometimes lead to faster reaction times.

10. *Clarity of Initiating Stimulation.* For automatic processes to operate effectively without numerous errors and false alarms, the ambiguity of the initiating stimulation probably has to be low. For example, we should not expect automatic detection to operate (well) in search tasks, if the stimulus clarity is dropped to threshold. In this case, the targets and distractors become ambiguous, and a careful decision may be required for a response.

11. *Simplicity.* Hirst et al. (1980) seem to regard *simplicity* as a defining characteristic of automatic processes, but this surely is inaccurate. We see no practical or theoretical reason why very complex processes could not be automatized. Everyday examples of largely automatized sequences certainly include very complex behaviors (e.g., driving, piano playing, typing, reading aloud). Of course, if complexity is defined by the presence of multiple decisions, then it must be a criterion for controlled processing; but we prefer not to use such a definition.

12. *Awareness.* Controlled processes generally involve consciousness of the various components. This is not surprising because these processes require attention and consist of strategies, decisions, and the like. The only exception may occur for controlled sequences that are so rapid that the awareness of

separate components is reduced or masked (as for controlled search at 40 msec per comparison).

Automatic processes do not usually require attention, unless they include an attention-calling component (and even then the components of the process might not reach consciousness, only the results). Even with this provision, we must be very careful in trying to use awareness or consciousness to classify processes as automatic or controlled. One problem arises because consciousness is often identified with memory, but this is not proper. For example, one can be quite "aware" that one sees *all* the characters in a briefly presented tachistoscopic display of letters, even though few of these can be recalled 2 seconds after display offset. It is possible that some automatic processes might achieve "awareness" in the momentary sense, even if they are not well remembered later. Usually, controlled processes will tend to be remembered (subject to all the well-known limitations on memory, of course). A more important problem lies in the following fact: There is often nothing preventing control processes from being assigned in parallel with automatic processes to the same task. The control process can be used to monitor the automatic process, thereby producing awareness, or to mimic or supplement the automatic process, thereby producing an awareness of its own.

13. *Attention and Intention.*   Attention and intention have been involved, directly or indirectly, in almost all the previous characteristics. Selective attention generally refers to the ability to operate upon certain information to the exclusion of other information sources at once (divided attention). We feel that automatic processing allows tasks to be performed as if attention could be divided among many inputs but may sometimes prevent focusing (because extraneous inputs may call attention due to prior training). Controlled processing is generally focused and can be divided only to the degree allowed by capacity limitations (see Shiffrin & Schneider, 1977, for a full discussion of the relationship of selective attention to controlled search and automatic detection).

Controlled processing involves intention by the subject (unless it is invoked by an automatic process), whereas automatic processing does not require intention (unless we are referring to a mixed sequence that is automatic except for an initiation that requires a control process).

Let us conclude this list of characteristics by pointing out that the present state of research and theory in this area does not allow us to discuss them with great assurance. Much work remains to be done, and it may eventually prove possible to use many of these characteristics (or others not considered) as defining characteristics for automatism and control. At this time, we are least unhappy with the capacity and control definition, as embodied in Rules 1 and 2.

We wish to reiterate that the theoretical division of processing into qualitatively differing components of automatism and control is unlikely to be settled by any single experimental test. Rather, concepts such as simplicity, elegance, breadth, and ability to generate predictions and experiments will determine the long-run success or failure of models embodying the two-process dichotomy. The one- versus two-process issue is analogous to the one- versus two-store question that developed about a decade ago in the memory area. At first, there were confusions between the *task* distinctions, STM and LTM, and the theoretical distinctions, STS and LTS, so that researchers sometimes lost sight of the fact that retrieval was almost always predicted to be a mixture of retrieval from the two stores. Furthermore, it was difficult to find defining features to distinguish STS from LTS, because what was stored in LTS was generally a reflection of what was rehearsed in STS. Similarly, we now find a confusion between tasks and theoretical components of tasks in the automatism literature. The defining characteristics are also difficult to set down, because they apply to the theoretical components, rather than the tasks. Also, any given task is likely to be accomplished by a mixture of automatic and controlled components. Over the years, the STS–LTS model for memory has become fairly standard, not because any single confirming test was carried out, but because the model is simple, predictive, and comprehensive. We suspect that the continuum versus automatism-control questions will be settled in a similar fashion, not by a crucial test, but by an overall comparison of alternative models and their ability to handle a wide variety of data.

In the rest of this chapter, the two-process view is assumed. Under this assumption, a number of important questions concerning automatism are discussed. These include: How does it develop? What is learned? How is it forgotten? How does it generalize? What role does it play in general skill development?

THE DEVELOPMENT OF AUTOMATISM

Consistency

In the earlier work on the development of automatism, only two training conditions were typically used. Training was either perfectly consistent (i.e., targets were always targets and never appeared as distractors), or it was inconsistent (i.e., targets and distractors varied randomly over trials). These two extremes, of course, occur only in controlled laboratory settings. In real life situations, training is unlikely to be perfectly consistent. In spite of this fact, automatic responses appear to develop. The degree to which automatism can develop when stimuli are usually relevant (to be attended to) but are occasionally irrelevant (to be ignored) is an important extension of the earlier work and is of utmost importance for practical applications.

In a recent series of experiments, Schneider and Fisk (1980b) have examined whether automatism will develop under varying ratios of consistency of training. They manipulated consistency by holding constant the number of times different items appeared as targets and varying the number of times they appeared as distractors. Five consistency conditions were used: (1) always target and never distractor—CM control (2) target twice as often as distractor; (3) target and distractor equally often; (4) target half as often as distractor; (5) target approximately one-seventh as often as distractor—VM control, because this is a typical ratio of target present to target absent trials in VM. During each block of 85 trials, four CM targets were each presented as a target 10 times. One appeared as a distractor 0 times (condition 1), one five times (condition 2), one 10 times (condition 3), and one 20 times (condition 4).

These experiments used a multiple-frame search detection task in which accuracy of spatial detection was the primary response measure. On each trial, a target was present in the series of frames, and the subject had to indicate in which of the four quadrants the target was presented. In one study, they gave 6000 trials of training (1200 per condition). Subjects were tested (under CM conditions) at several points during the course of training. By the end of training, performance was a monotonic function of the ratio of the target frequency to the distractor frequency of a given stimulus. Conditions 1, 2, and 3 were all superior to the VM control. However, performance in condition 4 did not improve much during the course of training despite the fact that target stimuli were presented as often in this condition as targets as in the other CM conditions. It appears that inconsistency can do more than simply slow the rate of development of automatism. When an item is searched for as target only half as often as it appears as a distractor, automatism may not develop at all.

The most important aspect of these results is that automatism can develop in conditions with less than perfect consistency. There was significant improvement in detection performance when an item was a target either twice as often or as often as it was a distractor (conditions 2 and 3, respectively).

Detecting versus Searching

As we have just seen, automatization of detection is dependent on the consistency of training. For a fixed level of consistency, several other factors may determine the rate of automatization. In particular, detection automatization may be determined by the number of times a particular character is searched for but not found; alternatively, it may be determined by the number of times the item is detected.

A multiple-frame detection task was used by Schneider and Fisk (1980d) to examine this issue. In all the CM conditions, the consistency was held at 100% (no target was ever a distractor). During the training phase of the experiment, two factors were varied. First, the absolute number of times that subjects searched for CM target items was either six or 20 (per block of 72 trials). Second, the number of times that an item that subjects searched for was actually present was varied (two or four out of six; and four or 16 out of 20). All conditions (including a VM control) were mixed within each block of trials. Subjects received seven blocks of training, with 72 trials per block. They were then tested in a condition in which a target was present on every trial.

Results from the test phase showed that detection accuracy increased as the number of detections increased (with the number of searches held constant). Detection accuracy increased from .64 to .71 as the number of target presentations increased from two to four (in the six trials of this type per block), and from .57 to .72 as the number of target presentations increased from four to 16 (in the 20 trials of this type per block). All of these detection rates were higher than the VM control, .45. These results show that the rate of automatization is a function of the number of times that an item is detected, when the total searches are held constant. However, when total detections are held about equal (the two conditions with four targets per block), an increase in the number of *non*detection searches decreases the rate of automatization. To be precise, when the trials without targets rose from two to 16, performance dropped from .71 to .57. Perhaps nondetections lead subjects to adopt poor control strategies, which in turn hinder automatization. These two effects taken together seem to suggest that the ratio of detection trials to nondetection trials is the single largest determiner of automatization. It hardly seems possible that this could be true in the extreme (could one detection in two attempts be as valuable as 500 detections in 1000 attempts?). Nevertheless, these results are intriguing and have important practical consequences (e.g., when learning tennis, on what proportion of swings should the learner be allowed to miss?). Further research is certainly called for.

It is also of interest that some automatization has occurred even in the condition with just two targets per block. The number of detections during all of training in this condition was just about 10, yet these 10 detections were sufficient to produce some automatization (i.e., raise detection accuracy above the VM level).

Other Factors Affecting Automatization

We cannot describe the results in any detail due to space restrictions, but it is useful to list several other factors affecting the rate of automatization. These include: (1) Similarity or feature overlap between the target set and distractor set. Learning is faster with greater dissimilarity; (2) The massing or distribution of training. This factor appears to have only minor effects; (3) History of training. Prior antagonistic CM training obviously hinders automatization. However, prior VM training also appears to slow automatization, compared with no prior training; (4) Type of task. Multiple-frame tasks involving accuracy measures appear to lead to faster automatization than single-frame tasks involving reaction times. The stress on processing speed and effort may be the reason; (5) Context. The availability and nature of context cues that help discriminate target from nontarget trials or help discriminate one type of CM condition from another seem to affect automatization.

What Can and Cannot Be Automatized?

Some researchers have equated simplicity and automatism. In fact, Hirst et al. (1980) have defined automatism by this characteristic. We, however, think that very complex tasks can become automatized to a surprisingly high degree. As evidence, we point to the Hirst et al. (1980) dual-task results, as well as numerous everyday examples (e.g., driving, musical instrument playing). Of course, to establish automatism experimentally, our intuitions are not acceptable, and we must turn to carefully constructed laboratory tasks. For this reason, the examples that follow are set in the search–detection paradigm.

Automatic attention responses can be attached to the name of a stimulus (Laberge, 1973; Shiffrin & Schneider, 1977), and the name is itself generated automatically. In addition, a category name may be generated automatically even for new categories learned in an experiment (Shiffrin & Schneider, 1977) as long as the category "name" is consistently assigned (or assignable) to the stimuli.

There has been a small amount of research directed toward the following question: Can automatized detection be learned for spatiotemporal combinations of items that are more complex than alphanumeric characters? For example, can automatic attention be directed to conjunctions of stimuli; to combinations of stimuli and spatial positions; to the absence of a feature; etc.? Some recent experiments have begun to explore these and related questions in an attempt to establish the limits of automatic processing.

Eberts (1979) and Eberts and Schneider (1980) have examined the automatic and controlled processing of spatial and temporal patterns. In their experiments, the target and distractor items were composed of three line segments at various inclinations that occurred in rapid temporal sequence in roughly superimposed spatial locations. A display consisted of four such sequences in four distinct spatial locations. Subjects were asked to discriminate a target from three distractor sequences. In the CM conditions, target sequences were always targets and never distractors; and in VM conditions, sequences were sometimes targets and sometimes distractors. After a lengthy training period (about 9000 trials in both CM and VM conditions), several of the characteristic CM/VM differences were observed. For example, CM sequences were less affected than VM sequences by changes in load; there was little deficit in doing a dual CM and VM search; and CM searches were unaffected by changes in temporal parameters. Interestingly, however, CM performance was disrupted by spatial transformations (e.g., rotation). As a cautionary note, we should point out that in spite of these quantitative differences, the automatic process that developed for these unfamiliar spatiotemporal patterns was relatively weak. Furthermore, VM performance continued to improve and had not asymptoted by the end of training.

Schneider and Eberts (1980) and Treisman and Gelade (1980) have reported experiments in which subjects searched for items that were specified by conjunctions of features. In particular, Schneider and Eberts (1980) compared single-feature search for either color or shape (e.g., "a red letter" or "a T") with conjunction-feature search for both color and shape (e.g., "a red T"). Because the dimensions of color and shape have been classified as separable dimensions according to several criteria (Garner, 1970), an interesting question concerns whether consistent training will result in the "unitization" of the separable dimensions and automatization of detection. Treisman and Gelade (1980) suggest the answer is no. In the Eberts and Schneider studies involving large amounts of training, CM conjunction search remained slower than CM shape search throughout training, but both conditions improved (i.e., automatized) at the same rate. (CM color search was practically perfect from the start of training.) In VM conditions, on the other hand, none of the conditions improved with practice (in terms of the slope of the search function). Using these results, one can argue that search for a conjunction of normally separable dimensions can be automatized, at least weakly. It must be admitted, however, that this is a very difficult result to achieve, involving careful training schedules for many trials.

The two experiments described previously suggest that simple spatiotemporal sequences of events and conjunctions of features can be automatically processed. A closely related question concerns the degree to which different automatic sequences can be initiated by the same stimuli in different contexts. Experiments by Dumais (1979, Experiment 3) and Schneider and Fisk (1980a) have examined this question. In the Dumais study, subjects were simultaneously trained in three visual search tasks. The three "cycle" conditions can be denoted: $A(B)$, $B(C)$, and $C(A)$, where capital letters refer to sets of characters (e.g., $A = \{D, R, Y, 7, \lambda, \phi, \text{ъ}\}$). The first letter in each case represents the memory set, and the letter in parentheses represents the distractor set. In this design, each set is used once as a target set and once as a distractor set. If considered as a whole, items are inconsistently trained in this experiment—appearing sometimes as targets and sometimes as distractors. However, the context for a character when it is a target differs from the context when it appears as a distractor. For example, when an item in set A is the target, items from set B are the distractors; however, when items from set A are distractors, the C items are targets. Thus, each target–distractor combination provides a unique stimulus configuration that is consistently trained.

The results are shown in Fig. 4.3, which gives the reaction-time difference between the display size of 16 and the display size of four. They show that subjects were not able to automatize their detection in all three of these conditions. However, performance was not like that observed in VM control conditions either. Subjects learned to respond automatically in one of the three conditions, use controlled (VM-like) search in another, and some combination in the third. Under these conditions (with the A, B, and C sets highly confusable), context was not sufficient to allow the development of automatic detection in all conditions. Schneider and Fisk (1980a) have, however, obtained preliminary evidence that if the target and distractor sets are highly discriminable, and if context is enhanced by adding distinctive colors and by first training subjects in

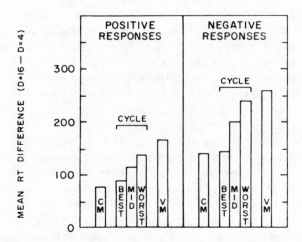

FIG. 4.3. Data from Dumais (1979, Experiment 3). Mean reaction-time difference between display size 16 and display size 4 is the response measure. Data
from the three cycle conditions are shown in the three intermediate bar graphs in
each panel; data from the CM control and from the VM control conditions are
shown on the far left and right, respectively.

one condition and then introducing the second, context can be used to trigger (or
withhold) automatic responses. Their results are subject to large individual differences, and more work is needed in this area before definitive statements can be
made.

What Cannot Be Automatized?   The context experiments that we have just
discussed suggest that there may be some limits to the development of automatism. Although more work is certainly needed in this particular area, there
are several situations in which we know that automatism will not develop. First,
if antagonistic responses are required, automatism (defined in terms of capacity
limitations) will never be observed. In addition, stimulus–response sequences
cannot be automatized if (beyond some point—see section on Consistency earlier) they are inconsistently trained. However, beyond these seemingly trivial
examples, little is known about the limits of automatism.

The Role of Controlled Processing in Automatization

We conclude the discussion of issues involved in the development of automatism
by considering the role of controlled processing in the development of automatism. In all the examples of automatization that we have discussed, subjects
initially use controlled processing. This would not be surprising if automatism was
simply controlled processing speeded up. However, we argue for two qualita-

tively different processes. Why, then, is controlled processing a prerequisite? Is something in controlled processing necessary for the development of automaticity, or does controlled processing coincidently produce the conditions necessary for automatism to develop?

Although there are no present data that directly address this question, we suspect the latter is the case. There appear to be several lines of research worth pursuing in this regard. First, we can ask whether controlled processing is indeed a prerequisite for automatism. Suppose, for example, that a subset of auditorily presented letters is consistently paired with shock while a simultaneous attention-demanding task is carried out. Suppose that after such training, this same subset of letters can be detected automatically in a visual search task. Such a result might indicate that automatism can be produced without prior controlled processing. Second, we might ask whether controlled processing in one task can lead to automatization in a very different type of task, requiring rather different controlled processing (were automatism not available). A weak example might involve transfer from an auditory search task to a visual search task for stimuli with the same "names." Although these are just speculations, they suggest that the role of controlled processing in automatization is open to experimental exploration.

WHAT IS LEARNED DURING AUTOMATIZATION?

Although the change with consistent training from a controlled to an automatic mode of processing has been well documented in search tasks, less is known about the process and mechanisms that underlie the resulting automatism (Kristofferson, 1977; Rabbitt, Cumming, & Vyas, 1977; Schneider & Shiffrin, 1977). What is learned in consistent mapping conditions that enables subjects to automatically detect target items? Do subjects learn to attend to relevant information (targets), ignore irrelevant information (distractors), or both? Does what is learned generalize to other situations?

Target versus Distractor Learning

In order to examine the relative importance of targets and distractors in automatism, a transfer of training design was used (Dumais, 1979, Experiments 1 and 2). A single-frame visual search task was employed and reaction time was the dependent variable of main interest. At the beginning of each trial, a single target item was presented to the subject; then a display of either 4 or 16 items was presented, and the subject indicated as quickly as possible whether the target item was or was not in the display.

Seven subjects were concurrently trained in two CM and one VM condition until stable differences between the CM and VM conditions were observed. We denote the two CM training conditions as T1(D1) and T2(D2)—where T1 and T2

TRANSFER EXPERIMENT DESIGN
_____

TRAINING: T1(D1)- CONSISTENT   (CM)
             T2(D2)- CONSISTENT   (CM)
                   - VARIED   (VM)

TRANSFER: T1(VM)- TARGET TRANSFER
                                        > POSITIVE
             VM(D1)- DISTR. TRANSFER

             VM(T2)- TARGET REVERSAL
                                        > NEGATIVE
             D2(VM)- DISTR. REVERSAL

             VM(VM)- CONTROL

FIG. 4.4. Summary of the experimental design for the transfer study (Dumais, 1979, Experiment 1). T1, T2, D1, D2, and VM each designate a five-item set containing two letters, one number, one Hebrew letter, and one Greek letter. The three training conditions are described in the upper part of the figure; the five transfer conditions are described in the lower portion. Each subject served in all three training and all five transfer conditions.

represent two different target sets and D1 and D2 represent two different distractor sets. The VM conditions is denoted as VM(VM), because targets and distractors are randomly interchanged over trials. After training, subjects are transferred to five different CM conditions for testing. Two of the conditions are examples of *positive transfer*. In the *target transfer* condition, the T1 target items remain the same, but the D1 distractor set is replaced with a set of VM items. In the *distractor* (or *background*) *transfer* condition, the D1 items are still distractors, and a VM target set is used. The next two conditions are *reversals*. In the *target reversal* condition, the T2 items (that had previously been trained as targets) are now used as distractors, and a VM target set is used. And, in the *background reversal* condition, the previously trained distractor set, D2, becomes the target set and a VM set is the distractor set. The final condition is a *control* condition in which both target and distractor sets had been trained only in VM conditions. The design is illustrated in Figure 4.4.

Training Data. Fig. 4.5 shows the mean correct RTs (averaged over seven subjects and the last five sessions of training) as a function of display size. Subjects were trained for approximately 4000 trials in each of two CM conditions and 12,000 in the VM condition; only the last 75 trials for each subject are used in Fig. 4.5, but the depicted results are highly representative. CM performance is better than VM performance in at least two respects. Mean RT is faster in the CM conditions, and more importantly, the slope of the search function is much flatter in the CM conditions than in the VM conditions. The fact that the slope is somewhat greater than zero (about 8 msec/item) even in the CM condition is probably the result of subjects simultaneously using a controlled search and automatic detection.

In Fig. 4.6, these same data are presented in a format that makes the transfer data easier to interpret. The bar graphs (top left panel) represent the mean difference in RT between display size 16 and display size four.

Transfer Data. RT differences from the transfer phase are shown in the right-hand panel of Fig. 4.6. First, consider the results of the two positive

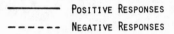

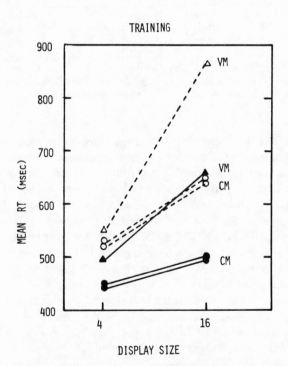

FIG. 4.5. Results from Dumais (1979, Experiment 1). Mean reaction time for correct responses is plotted as a function of display size. These data were obtained by averaging over subjects and over the last five sessions of training. Circles are used to represent the two CM conditions (T1(D1) and T2(D2)), and the triangles are used for the VM condition.

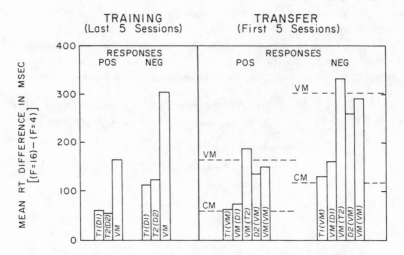

FIG. 4.6. In the left panel, data from Fig. 4.5 are replotted to show mean reaction-time difference between display size 16 and display size 4. Data in the right panel are from the transfer phase of the experiment (Dumais, 1979, Experiment 1).

transfer conditions. Performance in the target transfer condition is the same as that in the background transfer condition. Furthermore, performance in these two positive transfer conditions is not different from that observed in the CM training conditions. Essentially perfect transfer took place when *either* the targets or distractors remain the same and are paired with VM trained items. (We mention in passing the very interesting results from a companion study in which the transfer conditions did not use VM items. Instead, they used totally new items in place of the VM items. The results were identical.) These results show that both targets and distractors are affected by automatization (though we do not yet know the relative rates of learning).

We now consider the results of the two reversal transfer conditions. Performance in the background reversal condition is the same as that in the target reversal condition, and both of these conditions are the same as the VM control. Subjects appear to revert without harm to a normal controlled search when either the targets or distractors are reversed.

In sum, we observed excellent transfer for both the target and background sets, suggesting that the learning that underlies automatic detection depends on both target accentuation (target attending) and distractor inhibition (distractor ignoring).

A simple model of automatic attending can account for these and other transfer results. We assume that items newly introduced in a study have an average distribution of the strength with which they tend to attract attention. During training, this distribution is altered considerably. Items that are consistently targets and never appear as distractors (i.e., the CM target items) will accumulate the greatest attention strength. VM items that are sometimes targets and sometimes distractors will maintain an intermediate strength, perhaps not much different from the starting strength (because "new" items and VM items were equivalent). CM distractors that are never targets will lose a considerable part of their initial strength. Performance during both training and transfer is assumed to be based on the strength of the target items relative to the distractor items.

Fig. 4.7 shows how one might interpret such a strength model. Boldness of type indicates strength or tendency to draw attention. The boldest items come from the CM target distribution; the intermediate items from the VM distribution; and the narrowest items come from the CM distractor distribution. In the sample trial shown in each of the displays, A is the target item, and R, Σ, and 8 are the distractors.

How does this model explain the results? Consider first the training conditions (top two displays). After CM training, the target A has built up a large strength relative to the distractors and is easily detected. In the case of VM training, *all* items have intermediate strength, and the subject must use a controlled search of the display because no position preferentially attracts attention.

Consider next the two positive transfer conditions. In the target transfer condition, the consistently trained A target item (high strength) has a greater tendency to draw attention than do the VM distractors (medium strength). This results in performance that is much like that seen in CM training. A similar argument applies in the case of the distractor transfer condition, where the intermediate strength of the A target item is greater than that of the consistently trained background items that have low strength.

In both reversal conditions, on the other hand, the distractor items have a greater tendency to draw attention than does the target item. One might therefore expect attention to be drawn away from the target item and consequently for performance to be worse than in the control condition. However, we propose that subjects may find it difficult to attend simultaneously to items attracting attention in multiple spatial positions. If it is the case that attention cannot be drawn to multiple positions at once, then the subjects would revert to an ordinary controlled search for the target item. In this case, the two reversal conditions would result in performance that is the same as in the VM condition.

In summary, subjects learn to automatically detect CM target items both by attending to the target and by ignoring the distractors. The results follow from a model in which the consistency of training determines an item's tendency to draw attention.

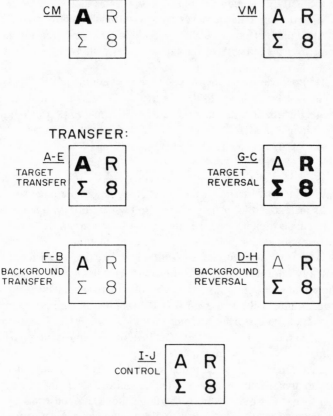

SAMPLE DISPLAYS FOR EACH CONDITION

Target: A
Distractors: R Σ 8

Darker Type Indicates Greater Tendency to Draw Attention

TRAINING:

CM

VM

TRANSFER:

A-E
TARGET
TRANSFER

G-C
TARGET
REVERSAL

F-B
BACKGROUND
TRANSFER

D-H
BACKGROUND
REVERSAL

I-J
CONTROL

FIG. 4.7.   Sample displays from each of the training and transfer conditions in
Dumais (1979, Experiment 1) are used to illustrate the model described in the text.
On the trial depicted here, the target item is A, and the distractors are R, Σ, and 8.
Bolder type face indicates greater strength or tendency to draw attention.

Generalization of Automatic Learning

The previously mentioned transfer of training experiment is certainly one measure of the generalizability of automatic learning. We now report a different, but
also interesting test of generalization (Dumais, unpublished). Subjects were ini-

tially trained in a search task in which they consistently searched for *A* target items in a *B* background [i.e., *A(B)*]. They were then transferred, not to another search task, but to counting task. Specifically, subjects were asked to count the number of *A* characters in a display composed of both *A* and *B* characters. The results are depicted in Fig. 4.8. The main finding of interest for present purposes is that the counting of A characters is less affected by the number of B characters in the display for subjects who had consistent training on these sets (right-hand panel, condition four). This suggests that automization of detection in the search task produces a perceptual saliency of the A characters that can be used in the counting task. When subjects who had not previously received *A(B)* search training were asked to perform the same counting task, there were marked effects of the number of *B* items (left-hand panel, condition four). (See also Francolini & Egeth, 1979.)

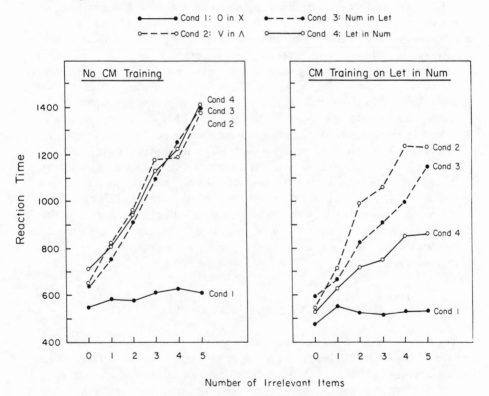

FIG. 4.8.   Data from the Dumais (unpublished) counting experiment. Mean time to count the number of target items (one, in the data presented here) as a function of the number of irrelevant items presented. Condition 4 is the condition of main interest. The right-hand panel presents data from three subjects who had been trained in CM conditions; and the left-hand panel presents data from three different subjects who had not been trained on the items used in condition 4.

THE LOSS OF AUTOMATISM

Evidence for the relatively permanent nature of automatic detection is found in reversal studies (Shiffrin & Schneider, 1977, Experiment 1). Subjects were trained in a CM condition for several thousand trials. When both the target and the distractor sets were reversed, dramatic decrements in performance were observed. Detection accuracy fell below that seen at the very beginning of training (when subjects were completely unpracticed). Subjects recovered only very gradually from this reversal. They needed about 2400 trials of reversal training to reach a level of performance equal to that seen after only 1500 trials of original learning. Thus, after reversal, subjects need considerable time to unlearn the original automatic attention responses (and to learn new ones). A related example of the permanent and obligatory nature of automatic attention responses comes from the focused-attention study described earlier: A CM trained target cannot be ignored.

In both of these examples, forgetting and unlearning occurred in the context of inconsistent training. What happens to an automatic attention response if no intervening laboratory training occurs? (It is certainly the case that much inconsistent nonlaboratory training occurs in any of these situations, because we assume our subjects occasionally read.) In a recent experiment, Dumais, Foyle, and Shiffrin (unpublished) examined this question. They first trained subjects in three CM visual search tasks. Subjects were retested on these conditions after delays of 7.2, 2.7, or 1.4 weeks. Performance in all of these delayed CM tests was better than that observed in a VM control. However, some forgetting did occur. The slope of the function relating RT to display size increased by about a factor of 3 after 7.2 weeks, by a factor of about 1.75 after 2.7 weeks, and actually decreased after 1.4 weeks. Thus, some forgetting of automatic detection occurs over a period of about 2 months, but a considerable amount is retained. Of course, much more research is needed to control for such factors as nonlaboratory inconsistent training and to explore many related issues.

AUTOMATIZATION IN SKILL DEVELOPMENT

The notion of skill acquisition can cover a wide range of activities, from "low-level" sensory discriminations (e.g., wine tasting), to motor skills (tracking tasks, typing, athletics), to perception and memory tasks (visual and memory search, letter matching), to very complicated cognitive skills (chess, go, computer programming, problem solving). As Chi and Glaser (in press) have noted, several types of changes are likely to occur during skill acquisition. Changes can occur in the knowledge or data base. These changes can take the form of more nodes, more relations defining a node, or more interrelations among nodes. In addition, changes in processing are certain to occur. These changes are of two types. Controlled processing can change quite markedly, as strategies develop, are added, and are deleted. In part, these strategies change because automatic processes develop to receive the demand upon limited capacity. Automatic processing will develop as skill acquisition proceeds, and some old automatic processes may be reconstituted. It is this phase of skill acquisition to which our present work speaks. We think automatization is a major component of skill acquisition in both the cognitive and motor domains and suggest that this factor be given prominent attention in research in these domains. Separating skilled performance into automatic and controlled components is surely a difficult and delicate matter. In the long run, the techniques that we and others are developing should help make this task easier.

REFERENCES

Atkinson, R. C., Holmgren, J. E., & Juola, J. F. Processing time as influenced by the number of elements in the visual display. *Perception & Psychophysics,* 1969, *6,* 321–326.

Broadbent, D. E. *Perception and communication.* London: Pergamon Press, 1958.

Chi, M. & Glaser, R. The measurement of expertise: Analysis of the development of knowledge skill as a basis for assessing achievement. To appear in E. L. Baker and E. S. Quellmalz (Eds.), *Design, analysis, and policy in testing and evaluation.* Beverly Hills, Calif.: Sage Publication, Inc., in press.

Dumais, S. T. *Perceptual learning in automatic detection: Processes and mechanisms.* Unpublished doctoral dissertation, Indiana University, September, 1979.

Dumais, S. T. *Perceptual selectivity with consistently trained items* (unpublished).

Dumais, S. T., Foyle, D. C., & Shiffrin, R. M. (unpublished data).

Eberts, R. *The automatic and controlled processing of sequences of events.* Human Attention Research Laboratory, University of Illinois (Report 7901), 1979.

Eberts, R. & Schneider, W. *The automatic and controlled processing of temporal and spatial patterns.* Human Attention Research Laboratory, University of Illinois (Report 8003), 1980.

Francolini, C. M. & Egeth, H. E. Perceptual selectivity is task dependent: The pop-out effect poops out. *Perception & Psychophysics,* 1979, *25,* 99–110.

Garner, W. R. The stimulus in information processing. *American Psychologist,* 1970, *25,* 350–358.

Hirst, W., Spelke, E. S., Reaves, C. C., Caharack, G., & Neisser, U. Dividing attention without alternation or automaticity. *Journal of Experimental Psychology: General,* 1980, *109,* 98–117.

James, W. *Principles of psychology.* New York: Holt, 1890.

Kristofferson, M. W. Effects of practice in character classification performance. *Canadian Journal of Psychology,* 1972, *26,* 54–60.

Kristofferson, M. W. The effects of practice with one positive set in a memory-scanning task can be completely transferred to a different positive set. *Memory & Cognition,* 1977, *5,* 177–186.

Laberge, D. Attention and the measurement of perceptual learning. *Memory & Cognition,* 1973, *1,* 268–276.

Logan, G. D. Attention in character-classification tasks: Evidence for the automaticity of component stages. *Journal of Experimental Psychology: General,* 1978, *107,* 32–63.

Logan, G. D. On the use of a concurrent memory load to measure attention and automaticity. *Journal of Experimental Psychology: Human Perception and Performance,* 1979, *5,* 189–207.

Posner, M. I. & Snyder, C. R. R. Attention and cognitive control. In R. L. Solso (Ed.), *Information processing and cognition: The Loyola symposium.* Hillsdale, N.J.: Lawrence Erlbaum Associates, 1975.

Rabbitt, P. M. A., Cumming, G., & Vyas, S. An analysis of visual search: Centropy and sequential effects. In S. Dornic (Ed.), *Attention & Performance* (Vol. VI), Hillsdale, N.J.: Lawrence Erlbaum Associates, 1977.

Reed, A. V. List length and the time course of recognition in immediate memory. *Memory & Cognition*, 1976, *4*, 16–30.

Schneider, W. & Eberts, R. *Automatic processing and the unitization of two features.* Human Attention Research Laboratory, University of Illinois (Report 8008), 1980.

Schneider, W. & Fisk, A. D. *Context dependent automatic processing.* Human Attention Research Laboratory, University of Illinois (Report 8009), 1980. (a)

Schneider, W. & Fisk, A. D. *Degree of consistent training and the development of automatic processing.* Human Attention Research Laboratory, University of Illinois (Report 8005), 1980. (b)

Schneider, W. & Fisk, A. D. *Dual-task automatic and controlled processing in visual search, can it be done without cost?* Human Attention Research Laboratory, University of Illinois (Report 8002), 1980. (c)

Schneider, W. & Fisk. A. D. *Visual search improves with detection searches, declines with non-detection searches.* Human Attention Research Laboratory, University of Illinois (Report 8004), 1980. (d)

Schneider W. & Shiffrin, R. M. Controlled and automatic human information processing: I. Detection, search, and attention. *Psychological Review*, 1977, *84*, 1–66.

Shiffrin, R. M. Capacity limitations in information processing, attention, and memory. In W. K. Estes (Ed.), *Handbook of learning and cognitive processes* (Vol. 4). Hillsdale, N.J.: Lawrence Erlbaum Associates, 1976.

Shiffrin, R. M. & Schneider, W. Controlled and automatic human information processing: II. Perceptual learning, automatic attending, and a general theory. *Psychological Review*, 1977, *84*, 127–190.

Solomons, L. & Stein, G. Normal motor automatism. *Psychological Review*, 1896, *3*, 492–512.

Spelke, E., Hirst, W., and Neisser, U. Skills of divided attention. *Cognition*, 1976, *4*, 215–230.

Sperling, G., Budiansky, J., Spivak, J. G., and Johnson, M. C. Extremely rapid visual search: The maximum rate of scanning letters for the presence of a numeral. *Science*, 1971, *174*, 307–311.

Sternberg, S. High-speed scanning in human memory. *Science*, 1966, *153*, 652–654.

Sternberg, S. Memory scanning: Mental processes revealed by reaction-time experiments. *American Scientist*, 1969, *57*, 421–457.

Sternberg, S. Memory scanning: New findings and current controversies. *Quarterly Journal of Experimental Psychology*, 1975, *27*, 1–32.

Treisman, A. M. Verbal cues, language and meaning in selective attention. *American Journal of Psychology*, 1964, *77*, 206–219.

Treisman, A. M. Strategies and models of selective attention. *Psychological Review*, 1969, *76*, 282–299.

Treisman, A. M. & Gelade, G. A feature-integration theory of attention. *Cognitive Psychology*, 1980, *12*, 97–136.

Townsend, J. T. A note on the identifiability of parallel and serial processes. *Perception & Psychophysics*, 1971, *10*, 161–163.

Townsend, J. T. Some results concerning the identifiability of parallel and serial processes. *British Journal of Mathematical and Statistical Psychology*, 1972, *25*, 168–199.

5 Skilled Memory

William G. Chase and K. Anders Ericsson
Carnegie-Mellon University

INTRODUCTION

In this chapter, we describe our analysis of a single subject (SF) who has become an expert at the digit-span task. Over the course of 2 years, involving over 250 hours of laboratory practice, SF has steadily increased his digit span from seven digits to about 80 digits. SF's current digit span exceeds that of normals by more than a factor of 10, and his span is four times higher than has ever been recorded in the literature before. In this chapter, we present our analysis of the cognitive processes underlying this memory feat, and we want to use this specific example to develop what we think are the important theoretical principles that we have discovered about skilled memory.

What we mean by skilled memory is the rapid and efficient utilization of memory in some knowledge domain to perform a task at an expert level. Without the knowledge base, task performance by a novice is poor or nonexistent. It is the goal of our present project to understand how memory skill is developed, and how memory is utilized by the expert to produce skilled performance.

The contrast between novice and expert memory performance is striking. Normal people's memory spans fall in a very narrow range (around 7 ± 2 items), and this span is fairly stable over a wide range of types of material (Miller, 1956). This relative invariance in the memory span is taken by most cognitive psychologists as an index of one of the most fundamental and stable properties of the human memory system: the limited capacity of short-term memory (Brown, 1958; Peterson & Peterson, 1959). This limit places severe constraints on people's ability to process information and solve problems (Miller, 1956; Newell & Simon, 1972). and further, memory span has been related to scores on intelligence tests (Bachelder & Denny, 1977a, 1977b).

141

The inability of normal people to hold more than about seven unrelated items in short-term memory stands in apparent contrast to reported feats of memory experts. Persons with trained memories can use mnemonic systems to memorize long lists of names, numbers, and other arbitrary items if they are given enough time between items to allow their systems to work (Bower, 1972; Yates, 1966). Chess masters are able to reproduce virtually an entire chess position of 32 pieces after a brief (5 sec) presentation of a chess board, whereas a novice can only remember the location of 3 or 4 pieces (Chase & Simon, 1973; de Groot, 1966). Mental calculation experts are able to store many intermediate computations in their head while doing mental arithmetic, and, as a side effect of their skill, they generally exhibit a digit span that is two or three times as large as normal (Hatano & Osawa, 1980; Hunter, 1962; Mitchell, 1907; Müller, 1911). Expert telegraphers are able to lag behind by as much as 15–20 words when receiving Morse code (Bryan & Harter, 1899).

In every case, memory performance of the expert seems to violate the established limits of short-term memory. How is it possible for experts to bypass the limits of short-term memory in the domain of their expertise? It is the analysis of this problem that we set out to study in the domain of memory span for digits.

It has often been disputed whether skills are the result of extensive practice or whether some exceptional ability is also necessary for their development. The standard approach for studying expertise has been to bring a recognized expert into the laboratory and study the scope and limits of his performance on a variety of tasks. This approach has some limitations, though. First, for advanced experts, there is little, if any, objective data on how they developed their skill. Second, there is a correlational problem of self-selection: With already-existing experts, one never knows how important initial abilities were for the eventual mastery of the skill. We avoid both these objections by studying the development of a skill from the beginning and by starting with someone with average memory abilities.

Studies of the development of memory skill are rare. In one early study in 1925, a group of kindergarten children was able to increase its average digit span from 4.3 to 6.4 digits after 78 days of practice (less than an hour a day), but this improvement was temporary and disappeared within 5 months (Gates & Taylor, 1925). In another early study (Martin & Fernberger, 1929), two motivated college students were able to increase their memory spans to 14 digits after about 50 hours of practice. These early studies, however, provide little insight into the cognitive mechanisms responsible for changes in the memory span. Nowadays, with better theories of memory and better techniques for studying memory, it is possible to analyze the underlying cognitive components of skill acquisition in the memory domain.

In what follows, we first describe our data on SF's memory span performance, and then we present our analysis of SF's skill in terms of the two principal cognitive mechanisms: the mnemonic system and the retrieval structure. In the final two sections of the chapter, we pursue the question of what additional mechanisms are involved in SF's skill and the implications of our findings for a theory of skilled memory.

THE LEARNING CURVE

An undergraduate (SF) with average memory abilities and average intelligence for a college student was paid on an hourly basis to participate in the experiment. SF was run on the memory span task for about an hour a day, 2 to 5 days a week, for over 2 years. The basic procedure was to read random digits to SF at the rate of one digit per sec, followed by ordered recall. If the sequence was reported correctly, the length of the next sequence was increased by one digit, otherwise the sequence length was decreased by one digit. Immediately after each trial, SF was asked to provide verbal reports of his thought processes during the trial.[1] At the end of each session, SF was also asked to recall as much of the material from the session as he could. On some days, experimental procedures were substituted for the regular sessions.

During the course of 25 months of practice, involving over 250 hours of laboratory testing, SF demonstrated a steady improvement in his average digit span from seven digits to over 80 digits (Fig. 5.1). Furthermore, there was a parallel improvement in his ability to remember digits following the session. In the beginning, SF could recall virtually nothing after an hour's session; now SF can recall well over 90% of the digits presented to him.

Figure 5.2 compares the early part of SF's learning curve with those of Martin and Fernberger's (1929) two subjects. This figure shows the maximum digit span as a function of the number of trials to obtain it. The interesting thing to notice about the figure is how similar the learning curves are.[2]

With only a couple of hundred hours of practice, SF would be classified as a beginner at most skills. However, in his field of expertise, memory for random

---

[1]There have been many changes in procedure over the 2 years of this study. For example, we used to ask for a verbal report after ½ the trials, randomly selected. Further, in the beginning we had some conditions with immediate recall and some conditions with 20-sec delays, because we were interested in various verbalization conditions in relation to verbal protocols. We eventually dropped all these delay conditions when it became apparent that they had no effect on the data.

[2]We find it surprising that subjects would not report using meaningful associations in that study, because we want to claim that improvements in memory span must necessarily involve mnemonic aids. Martin and Fernberger (1929) only discuss organization and the number of digits in the apprehended group and do not comment on whether or not subjects used meaningful associations. In another early study, Oberly (1928) discusses retrospective reports from normal subjects in the memory-span task, and he found that subjects with larger memory-span scores invariably reported using meaningful associations.

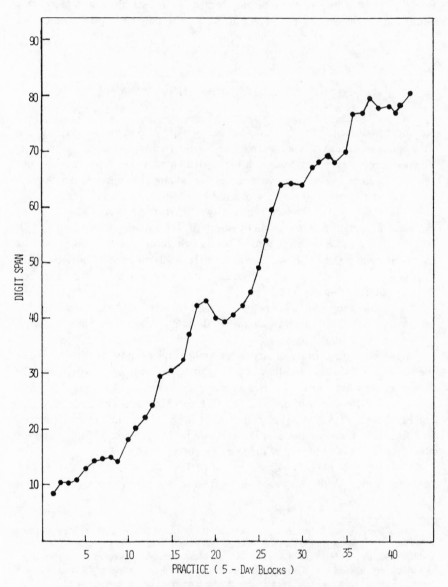

FIG. 5.1. Average digit-span for SF as a function of practice in 5-day blocks. Each day represents about 1 hour's practice and ranges from 55 trials per day in the beginning to 3 trials per day for the longest sequences. The 43 blocks of practice shown here represent about 215 hours of practice; interspersed among these practice sessions are approximately 75 hours of experimental sessions (not shown).

144

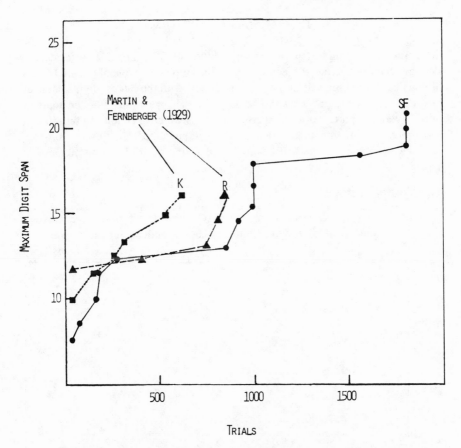

FIG. 5.2. This graph compares SF to Martin and Fernberger's (1929) two subjects on the same scale. Plotted here are the successive highest number of digits
recalled by each subject as a function of the number of trials it took each subject to
reach each maximum. Martin and Fernberger's subjects practiced about 3 months
before the experiment was terminated.

digits, SF compares favorably with the best-known mnemonists, such as Luria's
(1968) S and Hunt and Love's (1972) VP. For example, we gave SF the task of
recalling a matrix of 50 digits, because data on this task are also published for
both S and VP. After about 6 months of practice, SF's study times and recall
times were at least as good as those of the life-time memory experts, and after a
year and a half of practice, SF's performance was substantially better than the
experts' performance. There is one important difference between SF on the one
hand and S and VP on the other, in that SF's skill is limited to digits. For other
types of stimuli, like random consonants, SF's memory span is normal, about
seven symbols.

THE MNEMONIC SYSTEM

So far, we have simply reported the magnitude of SF's memory performance. We have seen an average subject who, with the help of a couple of hundred hours of practice, turned himself into a memory expert with the largest digit span ever recorded in the literature. How did he do it? The answer comes from an analysis of SF's verbal reports, various experimental tests we have conducted on SF, and a computer simulation model that we have constructed. In this section, we describe the most essential mechanism underlying SF's skill—his mnemonic system.

The Verbal Protocols

SF started out just like virtually all the naive subjects we have ever run. He simply attempted to code everything into a phonemic code, and then he rehearsed

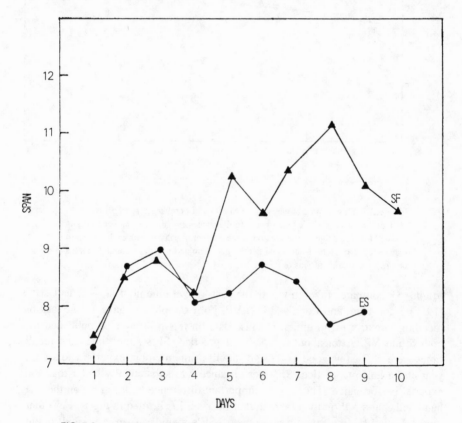

FIG. 5.3.   A comparison of SF with a subject who never developed a mnemonic. The jump in SF's performance from Day 4 to Day 5 is accompanied by the first report of mnemonic encodings at Day 5.

this code until recall. Like most subjects, SF noticed a few patterns (e.g., ascending sequences), and he utilized a rudimentary grouping strategy (to be described later), but for the most part, SF relied on the rehearsal buffer as the major mechanism for short-term retention.

Figure 5.3 compares SF with an unmotivated subject who quit after a couple of weeks. In contrast to SF, this subject never developed a mnemonic system and consequently was never able to improve very much. Notice that the performance of both subjects is very comparable through the first 4 days of the experiment. In fact, on Day 4, SF gave us a fairly lengthy verbal report about how he had reached his limit and no further improvement was possible.

And then, on Day 5, something very interesting happened. There was a large improvement in SF's digit span (a jump of 4 standard deviations from the day before), and, for the first time, SF began to report the use of a mnemonic aid. From this point on, SF showed a steady increase in his digit span as he developed his mnemonic system and the accompanying control structure.

To give an idea of the kind of protocols we obtained from SF, Table 5.1 shows a protocol from a fairly early session (Day 39). This is a trial on which SF achieved a new high of 22 digits. On this trial, the experimenter read the digits at a 1-sec rate; there was a 20-sec delay followed by recall, and then the experimenter requested a retrospective report. (The experimenter's comments are indicated by parentheses in the protocol.)

The most interesting thing to notice about the protocol is the mnemonic: SF is coding the digits as running times. It turned out that SF is a very good long-distance runner,[3] and he uses his knowledge of various times for events as a mnemonic aid.

From an analysis of SF's protocols, we were able to determine the coding rules used by SF to categorize groups of digits as running times. Table 5.2 shows the early development of SF's mnemonic coding scheme. This table shows, for each coding rule, the session number when it first appeared in the verbal protocols. The significant part of this coding scheme is the invention of the running-time mnemonic on Day 5, and its extension to four-digit running times on Day 20 and decimal times on Day 26. Additions to this basic code didn't occur until much later (around Day 60), when SF invented additional mnemonic rules to handle digit groups that cannot be converted to running times. For example, 896 can't be a time because the second digit is too big, and under these circum-

---

[3]To give some indication of SF's skill, he was a member of the university track and cross-country team, a member of a junior college national championship marathon team, and a member of the Human Energy Running Club. SF is now 22 years old, he trains 10–13 miles a day, and he has competed in numerous long-distance events in the eastern region of the U.S. for the past 9 years. SF's best events are the 3 mile, 5 mile, and marathon, and his best times in these events are 14:39, 25:40, and 2:39:36, respectively. SF rates himself in the top 2% of runners for events over 10 miles. In other respects, SF seems to have average memory abilities and average intelligence test scores (SAT = 990, GRE = 1140), although he has a high grade-point average (3.80).

TABLE 5.1
Protocol of SF Reaching a New High of 22 Digits
Session #39
July 11, 1978

[*Digits Presented* *1 per sec.*]	(4 1 3 1 7 7 8 4 0 6 0 3 4 9 4 8 7 0 9 4 6 2)

[*20 second delay*] [*"nine-four-six-two" rehearsed about 15 times rapidly in a whisper*]

[*Signal to recall*] *Time* *(sec)*
0

5	All right. All right. All right. All right. All right. All right. All right. Oh geez!
10	Ok. Ok. Ok. All right now . . . now this one is . . . un
15	it it . . . uh . . . oh.
20	ok. ok. ok. ok. Oh!
	Four thirteen point one
25	Seventy-seven eighty-four
30	Oh six oh three Four nine four, eight seven oh,
35	Nine forty-six Oh no!
40	Nine forty-six point . . . Oh!
45	Nine forty-six point . . .
50	two! (Can I please have it again once more please?)
55	Oh no. Oh no. Oh no. Oh no. What?
	(Can you take it once more, please?)
60	Oh. . . . Oh. All right. All right. All right.
1:05	It's four thirteen point one mile. Then seventy-seven eighty-four.
1:10	Then oh six oh three. Then four nine four.
	Eight seven oh.
1:15	Nine . . . forty-six. What'd you run it?
1:20	I ran it in nine forty-six point . . . two!
1:25	
	(Thank you. Please tell me everything you can remember.) All right. All right. All right. All right. All right.
1:30	Starting from the beginning. I made the four thirteen point one a mile time. I just remembered the seventy-seven eighty-four.

(Continued)

TABLE 5.1—*Continued*

Time	
1:35	Ok? Ok? Right. Seventy-seven eighty-four.
1:40	Then . . . then . . . then I . . .
	(Any pattern?)
	What?
	(Any pattern?)
1:45	No. No. Nothing. Just like seventy-seven eighty-four.
	Ok. Then I made the oh six oh three, I made that a mile time.
1:50	Then I remembered the four nine four and the eight seven oh.
	I just had to remember those.
1:55	Then I remembered the nine forty-six point . . . two!
	It's definitely point two, two-mile.
2:00	I said, so I said to myself "What did you run it in?"
	I ran it in nine forty-six point two. Nine forty-six point two. Right.
2:05	
2:10	(Uh . . . Could you uh . . . tell me about the last three groups of digits.
	I'm, I'm not sure that I . . .)
2:15	Um. It was, it was four nine four. Nothing. Eight seven oh. Nothing.
	Then nine forty-six point two two-mile.
2:20	
	(Did you rehearse anything?)
	Yea. Nine forty-six point two keeping in mind the first two sets of three.
2:25	
	(Uh. Were you unsure of any of the digits?)
2:30	
	(Sigh) No . . . No. No.
2:35	

stances, SF codes this group as "eighty-nine point six years old, very old man." To take another example, 1943 is coded as "near the end of World War II." These extra rules include AGE + DECIMAL for three-digit groups, and for four-digit groups, YEARS, AGE + AGE, or DIGIT + TIME. By the end of 6 months—100 sessions—SF had essentially completed his mnemonic scheme, and he was coding 95% of the digit sequences, of which the majority were running times (65%), a substantial minority were ages (25%), and the rest of the coded sequences were years or numerical patterns (5%). After 200 hours of practice, SF was coding virtually everything.

The next table (Table 5.3) shows the systematic nature of SF's running-time mnemonic system in semantic memory. After each session, SF is asked to recall as many groups of digits as he can from that session. (This table is a transcription of the recall on Day 39.)[4] First, notice that SF has 11 major categories of running

---

[4]Times in parentheses are ones that could not be found in the digits presented that day. Although there were a few of these false alarms in the early sessions (before Session 100), they are virtually nonexistent in his later sessions.

TABLE 5.2
Major Coding Structures

	Coding Structure	Example	First Reported (Session No.)
3-digit groups	Time	8:05	5
	Age & Decimal	49.7	70
4-digit groups	Time (3,4,5,10 MT)	13:20	20
	Time + Decimal	4:10.6	26
	Digit + Time	9–7:05	60
	Year	1955	64
	Age + Age	4676	64

times, ranging from half-mile times to marathon times, plus a few nontimes at the end. From SF's protocols, we know that he also has many subcategories within each category. For example, 3492 is coded as "Three forty-nine point two, near world-record mile time." And there are many other types of mile times, such as "very poor mile time," "average mile time for the marathon," and "average work-out mile time." Another thing to notice is the very systematic nature of SF's recall (left-to-right and top-to-bottom in the table). He begins with the shortest race and systematically works his way up, category by category, with very few reversals. Within each category, he uses the same procedure of systematically recalling from the shortest to the longest subcategory, with pauses separating subcategories. At the lowest level within each subcategory, SF still generally recalls times in an orderly way from smallest to largest times. On rare occasions, a running time will trigger episodic recall of other times from the same trial, such as a pair of mile times occurring together. In general, however, SF is unable to recall order information from the session.

TABLE 5.3
After-Session Recall: Day 39

Category									
½ mile	233.6	(257)							
¾ mile	(312)								
1 mile	343	354	413.1	418	432.1	507	(516)	529	601	641
2 miles	723	826	820	946.2	935				
3 miles	—								
4 miles	2252								
5 miles	2966								
10 kmt	3215								
15 kmt	—								
10 miles	5614	5649	6610						
Marathon	—								
Misc.	000	494	870	(057)	7784				

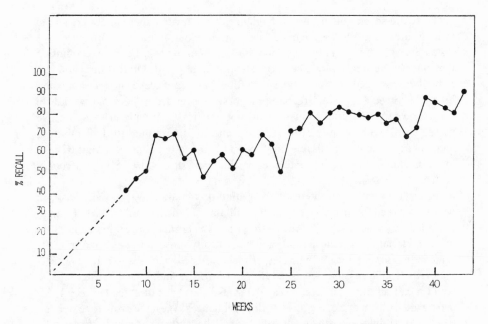

FIG. 5.4.   SF's average after-session percent recall in 5-day blocks. We first
started taking systematic measurements on this task around the 8th week. The
dotted line represents an extrapolation back to when SF was a normal subject;
normal subjects remember virtually nothing from an hours session.

We characterize SF's after-session recall as directed search through his
semantic memory categories at the highest levels and at the lowest level; we
characterize the mechanism as a generate-and-test procedure, in which the
number line is used as a retrieval device. We think this is an important property
of skilled memory—the ability to search systematically and efficiently through
the knowledge base.

A quantitative analysis of SF's after-session report shows a steady increase in
the amount recalled (Fig. 5.4), until at the present time, virtually everything from
an hour's session is in retrievable long-term memory. With about 4 months of
practice, SF was able to recall about 65% of the material in a session. There were
also some slight variations in recall, depending on the learning conditions. For
example, SF was able to recall about 10% more from the second half of the
session than from the first half; he was able to recall about 20% more from those
trials on which he gave a retrospective verbal report, and there are also some
slight variations in serial position. After 2 years of practice, however, these
effects have disappeared, as virtually everything from a session can be recalled.[5]

_____
[5]The after-session report is susceptible to motivational changes. For example, when SF has a bad
session, he doesn't try as hard in the after-session report, and his performance drops off.

There are several other lines of evidence that show that these codes are stored in long-term memory. In one experiment (after about 4 months of practice), we tested SF's memory after the session with a recognition test, because recognition is a much more sensitive measure of retention than recall. On that occasion, SF not only recognized perfectly three- and four-digit sequences from the same day, he also showed substantial recognition of sequences from the same week.[6] In another experiment (after about 4 months of practice) after an hour's session, we presented SF with three- and four-digit probes, but with the last digit missing, and he had to name the missing digit. SF was able to recall the last digit 67% of the time after 4 months of practice; after 250 hours of practice, SF was virtually perfect at this task.

Finally, we report an interesting variation on the after-session recall task, in which we asked for an extended recall (Williams, 1976). We first asked SF for an extended recall on Day 125. At this time, SF was normally recalling about 80% of the material from each session, and he typically took no more than 5 minutes for his after-session recall. In this experiment, after SF had recalled about 80% of the digits from a session, we asked him to try harder and to keep trying until he could recall all the digit sequences. After about an hour of extended recall, SF had recalled all but one of the missing digit sequences. We have asked for extended recall several times since then, and each time SF has shown virtually perfect recall. Also as SF became more practiced, extended recall became progressively easier until, after 250 hours of practice, SF recalls over 90% in his normal after-session recall.

Our analysis so far has shown that SF has invented a mnemonic system that relies on already-existing long-term memory knowledge of running times. We need, however, to establish that this knowledge system is *necessary* for SF's skilled memory performance; that is, would SF's memory performance return to normal without the use of his mnemonic system? We further need to specify the mnemonic system in more precise theoretical terms, and further, we need to subject our theory to more rigorous experimental verification.

The Theory and The Experiments

When we first started the study, we intended to run SF for a couple of weeks to see if it was possible to increase one's memory span with practice, and if so, could we discover how it was done by analyzing the verbal protocols. To our great surprise, SF revealed a steadily increasing skill in the memory-span task, and his verbal protocols were very rich and revealing about his mnemonic sys-

---

[6]There is an interesting anecdote worth mentioning here. Near the end of the recognition session, we deliberately presented SF with a few probes that he had been shown earlier in the session. For both old and new probes, SF would respond immediately (within a second or two) and with some irritation "I already told you that one," or something to that effect. The ability to retain this kind of information for at least an hour is a clear demonstration that these codes are stored in long-term memory.

tem. It took us about 40 sessions to analyze the protocols and develop a theoretical account of what SF was doing. At this point, we were ready to test our theory. From the protocols, we were able to simulate SF's mnemonic coding scheme with a few simple rules in the form of a production system, and our simulation was able to predict how SF would code digit sequences between 85% and 95% of the time. In fact, we have simulated SF's mnemonic coding scheme at several levels of practice, and we have discovered that the major advances in his mnemonic system occurred very early—within the first 100 hours of practice. Although there are occasional minor adjustments, the mnemonic system itself was essentially completed within a few months.

Because our theoretical analysis is based mainly on the verbal protocols, this evidence can be characterized as descriptive. A stronger test of our theory requires more direct experimental control. To this end, our first two experiments (Days 42 and 47) were designed to test our theory of the mnemonic system. We reasoned that if the mnemonic system were critical, then SF should perform poorly when the digit sequences were uncodable (Exp. I) and, conversely, if all the digit sequences could be coded as running times, SF's performance should improve (Exp. II).

In our first experiment on the basis of our analysis of the verbal protocols, we constructed digit sequences that could not be coded as running times (this was before SF started to use ages to supplement his running times). We also eliminated other easy sequences, such as patterns of ascending or decending sequences, repetitions, and triplets of odd or even digits.

When SF was faced with these uncodable sequences, his performance dropped back almost to his beginning level. Figure 5.5 compares the experimental session to the weekly averages preceding the experiment. The bottom curve (circles) is the initial ascending sequence until an error occurs,[7] and the top curve (triangles) is the average of the up-and-down procedure. The bottom curve shows an almost complete return to baseline, and the top curve shows a 20% drop from SF's normal performance.

Table 5.4 shows a more detailed analysis of performance on the experimental day (Friday) compared with the 4 preceding days. The first two columns are the digit span and the percentage of groups that were coded as running times. The means and standard deviation are shown at the bottom for the 4 prior days. Both the digit span and the number of mnemonic codes show substantial drops on the experimental day. The last three columns are the number of times, nontimes, and total digits recalled in the after-session report, and again, there are substantial drops on the experimental day.

---

[7]In the beginning, we started every session with an initial ascending sequence until SF made an error (as in the memory-span procedure on IQ tests), after which we used the more efficient up-and-down procedure. We eventually dropped this initial procedure because it became too time-consuming as SF's memory span increased.

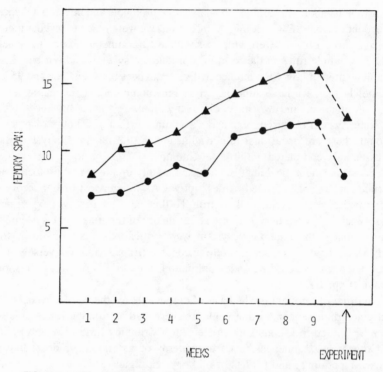

FIG. 5.5. SF's average digit span for Experiment 1 versus the 8 preceding
weeks. The top curve (triangles) shows SF's average digit-span with the up-and-
down method. The lower curve (circles) shows SF's digit-span on the initial
ascending sequence. Each session was started with an ascending sequence, starting
with five digits, until SF made an error (circles); the rest of the session was
conducted with the more reliable up-and-down procedure (triangles).

It is worth noting at this point that SF was still able to use his mnemonic
system in a clever way to avoid a complete regression in performance. SF was
able to change his strategy in two ways. First, he was able to augment his coding
scheme by converting nontimes to times. For example, the three-digit group 564
isn't a running time because the second digit exceeds five. However, SF converted this group in the following way: 564 → 6:04 mile time, and he remembered the additional fact that it is a converted time.[8] The second strategy change
occurred about half way through the session when SF hit on the idea of changing
his grouping structure. For example, we expected SF to code 13 digits as
3-3-3-4, but SF very cleverly learned to group 13 as 1-3-3-3-3, which allowed
him to find some running times.

[8]It is this experiment that apparently caused SF to induce this rule, which became a standard,
albeit small, part of the mnemonic system.

TABLE 5.4
Experiment I - NonTime Sequences

	Digit Span	% Times in Retrospective Reports	After-Session Report		
			Number of Times	Number of Non-Times	Number of Digits
Monday	13.1	65	26	7	110
Tuesday	18.8	62	24	5	98
Wednesday	16.2	70	31	4	123
Thursday	15.6	75	43	3	165
	15.9	68	31	4.75	124
	2.34	5.72	8.52	1.71	29.2
Friday	12.7	41	12	10	79

18 ← Regular   → 23 Converted

In our second experiment conducted a few days later, we did just the opposite. We reasoned that if the running time mnemonic is important, then SF's performance should improve if we gave him all running times. We therefore constructed sequences of digits that, according to our theory, should all be coded as running times.

Table 5.5 compares the results of this experiment with the 4 preceding days of the week. With these good sequences, SF's memory-span performance jumped by 27% (from 15.3 to 19.5), all his codes were running times (as expected), and there was a substantial jump in his after-session recall. In short, the results of this experiment support our theory of the importance of SF's mnemonic coding system.

TABLE 5.5
Experiment II - Good Sequences

	Digit Span	% Times in Retrospective Reports	After-Session Report		
			Number of Times	Number of Nontimes	Number of Digits
Monday	15.1	91.4	32	3	117
Tuesday	14.3	93.3	42	3	147
Wednesday	15.6	75.0	42	14	211
Thursday	16.3	87.2	34	5	145
	15.3	86.7	37.5	6.25	155
	.84	8.22	5.26	5.25	39.8
Friday	19.5	100.0	54	—	192

TABLE 5.6
Rehearsal Suppression Experiments

Recite Alphabet	(Day 62)	20.6 → 16.3
Visual Suppression - Copy	(Day 73)	25.7 → 26.5
Visual Suppression - Rotate	(Day 73)	25.7 → 24.5
Hya - Hya	(Day 75)	25.7 → 23.9
Shadowing	(Day 99)	31.6 → 2.05

In a third experiment, we were interested in establishing the reliability of SF's mnemonic coding rules. We presented SF with the same sequence on Day 103 that he had been presented with a month earlier (Day 85), and we compared the verbal protocols on these 2 days. SF used the same mnemonic code on 81% of the sequences (38 of 47). In addition, three of the nine discrepancies could be traced to changes in the mnemonic coding rules between Day 85 and Day 103, and four discrepancies were due to coding failures (i.e., no code) on one day or the other. In other words, in only two instances (4%) was there an unexplained discrepancy in the mnemonic rule system. Thus, there is good agreement from one occasion to the next in SF's mnemonic codes.

To summarize our analysis thus far, we have established that SF's performance is based on a mnemonic coding scheme in semantic memory, and we have modeled this coding scheme and experimentally verified it to our satisfaction. We next address the question of whether or not these semantic codes are stored in short-term memory; that is, do these semantic codes have to be held in short-term memory in order to be recalled?

The Rehearsal–Suppression Experiments

Exactly what is the role of short-term memory in SF's memory-span performance? The standard procedure for studying short-term memory in a given task is to prevent rehearsal and see how task performance deteriorates; any loss in performance is attributed to the absence of information in short-term memory. We initiated a series of rehearsal–suppression experiments to explore SF's use of short-term memory, and the results are summarized in Table 5.6. This table shows the experimental manipulation and the day of the experiment on the left, and on the right, the current memory-span level (the weekly average preceding the experiment) is compared with the experimental result.

In the first experiment, immediately after the list was presented, SF recited the alphabet repeatedly as quickly as he could for 20 sec, and then he recalled the list. The drop in performance corresponds almost exclusively to loss of the last group of digits at the end. This result makes perfect sense because, according to SF's verbal reports, he normally holds this last group in a rehearsal buffer. Again, about half way through the session, SF changed his grouping strategy to produce a smaller rehearsal group at the end, and this strategy change reduced the interference considerably.

The next two experiments were visual-suppression experiments that we conducted, because we thought that SF might be using some visual–spatial coding.[9] The interfering tasks in these two experiments were copying geometric shapes in the first case, and rotate and copy in the second case. In this latter task, SF had to mentally rotate a geometric shape 90° and then draw the rotated shape. These tasks had been previously designed by Charness (1976) to interfere with short-term visual retention. In these experiments, immediately after a list of digits was presented, SF was instructed to copy or rotate and copy a list of geometric shapes as quickly as he could for 20 sec before recalling the list of digits. The results were straightforward: These visual-suppression procedures had no effect at all on SF's performance.

The last two experiments were an attempt to occupy short-term memory during presentation of the digits, because we believe that the phonemic buffer is used during the coding process; that is, there must be some temporary storage of digits while a group is formed and semantic memory is searched for a mnemonic code, and we believe that SF initially codes digits phonemically for just such a purpose.[10] In the first experiment, we introduced a concurrent chanting task ("Hya–Hya") that has been used by Baddeley and his associates to suppress short-term memory (Baddeley & Hitch, 1974). In this task, SF was required to say "Hya" after each digit during presentation. To our great surprise, SF was able to say "Hya" between presentation of the digits without any trouble at all. In his verbal reports, SF said that he could organize this verbal chanting independently and somehow "hear" it in a different spatial location than where he was listening to and coding the incoming digits.

In the final rehearsal–suppression experiment, we imposed an attention-demanding shadowing task at the end of each group. From SF's protocols (and our model), we could predict how SF would group the digits, and the shadowing task was inserted in the 1-sec intervals between the last digit of one group and the first digit of the next group. One experimenter read digits to SF at a 1-sec rate and the other experimenter read a letter of the alphabet (randomly selected) to SF at the end of each group. SF's task was to listen to the digits, repeat back each letter as quickly as possible, and recall the digits at the end.

This experiment produced a very substantial decrement in performance (35%). It is interesting to compare this task with the concurrent chanting task that requires between three and four times as much verbalization, yet the concurrent chanting task did not produce any measurable interference. We interpret these results as follows. We think that concurrent chanting does not disrupt the

---

[9]In some of SF's early protocols, he would occasionally point to different spatial locations with his hand, in left-to-right order, when he recalled groups of digits. This behavior is also typical of normal subjects when recalling groups.

[10]This is the most commonly accepted view of short-term memory for verbal materials—that they are buffered in a phonemic code for several seconds (Baddeley, 1976, Chapter 7; Klatzky, 1980, Chapter 5).

phonemic buffer (as SF's introspections suggest). This is consistent with Levy's (1975) experiments on comprehension in reading and listening, in which she found that concurrent chanting disrupted reading but not listening. She suggested that concurrent chanting does not interfere with the phonemic buffer, but it does inhibit generation of phonemic codes.

We suggest that in the shadowing task, unlike the concurrent chanting task, SF was forced to retrieve a spoken letter from the phonemic buffer immediately after the last digit in each group was presented. This phonemic buffer operation eliminated SF's normal strategy of lagging behind the input and using the phonemic buffer as a temporary storage for the incoming group while processing semantically the previous group. In the following, we present evidence of SF's normal lagging strategy.

We conducted this experiment at about the same time as the rehearsal suppression experiments. Although this experiment does not involve rehearsal suppression, it has direct bearing on the role of short-term memory in SF's performance. In this task, we interrupted SF at some random point during a trial and asked for an immediate verbal protocol. Among other things, we were interested in how far behind the spoken sequence SF's coding lagged; that is, how many uncoded digits are kept in short-term memory; what is the running short-term memory load? Basically, we found that SF was actively coding the previous group of three or four digits while the digits for the current group were still coming in, a lag of about 4 to 7 sec in time. The contents of short-term memory were: (1) the most recent one, two, or three ungrouped digits in a phonemic code; (2) the previous group of three or four digits (it is not clear how these grouped items are coded); and (3) all the semantic information associated with the active mnemonic coding of the previous group.

From this experiment and the rehearsal–suppression experiments, we draw the conclusion that at any moment in time, the contents of short-term memory represent a very narrow window of the digit sequence. At recall, it appears that nothing except the rehearsal group is retrieved directly from short-term memory, and there is some evidence that, with further practice, even the rehearsal group was no longer stored exclusively in short-term memory.[11]

This concludes our experimental analysis of the role of short-term memory in SF's performance. Before moving on to a consideration of the theoretical mechanisms underlying SF's mnemonics, we briefly consider whether or not SF has increased his short-term memory capacity.

Short-Term Memory Capacity

After more than 250 hours of practice, has SF increased his short-term memory capacity? There are several reasons for thinking not. First, SF's mnemonically

---

[11]When these rehearsal-suppression experiments were conducted, the rehearsal group was often not coded, but eventually (after about 150 hours of practice), SF invariably coded every digit group, including the rehearsal group.

coded groups were almost always three and four digits, and he never generated a mnemonic code greater than 5 digits. Second, SF's phonemically coded rehearsal group never exceeded six digits, and a rehearsal group of six digits was always segmented into two groups of three digits. Thus, SF never kept a group larger than five digits *unattended* (coded but not rehearsed) in short-term memory, and even when attended (rehearsed), SF still only kept six or fewer digits in a phonemic code. We later show that SF almost never was able to keep the *order* straight for more than three or four coded groups, and he thus resorted to a hierarchical organization of groups (to be described later). After some initial difficulty in trying to keep the order straight for five groups, SF never allowed more than four groups to be clustered together. Third, after 3 months of practice on the digit-span task, we tested SF's memory span for consonants, and he showed no transfer at all from the digit-span task, and his consonant span was around six. Finally, in the literature, expert mental calculators and other memory experts seem to group digits into units of this size. Rückle's numerical codes are six-digit groups with a 3–3 substructure (Müller, 1911), and Aitkin's memory for digits is organized in five-digit groups (Hunter, 1962). There does not seem to be a single exception to this generalization in the mental calculation literature (Mitchell. 1907). For normal subjects, it appears that an optimum group size is three or four digits (Wickelgren, 1964).

These data suggest that the reliable working capacity of short-term memory is around three or four units, as Broadbent (1975) has recently argued. It is useful to distinguish the working capacity from the span. This latter term is defined as the size of the list that can be reported correctly 50% of the time. But the reliable capacity of short-term memory—the amount of material that is available almost all the time—is closer to three or four symbols. When we talk about skilled performance, this latter number is a more realistic estimate of the working capacity.

Meaning in Skilled Memory

At this point, we emphasize the first characteristic of skilled memory: *Experts use their knowledge structures in semantic memory to store information during skilled performance of some task.* The idea that mnemonic or other meaningful associations are necessary for skilled memory is consistent with the literature. The literature on memory performance of mental calculation experts suggests that these people invariably use their knowledge about mathematics to make extensive meaningful associations with numbers (Hunter, 1962, 1968; Mitchell, 1907; Müller, 1911). The literature on chess experts (Chase & Simon, 1973; de Groot, 1966) as well as a variety of other types of knowledge-based experts (Chase & Chi, 1980) suggests that meaningful patterns in long-term memory underlie superior memory. In short, expert memory performance in various semantically rich domains seems to involve coding and organized access to knowledge structures in long-term memory.

In the present study, we have presented a great deal of evidence that, in the memory-span task, SF invented a mnemonic system to take advantage of his knowledge of running times. However, we have not considered some of the broader issues, such as, what is a mnemonic and precisely how does it work? What accounts for the precision of mnemonic associations? How, for example, is it possible to recover the exact digit sequence 3492 from an abstract retrieval cue like "near world-record mile time?"

We should make it clear that a comprehensive coverage of these general issues is beyond the scope of this chapter. However, we do have some ideas about how mnemonics and other meaningful associations work, particularly in the context of skilled memory, and it is useful at this point to explore these ideas.

In general, a mnemonic is some mechanism for associating unknown material with something familiar; the advantage is that it relieves the burden on short-term memory, because recall can be achieved via a single association with an already-existing code in long-term memory. To understand *how* mnemonic associations work, however, requires an answer to the more general question of how meaningful associations work, and there is no definitive answer to that question in the literature, although the literature is filled with good ideas (see Bower, 1972, for a good review).

Early theoretical accounts tended to emphasize the encoding process, and most attention was focused on the power of contexts and interactive codes. For example, the most important principle to follow when using visual imagery mnemonics is to make the images *interactive*. If you want to remember COW and BALL, it is important to imagine them interacting in some way, viz., "The cow kicked the ball." When COW is presented at recall, it serves as a retrieval cue for the context, and BALL is derived from the context.

This idea is closest to the theoretical explanation we favor, namely that items to be remembered must be embedded within a hierarchical knowledge structure in semantic memory. To take another example, the three digits 325 are much easier to remember if they are interpreted as "Our meeting time this afternoon." Most people could confidently commit these digits to long-term memory without writing them down (unless there are competing times) and then have little trouble recalling them, given the retrieval cue "What time were we meeting this afternoon?"

Another way to think about this example is that the concept of a meeting time exists as a set of procedures in semantic memory for activating various semantic features that interpret this time. These procedures are used to build a semantic structure that is bound to the memory trace. In Fig. 5.6, we have depicted the meeting-time mnemonic in the form of a link-node structure. There are two parts to the structure: the time of day and the time during the hour. At encoding, it is assumed that something like a mid-afternoon feature is activated. It is assumed that the feature only responds to a small range of hours (say 2, 3, or 4), and the stimulus trace "three" activates this feature, and the stimulus trace is then bound to the MID-AFTERNOON node. Further, the stimulus trace for minutes is assumed

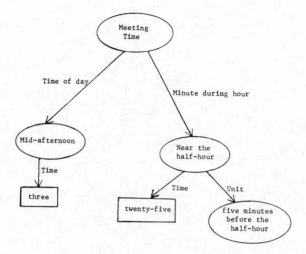

FIG. 5.6.   A link node structural representation of a mnemonic encoding of a meeting time.

to activate the nearest reference-point feature (say HOUR, QUARTER HOUR, HALF HOUR, THREE-QUARTERS HOUR), whether the time is BEFORE or AFTER the reference point, and further, because meeting times are often stated in 5- or 10-minute units, it is assumed that when a meeting time falls on one of these units, a further semantic feature is activated. In this case, these units are sufficient to uniquely specify the meeting time to the exact minute.

This example captures what we believe is the essential characteristic of meaningful associations: The stimulus trace is bound to a hierarchical semantic structure. The meaningful association or mnemonic provides a retrieval cue to the semantic structure, and once the semantic structure is activated, the trace is retrieved through the structure. Without such a structure, how is recall to be achieved? Unless the items are in short-term memory, about the only retrieval cue one can use is "What numbers have I heard recently?"; and this retrieval cue is not very specific, nor does it help to specify the order of the numbers in the unlikely event that a retrieval does occur.

Why are some mnemonics better than others? Why is "The cow kicked the ball" easier to remember than "Truth is good?" Besides the interactive principle, the next important principle about mnemonics is that they should be *concrete* (Paivio, 1971). Various theoretical explanations of this fact have emphasized the distinctiveness, uniqueness, redundancy, or elaboration of memory traces (Anderson & Reder, 1979). We illustrate this principle with a link-node structure representation of "The cow kicked the ball." It is assumed that when people generate a mental image of a cow kicking a ball (or comprehend the sentence), a set of procedures in semantic memory is activated that builds a hierarchical link-node structure something like the one depicted in Fig. 5.7. The

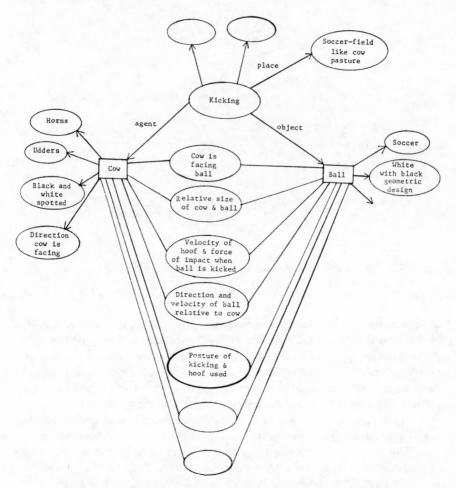

FIG. 5.7.   A schematic link node representation of a mnemonic encoding of ''A cow kicking a ball.'' The central node in this structure is the action node (KICK-ING), connecting COW and BALL by *agent* and *object* links, respectively.

traces of COW and BALL are bound to the central node KICKING in this structure by *agent* and *object* links.

Notice how much extra information is needed in this structure to fully specify the concept. Compared to this structure, the semantic structure for ''Truth is good'' is very impoverished, with nothing more than a *subject–predicate* relation and perhaps a single semantic feature of GOODNESS to link the traces. We have divided the features in Fig. 5.7 into two types: interactive and free. Interactive features are those needed to specify the relationship between COW and BALL in the context of kicking, and free features are those that aren't essential to the interaction.

There is a theoretical (and empirical) issue here as to why an elaborated memory trace is more memorable. If one believes that the memory trace in Fig. 5.7 is more memorable because it is more distinct or unique (Bower, 1972), then the noninteractive features are important. However, if one believes that the elaborations serve as redundant retrieval links between the trace items (Anderson & Reder, 1979; Bower, 1972; Stein & Bransford, 1979), then only the interactive features are important. We agree with Anderson and Reder (1979) that it is the interactive features that are important.

We should point out that according to our theory, an elaborated memory trace is important but not essential. We deliberately choose the meeting-time and COW–BALL examples to demonstrate this point. Both these associations work as mnemonics. The COW–BALL example is a better mnemonic because of the elaborated interactive links, but the meeting-time mnemonic works because, according to our theory, the trace is bound to a semantic structure in long-term memory. It is the semantic structure that is essential.

How are meaningful associations retrieved in the particular context of paired-associate learning? Following a recent proposal by Norman and Bobrow (1979), we suggest that at the time of retrieval the subject can rely on very much the same mechanism he used to generate the meaningful association. Norman and Bobrow (1979) labeled this the *constructability mechanism*. The skilled mnemonist has a set of well-practiced procedures for generating mental images, and given the retrieval cue (COW), he can use his procedural knowledge to retrieve the context (KICKING). The elaborated image provides many redundant retrieval cues to facilitate this retrieval. In our example, body parts, postures, and other interactive features serve to retrieve BALL from COW. We think that the ability to regenerate encoding features at the time of recall is a crucial characteristic of skilled memory.

SF's Mnemonic System

Now that we have introduced the appropriate theoretical context, we next take up the representation of SF's mnemonic system. It is traditional to describe memory in terms of the three logical phases: Encoding, Storage, and Retrieval. However, we postpone our discussion of retrieval until we have presented our analysis of SF's retrieval structure in the next section. In this section we outline our theory of SF's encoding and storage processes.

Basically, we assume that SF has an elaborate mechanism for recognizing running times, and we have modeled this mechanism as a production system. It is easier, however, to illustrate the encoding operation as a discrimination net (Chase & Simon, 1973; Simon & Gilmartin, 1973), and we claim without proof that discrimination net and production system models of pattern recognition are isomorphic.

In Fig. 5.8, we illustrate how SF's semantic memory might encode 3492. Each node in the discrimination tree corresponds to a production rule in our

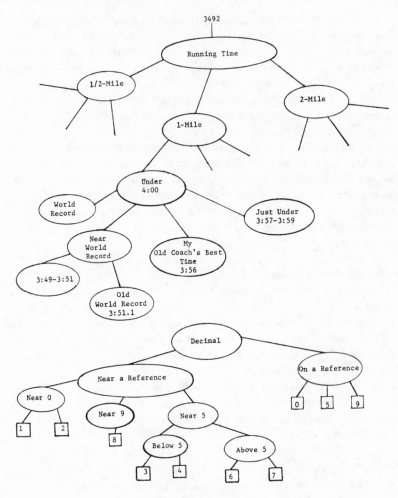

FIG. 5.8.   The relevant part of the discrimination net for accessing the mnemonic encoding for 3492. The net shown at the top contains procedures for encoding mile times under 4 minutes, and the separate net shown at the bottom contains procedures for encoding the decimal point.

production system. An interesting property of this discrimination tree is that SF can take advantage of the sequential presentation by conducting tests higher in the tree on the first digits. In most cases, categorization can take place with the first two digits regardless of the following digits. In this case, when SF has heard three and four, he can categorize this group as a RUNNING TIME, and it is either a 1-MILE TIME, a ¾-MILE TIME, or a 10,000-meter time. After hearing the third digit, nine, he can then recognize this sequence as a NEAR WORLD

RECORD, and we assume that there is further discrimination around the reference node 351.1. At this node, there are only three potential 1-mile times to choose from (3:49, 3:50, and 3:51). We assume that the first three digits are sorted separately from the decimal digit, and we assume that some structural representation based on reference points is needed for the decimal digit because of some remarks to that effect in the verbal protocols. The power of SF's mnemonic system, as we have characterized it here, is in its ability to derive a unique code.

What happens when another group activates the same category? What happens, for example, when SF hears another near world-record mile time? That category is no longer unique. We suggest that when a final node in the discrimination net is accessed, previously associated groups are *automatically* activated. In order to keep these similar groups distinct at recall, SF encodes the current group in relation to the old group. For example, 3492 is 1/10 sec *faster* than, say 3493. By this discrimination process, SF generates a unique code, even though the abstract code is not unique. In his verbal protocols, SF often reports that some digit groups are encoded in relationship to previous groups. Further, in his after-session recall, these similar groups are reported together without pauses between them.

At this point, it is worth mentioning that many normal subjects use some rudimentary mnemonics in the digit-span task. These mnemonics are typically such things, as "ascending sequence," "odd digits down," "the first two digits sum to the third one," and so on. When normal subjects are able to recall anything at the end of a session, it is invariably these kinds of patterns.[12] Compared to these numerical relation codes, SF's codes are unique. Because these numerical codes are imprecise, they have the additional disadvantage that they are susceptible to interference. They may work once or twice, but with repeated use, they quickly become overworked (i.e., associated with too many digit sequences). In contrast, the probability of getting more than one "near world-record mile time" during a session is very small, and when this does happen, there is evidence that SF automatically differentiates them.

It is instructive at this point to consider numerical codes that do work. Müller (1911, 1913, 1917) studied extensively the skills of Rückle, a mathematics professor, who was skilled at mental calculation and could commit many numbers to memory at a very rapid rate.[13] Rückle had extensive knowledge of numerical properties, and he used these properties (mostly factorizations) to code

---

[12]Fewer than half the college students we have tested can recall anything from a 20-minute session, and those who do recall only one or two groups.

[13]Most of Müller's stimuli were visually presented lists of digits. For example, Rückle could memorize a matrix of 25 digits in about 12 sec, although his auditory digit span at the 1-sec rate was only about 18 digits.

digits into five- or six-digit units. Müller reports the following four examples of Rückle's mnemonics (Müller, 1911, p. 216):

26169 -------------> 26 = 2 × 13; 169 = 13 × 13
451697 ------------> 451 = 11 × 41; 697 = 17 × 41
893047 ------------> 893 = 19 × 47; 047 = 47
286219 ------------> 219 = 3 × 73; log (73) = 1.86

Notice how unique these relations are. Hunter (1962) gives an almost identical picture of Professor Aitkin, the Edinburgh mathematics professor. In both these cases, and in many others in the literature, experts derive unique numerical relations very quickly to serve as mnemonic aids in their mental calculation skill. We point to uniqueness as the critical factor.

Having described the encoding process as a discrimination net, we next describe our *storage* assumptions. We assume that every time a production rule fires, a semantic feature is activated (i.e., stored in short-term memory). In this example, 3492 has activated semantic features corresponding to RUNNING TIME, 1-MILE TIME, NEAR WORLD RECORD, BELOW 3:50, and there are further structural features describing the decimal as NEAR ZERO. We assume that the trace 3492 (not the phonetic features, but the numerical features corresponding to their magnitude) is bound to a semantic structure like that depicted in Fig. 5.9.

Another way to say this is that all these features are stored together in one chunk by virtue of the fact that they are all active in short-term memory and attended to together as a unit; that is, in our model, the binding process is a chunking operation in short-term memory. This chunk can then be recalled by a retrieval process with the structure depicted by Fig. 5.9. This is another theoretical issue: whether mnemonics derive their advantage from storage or retrieval

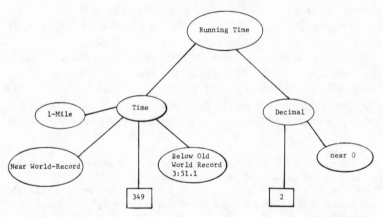

FIG. 5.9. The memory trace for 3492 is bound to a running time semantic structure containing semantic features derived from the discrimination net shown in the previous figure.

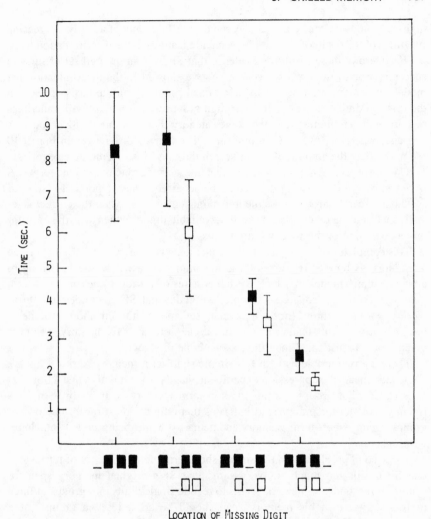

FIG. 5.10.   Time to retrieve a missing digit as a function of the location of the missing digit in the probe. (The location of the missing digit is indicated at the bottom of the figure. Open squares represent three-digit probes and darkened squares represent four-digit probes.) Brackets in the figure represent ± 1 standard deviation, based on 10 or fewer observations.

operations. We argue later that it is the interaction of storage and retrieval that is critical.

At this point, we mention one experimental result that is particularly relevant for our model of the structure of these memory traces. In this experiment after an hour's session, we presented SF with three- and four-digit probes from the session, but with one digit missing, and he had to name the missing digit. The latency data are shown in Fig. 5.10 as a function of the location of the missing digit. The mean latency and the variance are both monotonically decreasing functions of the depth of the missing semantic features in the discrimination tree.

We interpret these results as evidence that SF uses an ordered set of rules to successively narrow down the search. As we showed in the discrimination net model, the mnemonic category is determined primarily on the basis of tests on the first two digits. However, for four-digit groups, the third digit will sometimes be critical in determining the mnemonic category. For example, 5782 is coded as two ages whereas 5732 is a 10-mile time. The latency differences in Fig. 5.10 seem to reflect the amount of active search through SF's mnemonic categories.

The retrospective reports showed that the correct mnemonic category was retrieved before the missing digit could be accessed. These reports also showed systematic search through possible mnemonic categories, when the correct category could not be determined from the available digits, which was the case for probes with one of the first two digits missing.

This completes our analysis of SF's mnemonic coding system. The next issue we address is how SF retrieves these mnemonic codes. It would be wrong to adopt a simple model in which SF holds a set of retrieval cues in short-term memory. To take a concrete example, we claim that SF does not hold "near world-record mile time" (or the equivalent semantic feature) in short-term memory and then use this feature as a retrieval cue at recall. His memory system is much more sophisticated than this, as we hope to show.

There are two problems with this simple short-term memory retrieval model. First, the rehearsal–suppression experiments have proven to our satisfaction that SF's coded digit groups are not in short-term memory. Our analysis of SF's running short-term memory load indicates that only the most recent one or two groups occupy short-term memory momentarily while being coded into long-term memory.

The second problem with the simple short-term memory model of retrieval is that SF recalls too much. If we assume that SF's original memory span for symbols is around seven and he learns to recode single digits into groups of three or four digits, then his memory span should be around seven groups, or a maximum of 28 digits. In fact, because there is additional memory overhead associated with groups, the real memory-span limit is around three or four groups, or 16 digits. But SF's memory-span performance has increased steadily to over 80 digits (22 groups), and there is no sign of a limit. There must be some other mechanism besides the mnemonic coding. In the next section, we describe SF's retrieval structure.

THE RETRIEVAL STRUCTURE

A retrieval structure is a long-term memory structure that is used to make associations with material to be remembered. In effect, it serves the function of storing retrieval cues in addressable locations without having to use short-term memory. The retrieval structure can preserve the order of items to be remembered, although it is more versatile than that because it allows direct retrieval of any identifiable location.

The best example of a retrieval structure is the set of locations used in the method of loci. The way the method of loci works is to associate a list of concrete items with a predetermined set of locations (say the rooms in your house). An interactive mental image is generated successively for each item on the list with some known object in each corresponding location. Then, at recall, the object in each location is used as a retrieval cue to activate the mental image and recall the item to be remembered. The method of loci can be used for ordered recall, for reverse recall, for recall of the nth item, or for recall of any specified set of locations. All that is necessary is to know the locations of the items to be recalled. We assume that the recall mechanism is activation of the interactive links (illustrated earlier for the COW–BALL example), and that the same principle operates for any mnemonic system, such as the peg–word method and the chaining method.

The Verbal Protocols

Most of the details of SF's retrieval structure are revealed in his verbal protocols; Fig. 5.11 illustrates the development of the retrieval structure. In the beginning, like most people, SF simply tried to hold everything in a phonemically coded rehearsal buffer (R). By the second day of practice, however, SF demonstrated the first rudimentary use of a retrieval structure. Instead of holding everything in a rehearsal buffer, he tried to separate one or two groups of three digits each from the rehearsal group and recall these groups while rehearsing the last 4–6 digits. This rudimentary grouping strategy is also typical of normal subjects. The difference between SF and normal subjects is that SF invented a mnemonic (Day 5) and used the retrieval structure to store the mnemonic codes.

After SF invented his mnemonics, this grouping strategy worked well, and he gradually perfected it over the course of the first 30 sessions to the point where he could recall up to 18 digits by coding three groups of four digits each as running times and holding the last six digits in his rehearsal buffer. At this point, SF began to experience real difficulties in keeping the order straight for more than three or four running times. These difficulties are associated with the first plateau in his performance curve (Fig. 5.1, Blocks 8 and 9).

The next important advance came after SF introduced hierarchical organization (Day 32): he used two four-digit groups followed by two three-digit groups, and the rehearsal group. SF's performance improved rapidly as he perfected the use of this hierarchical retrieval structure, in parallel with improvements in his mnemonic system, until he began to experience the same difficulties as before. The second plateau in his performance curve (around Block 22, Fig. 5.1) is associated with difficulties in remembering the order of more than four groups of

First Reported (Session No.)	Retrieval Structures	Number of Digits

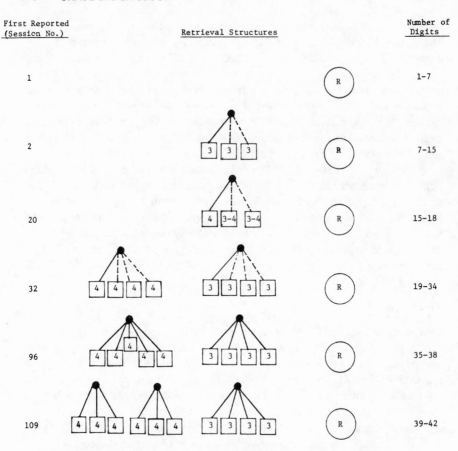

FIG. 5.11.   This graph illustrates the development of SF's retrieval organization. Shown on the left is the session number on which SF first reported the corresponding retrieval structure shown in the center. On the right is shown the range of digits for which the retrieval structure is designed. Each square corresponds to a digit group with number of digits given inside of it. Groups connected by lines to the same node (filled circle) belong to the same supergroup. The circle with R corresponds to the rehearsal group, which consists of four to six digits depending on the sequence length.

four digits followed by more than four groups of three digits. At this point (Day 96), SF tried unsuccessfully to tag the middle item of five groups as a "hitching post" or "peg." Then he finally introduced another level in the hierarchy by breaking these groups up into subgroups (Day 109), and his performance has improved rapidly ever since. SF is now using at least a three-level hierarchy: (1) digits → groups; (2) groups → supergroups; and (3) supergroups → clusters of supergroups; that is, it takes at least three features to locate a group within the hierarchy.

SF is currently averaging around 80 digits, and his grouping structure for 80 digits is illustrated in Fig. 5.12 for a typical trial. This figure represents our best guess about the hierarchical grouping structure, based on several sources of evidence.

The Experimental Evidence

Besides the verbal protocols, there is a great deal of additional evidence that SF uses hierarchical retrieval structures. Probably the most straightforward evidence comes from SF's speech patterns during recall, which almost invariably follow the same pattern. Digit groups are recalled rapidly at a normal rate of speech (about three digits per sec) with pauses between groups (about 2 sec between groups, on average, with longer pauses when he has difficulty remembering). At the end of hierarchical group, however, there is a falling intonation, generally followed by a longer pause.

Pauses, intonation, and stress patterns are well-known indicators of linguistic structures (Halliday, 1967; Pike, 1945). We carried out one study specifically designed to determine how reliably the prosodic features could predict the grouping patterns. This study was carried out before SF invented his mnemonic (Day 3), because after the first few sessions, the grouping patterns were so obvious from the speech patterns. In this study, one experimenter coded only the group boundaries as indicated by the prosodic features in SF's recall without listening to the verbal protocol, and the other experimenter coded the grouping patterns reported by SF in his verbal protocols without listening to recall, and there was virtually perfect agreement.

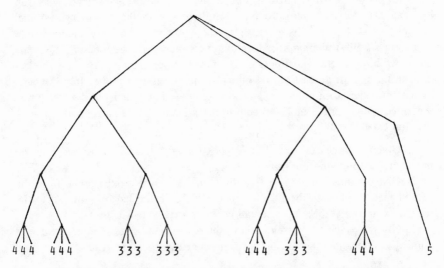

FIG. 5.12. This figure shows our best hypothesis about the hierarchical organization of SF's retrieval structure for 80 digits.

In another study after an hour's session, we presented SF with three- and four-digit groups from that session and asked him to recall as much as he could about that group. SF invariably recalled the mnemonic code he had used, and he often recalled a great deal about the hierarchy, such as which supergroup and where the group was located within the supergroup (first, middle, last). After an hour, SF was almost never able to recall which group preceded or followed the presented group. On rare occasions, SF was able to recall a preceding or following group. but this recall was invariably associated with some specific feature, such as two adjacent 1-mile times.

When SF recalls digits, he generally waits between 30 sec and 2 min after the digits have been presented before he begins to recall. In one study, we asked SF to indicate which digit groups he was thinking about during this interval. We found that SF rehearsed the digit sequence in reverse, supergroup by supergroup; that is, he rehearses the last supergroup, then the next-to-last supergroup, and so on. Within supergroups, he sometimes rehearses in reverse order, but generally he rehearses in forward order. The interesting thing about this experiment is that rehearsal is organized into supergroups.

We ran two experiments to determine if the group size was important for maintaining supergroups. We instructed SF to group all by four's or all by three's, and we found no decrement in performance, although SF did complain about having too much interference. We think this is an important result, because it suggests that the retrieval structure is associated with abstract mnemonic codes and not with some specific size-dependent digit patterns.

We have run several memory-search experiments that reveal, in a quantitative way, the nature of SF's retrieval operations. All these experiments were run between Day 98 and Day 116 on 30-digit lists with the following retrieval structure: 4-4-4-4-3-3-3-5. Three of these experiments were analogous to Sternberg's (1969) scanning-for-location experiment, and we asked SF to locate probes within the retrieval structure. The fourth experiment was to name the last digit in the group, given the first digits in the group as a probe. In all experiments, instead of asking for recall after presenting SF with a list of digits, SF was presented with a probe and we measured his latency. The three scanning-for-location experiments were as follows:

1. Given a three- or four-digit probe from the list, SF had to name the preceding or following group in the list.

2. Given a three-, four-, or five-digit (the rehearsal group) probe from the list, SF had to indicate the location of the probe in the list by pointing to the location within a graphic representation of the retrieval structure.

3. Given a graphis representation of the retrieval structure, the experimenter pointed to a location and SF had to name the corresponding group.

In two of these experiments, the latencies are very fast, and we claim that in these cases, SF uses the probe to directly access the memory trace in long-term

TABLE 5.7
Memory Search Experiments

Experiment	Grouping Structure							
	4	4	4	4	3	3	3	5
Name the last digit in the probe	1.6	1.5	1.7	1.8	2.3	2.2	1.7	2.1
Point to the location of the probe	1.2	1.4	2.0	1.2	1.0	.7	.9	
Name the group pointed to	5.0	9.3	8.9	11.7	8.1	5.1	4.3	2.9
Name the group preceding or			5.4		$\leftrightarrow$		3.3	
following the probe					10.1			

memory. Given all but the last digit in a group, SF can very quickly name the last digit (1.8 sec), and given a probe, SF can quickly point to its location in the retrieval structure (1.2 sec). In both cases, we claim that SF activates the memory trace in long-term memory and, in the one case, retrieves the missing digit, and in the other case, retrieves the location of the probe in the retrieval structure.

In contrast to the fast times associated with direct access, search through the retrieval structure is relatively slow, and further, search times depend on the location of the probe within the retrieval structure. Given a location, it took SF almost 7 sec to name the associated group, and he was considerably slower for groups in the middle of the retrieval structure. Further, when SF had to name the preceding or following group, it took him more than twice as long if the search crossed a hierachical boundary (10.1 versus 4.4 sec).

Table 5.7 compares the latencies of these various experiments as a function of the serial position of the probe. The top two rows give the results of the two direct-access experiments, and the bottom two rows give the results of the search experiments. The bottom row shows the average latencies within each supergroup and average latencies to cross the supergroup boundary. Notice that, compared to the search experiments, the direct-access latencies are fast and independent of the serial position within the retrieval structure.

Up to this point, we have presented evidence that groups are accessed through the hierarchical retrieval structures rather than through direct associations between groups. We next present an essential piece of evidence that these retrieval structures are necessary for SF's memory performance.

Figure 5.13 compares SF's performance with that of two other subjects that we have run for an extended period of time. One subject (triangles) is also a long-distance runner, and we have explicitly trained him to use SF's system. After about 75 hours of practice, he is performing slightly above SF's perfor-

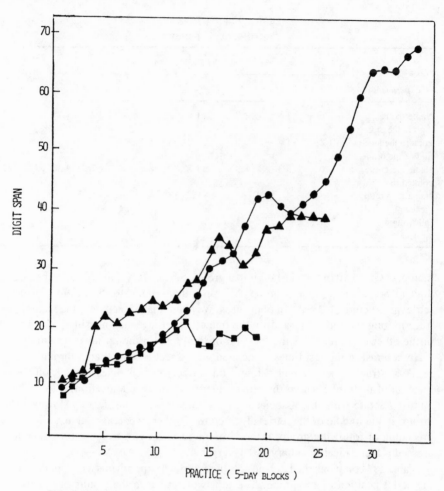

FIG. 5.13. This graph compares SF's learning curve (circles) with two other subjects. One subject (triangles) was explicitly trained to use SF's system, and the other subject (squares) was allowed to develop her own mnemonic.

mance curve,[14] and from all indications he is doing essentially the same thing as SF.

The other subject (squares) was run independently for about 100 hours, and in that time she invented a very elaborate set of mnemonic associations based mainly on days, dates, and times of day. For example, 9365342 = "September third, 1965, at 3:42 P.M." However, this subject never invented a retrieval structure.

---

[14]Part of this subject's initial jump in performance is due to a change in the up-and-down procedure, and part of it is due to the fact that because we explicitly trained him to use SF's system, he avoided the initial trial and error associated with SF's learning.

The difference in performance between this subject and the other two subjects is readily apparent in Fig. 5.13. Her mnemonic associations worked very well, and her performance curve was very similar to SF's until she reached about 18 digits. At that point, she showed no further improvements, and she stayed at that asymptote for several weeks and eventually quit due to loss of motivation.

The difference between this subject and SF is quite apparent from their protocols. Basically, this subject codes digit groups into mnemonics according to how they occur to her during presentation, on the basis of how the digits fall into good groups. In contrast, SF always decides beforehand how he will group the digits, and he tries never to deviate from his grouping structure. It seems apparent from the protocols that this subject's mnemonics are as good (i.e., uniquely determined) as SF's mnemonics, as well as Rückle's numerical-relation mnemonics.[15] But because she has not associated her mnemonic codes with a retrieval structure, her mnemonic codes are stored in long-term memory without a means of retrieving them in their proper order. Without a retrieval structure, she has to rely on short-term memory to remember the order, and she can only remember the order of about four independent groups. Hence, we take this study as evidence that a retrieval structure is necessary if memory-span performance is to exceed the limited ability of short-term memory to store the order of retrieval cues.

Retrieval in Skilled Memory

At this point, we emphasize the second characteristic of skilled memory: *Expert memory involves organized and direct retrieval from long-term memory*. There are two parts to this principle. First, experts seem invariably to know when to apply knowledge in a given task, whereas it is characteristic of novices that they often fail to apply what they know. In the literature, this characteristic has been demonstrated by de Groot (1966) for expert and novice chess players, and by Jeffries, Turner, Polson, and Atwood (this volume) for expert and novice programmers. In SF's case, we note that he can rapidly generate his mnemonic codes, and quickly and systematically search his semantic memory for his after-session recall.[16]

The second part of the principle is that, during the performance of some skilled task, experts store intermediate knowledge states for future reference in directly accessible locations in long-term memory. Chiesi, Spilich, and Voss (1979) have found that baseball fans are better able to remember sequences of baseball events because they understand the game better, which is to say, they relate the events to the game's goal structure. In SF's case, he invented a structure that we have called the *retrieval structure* for storing retrieval cues for

---

[15]Müller (1911) also reports evidence of hierarchical grouping by Rückle when he memorized long lists of digits.

[16]When SF has trouble recalling a group, he usually invokes the strategy of systematically searching semantic memory with the generate-and-test procedure.

his mnemonic codes, and this allowed him to bypass the limits of short-term memory.

It is this idea of a retrieval structure that we believe has important implications for a theory of skilled memory. Up until very recently, cognitive theories have generally assumed that short-term memory is the primary storage system for intermediate results in many mental tasks, and that everything else is stored in long-term memory. However, cognitive theorists are beginning to question this assumption. Both Baddeley (1976) and Shiffrin (1976) have questioned the role of short-term memory in complex tasks. Shiffrin, for example, makes the point that short-term memory simply does not have the capacity to store enough information to do anything useful in a complex task. Rather, intermediate knowledge states in long-term memory are tagged with the current context, which can then serve as a retrieval cue. Shiffrin has labeled this knowledge *temporal-contextual information*.

We agree with Shiffrin that directly retrievable knowledge states operate all the time in normal memory, and they allow people to build up sufficient context to do things like comprehend connected discourse, read text, solve problems, etc. The buildup of intermediate knowledge states undoubtedly underlies the phenomenon of warmup in cognitive tasks; that is, it simply takes time to search out knowledge states in semantic memory and build up enough *directly accessible* information to perform efficiently.

This problem is especially critical in skilled memory, where there is a premium on *rapid* access to large numbers of intermediate knowledge states. One of the intriguing aspects of our work is that it suggests that skilled memory involves rapid generation and direct retrieval of intermediate knowledge states. Later, we discuss more fully the importance of rapid access to intermediate knowledge states in skill.

There are several cases in the cognitive skills literature where our theory is relevant. First, current explanations of mental calculation experts in the literature stress that these people avoid the heavy memory overhead involved in mental computation in two ways: (1) by acquisition of special procedures that reduce memory load; and (2) by relying on recoding of digits into larger groups of meaningful numbers. For example, Bidder, the famous British mental calculation expert of the last century, was said to have recognized all four-digit combinations as "old friends." A three-digit number for a mental calculation expert is supposedly as familiar to him as single digits and familiar numbers, such as addresses and phone numbers, are to normal people.

In our preliminary analysis of a mental calculation expert, we have verified that these findings are true. However, these mechanisms are not sufficient. There is still a substantial memory overhead involved in storing and retrieving the results of intermediate computations. During a complex problem, intermediate computations must be temporarily stored, and then, at the right moment, they must be retrieved rapidly when needed. There is not enough time to recompute these intermediate products or to search for them, because these processes are too costly both in time and in the interference that they generate. Intermediate computations must be directly accessible—retrieval structures are necessary.

Second, in the chess literature, it has been a puzzle as to why chess masters have such good memories for chess positions. It has been known for some time that chess masters can remember almost an entire chess position after a brief (5 sec) glance at the chess board (de Groot, 1966), and Chase and Simon (1973) found that when they counted familiar, chunked patterns rather than single pieces, the master's span still exceeded his short-term memory capacity.

Finally, in a series of interference studies, Charness (1976) demonstrated that all these chess patterns, except perhaps for the last one, are not in short-term memory. It seems clear that these chess patterns are stored in a retrieval structure.

We might speculate that retrieval structures for intermediate knowledge states are particularly useful in problem solving. Current views of skill in chess, for example, place emphasis on the pattern-recognition system—our first principle; that is, the central mechanism that leads search through the problem space is the recognition of patterns in long-term memory, because they are associated with evaluations and procedural knowledge about good moves.

We suggest that a critical aspect of search in problem solving is the ability to store these intermediate knowledge states in a direct and rapid-access retrieval structure. As search proceeds through the problem space, we suggest that an important component of skill is the ability to reactivate these intermediate states *directly*. This ability is particularly useful when search involves backtracking to previous knowledge states. It is also apparent in another interesting way: when experts demonstrate their reconstructive abilities, and when they demonstrate their ability to generate extensive retrospective reports.

To summarize thus far, we have claimed that short-term memory does not have the capacity to store enough temporary knowledge to be useful in the performance of complex cognitive tasks. Rather, intermediate knowledge states are stored in directly addressable locations in a long-term memory structure that we have called a retrieval structure. Further, we have claimed that direct and rapid access to these intermediate knowledge states is characteristic of skilled performance in cognitive tasks. In short, there are good theoretical reasons for postulating the *usefulness* of retrieval structures.

We have not, however, discussed the mechanisms underlying retrieval. How is it possible to have direct access to long-term knowledge structures? This problem has been the central issue in recent reevaluations of the levels-of-processing literature (Jacoby & Craik, 1979; Nelson, 1979; Tulving, 1979). The original levels-of-processing claim was that meaningful codes are more memorable because they are processed at a deeper level, and most of the endeavor was an attempt to define what is meant by deeper. However conceived, most of the original emphasis was on encoding operations. But it has gradually become apparent that retrieval operations, are critical, and the current consensus is that meaningful associations and mnemonics are memorable because they can generate retrieval cues that reinstate the encoding operations. This is what is meant by the encoding–retrieval interaction, that retrieval cues should match or reactivate the original encoding operations as closely as possible.

There is still debate over whether it is necessary to postulate good versus poor encoding operations. It is consistent with our theory that encoding operations are critical, that the memory trace must be bound to a semantic structure, and that redundant interactive contextual features are important. However, we agree with the current levels-of-processing literature that retrieval operations that reactivate the original encoding operations are also critical.

At this point, let us raise a theoretical problem. How is it possible to use the same retrieval structure over and over? What happens to previous groups bound to the same structure? If we assume that the retrieval cues derived from the retrieval structure are sufficient to access the current digit group, it is not clear from traditional theories of long-term memory how the same retrieval cue can reliably discriminate earlier memory traces bound to the same cue. Our analysis of our subjects' encodings shows no sensitivity to the current context that would allow it to serve as a discriminating retrieval cue. Without any hard evidence of how the current group is discriminated, we can only speculate. We believe that the most recent memory trace associated with the retrieval structure overwrites the previous group, is tagged as most recent, or is discriminated by a strength cue. Our subjects report that they actively seek to speed up their retrieval as this information appears to decay fairly rapidly within a few minutes, and intrusion errors from the same location on a previous trial are not uncommon.

Although we have not yet specified retrieval assumptions in our computer simulation model, we conceive of them in the following way. Recall that during encoding, we assumed that SF activates a set of semantic features that specify, say, a "near world-record 1-mile time" (Fig. 5.9). In short-term memory, SF attends simultaneously to these semantic features and the grouped set of digits (3492), and this chunking operation is the mechanism that serves to bind the memory trace to these semantic features.

Our retrieval assumption is that the current location in the retrieval structure is used to activate traces in long-term memory that are associated with the current location. Notice in Fig. 5.12 that the retrieval structure is in the form of a hierarchical tree, which is a very efficient sorting structure. We assume that every branch in the tree is specified by a feature. Thus, in the tree structure in Fig. 5.12, it takes a maximum of four features to uniquely specify one of 22 groups. It is this set of features that we assume is activated during encoding and bound to the memory trace. In Fig. 5.14, we have illustrated the memory trace with the retrieval structure bound to it. The location is specified by a set of features (f_i) linked to the LOCATION node.

Notice that we have created links primarily between the running time structure and the location in the retrieval structure. Although there is virtually nothing in the verbal protocols about how memory traces are associated with the retrieval

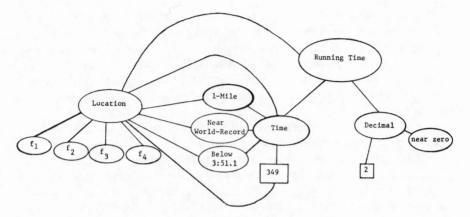

FIG. 5.14. A link-node structural representation of the full memory trace for 3492. The memory trace is bound to the hierarchical semantic structure for a running time (shown previously in Fig. 5.9) and the featural representation for the location in the retrieval structure is linked to the running-time structure.

structure, we must account for the major results, namely that SF remembers mnemonic codes; and his retrieval structure seems to work well only for the particular mnemonic codes that he has practiced (running times, ages, years, patterns). We have created a direct link from the retrieval structure node to the memory trace because SF very occasionally remembers uncoded sequences. The power of the retrieval structure, however, must derive from the nature of the interactive links between the mnemonic codes and the locational features of the retrieval structure. As yet, however, we do not have any evidence about the nature of these links.

The featural representation of the retrieval structure accounts for the major types of transposition errors that occur during recall, namely transposition of groups within a supergroup, transposition of the same position across two adjacent supergroups, and intrusion errors of a group from a previous trial (usually the prior trial) in the same location.

There is evidence that SF stores more information than simply the association between the group and the retrieval features. Most commonly, SF reports noticing relationships between adjacent groups, such as a pair of 1-mile times even though they may be given very different mnemonic codes (e.g., ''near world-record mile time'' and ''fair mile time for a warmup''). (For the case of identical mnemonic codes, see our earlier discussion.) SF almost invariably notes the relationship of order, such as, the first mile time was faster than the second in the pair. Another common report is that, given a mile time followed by a 2-mile time, the mile time is thought of as the time for the first half of the 2-mile time. These facts are stored as part of the memory trace and can serve as redundant retrieval cues as well as serve to determine the order.

We account for these reports as follows. First, because we have found that SF's short-term memory span includes the current group plus the previous group, we suppose that he automatically notices matches and other relations in short-term memory (e.g., two identical 1-MILE TIME features), and this noticing operation in effect binds the previous group to the current group. This noticing operation also sets up expectations for noticing strings of categories (e.g., all 1-mile times).

Up to this point, we have described the two most important mechanisms underlying SF's memory skill: the mnemonic associations and the retrieval structure. These, however, are still not sufficient to fully explain SF's performance. The problem is that both of these systems were essentially complete within the first 100 hours of practice. There have been minor improvements, but all major revisions took place within the first 100 hours. Yet SF continues to show steady improvement through 250 hours of practice and there is no sign of an asymptote. Something else must be happening.

ON THE SPEEDUP OF ENCODING AND RETRIEVAL OPERATIONS

We have reached the point where SF's verbal reports are of little direct help. Following Ericsson and Simon's (1980) theory of verbal reports, we suppose that SF is able to report the contents of short-term memory. Thus, SF is able to report semantic features and other knowledge states that become activated, but he cannot tell us where these came from or how they were activated; that is, mental structures and processes themselves are not directly observable, but only their results that appear as knowledge states in short-term memory.

We are at the point, we believe, where we need to know something about the details of SF's mental structures. We know from SF's verbal reports that very few new rules were added to the mnemonic system or the retrieval structure after 100 hours of practice. We need to know how these existing rules change with practice.

We have several lines of evidence that SF's coding operations have speeded up with practice. In one experiment, we were interested in obtaining some detailed timing data, so instead of reading digits to SF, we presented him with a computer-controlled video display. In this experiment, SF controlled the rate at which he received the digits by pressing a button each time he wanted a digit, and we measured the time between button pushes.

We have taken these timing data on SF several times over a 2-year period. As one might expect, SF pressed buttons very rapidly (200–300 msec/digit) until the end of a group was reached, and all the pauses occurred between groups. In Fig. 5.15, we show the pause time between groups as a function of the size of the list.

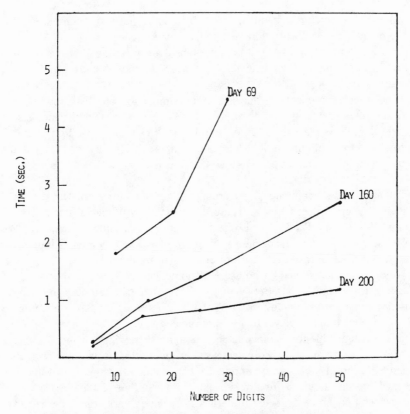

FIG. 5.15.   The average time that SF takes between groups as a function of the
length of the digit sequences. The parameter is the level of practice, which is
spaced over almost a 2-year period. The measure plotted is the average time SF
paused between visually presented digit groups when he controlled the presentation of digits. This time is virtually identical to the average time interval between
the presentation of the first digit in one group and the first digit in the next group,
with the minimal time to press keys for intermediate digits subtracted.

These data are shown for Days 69, 160, and 200, and SF's span on those days
was 26, 69, and 79 digits, respectively.

First, pause time increases with the size of the list. This result confirms what
has been known for many years, namely that longer lists take more time per item
to learn (Woodworth, 1938, p. 21); that is, there is more learning overhead with
larger lists.

Notice that over a 2-year period, SF's coding time has shown a very substantial decrease. Further, the last set of data (Day 200) shows much less of an
increase in pause time for larger lists. It is as if there is almost no overhead in
learning time for larger lists. We speculate that with practice, possibly the hierar-

chical retrieval structure is being displaced by a flat retrieval structure, analogous to the method of loci, with more distinctive location cues.

Finally, notice that with practice, the absolute encoding times are falling below 1 sec, a time that we believe approaches the range of short-term memory operations.

In another experiment, we have a direct comparison of SF's encoding and retrieval times, spaced 1 year apart, with those of several other mnemonists on the 50-digit matrix mentioned earlier. In this task, SF studies a 50-digit matrix of 13 rows and four columns until he has learned it, and then he is asked to recall the matrix and then to report various parts of the matrix, such as a given row, column, or a zigzag diagonal.

In Table 5.8, we compare SF's learning and retrieval times for Days 111 and 211 with several other subjects. These data on the two famous mnemonists S (Luria, 1968) and VP (Hunt & Love, 1972) are reported in the literature. We have also run this experiment on a subject who has had mnemonics training,[17] and we ran three normal subjects for comparative purposes.

Note that all the subjects who use mnemonics are comparable, both in their encoding times and their retrieval times, despite wide differences in their reported mnemonics. We note in passing that Luria's S claimed to be scanning a visual image, but his retrieval times seem inconsistent with such a strategy. His times are comparable to the other subjects who are retrieving mnemonic codes.

Mnemonics training markedly decreased encoding time (relative to normals), and in SF's case, a year's worth of practice has produced a large improvement in his encoding times, which are now substantially faster than all the other subjects. There does not, however, seem to be nearly as much variation in the retrieval times with practice.

In Fig. 5.16, we compare data on SF's learning time with Rückle's data, reported by Müller (1911). As far as we know, Rückle's data are by far the fastest learning times ever reported in the literature for digits (Woodworth, 1938, p. 21), and after 2 years of practice, SF's learning times seem comparable. As we noted earlier, Rückle's times are for simultaneous visual presentation, and SF's performance is far superior to Rückle's for fast auditory presentations.

We mention one final experiment on SF's coding times. In one of our early experiments, we presented SF with digits at a rapid rate (three digits/sec), and we found that SF was unable to code at this rate and his span dropped back to eight or nine digits, and for over a year and a half, SF was unable to code at these fast rates. However, we have found recently that SF is able to code one or two groups of three digits each at the fastest rates (about five digits/sec) and hold about five digits in a rehearsal buffer, for a total span of about 11 digits.

---

[17]This subject uses a standard mnemonic device picked up from the Lorayne and Lucas book (1974), for converting digits to phonemes, phonemes to concrete words, and concrete words to visual images, which he then links up via interactive images.

TABLE 5.8
Study and Recall Time (sec)
SF, Two Mnemonists, Subject with Mnemonics Training, and Three Normal Subjects on Luria's 50-Digit Matrix

	SF	SF (1 year later)	Mnemonists		Subject with Mnemonics Training	Normal Subjects		
			Luria's S	Hunt & Love's VP	AB	S1	S2	S3
Study time	187	81	180	390	222	1240	685	715
Recall time								
Entire matrix	43	57	40	42	51	95	42	51
Third column	41	58	80	58	56	117	42	78
Second column	41	46	25	39	40	110	31	40
Second column up	47	30	30	40	54	83	46	63
Zig zag diagonal	64	38	35		52	107	78	94

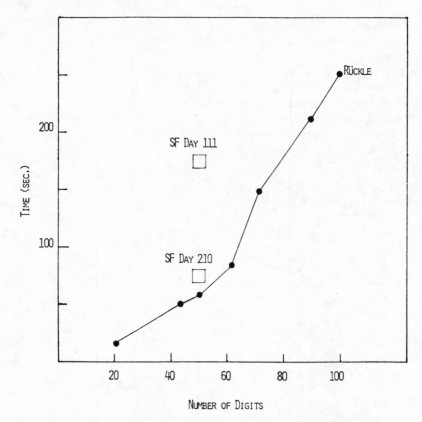

FIG. 5.16.   A comparison between SF (open squares) and Professor Rückle (circles). Shown is the time required to memorize visually presented digits as a function of number of presented digits. SF's data are taken from the experiment on the Luria-matrices (Table 5.8), and Rückle's data are derived from Müller (1911).

This set of experiments, taken together, provides good evidence that SF's encoding operations have speeded up considerably over the course of 2 years of practice. Although we have no data to confirm it as yet, we believe that SF's retrieval processes have also speeded up. In terms of absolute magnitudes, we think it is important that SF's encoding times and recognition times (experiment on missing digit) are falling below 1 sec, which brings them into the range of short-term memory operations.

This brings us to our third principle of skilled memory: *Skilled memory involves rapid storage and retrieval of intermediate knowledge states in long-term memory.*

Implications for a Theory of Skilled Memory

During the course of our analysis of SF, we have outlined three principles of skilled memory. The first principle—that skilled memory involves knowledge structures in semantic memory—is already well-documented in the literature. It is the second and third principles that we believe are important additional contributions to our understanding of skilled memory. These principles say that experts store and retrieve intermediate knowledge structures, and that they do it *fast*.

The key to skilled memory performance, we believe, is in the ability to rapidly store and reaccess intermediate knowledge states. This property is very useful because it relieves the burden on short-term memory, which normally serves the purpose of holding knowledge structures in an active (i.e., directly accessible) state for ready access. Practice causes these storage and retrieval operations to speed up to the point where, on an absolute scale, access times are less than a second, bringing skilled memory operations within the range of useful speeded skills.

The advantage of short-term memory is that a small set of information is directly accessible without search. Intermediate knowledge structures require skill in the sense that future situations, in which this information is relevant and should be retrieved, are anticipated at the time of encoding and associations are formed with relevant retrieval cues for those future situations. Skilled memory is thus only possible in situations where future retrieval can be anticipated. Short-term memory, on the other hand, does not require such anticipation of future use and is therefore a characteristic of novice performance. By extensive practice, coordination is developed between encoding processes and retrieval processes. This constitutes skilled memory.

This rapidly accessible intermediate knowledge structure in effect provides the expert with a large memory system that has the properties of short-term memory. The advantages are enormous. It frees up short-term memory for other processes. Direct accessibility reduces search, which costs time, takes up processing capacity, and dredges up interfering knowledge states. Finally, it allows the expert to organize and execute more complex mental operations than would otherwise be impossible with the small capacity of short-term memory. No wonder the reported feats of memory-based experts seem so astounding to the average person.

So far, we have described what we believe accounts for SF's continuing practice effects: a gradual speedup in his encoding and retrieval operations. But we have not said *how* this is possible. Although we have virtually no data on this problem, we speculate that SF is gradually learning a distinctive set of interactive links between his retrieval locations and his mnemonic codes (Fig. 5.14). These links are unique to each retrieval location, and their interactions with the mnemonic codes uniquely determine which mnemonic code is associated with the location.

We are reasoning by analogy with the method of loci, although there is a big difference: There are rich introspections about interactive features with visual imagery, whereas SF can report nothing about these numerical codes. The method of loci is also a much more time-consuming mnemonic (we estimate a minimum of 3 sec per image). Nevertheless, we believe that the principle is the same. As one learns to use the method of loci, one learns a set of distinctive locations, and one learns to use a set of distinctive interactive links between locations and objects to be remembered. At recall, when a practiced expert thinks of a location, he knows how to regenerate an image. In effect, at retrieval, he has learned how to reproduce as good a match as possible with the encoding operations. This is the encoding–retrieval interaction principle derived from the levels-of-processing literature, and the constructability principle discussed by Norman and Bobrow (1979).

In principle, our learning assumption is fairly simple. With practice, SF's encoding processes become faster and more reliable, and the links between his mnemonic codes and his retrieval structure are strengthened, resulting in more direct, reliable, and faster retrieval.

Although we have no evidence about the nature of the learning mechanism, the consequences of such a mechanism seem clear. During encoding, more time is left for other processes, such as noticing additional relationships among mnemonic groups. During recall, there is a smaller probability of a retrieval failure, and faster and more direct retrieval produces less retrieval interference. There is some evidence in the protocols that this might be the case, and this is one area where some experimental effort is needed.

CONCLUDING REMARKS

There are two aspects of this study that we think are important. First, the sheer magnitude of the memory feat is something that has never been accomplished before. As far as we know, SF's memory span is by far the largest ever reported in the literature. We were able to observe the development of this skill in a subject without any special memory abilities, and we were further able to train SF's system in another subject. Thus, we take this result as clear evidence that no special abilities are necessary for the development of memory skill. Practice, in conjunction with an appropriate mnemonic system and retrieval structure, is all that is necessary for the development of memory skill, and there is apparently no limit to improvements in memory skill with practice.

The second aspect of this study that we want to comment on is the implications of our results for a cognitive theory of skilled memory. Because we were able to observe the acquisition of SF's memory skill, we could analyze the underlying cognitive mechanisms, and we outlined what we thought were the three most essential components of that skill.

The most interesting implication of our results is that skilled memory seems to require rapid access to a large number of intermediate knowledge states, allowing the memory expert to bypass the limits of short-term memory. We propose that the traditional view by current cognitive theory that short-term memory is the storage mechanism for intermediate knowledge states must be reconceptualized. Short-term memory simply does not have the necessary capacity to handle the large number of intermediate knowledge states that are needed for skilled memory performance in some domain.

We have tried to sketch out the properties of a memory system that holds these intermediate knowledge states:[18] (1) Intermediate knowledge states are semantic structures in long-term memory; (2) they are stored in directly accessible locations in a retrieval structure, which is also in long-term memory; and (3) storage and retrieval operations in the retrieval structure are fast enough to bypass (or at least augment) short-term memory. Rapid access to such a large, versatile memory system allows the cognitive system of the expert to use complex operations that would not be possible using only a limited-capacity short-term memory. This is one reason why expert performance in semantically rich domains appears to be qualitatively superior to that of the novice.

ACKNOWLEDGMENTS

This research was supported by Contract N00014-79-C-0215 with the Advanced Research Projects Agency of the Office of the Secretary of Defense, which is monitored by the Office of Naval Research. We are grateful to J. R. Anderson, S. Faloon, and M. W. Schustack for comments on an earlier draft.

REFERENCES

Anderson, J. R., & Reder, L. M. An elaborative processing explanation of depth of processing. In L. S. Cermak & F. I. M. Craik (Eds.), *Levels of processing in human memory*. Hillsdale, N.J.: Lawrence Erlbaum Associates, 1979, 385–403.

Bachelder, B. L., & Denny, M. R. A theory of intelligence: I. Span and the complexity of stimulus control. *Intelligence*, 1977(a), *1*, 127–150.

Bachelder, B. L., & Denny, M. R. A theory of intelligence: II. The role of span in a variety of intellectual tasks. *Intelligence*, 1977(b), *1*, 237–256.

Baddeley, A. D. *The psychology of memory*. New York: Basic Books, 1976.

Baddeley, A. D., & Hitch, G. Working memory. In G. H. Bower (Ed.), *The psychology of learning and motivation* (Vol. 8), 1974, 47–90.

Bower, G. H. Mental imagery and associative learning. In L. W. Gregg (Ed.), *Cognition in learning and memory*. New York: Wiley, 1972.

Broadbent, D. A. The magical number seven after fifteen years. In A. Kennedy & A. Wilkes (Eds.), *Studies in long-term memory*. New York: Wiley, 1975.

---

[18]A good name for such a memory system is "working memory," but this term has traditionally been used to describe the temporary knowledge states that have the properties of short-term memory (Baddeley, 1976, Chapter 8; Klatzky, 1980, Chapter 5). This term is derived from the prevailing view that the intermediate knowledge states needed to perform cognitive tasks are stored in short-term memory.

Brown, J. Some tests of the decay theory of immediate memory. *Quarterly Journal of Experimental psychology*, 1958, *10*, 12–21.

Bryan, W. L., & Harter, N. *Psychological Review*, 1899, *6*, 345–375.

Charness, N. Memory for chess positions: Resistence to interference. *Journal of Experimental Psychology: Human Learning and Memory*, 1976, *2*, 641–653.

Chase, W. G., & Chi, M. T. H. Cognitive skill: Implications for spatial skill in large-scale environments. In J. Harvey (Ed.), *Cognition, social behavior, and the environment*. Potomac, Maryland: Lawrence Erlbaum Associates, 1980.

Chase, W. G., & Simon, H. A. Perception in chess. *Cognitive Psychology*, 1973, *4*, 55–81.

Chiesi, H. L., Spilich, G. J., & Voss, J. F. Acquisition of domain-related information in relation to high and low domain knowledge. *Journal of Verbal Learning and Verbal Behavior*, 1979, *18*, 257–273.

de Groot, A. D. Perception and memory versus thought: Some old ideas and recent findings. In B. Kleinmuntz (Ed.), *Problem solving: Research, method, and theory*. New York: Wiley, 1966.

Ericsson, K. A., & Simon, H. A. Verbal reports as data. *Psychological Review*, 1980, *87*, 215–251.

Gates, A. I., & Taylor, G. A. An experimental study of the nature of improvement resulting from practice in a mental function. *Journal of Educational Psychology*, 1925, *16*, 583–592.

Halliday, M. A. K. *Intonation and grammar in British english*. The Hague: Mouton, 1967.

Hatano, G., & Osawa, K. Digit span of grand experts in abacus-derived mental computation. Paper presented at the Third Noda conference on cognitive science, 1980.

Hunt, E., & Love, T. How good can memory be? In A. W. Melton & E. Martin (Eds.), *Coding processes in human memory*. Washington, D.C.: Winston, 1972.

Hunter, I. M. L. An exceptional talent for calculative thinking. *British Journal of Psychology*, 1962, *53*, 243–258.

Hunter, I. M. L. Mental calculation. In P. C. Wason & P. N. Johnson–Laird (Eds.), *Thinking and Reasoning*. Baltimore: Penguin, 1968.

Jacoby, L. L., & Craik, F. I. M. Effects of elaboration of processing at encoding and retrieval: Trace distinctiveness and recovery of initial context. In L. S. Cermak & F. I. M. Craik (Eds.), *Levels of processing and human memory*. Hillsdale, N.J.: Lawrence Erlbaum Associates, 1979.

Jeffries, R., Turner, A. A., Polson, P. G., & Atwood, M. E. The processes involved in designing software. In J. R. Anderson (Ed.), *Cognitive Skills and their Acquisition*. Hillsdale, N.J.: Lawrence Erlbaum Associates, 1981.

Klatzky, R. L. *Human memory: Structures and processes, Second ed.*, San Francisco: W. H. Freeman & Co., 1980.

Levy, B. A. Vocalization and suppression effects in sentence memory. *Journal of Verbal Learning and Verbal Behavior*, 1975, *14*, 304–316.

Lorayne, H., & Lucas, J. *The memory book*, New York: Ballantine books, 1974.

Luria, A. R. *The mind of a mnemonist*, New York: Avon, 1968.

Martin, P. R., & Fernberger, S. W. Improvement in memory span. *American Journal of Psychology*, 1929, *41*, 91–94.

Miller, G. A. The magical number seven, plus or minus two. *Psychological Review*, 1956, *63*, 81–97.

Mitchell, F. D. Mathematical prodigies. *American Journal of Psychology*, 1907, *18*, 61–143.

Müller, G. E. Zur Analyse der Gedachtnistatigkeit und des Vorstellungsverlaufes: Teil I. *Zeitschrift fur Psychologie, Erganzungsband 5*, 1911.

Müller, G. E. Zur Analyse der Gedachtnistatigkeit und des Vorstellungsverlaufes: Teil III. *Zeitschrift fur Psychologie, Erganzungsband 8*, 1913.

Müller, G. E. Zur Analyse der Gedachtnistatigkeit und des Vorstellungsverlaufes: Teil II. *Zeitschrift fur Psychologie, Erganzungsband 9*, 1917.

Nelson, D. L. Remembering pictures and words: Appearance, significance, and name. In L. S.

Cermak & F. I. M. Craik (Eds.), *Levels of processing in human memory*. Hillsdale, N.J.: Lawrence Erlbaum Associates, 1979, 45-76.

Newell, A., & Simon, H. A. *Human problem solving*. Englewood Cliffs, N.J.: Prentice-Hall, 1972.

Norman, D. A., & Bobrow, D. G. An intermediate stage in memory retrieval. *Cognitive Psychology*, 1979, *11*, 107-123.

Oberly, H. S. A comparison of the spans of 'attention' and memory. *American Journal of Psychology*, 1928, *40*, 295-302.

Paivio, A. *Imagery and verbal processes*. New York: Holt, Reinhart & Winston, Inc., 1971.

Peterson, L. R., & Peterson, M. J. Short-term retention of individual items. *Journal of Experimental Psychology*, 1959, *58*, 193-198.

Pike, K. *The intonation of American english*. Ann Arbor: Univ. of Michigan Press, 1945.

Shiffrin, R. M. Capacity limitations in information processing, attention, and memory. In W. K. Estes (Ed.), *Handbook of learning and cognitive process* (Vol. 4). Hillsdale, N.J.: Lawrence Erlbaum Associates, 1976, 177-236.

Simon, H. A., & Gilmartin, K. A simulation of memory for chess positions. *Cognitive Psychology*, 1973, *5*, 29-46.

Stein, B. S., & Bransford, J. D. Constraints on effective elaborations: Effect of precision and subject generation. *Journal of Verbal Learning and Verbal Behavior*, 1979, *18*, 769-778.

Sternberg, S. Memory scanning: Mental processes revealed by reaction-time experiments. *American Scientist*, 1969, *57*, 421-457.

Tulving, E. Relation between encoding specificity and levels of processing. In L. S. Cermak & F. I. M. Craik (Eds.), *Levels of processing in human memory*. Hillsdale, N.J.: Lawrence Erlbaum Associates, 1979, 405-428.

Wickelgren, W. A. Size of rehearsal group and short-term memory. *Journal of Experimental Psychology*, 1964, *68*, 413-419.

Williams, M. D. *Retrieval from very long-term memory*. Unpublished doctoral dissertation. University of California, San Diego, 1976.

Woodworth, R. S. *Experimental Psychology*. New York: Henry Holt & Co., 1938.

Yates, F. A. *The art of memory*. London: Rutledge & Kegan Paul, 1966.

6 Acquisition of Problem-Solving Skill

John R. Anderson
Carnegie-Mellon University

James G. Greeno
University of Pittsburgh

Paul J. Kline and David M. Neves
Carnegie-Mellon University

INTRODUCTION

This chapter presents some recent explorations we have made in the domain of learning to solve geometry proof problems. The background of these explorations consisted of two research programs: one investigating general principles of learning and the other investigating the nature of problem-solving skill in geometry. We have been conducting these two programs relatively independently since about 1976, but both programs have used versions of Anderson's (1976) ACT production system as a computational formalism. Our investigations of learning have included a discussion of general assumptions about learning and design issues (Anderson, Kline, & Beasley, 1980) and an analysis of prototype formation (Anderson, Kline, & Beasley, 1979). Our studies of geometry problem solving have included an analysis of forms of knowledge required for successful performance (Greeno, 1978), a discussion of goal representation (Greeno, 1976), and a discussion of schematic knowledge involved in planning (Greeno, Magone, & Chaiklin, 1979). The knowledge required to solve proof problems is moderately complex, but because its structure has been studied in some detail, it serves as a feasible target for a theoretical analysis of learning. In our investigations, we have found ways to extend both the previous analysis of learning and the previous analysis of problem-solving skill significantly.

The chapter is organized into five major sections and a summary. Each of the five major sections is devoted to a different aspect of our analysis of proof skills in geometry and their acquisition. The first section presents an analysis of how a student searches for a proof in geometry after he has acquired his basic skills. This provides a basic framework within which to understand each of the types of learning that we then discuss in the remaining four sections. The second section is concerned with what we call *text learning*. It is concerned with what the student directly encodes from the text and, more importantly, the processes that use this direct encoding to guide the problem solving. The third section is concerned with a process that we call *subsumption*, a means by which the student encodes new information into existing knowledge structures. Fourth, we discuss the processes of knowledge compilation by which knowledge is transformed from its initial encoded form, which is declarative, to a more effective procedural form. The final major section discusses how practice serves to tune and optimize the skill so that the proof search is performed more successfully.

The empirical information used in this research came from a number of sources. First, a 14-year-old student agreed to study geometry with our supervision and observation. This student, to whom we refer as subject R, met with one or two of us on quite a regular basis for 30 sessions covering 2 months. In each session, lasting for about 45 minutes, R read sections of a geometry textbook and worked problems from the text, thinking aloud as he proceeded. This work done by R was his only study of geometry; his mathematics work in school was on algebra, and this represented accelerated instruction for him. We also had access to a set of three interviews obtained from a 14-year-old student who was beginning to work on geometry as his regular school mathematics study. The other major source of information was a set of interviews obtained from six students who were taking a regular course in geometry. These interviews were obtained on an approximately weekly basis throughout the course.

A MODEL OF THE SKILL UNDERLYING PROOF GENERATION

Most successful attempts at proof generation can be divided into two major episodes—an episode in which a student attempts to find a plan for the proof and an episode in which the student translates that plan into an actual proof. The first stage we call *planning* and the second *execution*. It is true that actual proof-generation behavior often involves alternation back and forth between the two modes—with the student doing a little planning, writing some proof, running into trouble, planning some more, writing some more proof, and so on. Still we believe that planning exists as a logically and empirically separable stage of proof generation. Moreover, we believe that planning is the more significant aspect and the aspect that is more demanding of learning. Execution, while not necessarily trivial, is more "mechanical."

It is also the case that planning tends to pass without comment from the student. (We had one subject who preferred to pass through this stage banging his hands on his forehead.) However, we have tried to open this stage to analysis through the gathering of verbal protocols. These protocols indicate a lot of systematic goings-on that seem to fit under the title of planning.

A plan, in the sense we are using it here, is an outline for action—the action in this case being proof execution. We believe that the plan students emerge with is a specification of a set of geometric rules that allows one to get from the givens of the problem, through intermediate levels of statements, to the to-be-proved statement. We call such a plan a *proof tree*. This idea about the general nature of a plan is consistent with other discussions of planning such as Greeno, Magone, and Chaiklin (1979); Newell and Simon (1972); and Sacerdoti (1977).

Figure 6.1 illustrates an example geometry problem (a) and a proof tree (b). In the tree, the goal to prove two angles congruent leads to the subgoal of proving the triangles $\triangle XVZ$ and $\triangle WVY$ congruent. This goal is achieved by the side–angle–side (SAS) postulate. The first side $\overline{VX} \cong \overline{VW}$ is found directly from the givens. Because these sides form an isosceles triangle, they also imply $\angle VXZ \cong \angle VWY$, the second part of the SAS congruence pattern. The third part $\overline{XZ} \cong \overline{WY}$ can be found from the other given that $\overline{XY} \cong \overline{WZ}$. A proof can be obtained from Fig. 6.1 by unpacking various links in the proof tree. Such a proof follows. It

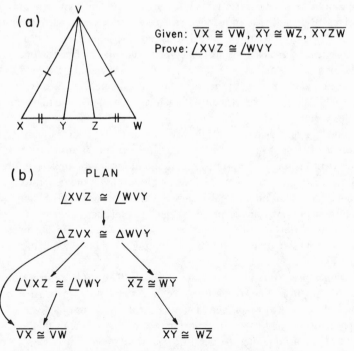

FIG. 6.1. A problem with its proof tree and detailed proof.

should be noted that some of these links map into multiple lines of proof. For instance, the link connecting $\overline{XY} \cong \overline{WZ}$ to $\overline{XZ} \cong \overline{WY}$ maps into the nine lines 4–12 in the proof. This is one of the important reasons why we characterize the proof tree as an *abstract* specification of a proof.

1.	$\overline{VX} \cong \overline{VW}$	given
2.	$\triangle XYZ$ is isosceles	definition
3.	$\angle VXZ \cong \angle VWY$	base $\angle$'s of isosceles
4.	$\overline{XY} \cong \overline{WZ}$	⁻ven
5.	$XY = WZ$	definition of $\cong$
6.	$YZ = YZ$	symmetric property of equality
7.	$XY + YZ = YZ + WZ$	addition property of equality
8.	$\overline{XYZW}$	given
9.	$XZ = XY + YZ$	segment addition
10.	$WY = YZ + WZ$	segment addition
11.	$XZ = WY$	substitution
12.	$\overline{XZ} \cong \overline{WY}$	definition of $\cong$
13.	$\triangle XVZ \cong \triangle WVY$	SAS
14.	$\angle XVZ \cong \angle WVY$	corresponding parts of congruent $\triangle$'s

The proof tree is, of course, not something that students typically draw out for themselves. Rather it is a knowledge structure in the head. Various remarks of students suggest to us that it is a real knowledge structure, not just a product of our theoretical fantasies. For instance, one student described a proof as "an upside-down pyramid." (For a student a proof tree would be upside down because the actual proof ends in the to-be-proved statement. However, we display the tree right side up (to-be-proven statement at the top) because that arrangement facilitates theoretical discussion).

As a pedagogical aside, we might say that we think it very important that the central role of such abstract plans be taken into account in instruction. It is very easy to direct instruction to proof execution and ignore the underlying plan that guides the writing of the proof. The idea of focusing on the general structure of the proof, rather than on its details, agrees with Duncker's (1945) suggestion of attempting to present organic proofs rather than mechanical ones. Because the proof tree is closely related to the main subgoals that arise during solution, instruction that used the proof tree explicitly might facilitate acquisition of useful strategic knowledge.

Creating a proof tree is not a trivial problem. The student must either try to search forward from the givens trying to find some set of paths that converge satisfactorily on the to-be-proved statement or try to search backward from the to-be-proved statement trying to find some set of dependencies that lead back to the givens. Using unguided forward or backward search, it is easy to become lost. We shall argue that students use a mixture of forward and backward search. This mixture, along with various search heuristics they acquire, enables students

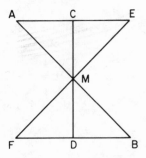

Given: M is the midpoint of $\overline{AB}$ and $\overline{CD}$
Prove: M is the midpoint of $\overline{EF}$

FIG. 6.2.   Problem for simulation of planning.

to deal with the search demands of proof problems found in high school geometry texts.

Example: The Simulation

We discuss an example problem taken from Chapter 4 of Jurgensen, Donnelly, Maier, and Rising (1975). This problem is shown in Fig. 6.2. It is among the most difficult problems found in that chapter. We first discuss the way that an ACT simulation performed on this problem. This serves to illustrate more fully our conception of the planning process in proof generation and how this planning is achieved in a production system. Then we shall see how ACT's performance compares with that of a high school subject.

ACT's search for a proof tree involves simultaneously searching backward from the to-be-proved statement and searching forward from the givens. An attempt is made to try to bring these two searches together. This search process creates a network of logical dependencies. When successful, ACT will eventually find in its search some set of logical dependencies that defines a satisfactory proof tree. This proof tree will be embedded within the search network.

Figure 6.3 illustrates the search at an early stage of its development. ACT has made forward inferences that there are two sets of congruent angles $\angle AMC \cong \angle BMD$ and $\angle CME \cong \angle DMF$ because of vertical angles and that there are two sets of congruent segments, $\overline{AM} \cong \overline{MB}$ and $\overline{CM} \cong \overline{MD}$ because of the midpoint information. (These inferences were made by specific productions in the ACT simulation, but we are postponing discussion of productions until the learning sections.) With this information in hand, ACT also makes the forward inference that $\triangle AMC \cong \triangle BMD$ because of the side–angle–side postulate. It has been our experience that almost everyone presented with this problem works forward to this particular inference as the first step to solving the problem. Note at this point

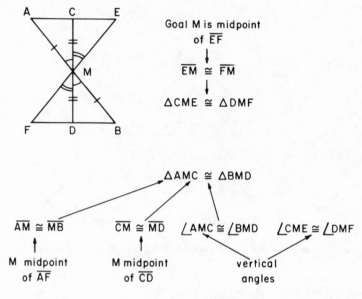

FIG. 6.3.   Problem net early in planning.

that neither ACT nor our subjects know how this inference will fit into the final proof of the problem.

Meanwhile, ACT has begun to unwind a plan of backward inferences to achieve the goal. It has translated the midpoint goal into the goal of proving the congruence $\overline{EM} \cong \overline{FM}$. In turn it has decided to achieve this goal by proving that these two segments are corresponding parts of congruent triangles, $\triangle CME$ and $\triangle DMF$. This means that it must prove that these two triangles are congruent—its new subgoal.

Note that the forward inferences have progressed much more rapidly than the backward inferences. This is because backward inferences, manipulating a single goal, are inherently serial whereas the forward inferences can apply in parallel. With respect to the serial–parallel issue it should be noted that the backward and forward searches progress in parallel.

Figure 6.3 illustrates the limit to the forward inferences that ACT generates. Although there are, of course, more forward inferences that could be made, this is the limit to the inferences for which ACT has rules strong enough to apply.

Figure 6.4 illustrates the history of ACT's efforts to reason backward to establish that $\triangle CME \cong \triangle DMF$. ACT first attempts to achieve this by the side–side–side (SSS) postulate (a basically random choice at this stage of learning). This effort is doomed to failure because the triangle congruence has been set as a subgoal of proving one of the sides congruent. When ACT reaches the goal of establishing $\overline{EM} \cong \overline{FM}$, it recognizes the problem and backs away. Our subject R, like ACT, had a propensity to plunge into hopeless paths. One component of learning (discrimination) would eventually stop it from setting such hopeless subgoals.

We shall skip over ACT's unsuccessful attempt to achieve the triangle congruence by side–angle–side (SAS) and look in detail at its efforts with the angle–side–angle (ASA) postulate. Two of the three pieces required for this— $\angle CME \cong \angle DMF$ and $\overline{CM} \cong \overline{MD}$ have already been established by forward inferences. This leaves the third piece to be established—that $\angle ECM \cong \angle FDM$. This can be inferred by supplementary angles from something that is already known—that $\triangle AMC \cong \triangle BMD$. However, ACT does not have the postulate for making this inference available. This corresponds to a blindness of our subject R with respect to using supplementary angles. Although the opportunity did not arise in this problem because he was following a different path to solution, many other times he overlooked opportunities to achieve his goals by the supplementary angle rule.

Having failed the three available methods for proving triangle congruence, ACT backed up and found a different pair of triangles, $\triangle AME$ and $\triangle BMF$,

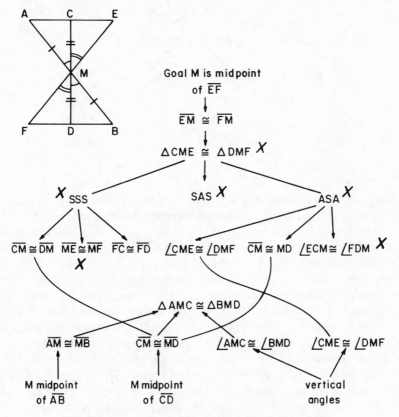

FIG. 6.4.   Trace of some backward-chaining efforts by ACT.

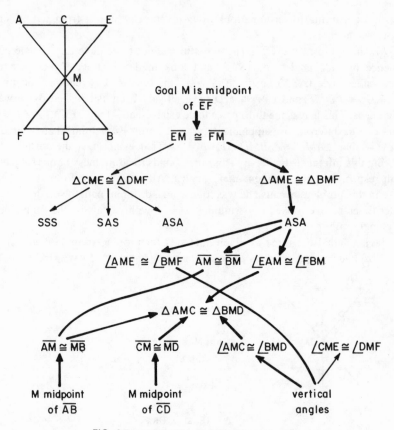

FIG. 6.5.   Application of ASA method by ACT.

whose congruence would establish the higher goal that $\overline{EM} \cong \overline{FM}$. (It turns out that, by failing on the supplementary angle needed to establish $\triangle CME \cong \triangle DMF$ and going on to try $\triangle AME \cong \triangle BMF$, ACT finds the shorter proof.)

Fortuitously, ACT chooses ASA as its first method. The attempt to apply this method is illustrated in Fig. 6.5. A critical congruence, that $\angle AME \cong \angle BMF$, is gotten because these are vertical angles. Note that this inference was not made by the forward-reasoning vertical-angle rules. This is caused by a difficulty that the ACT pattern matcher has in seeing that lines define multiple angles. The segments $\overline{AM}$ and $\overline{ME}$ that define $\angle AME$ were already used in extracting the angles $\angle AMC$ and $\angle CME$ for use by the forward-reasoning vertical-angle postulate.

ACT is also able to get the other parts of the ASA pattern. The side $\overline{AM} \cong \overline{BM}$ has already been gotten by forward inference. The fact that $\angle EAM \cong \angle FBM$ can be inferred from the fact that $\triangle AMC \cong \triangle BMD$ bcause the angles are corresponding parts of congruent triangles. With this, ACT has found its proof tree embedded within the search net. That proof tree is highlighted in Fig. 6.5.

Comparison of ACT to Subject R

It is of interest to see how ACT's behavior compares to that of a typical student. We have a more or less complete record of subject R's learning and work at geometry through Chapter 4 of Jurgensen, Donnelly, Maier, and Rising (1975). In particular, we have a record of his performance on the critical problem in Fig. 6.2.

Subject R's performance did not correspond to that of ACT in all details. This is to be expected because ACT's choices about what rules to apply have an important probabilistic component to them. However, we can still ask whether ACT and subject R made inferences of the same character. One way of answering this question is to determine whether ACT could have produced R's protocol if the probabilities came out correctly. By this criterion ACT is compatible with much of R's protocol.

Like ACT, R began by making the forward inferences necessary to conclude $\triangle AMC \cong \triangle BMD$ and then making this conclusion. Like ACT these inferences were made with little idea for how they would be used. Then like ACT, R began to reason backward from his goal to prove that M was the midpoint of $\overline{EF}$ to the goal of proving triangle congruence. However, unlike ACT he was lucky and chose the triangle $\triangle AME \cong \triangle BMF$ first. Unlike ACT again, but this time unlucky, he first chose SAS as his method for establishing the triangle congruence. He found $\overline{AM} \cong \overline{MB}$ from previous forward inference and the $\angle EAM \cong \angle FBM$ from the fact that $\triangle AMC \cong \triangle BMD$—just as ACT obtained this in trying to use ASA. However, he then had to struggle with the goal of proving $\overline{AE} \cong \overline{BF}$. Unlike ACT, subject R was reluctant to back up and he tenaciously tried to find some way of achieving his goal. He was finally told by the instructor to try some other method. Then he turned to ASA. He already had two pieces of the rule by his efforts with SAS and quickly got the third component $\angle AME \cong \angle BMF$ from the fact that they were vertical angles. Note that subject R also failed to make this vertical angle inference in forward mode and only made it in backward mode—as did ACT.

In conclusion, we think that R's behavior was very similar in character to that of ACT. The only major exception was R's reluctance to back up when a particular method was not working out.

When subject R worked on this problem, he had spent a considerable number of hours studying geometry. Thus, the version of ACT that simulates his performance represents knowledge acquired over some history of learning, although we discuss later some significant ways in which this version of ACT is less advanced than some others that have been programmed for geometry problem solving. We did not simulate the acquisition of skills represented in the version of ACT whose performance we have just described. However, we had certain learning processes in mind when we developed the simulation program, and its design was intended to be a plausible hypothesis about skill that could be acquired with those learning processes, as well as to simulate performance like that of subject R. We have developed simulations of various components of the learning process that lead to a skill product of the kind we simulated in this version of ACT. It is to this learning analysis that we now turn.

LEARNING FROM THE TEXT

Out of their initial interactions with the text and the teacher, students emerge with a rudimentary ability to solve proof problems in geometry. One might suppose that students are directly instructed as to what the procedures are that underlie proof generation. However, there is no such instruction in standard texts and yet students can learn from these texts. The texts provide only indirect information about how to generate proofs. We have been able to identify three sources of the knowledge that permits students their initial success in solving problems. These sources can be ordered on a continuum of sophistication and power. Lowest on this continuum, students use worked-out examples as an analogical base for solving further problems.[1] Next on the continuum students can apply general problem-solving methods to apply their understanding of the postulates and definitions of geometry. Highest on the continuum, students can extend general concepts that they have to incorporate the new material of geometry (subsumption). We discuss the first two kinds of learning in this section and the other kind of learning in the next section. We organize the first two together because they involve more direct encoding of knowledge from the text. The issue here turns out to be not encoding the knowledge but rather how the knowledge is used once encoded. With respect to the third kind of learning, the subsumption processes underlying the encoding proves to be of considerable interest.

Analogy: Use of Examples

A good deal of a typical student's time is spent studying worked-out examples of proofs or going over examples that he/she has worked out. Students are able to commit a good bit of these examples to memory, and what they cannot remember, they refer back to the text for. Many students make heavy use of the examples (recalled from memory or read from the text) to guide solutions to new problems. Students are able to detect similarities spontaneously between past

---

[1] Another form of learning based on worked-out examples is possible, but the authors of this paper differ in our opinions about whether it is plausible. The possibility is that learners acquire new problem-solving procedures directly from observation of the solutions of example problems. We have worked out some simulations of learning based on this idea, but we do not describe them in this chapter, partly because of space limitations and partly because we do not all agree that the mechanism of production designation used in that learning psychologically plausible.

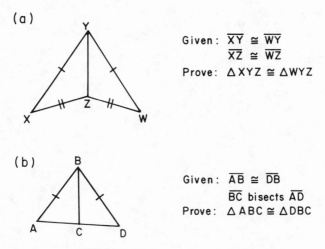

(a)

Given: $\overline{XY} \cong \overline{WY}$
$\overline{XZ} \cong \overline{WZ}$

Prove: $\triangle XYZ \cong \triangle WYZ$

(b)

Given: $\overline{AB} \cong \overline{DB}$
$\overline{BC}$ bisects $\overline{AD}$

Prove: $\triangle ABC \cong \triangle DBC$

FIG. 6.6. Two Problems with obvious similarity.

problems they remember and new problems they are facing. Once having detected the similarities, they enjoy fair success in mapping/transforming proofs for one problem to another problem. This use of prior examples we refer to as *analogy*, which seems an appropriate label and is consistent with others' uses of the term (Rumelhart & Norman, this volume; Winston, 1978). One such pair of problems for which analogy is successful is illustrated in Fig. 6.6. The text provides a solution to Problem (a) and then presents Problem (b) as the first problem for proof in the section. Our subject R noticed the similarity between the two problems, went back to the first, and almost copied over the solution.

To account for successful solution of Problem (b) by analogy using Problem (a), we must assume that the student has a facility to match partially the diagram and given statements of one problem to the diagram and given statements of another problem. We have recently developed such partial matching facilities for the ACT theory.

One problem with analogy to specific problems is that it appears to be effective only in the short run because students' memory for specific problems tends to be short-lived. All examples we have of analogy in R's protocols come within the same section of a chapter. We have no examples of problems in one section reminding R of problems in an earlier section.

A second problem with pure analogy is that it is superficial. Any point of similarity between two problems increases the partial match. It is no accident that the two pairs of triangles in Fig. 6.6 are oriented in the same direction, although this is completely irrelevant for the success of the analogy.

In ACT, analogy depends on partial matching processes that are quite "syntactic" in character; that is, the partial matching processes just count up the degree of overlap in the problem descriptions without really evaluating whether

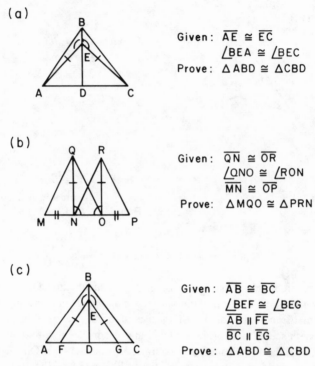

(a)

Given: $\overline{AE} \cong \overline{EC}$
$\angle BEA \cong \angle BEC$
Prove: $\triangle ABD \cong \triangle CBD$

(b)

Given: $\overline{QN} \cong \overline{OR}$
$\angle QNO \cong \angle RON$
$\overline{MN} \cong \overline{OP}$
Prove: $\triangle MQO \cong \triangle PRN$

(c)

Given: $\overline{AB} \cong \overline{BC}$
$\angle BEF \cong \angle BEG$
$\overline{AB} \parallel \overline{FE}$
$\overline{BC} \parallel \overline{EG}$
Prove: $\triangle ABD \cong \triangle CBD$

FIG. 6.7. Problems illustrating limited validity of superficial analogy.

the overlaps are essential to the appropriateness of the solution or not. In our own selves we note a tendency to respond to overlap between problems in this same superficial way. Consider the three problems in Fig. 6.7. At a deep level the first two problems are really quite similar. Larger triangles contain smaller triangles. To prove the containing triangles congruent it is first necessary to prove the contained triangles congruent. The contained triangles in the two problems are congruent in basically the same way and they overlap with the containing triangles in basically the same way. However, on first glance the two problems seem quite different. In contrast, on first glance, the two problems in Fig. 6.7 a and c appear to have much in common. Now it is true that upon careful inspection we can determine that the first pair provides a more useful analogy than the second pair. However, it seems that the function of analogy in problem solving of this sort is that of a *noticing* function. Similar problems spontaneously come to mind as possible models for solutions. If the superficial similarity between Problems (a) and (b) is not sufficient for the analogy to be noticed, there will never be the opportunity for careful inspection to realize how good the deep correspondence is.

There is one very nice illustration of the problem with the superficiality of analogy in the protocol of R. This concerns a pair of problems that come in the first chapter. Figure 6.8 illustrates the two problems. Part (a) illustrates the initial problem R studied along with an outline of the proof. Later in the section R came across Problem (b) and immediately noticed the analogy. He tried to use the first proof as a model for how the second should be structured. Analogous to the first line $RO = NY$ he wrote down the line $AB > CD$. Then analogous to the second line $ON = ON$ he wrote down $BC > BC!$ His semantic sensitivities caught this before he went on and he abandoned the attempt to use the analogy.

Interpretation of Definitions and Postulates

We have found a schemalike representation to be very useful for representing a student's initial declarative encoding of some of the geometry postulates and definitions. (As we explain shortly, we have also found schemata to be useful structures for encoding prior knowledge.) Table 6.1 illustrates a schema encoding for the SAS postulate that is stated in the text as:

> If two sides and the included angle of one triangle are congruent to the corresponding parts of another triangle, the triangles are congruent.

The diagram in Fig. 6.9 accompanied this statement.

We propose that a student creates a declarative representation like the schema in Table 6.1. The schema in Table 6.1 is divided into four categories of information: background, hypothesis, conclusion, and comment. The background includes relevant descriptive information about the diagram and contains the con-

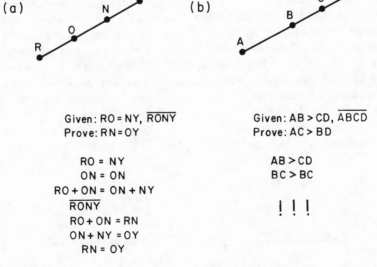

FIG. 6.8.   A Problem in which superficial analogy goes wrong.

TABLE 6.1
SAS Schema

Background	
	s1 is a side of $\triangle XYZ$
	s2 is a side of $\triangle XYZ$
	A1 is an angle of $\triangle XYZ$
	?A1 is included by s1 and s2?
	s3 is a side of $\triangle UVW$
	s4 is a side of $\triangle UVW$
	A2 is an angle of $\triangle UVW$
	?A2 is included by s3 and s4?
Hypothesis	
	s1 is congruent to s3
	s2 is congruent to s4
	A1 is congruent to A2
Conclusion	
	$\triangle XYZ$ is congruent to $\triangle UVW$
Comment	
	This is the side–angle–side postulate

straints that allow the variables (sides and angles) to be properly bound. The hypothesis specifies propositions that must be asserted in previous statements of the proof. The comment contains additional information relevant to its use. Here we have the name of the postulate that prescribes what the student should write as a reason.

In reading such a postulate subject R would typically read through at a slow but constant rate and then go to the diagram trying to relate it to the statement of the postulate. More time would be spent looking at the diagram and relating it to the postulate statement than on anything else. We take this to indicate time spent extracting the background information that is not very saliently presented for a particular problem. Students are not always successful at extracting the relevant background information. For instance, subject R failed to appreciate what was meant by "included angles" (hence the question marks around these clauses in the clauses in the background in Table 6.1). It was only sometime later, after direct intervention by the experimenter, that R got this right.

We regard the knowledge structure in Table 6.1 to be schemalike in that it is a unit organized into parts according to "slots" like background, hypothesis,

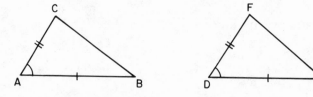

FIG. 6.9.   Diagram accompanying the SAS postulate.

conclusion, and comment. The knowledge structure is declarative in that it can be used in multiple ways by interpretative procedures. For instance, the following production would be evoked to apply that knowledge in a working-backward manner:

> IF   the goal is to prove a statement
> and there is a schema that has this statement as conclusion
> THEN   set as subgoals to match the background of the schema
> and after that to prove the hypothesis of the schema

If the schema is in working memory and its conclusion matches the current goal, this production will start up the application of the schema to the current problem. First the background is matched to bind the variables and then the hypotheses are checked.

A schema of this kind can be evoked in several ways in a working-forward mode. In this way, it is similar to a constraint, in Steele and Sussman's (1978) sense. For instance, the following production would serve to evoke the schema in this manner:

> IF   a particular statement is known to be true
> and there is a schema that includes this statement in its hypothesis
> THEN   set as subgoals to match the background of the schema
> and then to match the remaining hypotheses of the schema
> and if they match, to add the conclusion of the schema

This production is evoked when only part of the hypothesis is satisfied. Because there can be any number of statements in a hypothesis, it is not possible to have a general interpretive production that matches all the statements of any hypothesis (because a production only matches a fixed number of statements in its condition). Rather it is necessary to evoke on a partial match and then to check if the remaining statements match. This is one instance of many that illustrates the need for piecemeal application when knowledge is used interpretively. Before the rest of the hypotheses can be checked, the background must be matched to bind variables. If the hypotheses do match, the conclusion is added as an inference.

Note that whether the knowledge is used in reasoning forward or reasoning backward, the background must be matched first. In reasoning forward, the hypotheses serve as a test of the applicability of the schema and the conclusion is added. In reasoning backward, the conclusion serves as the test and the hypotheses are added as subgoals. However, in either mode the background serves as a precondition that must be satisfied.

SUBSUMPTION: LEARNING WITH UNDERSTANDING

In this section we present an analysis of meaningful learning. in the sense that was used by Katona (1940) and Wertheimer (1945/1959). Discussions of mean-

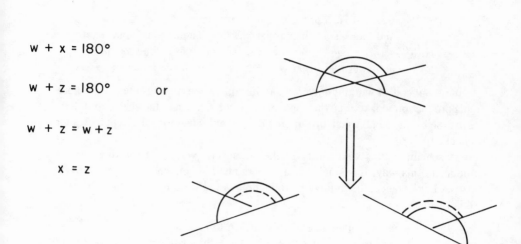

$w + x = 180°$

$w + z = 180°$ or

$w + z = w + z$

$x = z$

FIG. 6.10.   The Vertical angles problem. [After Wertheimer (1945/1959).]

ingful learning have distinguished between learning that results in relatively mechanical skill and learning that results in understanding of the structure of the problem situation. We have developed a system that learns meaningfully by acquiring a structure in which problem-solving procedures are integrated with general concepts the system already has. The outcome of learning is a schema that provides a structure for understanding a problem situation in general terms, as well as guiding problem-solving performance. We believe that in working out this implementation we have reached a more specific and clearer understanding of the processes and prior knowledge required for meaningful learning of problem-solving procedures.

Wertheimer and Katona gave numerous examples of the distinction between mechanical and meaningful learning. One of Wertheimer's is particularly relevant to our discussion. The problem is to prove that the opposite vertical angles in Fig. 6.10 are equal: for example, to show $x = z$. There is a simple algebraic proof, shown in the lower left portion of Fig. 6.10. Wertheimer argued that this algebraic solution could be learned without the student understanding the problem well. He advocated teaching in a way that would call attention to important spatial relationships in the problem, shown in the lower right portion of Fig. 6.10. The idea that understanding is strengthened by appreciation of these spatial relationships seems intuitively compelling. There is a problem of specifying the nature of understanding in a way that clarifies how it is strengthened, and we hope that our discussion in this section contributes to an improvement in clarifying specificity of this issue. We describe some general features of the system we developed to investigate meaningful learning and then describe the learning that this system accomplishes in two different learning tasks.

Schema-Based Problem Solving.   The system that we developed to investigate meaningful learning represents problems schematically. The schema used in debugging the system has the relationships between two objects that are joined together to form another object; we call the schema WHOLE/PARTS. The structure of a schema is consistent with recent proposals, especially of Bobrow and Winograd (1977) in their KRL system. A schema is used to represent relationships among a set of objects that fit into the schema's *slots*. The schema has some application conditions that are procedural in our system, implemented as *schematizing productions*. A schema also has *procedural attachments,* which are schematic descriptions of procedures that can be performed on objects of the kinds that the schema can be used to interpret. Finally, a schema has *contextual associations,* which provide information about features of the schema's application that vary in different contexts.

An example is in Table 6.2, where we show the main components of the schema in the state we used as initial knowledge prior to learning in the context of geometry problems. The schema provides a structure for understanding problems such as: "There are 5 girls and 3 boys; how many children are there?" or "There are 6 dogs and 8 animals; how many cats are there?" The schematizing production requires that two of the sets be related to the third through a "kind-

TABLE 6.2
The WHOLE/PARTS Schema

Slots:
PART 1, PART 2, WHOLE
Procedural Attachments:
COMBINE/CALCULATE
SEPARATE/CALCULATE
ADJUST/SAME-WHOLE
Contextual Associations:
SET $\rightarrow$ NUMBER
Schematizing Production
IF   V1 is a set,
and V2 is a set,
and V3 is a set,
and V1 is a kind of V3,
and V2 is a kind of V3,
THEN   Instantiate WHOLE/PARTS,
with V1 in PART 1, V2 in PART 2,
and V3 in WHOLE.

TABLE 6.3
COMBINE/CALCULATE Procedural Attachment

Prerequisites:

    Vrelation of PART 1 is known.

    Vrelation of PART 2 is known.

Consequence:

    Vrelation of WHOLE is found.

Performance:

    Add numbers (Vrelation of PART 1, Vrelation of PART 2)

---

of'' relation and uses these relations in determining which sets are the parts and which is the whole. (Other schematizing productions could easily be added, for example, sets that are located in separate places for problems such as "There are 3 cookies on the counter and 4 cookies in the jar; How many cookies are there in all?'') More systematic studies of the use of schemata in understanding arithmetic word problems have been conducted by Heller (1980) and by Riley (1979).

One of the procedural attachments of the schema is shown in Table 6.3. This is organized in the way proposed by Sacerdoti (1977), with information that specifies prerequisites, consequences, and actions that are performed in order to execute the procedure. These procedural attachments are schemalike themselves and have some similarity to the types of schema discussed earlier (e.g., in Table 6.1).[2] In Table 6.3, Vrelation refers to a variable whose value is determined by the contextual association of the schema; for problems about sets, Vrelation would be the number associated with a set. Therefore, if the problem is about sets, the prerequisite of COMBINE/CALCULATE is that numbers of the parts are known, the consequence is that the number of the whole will be found, and the action to perform is addition of the known numbers.

The other procedural attachments in the WHOLE/PARTS schema are organized similarly. The procedure SEPARATE/CALCULATE has a prerequisite of known values associated with the whole and one of the parts, and the consequence of finding the other part. The procedure ADJUST/SAME-WHOLE is used when one of the parts is too large or too small for some reason, and a shift of members between the two parts is made in a way that keeps the value of the whole constant.

To solve problems using schemata, ACT has a strategy implemented as a set of productions similar to the productions on pp. 205. The specific strategy that

---

[2]Our use of the term *schema* is somewhat different here than in the earlier presentation (Table 6.1). This is similar to the general literature, where schema is used to refer to various kinds of structures; however, we may be unusual in adopting two different meanings in the same article. The difference reflects the fact that the implementation described in these two sections were in the hands of different authors (Table 6.1: Anderson; this section: Greeno). We believe that the two kinds of schematic structures are quite compatible. The background information in Table 6.1 corresponds to the condition of a schematizing production here, the hypotheses in Table 6.1 to the prerequisites of procedural attachment, and the conclusion to the consequence of a procedural attachment.

we implemented for this system uses one step of backward chaining if it can; otherwise it is a forward-chaining strategy. ACT first tries to find a procedure whose consequence matches its current problem goal. If one is found, ACT checks the prerequisites of that procedure, and if they are satisfied, ACT performs the actions of that procedure. If prerequisites are not satisfied, ACT looks for another procedure whose consequence matches the goal of the problem. Any time ACT fails to find a procedure with a consequence matching its current goal, it tests prerequisites of its procedures and attempts to work forward.

Learning Tasks.   Several different forms of learning can be considered in relation to schemata of the kind we are using. We discuss three here. First, we simulated generalization of a schema to a new problem domain. The system initially had the schema shown in Table 6.2, which it could use to schematize problems about sets. It was shown an example problem involving segments and learned a new schematizing production and contextual association enabling it to use the WHOLE/PARTS schema to schematize problems about segments.

A second task that we have simulated involved adding new structure to an existing schema. The added structures were new procedural attachments that enable ACT to solve a new kind of problem. Initially the only procedures attached to the WHOLE/PARTS schema involved numerical calculations or adjustments. ACT was shown an example problem involving proof and acquired new procedures for writing steps in the proof. These new procedures were attached to ACT's WHOLE/PARTS schema, so that ACT's later solution of other proof problems included its general understanding of part–whole structural relations.

The third task for which we have performed a simulation involved synthesizing new schematic structure. A problem was presented for which the existing WHOLE/PARTS schema is too simple to provide a complete interpretation. The system acquired a more complex schema in which two WHOLE/PARTS structures are included as subschemata and in which the previously learned proof procedures were available for use in solving more complex problems.

Task Application in a New Domain.   Initially the WHOLE/PARTS schema was coded for the model and debugged on problems involving numbers of objects in different sets, such as the "There are 5 children and 2 boys; how many girls are there?" A new example problem was presented to the model, consisting of a diagram consisting of a segment with endjoints A and C, and a point on the segment marked B. The following propositions were also presented: "Given: $AB = 5$, $BC = 3$; find AC." The solution was also presented: "$AC = 5 + 3 = 8$." The model included a production for interpreting the given information as lengths of segments in the diagram. It also had a production for interpreting "Find AC" by setting a goal to find the length of that segment.

The new knowledge required for the schema to be applied in the domain of segments is a new schematizing production whose action assigns objects in the segment problem to slots in the WHOLE/PARTS schema. There is a difficulty with formulating such a production and that difficulty arises from the fact that the learner is not directly told to incorporate this situation as an instance of his WHOLE/PARTS schema. We assumed that activation of the appropriate schema would require some relatively specific cue, which is consistent with evidence that indicates that human problem solvers are unlikely to notice structural similarities among problems unless there are fairly obvious signals available (Gick & Holyoak, 1980). We provided the needed cue in the form of the WHOLE/PARTS schema's name; this might correspond to a situation in a class where the teacher points out that the whole segment is composed of other segments as its parts.

Our simulation identifies the schema that is named in the explanation of the solution step that is presented. The respective slot roles of the varoius objects in the problem are sorted out by examining the problem-solving action. A production is built whose performance matches the action that is shown, and the slots mentioned in the procedure are matched to the objects that are associated with the values in the action. The action of the new production is determined by these identifications: it refers to the objects in the problem that is to be schematized and associates them with the slots they should occupy.

Table 6.4 shows the schematizing production that the system learned. We also programmed the system to store a new contextual association, so that for future problems involving segments the problem solver would use the lengths of segments as the relevant properties. Thus, by acquisition of the schematizing production the system is able to bring to bear its knowledge about WHOLE/PARTS relationships to the solving of geometry problems.

We believe that the ability to solve WHOLE/PARTS problems of the kind we discuss here is probably learned well before students begin studying geometry and that they probably understand the part–whole relationship involved. We have

TABLE 6.4
Schematizing Production Learned from the
Example Problem

IF	V112 is a segment
	and V116 is a segment
	and V120 is a segment
	and V120 contains V112
	and V120 contains V116
	and V119 and V121 are endpoints of V112
	and V119 and V122 are endpoints of V116
	and V121 and V122 are endpoints of V120
THEN	Instantiate WHOLE/PARTS,
	with V112 in PART 1, and V116 in PART 2,
	and V120 in WHOLE.

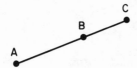

Given: $\overline{ABC}$
Prove: AB = AC − BC

Statement	Reason
1. $\overline{ABC}$	1. Given
2. AC = AB + BC	2. Segment addition (Step I)
3. AB = AC − BC	3. Substraction property (Step 2)

FIG. 6.11.   An Example used to teach problem-solving procedures.

not observed any students in their work on geometry whose performance indicates a lack of the knowledge modeled in this section. On the other hand, the extension of this knowledge and understanding to the early problems of geometry is by no means automatic for all students, as we discuss later.

Acquiring New Procedural Attachments.   The second meaningful learning task that we simulated used the problem shown in Fig. 6.11. The performance simulated in this situation was similar to that discussed on pp. 203–205.

In this task, ACT began with the WHOLE/PARTS schema and the schematizing production shown in Table 6.4, so it represented the part–whole structure of the segments in the diagram. Steps 2 and 3 represented new actions for ACT— that is, ACT did not have knowledge of procedures that would produce these proof steps. Using its representation of the problem situation and the statements in the proof steps, ACT stored new descriptions of procedures and attached them to its WHOLE/PARTS schema. As a result, ACT had structures similar to the SAS schema shown in Table 6.1 corresponding to the segment-addition postulate and the subtraction property of equality. However, these new structures were integrated with ACT's general understanding of structures that involve part–whole relationships.

A consequence of attaching the segment-addition procedure to the WHOLE/ PARTS schema is that it is available for use in more complicated problem situations, when the WHOLE/PARTS schema is invoked in ACT's understanding of more complex problems. We discuss an extension of that kind in the next section.

Building a New Schema from Old Schemata.   Another task that we have used to simulate learning is shown in Fig. 6.12 (also discussed in Fig. 6.8). Conceptual understanding of this problem involves seeing the given segment *RY* as two

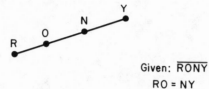

Given: $\overline{RONY}$
RO = NY
Prove: RN = OY

FIG. 6.12.   Problem for learning a new schema.

overlapping WHOLE–PARTS structures, each having a distinct part as well as a part that the two structures share. Table 6.5 shows a schema that we have partially implemented with the required structure. The important new idea in this simulation is the inclusion of subschemata as components of the schema. The main consequence is that the procedures already attached to the subschema are automatically available in situations schematized with the superschema. For example, the segment-addition procedure, attached to the WHOLE/PARTS schema because of the learning just discussed, is available in solving problems that can be schematized with the OVERLAP/WHOLE/PARTS schema. In the problem-solving strategy that we implemented, the problem solver first tries to apply procedures that are attached to the main schema, and when none are applicable, procedures attached to the subschemata are tested.

TABLE 6.5
OVERLAP/WHOLE/PARTS Schema

Slots
        PARTA, PARTAB, PARTB, WHOLEA, WHOLEB, WHOLE
Subschemata
        WHOLE/PARTSA, WHOLE/PARTSB
Procedural Attachments:
        SUBSTITUTION
        ADDITION-PROPERTY
        SUBTRACTION-PROPERTY
Contextual Association:
        Segment ⟶ Length
        Schematizing Production
        IF   V1, V2, V3, V4, V5, and V6 are segments
                and V6 includes V1, V2, V3, V4, and V5,
                and V4 includes V1 and V2,
                and V5 includes V2 and V3,
        THEN   Instantiate WHOLE/PARTS (= schema1) with V1 as PART1, V2 as PART2,
                V4 as WHOLE;
                and instantiate WHOLE/PARTS (= schema2) with V3 as PART1, V2 as PART2,
                V5 as WHOLE;
                and instantiate OVERLAP/WHOLE/PARTS with V1 as PARTA, V2 as PARTB,
                V3 as PARTB, V4 as WHOLEA, V5 as WHOLEB, V6 as WHOLE,
                schema1 as WHOLE/PARTSA, and schema 2 as WHOLE/PARTSB.

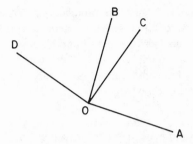

Given: $\angle$AOB and $\angle$COD are right angles
Prove: m$\angle$AOC = m$\angle$BOD

FIG. 6.13.   Transfer problem.

There are powerful consequences of schematizing line-segment problems as instances of WHOLE/PARTS or OVERLAP/WHOLE/PARTS structures. At this level of representation a wide variety of problems have essentially the same character. For instance, consider the angle problem presented in Fig. 6.13. From the point of view of the OVERLAP/WHOLE/PARTS schema it is essentially isomorphic to the segment problem in the earlier Fig. 6.12. An interesting question is to what degree do students conceptualize these problems in terms of the general schema and how much success do they enjoy in their problem solving if they do.

The protocols that we obtained from the six students who were studying a regular course in geometry are relevant here. One of the sessions occurred soon after students had completed work on proofs of the kind shown in Fig. 6.12 involving line segments. Students had been introduced to a concept of additive combination of angles, called the angle-addition property, but they had not yet worked on proof problems of the kind shown in Fig. 6.13, which was the first problem presented in the interview session.

We found a full range of performance from these students in terms of their ability to recognize the similarity between the angle and segment problems. Four of the six noticed some similarity, one (who successfully solved the problem) noticed no similarity, and the final student had so many gaps in knowledge that it is difficult to diagnose exactly what this student knew. At least two students gave evidence of quite deep appreciation of the underlying similarity. One of them spontaneously remarked "Okay, well, it's basically the same kind of thing. . . . Well, it's just working kind of the same thing. Except over a curve, kind of, the measure of angles instead of distances." The other remarked "Well, its the same problem again. You know something? I'm getting kind of tired of that problem." Although only the second of these two solved the problem, both showed evidence of trying to use the general conceptual structure on their problem solving. We conclude from these protocols and others that at least some students make active use of these general schemata in their geometry problem solving, that these schemata can be helpful in problem solving, but that they are not essential. On the last point, our subject R, whom we have studied most extensively, made slow but sure progress stubbornly refusing to try to relate the geometry material to prior knowledge.

KNOWLEDGE COMPILATION

In this section we discuss learning mechanisms that accomplish a transition from declarative to procedural knowledge. In the simulations of geometry learning that we have discussed in this chapter, we have assumed that the initial cognitive encoding of information for problem solving is declarative. There is room for disagreement on the question of whether problem-solving knowledge always has an initial declarative encoding (in fact the authors of this chapter disagree on this question—see footnote 1). Even so, descriptions of procedures constitute an important source of information for human learners, and the development of cognitive procedures from initial knowledge in declarative form is an important requirement of much human learning.

One advantage of declarative representations over corresponding representations in the form of productions is that declarative representations are more concise. The same facts can give rise to a great many possible productions reflecting various ways that the information can be used. For instance, consider the textbook definition of supplementary angles:

"Supplementary angles are two angles whose measures have sum 180."

Below are productions that embody just some of the ways in which this knowledge can be used. These productions differ in terms of whether one is reasoning forward or backward, what the current goal is, and what is known.

IF $m\angle A + m\angle B = 180°$
THEN $\angle A$ and $\angle B$ are supplementary

IF   the goal is to prove $\angle A$ and $\angle B$ are supplementary
THEN   set as a subgoal to prove $m\angle A + m\angle B = 180°$

IF $\angle A$ and $\angle B$ are supplementary
THEN $m\angle A + m\angle B = 180°$

IF $\angle A$ and $\angle B$ are supplementary
and $m\angle A = X$
THEN $m\angle B = 180° - X$

> IF $\angle A$ and $\angle B$ are supplementary
>   and the goal is to find $m\angle A$
> THEN   set as a subgoal to find $m\angle B$

> IF   the goal is to show $\angle A \cong \angle B$
>   and $\angle A$ is supplementary to $\angle C$
>   and $\angle B$ is supplementary to $\angle D$
> THEN   set as a subgoal to prove $\angle C \cong \angle D$

A basic point is that the definition of supplementary angles is fundamentally declarative in the sense that it can be used in multiple ways and does not contain a commitment to how it will be used. It is unreasonable to suppose that, in encoding the definition, the system anticipates all the ways in which it might be used and creates a procedural structure for each.

A related difficulty has to do with encoding control information into working-backward productions. The actual implementations of a working-backward production require rather intricate knowledge and use of goal settings that might exceed the knowledge or information-handling capacities of many learners.

Interpretive Application of Knowledge

Rather than assuming that students directly encode such information into procedures, we have assumed that they first encode this information declaratively. In the ACT system, encoding information declaratively amounts to growing new semantic network structure to encode the information. We suppose general *interpretative* procedures then use this information according to the features of the particular circumstance. In earlier sections we discuss how this declarative knowledge was encoded in schema-like format and how some interpretive procedures would use this knowledge. As we now describe, when declarative knowledge is used many times in a particular way, automatic learning processes in ACT will create new procedures that directly apply the knowledge without the interpretative step. We refer to this kind of learning as *knowledge compilation*.

In individual subjects we see a gradual shift in performance that we would like to put into correspondence with this compilation from the interpretative application of declarative knowledge to direct application of procedures. For instance, after reading a particular postulate, students' applications of that postulate are both slow and halting. Students will often recite to themselves the postulate before trying to apply it—or even go back and reread it. It seems that they need to activate the declarative representation in their working memory so that interpretative procedures can apply to the data of this representation. They typically match separately fragments of the postulate to the problem. We shall see that such fragmentary application is typical of a general knowledge interpreter applying to

TABLE 6.6
SAS Schema

Background

   s1 is a side of ΔXYZ

   s2 is a side of ΔXYZ

   A1 is an angle of ΔXYZ

   A1 is included by s1 and s2

   s3 is a side of ΔUVW

   s4 is a side of ΔUVW

   A2 is an angle of ΔUVW

   A2 is included by s3 and s4

Hypothesis

   s1 is congruent to s3

   s2 is congruent to s4

   A1 is congruent to A2

Conclusion

   ΔXYZ is congruent to ΔUVW

Comment

   This is the side-angle-side postulate

---

a declarative representation. With repeated use, however, application of the postulate smooths out. It is no longer explicitly recalled and it is no longer possible as observer or subject to discriminate separate steps in the application of the procedure.

We use the side-angle-side schema of Table 6.1 to discuss how the student switches from the initial piecemeal interpretive application of knowledge to direct, unitary procedures. For convenience that table is reproduced as Table 6.6. The following are some of the productions that are used to apply the schema knowledge in working backward mode:

   P1: IF the goal is to prove a statement
        and there is a schema that has this statement as conclusion
     THEN set as subgoals to match the background of the schema
        and after that to prove the hypothesis of the schema

This production recognizes that the schema is relevant to proving the problem. It would invoke the SAS schema in situations where the goal was to prove two triangles congruent. The next production to apply is:

   P2: IF the goal is to match a set of statements
     THEN match the first statement in the set

Production P1 had set the subgoal of matching the statements in the background. This production starts that process going by focusing on the first statement in the background. This production is followed by a production that iterates through the statements of the background.

    P3:   IF   the goal is to match a statement in a set
                and the problem contains a match to the statement
          THEN go on to match the next statement in the set

(Actually, there is a call to a subroutine of productions that execute the matches to each statement. See Neves & Anderson, this volume). After all statements in the background have been matched, the following production sets the goal to prove the hypotheses:

    P4:   IF   the goal is to match a set of statements
                and the last statement in that set has been matched
          THEN go on to the goal that follows

Composition

There are two major processes in knowledge compilation—*composition* and *proceduralization*. When a series of productions apply in a fixed order, composition will create a new production that accomplishes the effect of the sequence in a single step (Neves & Anderson, this volume). Composition, operating on the sequence of P1, P2, and P3, applied to the SAS schema, would put forth the production:

    P5:   IF   the goal is to prove a statement
                and there is a schema that has this statement as conclusion
                and the schema has a statement as the first member of its
                    background
                and the problem contains a match to the statement
          THEN set as subgoals to match the background
                and within this subgoal to match the next statement of the
                    background
                and after that to prove the hypotheses of the schema

This production only applies in the circumstance that the sequence P1, P2, and P3 applied and this production will have the same effect in terms of changes to the data base. The details underlying composition are discussed in Neves and Anderson, this volume, but the gist of the process is easy to describe. The composed production collects in its condition all those clauses from the individual productions' conditions except those that are the product of the actions of earlier productions in the sequence. As an example of this exception P2 has in its condition that the goal is to match the set of statements. Because this goal was set by P1, earlier in the sequence, it is not mentioned in the condition of the composed production P5. Thus, the condition is a test of whether the circumstances are right for the full sequence of productions to execute. The action of the composed production collects all actions of the individual productions except those involved in setting transitory goals that are finished with by the end of the sequence. As an example of this exception, P2 sets the subgoal of matching the first statement of the background but P3 meets this subgoal. Therefore, the sub-goal is not mentioned in the action of the composed production P5.

This composition process can apply to the product of earlier compositions. Although there is nothing special about compositions of three productions, consider what the resulting production would be like if P5 were composed with two successive iterative applications of P3:

> P6:   IF   the goal is to prove a statement
> and there is a schema that has the statement as conclusion
> and the schema has a statement as the first member of the
>   background
> and the problem contains a match to this statement
> and the schema has another statement as the next member of its
>   background
> and the problem contains a match to this statement
> and the schema has another statement as the next member of its
>   background
> and the problem contains a match to this statement
> THEN   set as subgoals to match the background
> and within this the next statement of the background
> and after that to prove the hypotheses of the schema

It should be noted that such productions are not really specific to the SAS schema. Indeed, productions such as P5 and P6 might already have been formed from compositions derived from the productions applying to other, earlier schemata. If so, these composed productions would be ready to apply to the current schema. Thus, there can be some general transfer of learning produced by composition. However, there is a clear limit on how large such composed productions can become. As they become larger, they require more information in the schema be retrieved from long-term memory and held active in working memory. Limits on the capacity of working memory imply limits on the size of the general, interpretive conditions that can successfully match.

Proceduralization

Proceduralization is a process that eliminates retrieval of information from long-term memory by creating productions with the knowledge formerly retrieved from long-term memory built into them. To illustrate the process of proceduralization, consider its application to the production P6. This statement contains in its condition four clauses that require retrieval of information from long-term memory:

1. There is a schema that has the to-be-proved statement as its conclusion.
2. The schema has a statement as the first member of its background.

3. The schema has another statement as the next member of its background.
4. The schema has another statement as the next member of its background.

Applied to the SAS schema these statements match the following information:

1. The SAS schema has as its conclusion "$\triangle XYZ \cong \triangle UVW$."
2. The first statement of its background is "S1 is a side of $\triangle XYZ$."
3. The next statement of its background is "S2 is a side of $\triangle XYZ$."
4. The next statement of its background is "A1 is an angle of $\triangle XYZ$."

What is accomplished by matching these statements in P6 is to identify the SAS schema, its conclusion, and the first three statements of its background. A specialized production can be built that contains this information and does not require the long-term memory retrievals:

P7:   IF   the goal is to prove that $\triangle XYZ \cong \triangle UVW$
            and S1 is a side of $\triangle XYZ$
            and S2 is a side of $\triangle XYZ$
            and A1 is an angle of $\triangle XYZ$
      THEN set as subgoals to match the background of the SAS schema
            and within this to match the next statement in the schema
            and after that to prove the hypothesis of the schema

This production is now specialized to the SAS schema and does not require any long-term memory retrieval. Rather, built into its condition are the patterns retrieved from long-term memory.

The effect of this proceduralization process is to enable larger composed productions to apply because the proceduralized productions are not limited by the need to retrieve long-term information into working memory. This in turn allows still larger compositions to be formed. The eventual product of the composition process applied to the top-down evocation of the SAS schema, initially via productions P1, P2, P3, and P4, would be:

P8:   IF   the goal is to prove that $\triangle XYZ$ is congrent to $\triangle UVW$
            and S1 is a side of $\triangle XYZ$
            and S2 is a side of $\triangle XYZ$
            and A1 is an angle of $\triangle XYZ$
            and A1 is included by S1 and S2
            and S3 is a side of $\triangle UVW$
            and S4 is a side of $\triangle UVW$
            and A2 is an angle of $\triangle UVW$
            and A2 is included by S3 and S4
      THEN set as subgoals to prove
            S1 is congruent to S3
            S2 is congruent to S4
            A1 is congruent to A2

This production serves to apply the SAS postulate in working backward mode. When the knowledge reaches this state, it has been completely proceduralized.

As we discuss in later portions of the chapter, composition need not stop when the postulate has been completely incorporated into a single production. Composition can continue to merge productions to compress even longer sequences of actions into a single production. For instance, consider what would happen should production P8 compose with later productions that attempted to prove the hypothesis parts. Suppose, furthermore, that the first two parts of the hypothesis could be established directly because they were already true. The composition process would produce the following working backward production:

P9: IF   the goal is to prove that $\triangle XYZ$ is congruent to $\triangle UVW$
          and S1 is a side of $\triangle XYZ$
          and S2 is a side of $\triangle XYZ$
          and A1 is an angle of $\triangle XYZ$
          and A1 is included by S1 and S2
          and S3 is a side of $\triangle UVW$
          and S4 is a side of $\triangle UVW$
          and A2 is an angle of $\triangle UVW$
          and A2 is included by S3 and S4
          and S1 is congruent to S3
          and S2 is congruent to S4
     THEN   set as a subgoal to prove that A1 is congruent to A2

This production checks that two sides of the triangles are congruent and sets the goal to prove that the included angles are congruent. P9 is obviously much more discriminant in its application than P8 and is therefore much more likely to lead to success.

Evidence for Composition and Proceduralization

So far we have offered two lines of argument that there are these processes of composition and proceduralization. One is that it creates a sensible connection between declarative knowledge and procedural knowledge; that is, knowledge starts out in a declarative form so that it can be used in multiple ways. However, if the knowledge is repeatedly used in the same way, efficient procedures will be created to apply the knowledge in that way. The second argument for these processes is that they are consistent with the gross qualitative features of the way application of knowledge smooths out and speeds up; that is, with practice, explicit verbal recall of the geometry statements drop out and the piecemeal application becomes more unitary.

The idea is a natural one, that skill develops by collapsing together multiple steps in one. Lewis (1976), who introduced composition applied to productions, traces the general concept back to Book (1908). However, there is more than intuitive appeal and general plausibility going for this learning mechanism. It is capable of accounting for a number of important facts about skill development. One feature of the knowledge compilation is that procedures can develop to apply the knowledge in one manner without corresponding procedures developing to apply the knowledge in other ways. It is somewhat notorious that people's ability to use knowledge can be specific to how the knowledge is evoked. For instance, Greeno and Magone (in preparation) have found that students who have a fair facility at proof generation make gross errors at proof checking, a skill that they have not practiced.

Neves and Anderson (this volume) provide an extensive discussion of how composition and proceduralization serve to account for a range of results in the experimental literature—for the speedup of a skill with practice, for the growing automaticity of a skill, for the Einstellung effect (Luchins, 1942), and for the dropout of self-reports with practice.

KNOWLEDGE OPTIMIZATION

Having operators proceduralized is not enough to guarantee successful proof generation. There is still a potentially very large search space of forward and backward inferences. Finding the proof tree in this search space would often be infeasible without some search heuristics that enable the system to try the right inferences first.

In our observations of student subjects as they learned geometry, we saw very little success in discovering such heuristics. Therefore, these observations do not provide a strong basis for the assertion that acquisition of such heuristics is an important part of learning geometry. However, the performance of students at more advanced stages of learning included many examples of problem-solving activity organized according to quite strong heuristic methods. An additional basis for our beliefs on this matter come from comparing our own performance on proof problems with that of the subjects whom we observed in their early stages of learning. Although the title "expert" is a little overblown in our case, we have something of a novice-expert contrast here. Our two beginning subjects barely managed to get their knowledge beyond the initial proceduralization and often made choices in search that seemed transparently wrong to us. Presumably, our more tuned judgment reflects the acquisition of appropriate heuristics with experience. Therefore, in discussing particular heuristics we shall be drawing on: (1) those rare instances of learning of heuristics identifiable in our beginning subjects; (2) performance of more advanced students that has been analyzed previously; and (3) our own intuitions about the kinds of heuristics we use.

One kind of heuristic amounts to adding some discriminative conditions to a production to restrict its applicability. For instance, production P9 differs from P8 (pp. 219–220) by the addition of tests for two out of three of the conditions of

SAS. Although satisfying these conditions does not guarantee that SAS will be satisfied, it does make it more likely. This is the nature of a heuristic—to select an operator on the basis of tests that suggest that it has a higher probability of success in this circumstance than other operators.

It is interesting to note that novices do not deal with proofs by plunging into endless search. They are very restrictive in what paths they attempt and are quite unwilling to consider all the paths that are legally possible. The problem is, of course, that the paths they select are often nonoptimal or just plain deadends. Thus, at a general level, expertise does not develop by simply becoming more restrictive in search; rather it develops by becoming more appropriately restrictive.

There are four ways that we have been able to discover by which subjects can learn to make better choices in searching for a proof tree. One is by analogy to prior problems—using with the current problem methods that succeeded in similar past problems. Use of such analogy is limited in ways that we discussed earlier and we shall not discuss it further here. The second, related technique, is to generalize from specific problems operators that capture what the solutions to these specific problems have in common. The third is a discrimination process by which restrictions are added to the applicability of more general operators. These restrictions are derived from a comparison of where the general operators succeeded and failed. The fourth process is a composition process by which sequences of operators become collapsed into single operators that apply in more restrictive situations. We now discuss the last three of these methods.

Generalization

We have characterized solving problems by analogy as superficial. Part of what is superficial about the approach is that the analogy is based only on the statement of the problems and not on the structures of their solution. Analogy, in the sense discussed, cannot use the structure of the solution, because the proof for the second problem is not available when the analogy has to be made. Analogy is being used in service of finding the second proof.

Generalization, on the other hand, is based on a comparison between two problems and their solutions. By using the structure of the solution it is possible to select out the relevant aspects of the problem statement. A rule is formulated by the generalization process that tries to capture what the two problems and their solutions have in common. That rule can then be used should similar problems appear. For instance, consider the two problems in Fig. 6.14. The generalization process applied to these two examples would encode what they have in common by the following schema:

GENERALIZED SCHEMA:

Background
$\triangle XYZ$ contains $\triangle SYZ$
$\triangle UVW$ contains $\triangle TVW$

Givens

$\overline{SY} \cong \overline{TV}$

$\angle YSZ \cong \angle VTW$

Goal

$\triangle XYZ \cong \triangle UVW$

Method

$\triangle SYZ \cong \triangle TVW$	by SAS
$\overline{YZ} \cong \overline{VW}$	by corresponding parts
$\angle XYZ \cong \angle UVW$	by corresponding parts
$\triangle XYZ \cong \triangle UVW$	by SAS

In our opinion, these generalizations are based on the same partial-matching process that underlies analogy. However, the partial matching occurs between solved problems and not just between problem statements. Because the product of the partial match is a fairly general problem description, it is likely to apply to many problems. Thus it is likely to be strengthened and become a permanent part of the student's repertoire for searching for proofs. This contrasts to the specific examples that serve as the basis for analogy. These specific examples are likely to be forgotten.

We have been able to identify two moderately clear cases of generalization in R's protocols. One has to do with problems of the variety illustrated in Fig. 6.6a. Many variations on this problem appeared in the early part of the text and R came to recognize this general type of problem when it appeared later. The other example has to do with the use of the hypotenuse–leg theorem for right-angle triangles. After some examples R formulated the generalized rule that he should use this theorem if he was presented with two right-angle triangles whose hypotenuses were given as congruent. This is the feature that all the hypotenuse–leg problems had in common.

(a)

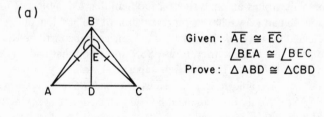

Given: $\overline{AE} \cong \overline{EC}$

$\angle BEA \cong \angle BEC$

Prove: $\triangle ABD \cong \triangle CBD$

(b)

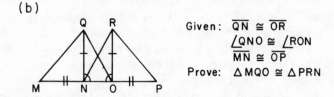

Given: $\overline{QN} \cong \overline{OR}$

$\angle QNO \cong \angle RON$

$\overline{MN} \cong \overline{OP}$

Prove: $\triangle MQO \cong \triangle PRN$

FIG. 6.14.   Two proof problems whose generalization leads to a useful operator.

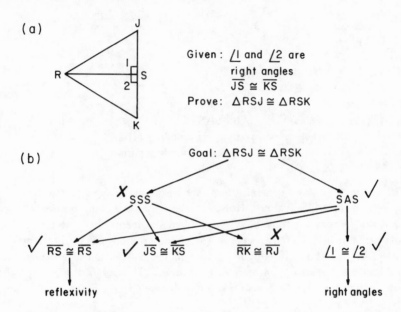

FIG. 6.15.   Problem leading to a discrimination.

Discrimination

Discrimination provides a complementary process to generalization. It takes operators that are too general and thus are applying in incorrect situations and it places restrictions on their range of applicability. If the operator to be discriminated is embodied as a production, discrimination adds an additional clause to restrict the range of situations where the production condition will match. ACT determines what additional clauses to add by comparing the difference between successful and unsuccessful application of the rule.

Figure 6.15 illustrates an analysis of a problem that led subject R to form a discrimination. In part (a) we have a representation of the problem and in part (b) we have indicated the network of backward inferences that constitute R's attempt to solve the problem. First he tried to use SSS, a method that had worked on a previous problem that had a great deal of superficial similarity to this problem. However, he was not able to get the sides $\overline{RK}$ and $\overline{RS}$ congruent. Then he switched to SAS, the only other method he had at the time for proving triangles congruent. (Interestingly, it was only in the context of this goal that he recognized the right angles were congruent.) After he had finished with this problem, he verbally announced the rule to use SSS only if there was no angle mentioned. This can be seen to be the product of discrimination. The "don't use SSS if angle" comes from a comparison of the previous problem in which no angle was mentioned with the current problem that did mention angles.

ACT's generalization and discrimination processes were described in considerable detail in Anderson, Kline, and Beasley (1979). There we were concerned with showing how they applied in modeling the acquisition of category schema or prototypes. That data provided pretty strong evidence for the ACT mechanisms and further new data is contained in Elio and Anderson (in preparation). It is partly the success of that enterprise that leads us to believe they play an important role in the development of expertise in geometry proof generation. Basically, the claim is that from examples students develop schemata for when various proof methods are appropriate just as they develop schemata for what are examples of categories.

Composition

We feel that composition has an important role to play in forming multiple-operator sequences just as it played an important role in the initial proceduralization of operators. Figure 6.16 illustrates an example where composition can apply. The first production to apply in solving this problem would be:

P1: IF the goal is to prove $\angle X \cong \angle U$
     and $\angle X$ is part of $\triangle XYZ$
     and $\angle U$ is part of $\triangle UVW$
  THEN the subgoal is to prove $\triangle XYZ \cong \triangle UVW$

This production would set as a subgoal to prove $\triangle ABC \cong \triangle DBC$. At this point the following production might apply:

P2: IF the goal is to prove $\triangle XYZ \cong \triangle UVW$
     and $\overline{XY} \cong \overline{UV}$
     and $\overline{ZX} \cong \overline{WU}$
  THEN the subgoal is to prove $\overline{YZ} \cong \overline{VW}$

This production, applied to the situation in Fig. 6.16, would set as the subgoal to prove $\overline{BC} \cong \overline{BC}$ as a step on the way to using SSS. At this point the following production would apply:

P3: IF the goal is to prove $\overline{XY} \cong \overline{XY}$
  THEN this may be concluded by reflexivity

This production would add $\overline{BC} \cong \overline{BC}$ and allow the following production to apply:

P4: IF the goal is to prove $\triangle XYZ \cong \triangle UVW$
     and $\overline{XY} \cong \overline{UV}$
     and $\overline{YZ} \cong \overline{VW}$
     and $\overline{ZX} \cong \overline{WU}$
  THEN the goal may be concluded by SSS

where $\overline{XY} = \overline{AB}$, $\overline{UV} = \overline{DB}$, $\overline{YZ} = \overline{BC}$, $\overline{VW} = \overline{BC}$, $\overline{ZX} = \overline{CA}$, and $\overline{WU} = \overline{CD}$. This adds the information that $\triangle ABC \cong \triangle DBC$. Finally, the following pro-

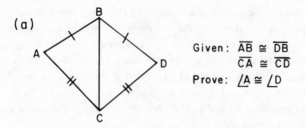

FIG. 6.16.   Problem leading to a composition.

duction will apply that recognizes that the to-be-proved conclusion is now established:

P5:   IF   the goal is to prove $\angle X \cong \angle U$
             and $\triangle XYZ \cong \triangle UVW$
       THEN the goal may be concluded because of congruent parts of congruent triangles

The composition process, operating on this sequence of productions, would eventually produce a production of the form:

P6:   IF   the goal is to prove $\angle A \cong \angle D$
             and $\angle A$ is part of $\triangle ABC$
             and $\angle D$ is part of $\triangle DBC$
             and $\overline{AB} \cong \overline{DB}$
             and $\overline{CA} \cong \overline{DC}$
       THEN conclude $\overline{AB} \cong \overline{AB}$ by reflexivity
             and conclude $\triangle ABC \cong \triangle DBC$ by SSS
             and conclude the goal because of congruent parts of congruent triangles

The variables in this production have been named to correspond to the terms in Fig. 6.16 for purposes of readability. This production would immediately recognize the solution to a problem like that in Fig. 6.16. Another feature of composition, illustrated in this example, is that it transforms what had been a basically working-backward solution to the problem into something much more of the character of working forward. Indeed, all the methods that we have discussed for tuning search operators, to the extent that they put into the conditions additional tests for applicability and into the action additional inferences, have the effect of converting working backward into working forward. Larkin, McDermott, Simon, and Simon (in press) and Larkin (this volume) have commented on this same transformation in the character of physics problem solving with the development of expertise.

SUMMARY

By way of a summary, Fig. 6.17 provides an overview of the progress that we think a student makes through geometry learning. There are two major sources of knowledge in the learning environment—these are the general rules stated in the instructional portion of the text and the examples of proofs worked out and provided as exercises. Both rules and examples are given declarative encodings. The declarative representation of rules can be used to solve problems by general problem-solving procedures. The declarative encoding of the examples can be used to guide the solution to problems through a declarative interpreter. The twin processes of knowledge compilation, composition and proceduralization, can transform either of these declarative representations into a procedural form. The procedures compiled from the declarative representation of the rules are general and the procedures compiled from examples are specific. The generalization mechanism provides a way of transforming the specific procedures into general form.

There is another route to learning and this is the process of subsumption, which involves the development of new problem-solving schemata out of old ones. We see this as a form of learning with structural understanding. We

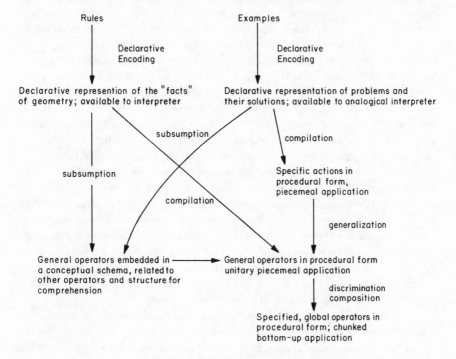

FIG. 6.17.   Summary of learning processes.

discussed two types of learning of this variety—elaborating existing schemata to apply to new situations or building new schemata out of existing schemata. These schemata are basically declarative in character and the compilation process should be able to apply to these to form general procedures also.

Note that there are many routes by which a student can arrive at general operators for solving geometry problems. This corresponds to the diversity we see in individual students: Some lean heavily on prior knowledge in learning; others try to apply the general rules of geometry directly; still others (probably the majority) lean heavily on past examples to guide their problem solving and learning.

Whatever means the student takes to achieve general operators for solving geometry problems, there remains a great deal of learning about heuristic features of the problem environment that are predictive of solution steps. To some extent, general operators that arise from specific examples through generalization may still preserve some of these heuristic features of the examples. Other methods of acquiring these heuristic features involve the processes of discrimination and composition that create larger multiple-inference operators that are much more discriminant in their range of applicability. In the extreme we obtain special rules that outline full proof trees for certain kinds of problems. The character of these operators is, as we have noted, working forward more than working backward. To the extent that new problems fit the specifications of these advanced operators, solution will be quick and efficient. However, to the extent new problems pose novel configurations of features not covered by the advanced operators, the student will have to fall back to the slower and more general operators for working backward. We certainly notice this variation in our own behavior as "experts" depending on how unique a geometry problem is. Our view of expertise then, is very much like the one that was developed for chess (Chase & Simon, 1973; Simon & Gilmartin, 1973); that is, experts in geometry proof generation have simply encoded many special case rules.

In conclusion, we should make some remarks to avoid an overly impressive interpretation of Fig. 6.17: Nowhere does there reside a single version of the ACT system containing all the components in Fig. 6.17 that progresses from the initial input of a geometry text to the final status of a geometry expert. Rather we have simulated bits and pieces of Fig. 6.17 separately. All the major components have been tested on problems and we would like to believe they would all work together if put into a complete system. However, undoubtedly interesting new issues would come up if we tried to put it all together. So, Fig. 6.17 represents a partial sketch of what is involved in geometry learning.

There are two basic reasons for the current disjointed character of our simulations. One is that the size and complexity of the full system is staggering. We run out of PDP 10 conventional address space just simulating components. The other reason is that we all took on separate parts of the task, and although we certainly talked to each other, our implementation efforts were separate. While on this topic we should indicate who was mainly responsible for implementing which components: John Anderson implemented the general control structure for proof searches; Jim Greeno, the processes underlying schema subsumption; Paul Kline, the analogy components; David Neves, the knowledge compilation processes; and John Anderson and Paul Kline, the processes of generalization and discrimination. Perhaps someday, technology and ourselves willing, there will be implemented an integrated version of Fig. 6.17.

ACKNOWLEDGMENTS

This research was supported by the Personnel and Training Research Programs, Psychological Services Division, Office of Naval Research, under Contract No.: N00014-78-C-0725, Contract Authority Identification, NR No.: 154-399 to John Anderson and under Contract No.: N00014-78-C-0022, Contract Authority Identification Number, NR No.: 157-408 to James Greeno.

REFERENCES

Anderson, J. R. *Language, memory, and thought.* Hillsdale, N.J.: Lawrence Erlbaum Associates, 1976.

Anderson, J. R., Kline, P. J., & Beasley, C. M. A general learning theory and its application to schema abstraction. In G. H. Bower (Ed.), *The psychology of learning and motivation* (Vol. 13). New York: Academic Press, 1979.

Anderson, J. R., Kline, P. J., & Beasley, C. M. Complex learning processes. In R. E. Snow, P. A. Federico, & W. E. Montague (Eds.), *Aptitude, learning, and instruction: Cognitive process analyses.* Hillsdale, N.J.: Lawrence Erlbaum Associates, 1980.

Bobrow, D. G., & Winograd, T. An overview of KRL, a knowledge representation language. *Cognitive Science,* 1977, *1,* 3–46.

Book, W. F. The psychology of skill with special reference to its acquisition in typewriting. Missoula, Montana: University of Montana, 1908. Facsimile in *The Psychology of Skill,* New York: Armo Press, 1973.

Chase, W. G., & Simon, H. A. The mind's eye in chess. In W. G. Chase (Ed.), *Visual information processing.* New York: Academic Press, 1973.

Duncker, K. On problem solving. *Psychological Monographs,* 1945, *58,* Whole No. 270.

Elio, R., & Anderson, J. R. Effects of category generalizations and instance similarity on schema abstraction, in preparation.

Gick, M. L., & Holyoak, K. J. Analogical problem solving. *Cognitive Psychology,* 1980, *12,* 306–355.

Greeno, J. G. Indefinite goals in well-structured problems. *Psychological Review,* 1976, *83,* 479–491.

Greeno, J. G. A study of problem solving. In R. Glaser (Ed.), *Advances in instructional psychology (Vol. 1).* Hillsdale, N.J.: Lawrence Erlbaum Associates, 1978.

Greeno, J. G., & Magone, M. E. *The concept of formal proof.* Manuscript in preparation.

Greeno, J. G., Magone, M. E., & Chaiklin, S. Theory of constructions and set in problem solving. *Memory and Cognition,* 1979, *7,* 445–461.

Heller, J. I. *The role of "focus" in children's understanding of arithmetic word problems.* Paper presented at the meeting of the American Educational Research Association, Boston, April 1980.

Jurgensen, R. C., Donnelly, A. J., Maier, J. E., & Rising, G. R. *Geometry*. Boston, Mass.: Houghton Mifflin, 1975.

Katona, G. Organizing and memorizing. New York: Columbia University Press, 1940.

Larkin, J. H., McDermott, J., Simon, D. P., & Simon, H. A. Models of competence in solving physics problems. *Cognitive Science,* in press.

Lewis, C. H. *Production system models of practice effects*. Unpublished Ph.D. dissertation, University of Michigan, 1978.

Luchins, A. S. Mechanization in problem solving. *Psychological Monographs,* 1942, *54,* No. 248.

Newell, A., & Simon, H. *Human problem solving*. Englewood Cliffs, N.J.: Prentice-Hall, 1972.

Riley, M. S. *The development of children's ability to solve arithmetic word problems*. Paper presented at the meeting of the American Educational Research Association, San Francisco, April 1979.

Sacerdoti, E. D. *A structure for plans and behavior*. New York: Elsevier North-Holland, 1977.

Simon, H. A., & Gilmartin, K. A simulation of memory for chess positions. *Cognitive Psychology,* 1973, *5,* 29–46.

Steele, G. L., Jr., & Sussman, G. J. *Constraints* (AI Memo No. 502). Cambridge, Mass.: Massachusetts Institute of Technology, Artificial Intelligence Laboratory, November, 1978.

Wertheimer, M. *Productive thinking*. New York: Harper & Row, 1945. (Enlarged edition, 1959)

Winston, P. H. Learning by creating transfer frames. *Artificial Intelligence,* 1978, *10,* 147–172.

7

Advice Taking and Knowledge Refinement: An Iterative View of Skill Acquisition

Frederick Hayes-Roth, Philip Klahr, and David J. Mostow
The Rand Corporation
Santa Monica, California

ABSTRACT

We consider knowledge acquisition and skill development as an iterative process. In the first phase, an initial capability is achieved by understanding instructions and following advice. Once a person (or machine) tries out its new knowledge, a variety of potential problems and learning opportunities arise. These simulate refinements to previous knowledge that, in turn, reinitiate the entire cycle. This learning paradigm has led to new work in knowledge representation, operationalization, expectation-driven bug detection, and knowledge refinement techniques. This chapter explains how advice is converted into operational behavior, how unexpected or undesirable behavioral outcomes stimulate learning efforts, and how the bugs responsible can be diagnosed and repaired. These phenomena are illustrated with examples of human and machine skill development in a familiar card game. The proposed learning methods provide a basis for a deeper understanding of skilled behavior and its development than previously possible.

What is Learned?

When we acquire an intellectual skill, what is learned? In this chapter, we focus on three types of learned knowledge. The first includes improved concepts and heuristics that characterize the problem domain. The second includes increasingly effective means for achieving goals in the problem domain. The third type includes improved knowledge of the expectable consequences of our plans. In this context, skill development means improving the quality and increasing the

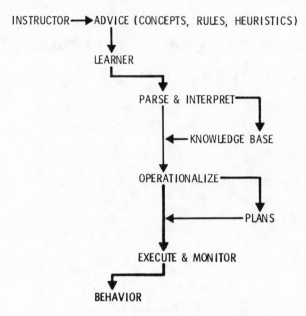

FIG. 7.1.   The learning cycle: phase 1, following advice.

coverage of these three kinds of knowledge as well as the capability to apply them appropriately.

Nearly all our skills develop in part by instruction and in part by experience. We elaborate this notion as a two-phase learning cycle. The first phase requires a learner to follow the advice of the instructor, as illustrated in Fig. 7.1.

In the first phase, an instructor advises the learner about a problem domain. The advice specifies the basic concepts of the domain, rules that restrict behavior, and suggested heuristics to guide problem-solving behavior. Before the learner can employ this advice in the generation of behavior, he/she needs to convert it into useful forms. First, the learner needs to parse and interpret the advice. To understand each concept, rule, and heuristic, the learner must relate it to his/her existing knowledge of the problem domain. We refer to this collection of knowledge as the *learner's knowledge base*. The learner's understanding transforms the advice from its initial linguistic form to a declarative knowledge representation. At this point, the learner must operationalize the advice by transforming the declarative knowledge into executable or procedural forms. Operationalization means finding plans for carrying out the actions that the advice prescribes. Finally, the learner must execute and monitor the plans. This final step produces the behavior that the initial advice dictated.

As we all know, learning a new skill is rarely as simple or effective as the preceding discussion suggests. More often than not, our initial efforts at carrying out someone's advice lead to several problems. We may fail to carry out the instructor's true wishes because we misunderstood the advice. We may err because our plans fail to work as supposed. Or we may find it difficult to execute our plans as we hoped. When we begin to act, our behavior reveals such shortcomings. These weaknesses in behavior stimulate the second phase of the learning cycle.

In the second phase (Fig. 7.2), we diagnose the problems in behavior and refine the knowledge that underlies them. These processes may be carried out by either the instructor or the learner, or both. Diagnosis in this context means attributing responsibility for errors to units of knowledge that supported erroneous reasoning or procedures. Refinement means modifying previous knowledge to prevent similar negative experiences in the future. The refinement process may suggest new advice to eliminate ambiguities in the instruction, new concepts or heurisitcs for approaching problems, new plans for avoiding undesirable events,

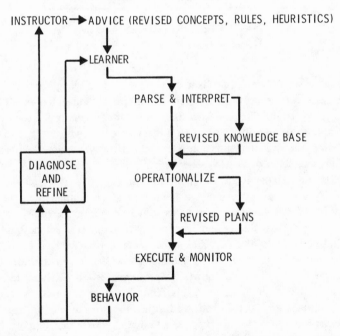

FIG. 7.2. The learning cycle: phase 2, diagnosing behavior and refining knowledge.

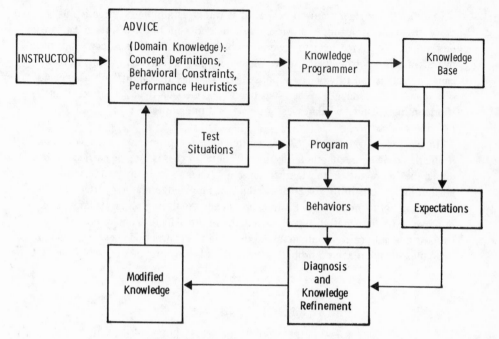

FIG. 7.3.   Learning research methodology.

etc. In each case, the learner needs to reevaluate his knowledge base and plans in accordance with the diagnosed deficiencies and proposed refinements. Our principal objective in this chapter is to explain each of these processes. We shall largely ignore the role of positive learning experiences whose diagnosis should lead to strengthening of responsible elements. However, some similarities between the treatments of positive and negative learning experiences are readily apparent (Lenat, Hayes-Roth, & Klahr, 1979a, 1979b).

To study the learning cycle, we have pursued a simple methodology, as shown in Fig. 7.3. An instructor provides advice of the sort previously described. In the given problem domain, the advice covers the concept definitions, the behavioral constraints or rules, and some specific performance heuristics that prescribe particular methods for achieving goals. To model the advice-taking process, we are developing a knowledge programmer, an Artificial Intelligence (AI) system that assimilates such advice and converts it into an executable program for performing the instructed skill. In this conversion process, the knowledge programmer should produce a knowledge base that supports expectations about what its program will accomplish in various situations. When the program is allowed to perform in test situations, its behavior will reveal how well the knowledge programmer has followed the advice.

To model the second phase of learning, we are developing AI systems for diagnosis and knowledge refinement. These systems must compare the actual program behaviors with the expected ones to diagnose weaknesses in the knowledge base. For each weakness, knowledge refinement strategies propose ways to modify the knowledge that will bring observed and predicted outcomes closer. The modified knowledge then must be fed back to the learner in the form of new advice, which reinitiates the learning cycle.

We have designed and implemented AI programs for a portion of each of these capabilities. Our systems are described in several technical papers (Hayes-Roth, Klahr, Burge, & Mostow, 1978; Hayes-Roth, 1980; Hayes-Roth, Klahr, & Mostow, 1980; Mostow & Hayes-Roth, 1979a, 1979b). In this chapter, we focus more on the "what" of these skill development processes than on the "how." Advice taking and knowledge refinement seem to us ubiquitous aspects of skill development, and our research methodology emphasizes those aspects that require greatest advance. We discuss our specific research applications where appropriate, but otherwise we emphasize more general problems and the learning principles they suggest.

The proposed research methodology emphasizes four principal problems. First, we must specify what we mean by *advice:* What is advice and how shall we represent it? The second major problem concerns the conversion of advice into executable procedures: How can a learner operationalize advice? Third, we must specify the events that should initiate learning: What kinds of situations trigger learning? Fourth, we need to explain how to modify previously erroneous behaviors: What can be learned, and how can this be done? In the following sections, each of these problems is considered in turn.

What is Advice?

Advice consists of concept definitions, behavioral constraints, and performance heuristics. Concept definitions describe the elements of a problem domain, such as objects, actions, and properties. Behavioral constraints prescribe necessary qualities and proscribe disallowed characteristics of behavior. These constraints are typically mandatory rules that govern behavior in a problem domain. Performance heuristics, on the other hand, suggest ways to solve the domain problems and achieve desired results. These heuristics prescribe ways a learner should attempt to behave if possible.

Our research has been motivated, in part, by a desire to understand learning as a domain-independent capability. Nevertheless, we believe strongly that expertise in any domain requires considerable domain-specific knowledge. To bridge this gap, we have been developing general methods for assimilating domain-specific knowledge (as have Barr, Bennett, & Clancey, 1979; Davis, 1978, 1979, among others). In particular, we interpret domain-specific rules and heuristics as specific "compositions" of the domain concepts. From this perspective, advice consists of the primitive concepts of a domain plus the constraints and heuristics that are expressions composed in terms of these primitive concepts. The general capabilities that underlie this view include a scheme to represent concept definitions and a method to express rules and heuristics as composite expressions of the more primitive terms. In a sense, the domain concepts define a lexicon in which the rules and heuristics are expressed.

To illustrate, we consider the familiar card game *hearts*. The following text would be representative of an instructor's advice to a learner.

The goal of this game is to avoid taking points. In each round, the deck of cards is initially dealt out among three or four players. Each player's cards constitute the player's hand. Play in a round consists of a series of tricks. Each player, clockwise in turn, plays once in a trick by moving a card from his or her hand into the pot. The player who has the two of clubs (2C) leads the first trick. Each player must follow suit if possible (i.e., must play a card of the same suit as that led). The player who plays the highest card in the suit led wins the trick and leads the next trick. A player who wins a trick takes all cards in the pot and is charged with any points that those cards have. Each heart has one point (hence the name of the game). The queen of spades (QS) has 13 points. The worst a player can do in one round is take all but 1 point, in which case he or she takes 25 points. If the player takes 26 points (i.e., "shoots the moon"), every other player is charged with the 26 points. Shooting the moon is the best a player can do; taking 0 points is second best. You can prevent someone from shooting the moon by taking a point yourself. Whenever it is out, flush the queen of spades to make sure it isn't given to you.

A complete description of the game can be found elsewhere (Balzer, 1966; Hayes-Roth, Klahr, Burge, & Mostow, 1978).

The preceding description illustrates all three kinds of advice elements. In the hearts domain, the concept definitions include the following:

deck, hand, card, suit, spades, clubs, diamonds, hearts, deal, round, trick, avoid, point, player, play, take, lead, win, follow suit, shooting the moon, . . .

In terms of these concepts, the behavioral constraints include:

The player with 2C leads.
Each player must follow suit.
The player of the highest card in the suit led wins the trick.
The winner of a trick leads the next trick.

The performance heuristics include:

Avoid taking points.
Take all the points in a round.
If you can't take all the points in a round, take as few as possible.
Take a point if necessary to prevent someone from taking them all.
If the queen of spades is out, flush the queen of spades.

Now let's consider how these domain concepts can be represented and used to understand the domain-specific advice. In particular, consider the concepts of *trick* and *avoid*. A trick is defined as a scenario in which each player plays a card and the winner takes the pot. Similarly, we define avoid by saying that avoiding an event during a scenario means not letting it happen then. In our work on knowledge programming, we have adopted specialized forms of the lambda calculus to represent such concepts (Allen, 1978). In our representation scheme, we would represent these domain concepts as follows:

(trick) = (scenario (each p (players) (play-card p))
                    (take-trick (trick-winner)))

(avoid e s) = (achieve (not (during s e)))

These representative definitions highlight our methods. First, each concept is viewed as a LISP expression, and the equality means that the expression on the right can be substituted for the one on the left. Each domain-specific concept is represented using a lexicon of approximately 100 domain-independent primitive concepts, such as *scenario, each, achieve, not,* and *during.* Thus, the definition of trick expresses exactly:

A trick is a scenario of two sequential steps.
First, each p in the set of players plays a card.
Second, the trick-winner takes the trick

In this definition, "play-card," "take-trick," and "trick-winner" are stand-ins for other domain concepts that are similarly represented in terms of lower-level definitions. Play-card, for example, denotes the action of playing a card; similarly, take-trick denotes winning the trick and taking the pot.

The definition of *avoid* expresses the notion that some event e is to be avoided in some scenario s. In particular, it states that avoid e in s is equivalent to achieving the negation of the proposition that e occurs during s.

In our research, we have studied advice taking in several domains, including hearts and music. The same core set of primitive concepts is used to define the domain concepts. In hearts, all the basic domain concepts are represented as LISP expressions like those shown previously. Moreover, each bit of behavioral advice is represented as a LISP expression as well. However, simply representing advice in the form of such expressions is not sufficient to follow the advice; the expressions must be executable. Making such expressions executable is the goal of *operationalization.*

How Can a Learner Operationalize Advice?

Even if a learner can map behavioral advice into LISP expressions or other representation formalisms, he/she may have no effective means of carrying out the actions needed to achieve what the expression denotes. In this framework, however, operationalization has a simple meaning: Expressions representing behavioral prescriptions must be transformed into operational forms (Balzer, Goldman, & Wile, 1977; Barstow, 1977; Heidorn, 1974). In our context, an expression of the form (F e_1 . . . e_2) is operational only if F has an effective procedure and each e_1 is operational or denotes a constant. Although this may sound quite abstract, it really is quite simple: A prescribed behavior is operational if we can express it in terms of procedures and objects we know how to evaluate.

Again, a specific example will help clarify these points. Suppose, for example, a learner wants to follow the heuristic, "avoid taking points." The learner might reason as follows:

1. To avoid taking points in general, I should find a way to avoid taking points in the current trick.
2. This means I should try not to win the trick if it has points.
3. I can do this by trying not to play the winning card.
4. This I could do by playing a card lower than some other card played in the suit led.
5. Thus, I should play a low card.

Each successive statement in this line of reasoning represents a specific way to achieve the effect described in the preceding one. The last statement, however, is the only one that fits our definition of operational. Statement 5 represents an effective operationalization of the initial advice. In our opinion, "learning" often depends primarily on the learner's ability to find ways for carrying out an instructor's advice. As this example shows, a "problem-reduction" strategy may prove sufficient to convert an unoperational goal expression into an effective, sufficient, operational procedure.

This example may seem to suggest that operationalization may be quite straightforward and simple. We have found, however, that it requires substantial analytical techniques that may give rise to considerable complexity. To convert one expression into its next-level representation, the learner can use a variety of methods. Basically, the learner substitutes a new expression that he/she thinks will suffice to achieve the previous one. Three different types of substitutions can arise. Each substitution may replace an initial expression by a logically equivalent one, by a description of some state whose realization should entail the initial one, or by a set of actions that supposedly can produce the desired result. Two kinds of knowledge are required to accomplish these transformations. First, the learner manipulates all the domain-specific knowledge to determine various relations of interest. Second, the learner must also apply general transformational rules that determine plausible and correct substitutions. We have, to this date, developed about 200 of these transformational rules.

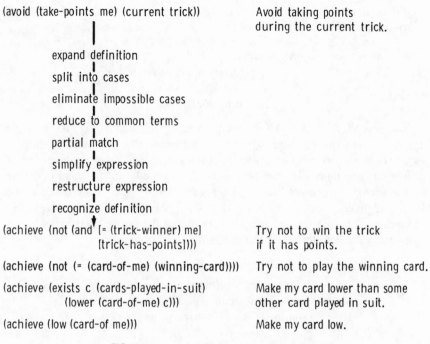

(avoid (take-points me) (current trick))   Avoid taking points
                                                        during the current trick.

    expand definition

    split into cases

    eliminate impossible cases

    reduce to common terms

    partial match

    simplify expression

    restructure expression

    recognize definition

(achieve (not (and [= (trick-winner) me]   Try not to win the trick
            [trick-has-points])))   if it has points.

(achieve (not (= (card-of-me) (winning-card))))   Try not to play the winning card.

(achieve (exists c (cards-played-in-suit)   Make my card lower than some
       (lower (card-of-me) c)))   other card played in suit.

(achieve (low (card-of me)))   Make my card low.

FIG. 7.4. Operationalize "avoid taking points."

Figure 7.4 illustrates at a fairly high level the successive expressions that result from the knowledge programmer's efforts to operationalize the "avoid taking points" heuristic. On the left, five LISP expressions are shown in correspondence with the five steps a typical human learner takes. Between the first and second expression, we have shown eight distinct types of transformations that play a role in transforming expression 1 into expression 2. Although a detailed explanation of each transformation would exceed the scope of this chapter, we describe each of these kinds of operations briefly here.

The first kind of transformation expands the definition of a term in an expression. For example, the initial expression would be matched to the form (avoid e s) so that (take-points me) would replace e and (current trick) would replace s. The resulting expression would be an expanded expression for the idea that the learner should prevent taking points during the current trick.

(achieve (not (during (current trick) (take-points me))))

This kind of definitional transformation simply reexpresses a compact idea in terms of its equivalent and more elaborated elementary concepts. Definition expansion plays a major role in operationalization because a learner must frequently unpack and manipulate advice that is initially packed in terse compositions of domain concept. By similarly expanding the concept of trick, the previous operationalization becomes:

```
(achieve (not (during (scenario
                      (each p (players) (play-card p))
                      (take-trick (trick-winner)))
               (take-points me))))
```

The second kind of transformation, called *case analysis,* breaks a single expression into two or more expressions that depend on alternative additional assumptions. In operationalization, case analysis reformulates one meaning as different expressions that can be evaluated separately. In the context of our current example, to ensure against taking points during the two-step scenario. the learner might consider two cases: (1) that taking points occurs during the playing of cards; or (2) that taking points occurs during the taking of the trick. This transformation would produce the following new expression:

```
(achieve (not (or
               (during  (each p (players) (play-card p))
                (take-points me))
               (during (take-trick (trick-winner))
                (take-points me)))))
```

The third type of transformation eliminates impossible cases. The learner must recognize that some expressions cannot be achieved and thus should be eliminated from further consideration. In the current example, case 1 should be ignored because there is no cotemporaneous relation between playing cards and taking points. More generally, impossible cases arise when expressions represent unachievable conditions. Our knowledge programmer detects these in various ways. In this particular example, because it can find no relationship between the definitions of playing cards and taking points, it decides to drop that case from consideration.

The fourth kind of transformation reduces different expressions to common terms. This general transformation helps coerce comparability between seemingly different entities. In the current example, such a transformation helps reexpress case 2. This case represented the possibility that taking points would occur during the action of taking the trick. This case follows from our definitions of the game, because a person takes points when he or she takes a pot containing point cards. The knowledge programmer recognizes this relationship as a path in a semantic network it constructs to represent part–whole relationships among domain action definitions. Because take-points is a part of take-trick, the knowledge programmer can reexpress (during (take-trick (trick-winner)) (take-points me)) as follows:

```
(exists c1 (cards-played)
  (exists c2 (point-cards)
    (during (take (trick-winner) c1)
            (take me c2))))
```

This expression characterizes the meaning of "me taking points during the trick-winner's taking a trick." This can only make sense, according to the domain concepts, if me takes a point card c2 during the period that the trick-winner takes the cards played. Our transformation has introduced two variables, c1 and c2, which remain to be made operational before the operationalization is complete.

The fifth general transformation method used is partial matching (Hayes-Roth, 1978). Partial matching compares two descriptions to identify their similarities and differences. When two expressions occurring within some relationship match perfectly, the relationship between them often can be greatly simplified. When this isn't possible, we can often achieve comparable simplifications by first finding ways to reduce the differences between the two expressions to common terms. By using a rule of partial matching plus a semantic network of relationships among concepts, our knowledge programmer transforms the preceding expression into the requirement:

```
(exists c1 (cards-played)
  (exists c2 (point-cards)
    (and (= (trick-winner) me) (= c1 c2))))
```

This requirement establishes necessary conditions for me to take points while the trick winner was taking the cards played, namely that the trick winner *is* me and that me takes the point cards that the trick winner does.

The sixth type of transformation is simplification. Much general analytical knowledge concerns the types of expressions that can be replaced by simpler ones. De Morgan's laws in logic are examples of the kinds of simplifications a learner implicitly uses to replace a complex expression by an equivalent, simpler one. Other kinds of simplifications include replacing symbolic expressions by constants or removing quantifiers when appropriate. In the current example, this last kind of simplification can exploit the fact that the two variables c1 and c2 are equal. To simplify the expression, the symbol c2 can be replaced by c1, and at the same time the condition that c1 and c2 should be equal can simply be dropped.

The seventh type of transformation restructures expressions to make them more amenable to the other types of analysis. These restructuring operations only serve the purpose of reconfiguring expressions, but such reconfigurations can make the difference between a hard and an easy operationalization. Depending on the domain knowledge and general transformations available, some expression patterns will sustain continued operationalization, whereas others, perhaps equivalent, will not be noticed. In the current example, the learner profitably moves the existential quantifier to an interior position in the expression to restructure part of the expression as shown here:

    (and [= (trick-winner) me]
        [exists c1 (cards-played)
            (in c1 (point-cards))])

This expresses the requirement that the trick winner is me and some c1 among the cards played is in the set of point cards.

The eighth type of transformation is the inverse of the first. These transformations recognize instances of higher-level definitions and replace the more complex, lower-level expressions by the corresponding higher-level ones. The resulting expressions may simplify otherwise complex expressions and may lead more directly to the identification of effective procedures. In the current illustration, for example, the last two lines of the preceding expression represent exactly the concept that "the trick has points." This concept occurs in the second line of the derivation in Fig. 7.4 as [trick-has-points]. By substituting this concept, the overall derivation to this point becomes:

    (achieve (not (and [= (trick-winner) me]
                    [trick-has-points])))

In operationalizing the remaining three steps, several other general types of transformations are involved. Approximately 40 transformational steps are required to operationalize this single heuristic bit of advice. Other lines of reasoning could also be pursued successfully and several of these produce alternative operationalizations for "avoid taking points."

The one example we have followed should illustrate both the variety of techniques involved in operationalization and the complexity of the detailed processes that the knowledge programmer models. This particular example was chosen because of the variety of operationalization methods it reveals.

A second example of operationalization will provide the basis for illustrating the second phase of learning, involving diagnosis and refinement. In this example, the learner attempts to follow the instruction, "If the queen of spades is out, try to flush it." To follow this advice, the learner must develop a method for: (1) deciding if the queen of spades is out; and (2) forcing the player who has it to play it. Our knowledge programmer uses a "pigeon-hole principle" to solve the first problem: A thing must reside momentarily in just one of its possible loci. In this example, the card is "out" if it has not been played and is not in the learner's own hand.

To flush the queen, a more complex operationalization effort is required. In overview, the knowledge programmer develops the following plan:

1. Flush the queen of spades.
2. This means forcing the owner of the queen of spades to play it.

3. This requires me to reduce the owner's options to just that one action.

4. This can be done by leading spades until the owner of the queen is forced to play it.

5. To do this, I should win the lead and then continue leading spades.

The kind of reasoning the program uses to develop its plan is as follows: By substituting the definition of "flush," it infers that it needs to establish the condition "some player p must play the queen of spades." It uses its concept of "must" and the rule that players must follow suit to infer that p can have only one legal card to play—the queen of spades. This in turn entails either p has only the queen of spades or player me leads a spade, and p's only spade is the queen. It focuses on the second case and then develops a plan for how player me could force such a situation. In brief, it develops a plan for me to win a trick to take the lead. Then as long as player me retains the lead, player me continues to lead spades. As players familiar with the game will realize, this is an effective method for flushing the queen. However, as we discuss in the following, this plan will probably lead to some disappointments that should stimulate learning.

What Kinds of Events Trigger Learning?

We presume that learning is often triggered by violated expectations. Expectations vary from weak, general ones to strong, specific ones. The weak expectations a learner may have arise from the general belief that following advice should produce favorable results. Equivalently, the learner may expect only good consequences when he/she follows the plans that operationalize an instructor's advice. Strong expectations on the other hand are consequences of actions that can be deduced from the learner's knowledge base. In particular, the learner operationalizes expressions to achieve particular results. Presumably then, executing the operationalizations should achieve the conditions they purport to.

Violated expectations are the triggering events for learning. These violations include both unexpected and unfavorable consequences of successfully executed plans. In addition, the unexpected but desirable outcomes of behaviors should trigger efforts to learn what these outcomes might be attributed to. Finally, disconfirmations of assumptions also motivate learning (Lakatos, 1976). In toto, we can think of behavior as theory-driven, because behaviors derive from assumptions, plans, and theoretically appropriate transformations of expressions; learning is triggered by events that disconfirm the expectable consequences of such theories. A deep and more formal exposition of theory-driven learning appears in Hayes-Roth (1980).

A simple example illustrates these concepts. Consider the previously derived plan for "flush the queen of spades." The plan developed for this advice was, roughly, take the lead and then lead spades until a player is forced to play the queen. Suppose that this plan worked well when executed in several games, but then during one game a sequence like the following unexpectedly occurred: The learner wins a trick. He or she then leads the jack of spades, and the other players follow suit. The queen is still held by one of the players. On the next trick, the learner chooses another spade to lead. This time, he/she has only two spades left, the four and the king, and chooses arbitrarily to play the king. The next player plays the five, the one after him plays the queen, and the last plays the ten. The learner has just won a trick according to its plan, and has even flushed the queen. Unfortunately, the learner has also taken 13 points, a very undesirable outcome.

What might the learner do at this point? With apparently little effort, a person would recognize that the plan was buggy, because it achieved an undesirable result that was unexpected. Implicit in the plan was the notion that the player with the queen would be coerced into playing it and, presumably, would win the spade trick with it. Having discovered this insight, a human learner would attempt to amend the buggy plan accordingly. The fix in this case would require that, when trying to flush the queen, a player must lead only spades below the queen to avoid winning the queen. In the next section, we describe learning techniques that produce this sort of knowledge refinement.

What Can Be Learned, and How Is This Done?

A learner can increase its knowledge in any of the areas knowledge is currently possessed. This means learning new domain knowledge, new operationalizations, or new operationalization methods. We consider only the first two of these types of learning, because the last surpasses our current understanding. Thus, a learner can discover new and generalized domain concepts (Lenat, 1976; Lenat & Harris, 1978), additional behavioral goals, and improved heuristics for problem solving in the domain. Each newly formulated unit of knowledge domain typically corresponds to unoperational advice. On the other hand, the learner can formulate new and improved plans for more effectively operationalizing previous advice.

We view learning of this sort as *knowledge refinement*. The learner progresses by iteratively modifying the current knowledge base to accommodate experience. The improvements to knowledge arise from two principal sources: heuristic rules for diagnosis and heuristic rules for learning. The diagnosis rules identify problematic knowledge base elements (Sussman & Stallman, 1975). The learning rules suggest particular knowledge refinements. These elements support steps 3 and 4 of an overall five-step process, as shown in Table 7.1.

Let us pursue the example from the preceding section. We supposed that a learner would attempt to fix the apparently buggy plan for "flush the queen of spades" by asserting an additional goal for that plan to achieve. That additional goal, or constraint, was that the learner should not itself win the trick in which the queen of spades is played. That kind of advice could arise externally, from an instructor, or internally, from the learner's own diagnosis procedures. We explore this latter alternative further.

TABLE 7.1
Knowledge Refinement Approach

Step	Source or Mechanism
1. Establish expectations	During knowledge programming, planning establishes plausible antecedents and consequences of actions; these beliefs represent expectations.
2. Trigger analysis	When an actual event violates an expectation, the reasoning behind the expectation is reanalyzed in light of observable data.
3. Locate faulty rules	A set of diagnostic rules debug the planning logic by contrasting the a priori beliefs with actual data. If a heuristic rule used by the plan assumes a false premise or entails a false conclusion, it is faulty.
4. Modify faulty rules	A set of learning rules suggest plausible fixes to the erroneous heuristic rule. These might alter its preconditions, assumptions, or expectations to keep it from producing the same faulty result in a subsequent situation.
5. Reimplement and test	Incorporate a modified heuristic rule into a new behavior by reinvoking the knowledge programmer. Verify that the rule eliminates the previous problem and test it in new situations.

First let us suppose that the learner had no precise expectation regarding the queen-flushing plan. However, because the learner followed supposedly expert advice, he/she has a general expectation that bad consequences should not result. When, as in this case, undesirable results occur, the learner tries to understand why he/she suffered such a regrettable outcome and how to prevent it.

The learner analyzes the last trick to infer cause–effect relations, based on its current knowledge. According to the domain concepts and constraints, to take 13 points in the trick, the learner had to win the trick during which the queen was played. So the learner conjectures some refined advice for himself: "Flush the queen of spades but do not win a trick in which the queen is played." Because this refined advice surpasses the original advice in quality. the learner has already improved its knowledge. On the other hand, this high-level advice requires operationalization if it is to be useful. This type of advice can be operationalized with exactly the same methods we previously described. Our current knowledge programmer correctly operationalizes this advice by producing a plan corresponding to the following: "Take the lead; then continue leading spades that rank below the queen." Thus, this type of bug could be eliminated by formulating a desired refinement directly in terms of a new high-level prescriptive heuristic. The refined heuristic, in turn, is implemented by the same knowledge programming methods previously used for accepting advice from an instructor. (In some cases, as in this example, the refined heuristic can also be operationalized directly by modifying the previous plan, as opposed to starting over from scratch.)

To continue the illustration, let us suppose that the learner begins to apply its refined plan. Because the learner knows that the plan has been refined to prevent it from taking the queen of spades itself, it notes this specific expectation in the knowledge base as a predicted consequence of the plan. In a new game, however, suppose the learner has the ten, jack, and king of spades. It wins a trick and then leads the ten. All players follow suit with lower cards, so the learner leads again with the jack. Again it wins the trick. At this point, its revised plan proscribes leading spades, so it leads a diamond. Another player wins the trick, and that player continues to lead spades. The learner is forced to play the king, and the next player follows suit with the queen of spades.

Again, contrary to its specific expectation, the learner wins the trick and takes 13 points. Now the learner attempts to discover why its expectation was violated. It constructs a cause–effect model of the events leading to the disaster. In this model, it notes that at the time it played the king, it had no other choices. So apparently, by that time, only by keeping the other player from leading spades could it have prevented the disaster. Alternatively, it reviews events prior to that trick to see what, if anything, it did that causally contributed to creating a situation in which no options existed. It notices that playing the ten and jack of spades earlier produced the state where it had only the king of spades. It notes that these actions were taken with the express intention of preventing it from taking the queen, but apparently they contributed directly to just that outcome.

The learner now proposes to itself another refinement. It should prevent a reoccurrence of this type of situation in the future. Its proposed advice: "Do not lead low spades if you can be forced subsequently to play a spade higher than the queen."[1] This, in turn, leads to an operationalization that requires an estimation of the probable distributions of spades among players. Although we have developed some methods for handling such probability functions, we have not yet implemented those needed for this particular problem. However, as persons knowledgeable in the game will notice, the proposed concept of a card that is "safe" vis-à-vis the opposing distributions is quite sophisticated. In fact, generalizations of this "safe spade" concept, such as "safe in suit x" or "safe with respect to all suits," play major roles in expert strategies.

As another example of knowledge refinement, consider again the plan developed in a previous section to avoid taking points. That plan proposed playing the lowest possible card. Using this plan, the learner expects it will avoid taking points, but there are numerous ways that this plan leads to violated expectations, each of which reflects characteristics similar to the queen-flushing examples. For example, the learner may play its lowest card (a five, say) and still win a trick with points. This causes the learner to weaken its expectations (i.e., to associate some uncertainty with this predicted outcome). Pursuant to such a play, it may take another trick with its current lowest card (a ten, say), again with points.

---

[1]This example has not actually been performed by a machine implementation. Before it could be implemented, several difficult issues would arise. Foremost among these, the diagnostic system would need to conjecture several alternative problems and solutions. Each of these proposed solutions would require, in turn, experimental testing through additional play. For example, the program might have hypothesized the remedy, "Do not begin to flush the queen of spades if you cannot retain the lead." This heuristic seems beneficial, but we cannot be certain. Empirical validation of alternative heuristics seems unavoidable.

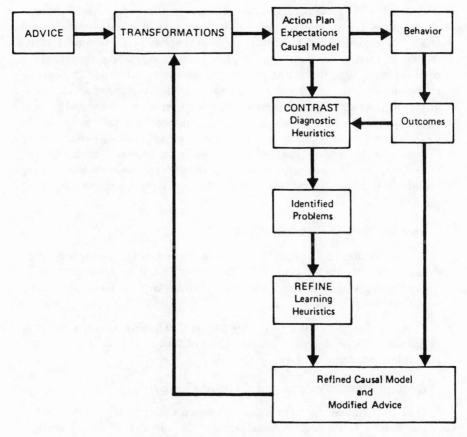

FIG. 7.5.   Knowledge refinement strategy.

However, if it had played the ten before the five, it might have avoided winning the second trick, because in the second trick the five might have been lower than other players' remaining cards. Each of these problems gives rise to new attempts to refine both the expectations and the plan, in a manner similar to that previously described.

Our general model of knowledge refinement can be portrayed as shown in Fig. 7.5.

The contrast between expectations and actual outcomes serves to focus the learning system directly on specific problems. The learner then attempts to diagnose the flaws in its original causal model in light of the new data in hand. The diagnosed problem dictates additional conditions or new goals for operationalization.

The overall approach we have taken to this knowledge refinement employs three basic elements: (1) proofs; (2) diagnostic rules; and (3) learning rules. Although not actually implemented on a computer, we have hand-simulated all the steps. The knowledge programmer associates with each plan and its expectations a proof (or an informal rationale). The *proof* of a plan links assumed conditions to expectations by deductively following paths representing the transformations used to operationalize the plan. Links along these paths reflect the equivalence of logical transformations, the plausible sufficiency of heuristic transformations, or the antecedent–consequent relations of incorporated instrumental acts. At each point, a transformation links premises to expectations, and these expectations may become part of the premises for a later inference. In short, a proof maps a general model of cause–effect relations into a specific derivation of the expected consequences of particular planned actions.

Diagnostic rules examine the proof in light of the evidence and identify hypothetical deficiencies in the knowledge base. A typical diagnostic rule is as follows:

Invalid Premise Diagnostic Rule

If an expectation is violated, find a premise in the proof of the expectation that is falsified by the data. If the false premise follows from some inference rule whose own antecedent premises (necessary conditions) are true, declare that rule faulty.

Learning rules, on the other hand, specify ways to modify heuristics to correct deficiencies. We have generated a sizable set of such rules to date. Two examples of learning rules are shown below:

Require Implicitly Assumed Premise Explicitly

If an implicit assumption of a rule is falsified during proof analysis, add the premise to the required conditions of the rule and delete any other premises that it implies.

Guarantee Assumed Conditions

If an assumed premise is falsified during proof analysis, identify sufficient conditions for its validity and make these required conditions for the associated plan component.

Figure 7.6 demonstrates how these diagnostic and learning rules are used to refine the original "flush the queen of spades" plan as discussed previously. Figure 7.6 also exemplifies the knowledge refinement approach outlined in Fig. 7.5.

Thus, we have found several ways to evaluate a plan against observable outcomes to identify weaknesses, conjecture refinements, and evaluate these refinements experimentally. Very little of this work has been implemented in applications software, because of the large number of plausible learning strategies (Hayes-Roth, Klahr, & Mostow, 1980) and the wide variety of specific possible applications. Any efforts to implement these concepts in a realistically complex task will encounter considerable combinatorial difficulties. Each observed error may indicate several hypothetical bugs and fixes. Each of these will require independent empirical (or formal) validation, usually accomplished best by experimental testing. The need for testing hypothetical concepts and rules will lead to alternative plausible knowledge bases and associated operational procedures. Managing multiple configurations of this sort, of course, can be very difficult. Understanding how humans narrow this combinatorial space should be a principal goal of subsequent studies of human learning.

In summary, once a plan is executed, much can be learned from a retrospective analysis. During initial advice taking, two important ingredients are missing that later can support evaluation and discovery. The first new source of information is the actual situation description. The details of the actual situation in which the plan executes reveal and implicitly define important special cases that the general operationalization overlooks. Second, having acted, we can see the true effects of our behavior on the environment. This provides sources of confirmation or disconfirmation of parts of our plans, which then stimulate focused efforts at diagnosis and knowledge refinement. These provide numerous opportunities for concept formulation and each, in turn, initiates a new cycle of advice taking, knowledge programming, and knowledge refinement.

Conclusions

We have formulated skill development as an iterative process that converts advice into plans and, ultimately, converts these plans into behaviors. The overall model we have presented is summarized in Fig. 7.7. Although this framework treats learning as a largely domain-independent enterprise, it motivates two caveats. First, we believe every skill is largely domain-dependent. Whatever domain independence exists is attributable to the general skills that underlie initial skill acquisition and subsequent skill improvement. Initial skill acquisition depends on the general and complex advice-taking skills of understanding and knowledge programming. In this chapter, we have developed many aspects of the advice-taking process. The second phase of learning also employs numerous and relatively general skills. In this phase, diagnostic and learning rules identify and rectify erroneous bits of knowledge. The second caveat on domain independence recognizes the important role that domain knowledge plays in diagnosis and refinement. A learner's ability to apply diagnosis and learning rules will also depend on his/her familiarity with and expertise in the problem domain. Although these heuristic and learning rules are domain-independent, to apply these rules a learner must be able to reason deductively about and with the entailments of his/her domain knowledge; that is, he/she must understand how specific expectations derive from particular assumptions, plans, and proofs. Furthermore, to refine erroneous knowledge, the learner must be able to reason about the

PLAN:

Flush queen of spades:

If	player P takes the lead
and	P doesn't have the queen of spades
then	P continues leading spades

Expectation:
P doesn't take the queen of spades

Proof of expectation:

1. Play P takes the lead — Premise (condition of plan)
2. P doesn't have the queen of spades — Premise (condition of plan)
3. P continues leading spades — Premise (action of plan)
4. If player P takes the lead and P doesn't have the queen of spades and P continues leading spades then opponent will play queen of spades. — Heuristic rule
5. Opponent will play queen of spades — Derived premise from 1,2,3,4
6. If an opponent plays queen of spades then the opponent wins the trick and opponent takes the queen of spades — Heuristic rule
7. Opponent takes the queen of spades — Derived premise from 5,6
8. If opponent takes the queen of spades then player P doesn't take queen of spades — Heuristic rule
9. Player P doesn't take the queen of spades — Derived premise from 7,8

Behavior in actual play: P leads king of spades;
                      Opponent plays queen of spades
Outcome: P wins the trick; P takes the queen of spades.

Expectation of "Flush queen of spades" plan is violated.

Apply diagnostic rules to identify problems:
    Using "Invalid Premise" diagnostic rule, the derived premise in Statement 7 is falsified by the data. The inference rule used to derive this false premise is the rule specified in Statement 6. Its premise is true, but its conclusion is false. Declare this rule faulty.

Apply Learning Rules to modify plans and heuristics:
    Using "Guarantee Assumed Conditions" learning rule, the system looks

FIG. 7.6. Knowledge refinement example.

for other rules in the knowledge base that identify conditions for infer-
ring Statement 7. It may find, for example, the inference rule:

> If opponent player plays a high card C
> and player P plays below C
> then opponent wins trick and takes C

In our current example, C is the queen of spades.
This rule now replaces the faulty rule in Statement 6 with the new premise

> Player P plays below the queen of
> spades

added as a premise to the plan and the proof. The resultant plan is

> If   player P takes the lead
> and   P doesn't have the queen of spades
> then   P continues leading spades
>   below the queen of spades

FIG. 7.6. (*Continued*)

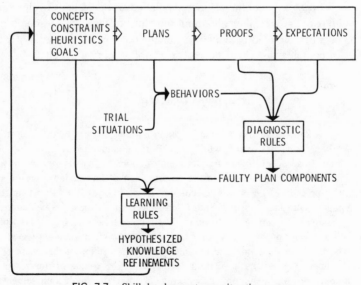

FIG. 7.7. Skill development as an iterative process.

251

knowledge and consider alternatives to it. Although these are general skills, differential experience in particular problem domains will presumably affect the difficulty of learning in those domains.

We believe our model of learning processes can be translated into a practical instructional program. Humans regularly perform the functions of understanding advice, knowledge programming, diagnosis, and refinement. Students could benefit from instruction on improved methods for each of these tasks. The concepts of domain definitions, constraints, heuristics, goals, plans, proofs, expectations, and violations should form the basis for a deeper understanding of one's own learning functions. Because these concepts make intuitive as well as analytical sense, they may support practical efforts to develop learning skills.

On the other hand, much remains to be done within the proposed learning research paradigm. Although the processes we have described in this chapter shed some light on advice taking and knowledge refinement, they do not constitute a complete model. For the goals of experimental psychologists, many additional assumptions would need to be introduced to transform our current model into a more predictive and vulnerable theory. To make the model valuable in computer applications, many more of the functions need to be programmed. This is hard for two reasons. First, each of the functions we have described is a state-of-the-art objective for AI. And, if that is not enough, learning programs must cope with combinatorics arising from ambiguities inherent in advice and the alternative possibilities for operationalizing each bit of knowledge. For these reasons, we expect only continual, incremental advances in our development of this research paradigm. In short, learning functions of the sort considered in this chapter appear to yield readily to analysis; on the other hand, synthesis of learned behaviors in complex tasks will prove considerably more difficult.

ACKNOWLEDGMENTS

We gratefully acknowledge the substantive contributions of our Rand, Stanford, and Carnegie-Mellon colleagues to this work. John Burge collaborated with us on learning heuristics. Stan Rosenschein made frequent contributions to our efforts on knowledge representation. Doug Lenat assisted in the development of knowledge representations, heuristics, and procedures for cognitive economy (Lenat, Hayes-Roth, & Klahr, 1979a, 1979b). As advisors to Jack Mostow, both Allen Newell and Jaime Carbonell contributed to our understanding of operationalization. The report, however, represents only the authors' attitudes and not the opinion of others with whom we have collaborated.

Perry Thorndyke made major contributions to the organization of this chapter.

Several computer programs have been developed in the course of this research by various combinations of the authors or their collaborators. Mostow has implemented the knowledge programming system as part of his dissertation research supervised by Hayes-Roth. Hayes-Roth and Klahr have implemented three different programs for representing and applying the knowledge of the hearts domain. Although these programs actually play the game moderately well, their interest for us lies in their alternative approaches to knowledge representation and control.

REFERENCES

Allen, J. *Anatomy of LISP,* New York: McGraw Hill, 1978.

Balzer, R. A mathematical model for performing a complex task in a card game. *Behavioral Sciences,* 1966, *2* (3), 219-236.

Balzer, R., Goldman, N., & Wile, D. Informality in program specifications. *Proceedings of the Fifth International Joint Conference on Artificial Intelligence.* Cambridge, Mass., 1977, 389-397.

Barr, A., Bennett, J., & Clancey, W. *Transfer of expertise: A theme for AI research.* Technical Report HPP-79-11, Stanford University, 1979.

Barstow, D. A knowledge-based system for automatic program construction. *Proceedings of the Fifth International Joint Conference on Artificial Intelligence.* Cambridge, Mass., 1977, 382-388.

Davis, R. Knowledge acquisition in rule-based systems: Knowledge about representation as a basis for system construction and maintenance. In D. A. Waterman & F. Hayes-Roth (Eds.). *Pattern-directed inference systems,* New York: Academic Press, 1978.

Davis, R. Interactive transfer of expertise: Acquisition of new inference rules. *Artificial Intelligence,* 1979, *12*(2), 121-158.

Hayes-Roth, F. The role of partial and best matches in knowledge systems. In D. A. Waterman & F. Hayes-Roth (Eds.), *Pattern directed inference systems,* New York: Academic Press, 1978.

Hayes-Roth, F. *Theory-driven learning: Proofs and refutations for concept discovery.* Rand Technical Note N-1543, Santa Monica, Calif.: The Rand Corporation, 1980.

Hayes-Roth, F., Klahr, P., Burge, J., & Mostow, D. J. *Machine methods for acquiring, learning, and applying knowledge.* P-6241, Santa Monica, Calif.: The Rand Corporation, 1978.

Hayes-Roth, F., Klahr, P., & Mostow, D. J. *Knowledge acquisition, knowledge programming, and knowledge refinement.* R-2540-NSF, Santa Monica, Calif.: The Rand Corporation, 1980.

Heidorn, G. E. English as a very high level language for simulation programming. *Proceedings of the ACM SIGPLAN Symposium on Very High Level Languages.* Santa Monica, Calif.: 1974, 91-100.

Lakatos, I. *Proofs and refutations.* Cambridge: Cambridge University Press, 1976.

Lenat, D. AM: *An artificial intelligence approach to discovery in mathematics as heuristic search.* SAIL AIM-286. Stanford,CAlif.: Stanford Artificial Intelligence Laboratory, 1976. Jointly issued as Computer Science Dept. Report No. STAN-CS-76-570.

Lenat, D., & Harris, G. Designing a rule system that searches for scientific discoveries. In D. A. Waterman & F. Hayes-Roth (Eds.), *Pattern-directed inference systems,* New York: Academic Press, 1978.

Lenat, D. B., Hayes-Roth, F., & Klahr, P. *Cognitive economy.* N-1185. Santa Monica, Calif.: The Rand Corporation, 1979. (a)

Lenat, D. B., Hayes-Roth, F., & Klahr, P. Cognitive economy in AI systems. *Proceedings of the Sixth International Joint Conference on Artificial Intelligence.* Tokyo, Japan, 531-536, 1979. (b)

Mostow, D. J., & Hayes-Roth, F. *Machine-aided heuristic programming: A paradigm for knowledge engineering.* N-1007. Santa Monica, Calif.: The Rand Corporation, 1979. (a)

Mostow, D. J., & Hayes-Roth, F. Operationalizing heuristics: Some AI methods for assisting AI programming. *Proceedings of the Sixth International Joint Conference on Artificial Intelligence.* Tokyo, Japan, 601-609, 1979. (b)

Sussman, G. J., & Stallman, R. *Heuristic techniques in computer aided circuit analysis.* Memo 328. Cambridge, Mass.: MIT AI Laboratory, 1975.

8 The Processes Involved in Designing Software

Robin Jeffries, Althea A. Turner, Peter G. Polson
University of Colorado

Michael E. Atwood
Science Applications, Inc., Denver

INTRODUCTION

The task of design involves a complex set of processes. Starting from a global statement of a problem, a designer must develop a precise plan for a solution that will be realized in some concrete way (e.g., as a building or as a computer program). Potential solutions are constrained by the need to eventually map this plan into a real-world instantiation. For anything more than the most artificial examples, design tasks are too complex to be solved directly. Thus, an important facet of designing is decomposing a problem into more manageable subunits. Design of computer systems, software design, is the particular design task to be focused on in this chapter.

Software design is the process of translating a set of task requirements (functional specifications) into a structured description of a computer program that will perform the task. There are three major elements of this description. First, the specifications are decomposed into a collection of modules, each of which satisfies part of the problem requirements. This is often referred to as a modular decomposition. Second, the designer must specify the relationships and interactions among the modules. This includes the control structures, which indicate the order in which modules are activated and the conditions under which they are used. Finally, a design includes the data structures involved in the solution. One can think of the original goal-oriented specifications as defining the properties that the solution must have. The design identifies the modules that can satisfy these properties. How these modules are to be implemented is a programming task, which follows the design task.

This chapter presents a theory of the global processes that experts use to control the development of a software design. After a review of some relevant literature, the theory is described in detail. Thinking aloud protocols collected from both expert and novice designers on a moderately complex problem provide evidence for these theoretical ideas. Finally, we speculate on how such processes might be learned.

RESEARCH ON DESIGN AND PLANNING

Although there has been little research that focuses directly on problem-solving processes in software design, there are a number of research areas that are peripherally related. The first of these, formal software design methodologies, is indicative of the guidelines that experts in the field propose to structure the task of designing. The second area, automatic programming, provides a detailed analysis of the task from an artificial intelligence viewpoint. Finally, research on planning and design gives insight into planning processes that may be general across domains.

Software Design Methodologies

There are two reasons for considering the professional literature in this field. A reasonable model of performance in any domain ought to relate to accepted standards of good practice in that domain. These formalized methods were written by experts in the area trying to convey to others the procedures they use to perform the task. In addition, most expert designers are familiar with this literature and may incorporate facets of these methodologies into their designs.

Software design involves generating a modular decomposition of a problem that satisfies the requirements described in its specifications. Design methods provide different bases for performing modular decompositions. There are two prevailing views in the literature as to what this basis should be. Both positions prescribe problem reduction approaches to the design process. One focuses on data structures and the other on data flow. The various methodologies differ in the nature and specificity of the problem reduction or decomposition operators and of the evaluation functions for determining the adequacy of alternative decompositions.

With the data-structure–oriented approaches (e.g., Jackson, 1975; Warnier, 1974), a designer begins by specifying the input and output data structures according to certain guidelines. A modular decomposition of a problem is identified by deriving the mapping between the input and output data structures. Because such methods involve the derivation of a single "correct" decomposition, there is no need for evaluation criteria or the comparison of alternative decompositions.

Data-flow oriented approaches (Myers, 1975; Yourdon & Constantine, 1975) are a collection of guidelines for identifying trial decompositions of a problem.

Thus, these methods are more subjective, allowing a designer to exercise more judgment. As a result, numerous heuristics for evaluating potential decompositions are used with these methods. Examples of such evaluation guidelines include: maximizing the independence and cohesion of individual modules, providing a simple (as opposed to general) solution to the current subproblem, etc. These guidelines control the evaluation of possible solutions to a design problem and the generation of new alternative designs.

Most formal software design methodologies require that the design proceed through several iterations. Each iteration is a representation of the problem at a more detailed level. Thus, the initial decomposition is a schematic description of the solution. This becomes more detailed in the subsequent iterations. In general, this mode of decomposing the problem leads to a top-down, breadth-first expansion of a design.

There are competing views that prescribe different modes of expansion. Some of these are characterized by such terms as *bottom-up, middle-out,* or *inside-out* (Boehm, 1975). Such positions have been developed in response to what some individuals feel are unsatisfactory properties of a top-down expansion. There are problems in which it is necessary to understand certain crucial lower-level functions in order to identify high-level constraints on the design. These alternative modes of expansion may be used by a designer in problems for which an initial decomposition is difficult to derive. There are undoubtedly problems for which each of these methodologies is particularly suited. However, the formal literature on software design lacks a mapping between types of problems and the appropriate design methodology.

Automatic Programming Systems

Another source of information about the task of software design comes from automatic programming systems. The term *automatic programming* has been used to refer to activities ranging from the design and development of algebraic compilers to systems that can write a program from information given in the form of goal-oriented specifications (Biermann, 1976; Heidorn, 1976). The latter represent attempts to specify the procedures of software design in a mechanizable form.

Simon's (1963, 1972) Heuristic Compiler was one of the earliest proposals for a programming system that generated code from abstract specifications. This program's task was to generate IPL–V code for subroutines that were components of some larger program. It was implicitly assumed that the original specifications had been decomposed into detailed functional descriptions for a collection of routines that would make up the complete program.

The definitions of routines to be generated by the Heuristic Compiler could take one of two forms, with each form being handled by a separate special compiler. The first form involved a before and after description of the states of certain cells in the IPL system. The specification described the inputs and outputs of a routine. The state description compiler's task was to derive the sequence of IPL instructions that brought about that transformation. The other form of definitions was in terms of imperative statements describing the function to be performed by a given subroutine, which was handled by the function compiler. Both specialized compilers used suitably generalized forms of means–ends analysis to generate sequences of IPL instructions that would meet the input specifications.

One branch of current research on automatic programming can be viewed as attempts to generalize the ideas that were originally contained in the state description compiler. Biermann (1976) describes several automatic programming systems that derive programs from examples of input–output behavior for a routine or from formal descriptions of inputs and outputs. Note that the data-structure-oriented software design methodologies discussed earlier resemble these systems in their focus on deriving detailed actions from inputs and outputs.

Other automatic programming systems have been developed that generate routines from information supplied through a natural language dialogue with the user (Heidorn, 1976). These efforts can be viewed as generalizations of the function compiler. Such systems consist of four components (Balzer, 1973; Green, 1977; Heidorn, 1976). First, the system acquires a description of the problem to be solved, frequently via interactions with a relatively naive user. Second, this information is synthesized into a coherent description of the program to be written (Green, 1977). This description is then verified, and additional information, if necessary, is acquired through further interactions with the user (Balzer, Goldman, & Wile, 1977). Finally, the refined description is used as input to a subsystem that synthesizes the program in the high-level language, making decisions about data structures, algorithms, and control structures. Much of the current work in automatic programming focuses on the last of these components.

Balzer and his colleagues have considered the task of transforming an informal natural language specification of a program into a formal description of a design. This design would then be input into a code generation subsystem. There are two aspects of Balzer's work that are relevant here. First, he attempts to develop techniques that enable one to carry out the initial phases of the design effort. Incomplete goal-oriented specifications are first translated into abstract, incomplete functional specifications and then refined into a complete set of formal specifications for the program. Second, the knowledge used by Balzer's system is domain independent. This system can be contrasted with the programs of Long (1977) and Mark (1976) that are strongly domain dependent, and where design problems are proposed in a single microworld.

A system that is designed to deal with the problems of detailed design and code generation is a program called PECOS (Barstow, 1977, 1979). PECOS generates LISP code from a high-level description of input and output data structures and the algorithms to be used to solve the problem. A distinguishing feature of PECOS is that the program uses a collection of rules. It encodes both general knowledge and specific information about LISP to guide its problem-solving efforts, rather than using a uniform strategy like means–ends analysis.

PECOS' knowledge base is in the form of a large set of rules. General rules deal with representation techniques for collections, enumeration techniques for collections, and representation techniques for mappings. Each of these subsets of rules can be organized into a hierarchical structure with a number of intermediate levels between the most abstract concepts (e.g., collection) and information about specific procedures or data structures (e.g., linked free cells).

PECOS employs problem-solving mechanisms that iteratively refine each component of the specifications. A partially refined subproblem is selected, and then a rule is applied to it. Each rule application can produce one of three outcomes. First, the subproblem can be refined to the next lower level of detail. Second, crucial properties of some component of the subproblem can be identified and included in the description. Third, additional information about the subproblem can be gathered.

This review of automatic programming demonstrates that there are two components to the task of software design. The first is the translation of the initial goal-oriented specifications into a high-level functional decomposition of the original problem. This incomplete, abstract description of the problem must then be refined into a set of formal specifications that precisely define data structures, control structures, and the functions performed by various modules in the program. The second stage of the design process involves a collection of implementation decisions. These decisions specify data structures and algorithms that satisfy the functional descriptions and efficiency criteria. The first phase requires powerful problem-solving strategies that can factor the original problem into a collection of subproblems. It also requires the generation of successive refinements of each subproblem, incorporating more and more detail about the developing solution.

Models of Planning and Design

There exist two problem-solving systems (Hayes–Roth & Hayes–Roth, 1979; Sacerdoti, 1975) that contain mechanisms that seem adequate to carry out the processes required in the initial phase of the design process. Both of these systems generate a plan of action.

Sacerdoti's (1975) NOAH solves robot planning problems by a process of successive refinement. Sacerdoti assumes that the knowledge necessary to generate a plan is organized in a collection of knowledge structures, each of which contains the specification of some subgoal and the actions necessary to accomplish that subgoal. Each unit of knowledge has the information necessary to take one element of a developing plan and produce its next more detailed refinement. Sacerdoti assumes that the complete plan is generated iteratively. At any stage of the planning process, each segment of the plan is expanded to its next level of refinement. Then generalized problem-solving processes, called *critics,* are used to reorganize this more detailed plan into an internally consistent and efficient sequence of actions. The process repeats itself at the next level, terminating with a plan whose individual steps can be executed to solve the initial problem.

Hayes–Roth & Hayes–Roth (1979) describe a HEARSAY-like system that plans routes for performing a collection of everyday errands. Knowledge about the planning of errands is organized into a collection of pattern-directed modules, called *specialists,* that communicate through a global data structure called the *blackboard.* The behavior of this system is opportunistic in the sense that data currently on the blackboard can trigger a specialist that makes a decision at some arbitrary level of abstraction in the developing plan.

Hayes–Roth and Hayes–Roth point out that a system like NOAH is quite rigid, in that it is restricted to a purely top-down, breadth-first expansion of a solution. Their system, in contrast, is capable of making a best or most useful decision at any level of abstraction; is capable of incremental or partial planning; and can adopt different planning methods depending on the specifics of a given problem.

Many of Hayes–Roth and Hayes–Roth's criticisms concerning the rigidity of a program like NOAH are well taken. On the other hand, many of the phenomena that they have observed in their protocols may be due to the task and the level of expertise of their subjects. None of their subjects had extensive experience with errand-planning tasks. It may be the case that one would observe quite different behavior in an environment that required the solution of a large number of subproblems and the integration of these solutions. One might also expect more orderly kinds of behavior in situations where successful performance required the integration and utilization of a large, well-organized body of relevant knowledge.

There has been a limited amount of research on the process of design or on problems that are difficult enough to require the construction of an elaborate plan. Much of the work on expert problem solving in thermodynamics (Bhaskar & Simon, 1977), physics (Larkin, 1977), and other semantically rich domains is not directly relevant to processes involved in solving design problems, because these studies all use problems that can be solved by a single, well-understood problem method, or schema. An expert in these domains first has to identify the relevant schema and then apply the schema to the problem. In contrast, the major task in design is the reduction of the original problem into a collection of sub-problems.

Levin (1976) has attempted to develop a theory of software design processes that is consistent with current thinking on the structure of the human information-processing system and known problem-solving methods. Levin (1976) postulates that design can be viewed as involving three fundamental processes: "selecting problems to work on, gathering information needed for the solution, and generating solutions [p. 2]." Levin argues that the problem selection process is controlled by a set of global strategies and local information about constraints that are directly relevant to the current subproblem. He developed a simulation model that takes as input the protocol of an expert designer working on a fairly difficult problem and produces a list of subgoals generated by that designer during the process of solving the problem.

Simon (1973) sketches out a theory of psychological processes involved a design task in the context of discussing the distinction between well-structured and ill-structured problems.

> The whole [architectural] design then, begins to acquire structure by being decomposed into various problems of component design, and by evoking, as the design progresses, all kinds of requirements to be applied in testing the design of its components. During any given short period of time, the architect will find himself working on a problem which, perhaps being in an ill structured state, soon converts itself through evocation from memory into a well structured problem [p. 190].

Simon's view of the design process is that the original design problem is decomposed into a collection of well-structured subproblems under the control of some type of executive process that carries out the necessary coordination functions. Also note that information retrieved from long-term memory is incorporated into the developing solution; it is this additional information that converts the original ill-structured problem into a collection of well-structured problems.

Much of the work discussed previously focuses on the decomposition of complex tasks into more manageable subtasks. Our interpretation of the literature on software design is that this decompositional process is central to the task. Moreover, we believe that the mastery of decomposition should be what differentiates experts from novices. The theory to be presented next is built on the process of decomposition and its associated control strategies.

A THEORY OF PROBLEM SOLVING IN SOFTWARE DESIGN

The following is an outline of a theory of processes involved in solving a software design problem. The successful performance of this task involves the coordination of a complex set of processes. Some apply abstract knowledge about the task. Others retrieve computer science knowledge or information about the design problem or are involved in the storage of relevant information for later use in solving problems. The focus of this discussion is on the global structure of the design task, particularly its guiding control processes, and on the manipulation of knowledge within the problem-solving effort.

Experts have knowledge concerning the overall structure of a good design and of the process of generating one. Using this knowledge, they direct their actions to insure that their designs will satisfy these structural constraints. This implies that skilled designers have knowledge describing the structure of a design independent of its content. This abstract knowledge about design and design processes, along with the set of procedures that implement these processes, will be referred to as the *design schema*. This schema, which develops through experience with software design, enables efficient management of a designer's resources in doing this particular specialized and complex task. We propose that the generation of a design is controlled by the interaction between the design schema and the more specific knowledge that describes how to accomplish particular goals.

A schema is a higher-order knowledge structure that governs behavior in a particular domain or activity, providing a broad abstract structure onto which an exemplar is to be mapped. These knowledge structures specify principal elements of a given domain and include mechanisms that drive the generation process and that lead to outcomes that are structured according to conventions shared by expert members in a discipline. A schema can be used to organize complex material into constituents and may be applied recursively to break some of these constituents down further. These same structures also guide the comprehension process by arranging incoming information so that it is structured according to the underlying abstract schema. Absence of an appropriate schema can interfere with both the initial comprehension and subsequent recall of a text.

The design schema is used in both the generation and comprehension of software designs. The design schema is not tied to any specific problem domain but consists instead of abstract knowledge about the structure of a completed design and the processes involved in the generation of that design. It accounts for the overall structure of expert design behavior and the similarities among experts. Of course, the design schema will differ from expert to expert, because their experiences with software design will not be identical. However, the overall nature of these schemata will be similar for most people. Therefore, we choose to simplify this discussion by referring to a single, modal design schema.

The design schema develops as a result of experience with software design. Originally, a designer's approach to this task is assumed to involve general problem-solving strategies, such as "divide and conquer." As an individual has more and more experience with this activity, these general strategies are transformed into a specialized schema. The schema is developed through the addition of domain-specific concepts, tactics, and evaluative criteria. Whenever a designer's specialized schema is inadequate to solve a problem, more general strategies take over.

The design schema is assumed to include: (1) a collection of components that partition the given problem into a set of meaningful tasks; (2) components that add elements to tasks in order to assure that they will function properly (e.g., initialization of data structures or of loops); (3) a set of processes that control the generation and/or comprehension of designs; and (4) evaluation and generation procedures that ensure effective utilization of knowledge. Each component of the design schema is composed of both declarative and procedural knowledge about the abstract nature of the design process. The schema can be applied recursively, which leads to a modular decomposition of the problem into more and more detailed modules.

The schema can be viewed as driving the generation of a software design by breaking up the initial task into a set of subproblems. Knowledge of the particular subproblems that are identified during this decomposition interacts heavily with the schema. However, the design schema itself does not contain knowledge about any particular class of problems. The schema can be applied to the original problem or to any subproblem at a lower level. The recursive application of the design schema to subproblems enables decomposition of each problem into a manageable set of tasks.

How the decomposition proceeds depends on the designer, the designer's experience, and the problem at hand. There are several decomposition strategies that a designer can use to guide the process. One strategy is to break the problem into input, process, and output elements. Whereas there are other strategies that could be used to decompose some problems, the input-process–output strategy is preeminently used. In order to keep this discussion more concrete, we describe decomposition in terms of this prevailing strategy.

The initial pass at decomposition results in a representation of the problem that is a simplified "solution model" of the system; that is, a model is devised specifying a set of tasks that will solve the problem and a control structure for these tasks. It is then expanded into a set of well-defined subproblems. The solutions to these subproblems represent a solution to the original design problem. This process of decomposition is now applied to each subproblem in turn, resulting in more and more detailed plans of what should be done to accomplish the task. Once an individual selects a given element to refine further, the schema is assumed to execute to completion, developing a solution model for that element and refining it into a more detailed plan. If any of the elements resulting from this process are complex (i.e., accomplish multiple functions that are not recognized as having known solutions), the schema is called recursively to reduce them to the next level of detail.

The application of the schema to an element of a design causes a set of high-level goals and procedures for accomplishing those goals to be activated. Thus, the schema includes procedures that examine information relevant to the expansion of a given element, critique potential solutions, generate alternative solutions for a subproblem, etc. The input component, for example, finds information that must be passed to a process component before the actual processing can be initiated. If the chosen input data structure is complex, that is, requires some degree of processing itself to generate the appropriate data structure, then a new subproblem is generated as a descendant of the original one.

The design schema represents the global organization of a designer's professional knowledge. As such, it will impact almost every facet of the designer's behavior in the domain. Nevertheless, the design schema does not encompass a person's knowledge of specific facts in computer science or understanding of how things function in the real world. There are undoubtedly other aspects of this domain that should not be subsumed under the schema, but our theory is not sufficiently developed to isolate them at this point.

The decomposition process uses two additional problem-solving strategies. The first can be described as problem solving by analogy, or, to use Sussman's (1977) term, "the debugging of almost right plans." When the solution model generated for a given subproblem, or some part of it, is recognized as being analogous to an already understood algorithm, that algorithm is evaluated for applicability in the current context. If it is found to be reasonably applicable, it is debugged and incorporated into the developing solution. This attempt to retrieve previous solutions is invoked once a solution model has been derived, but before any further refinement takes place.

The second method can be characterized as problem solving by understanding. This is prominent in cases where an element identified by application of the design schema is not understood in enough detail for the design schema to be applied to it. The designer's knowledge of the problem area in question, as well as of computer science, is then used to refine the understanding of this element. This method may be employed at any point in the solution. It is most frequently applied when developing a solution model but can also be applied during refinement of a subproblem.

In addition to controlling the overall problem-solving process, the design schema has some coordination and storage functions. Successful solution of a design problem requires that information generated during each problem-solving episode be stored in long-term memory. This information must be interconnected with the expert's knowledge about computer science as well as with the developing solution. Much of what goes on can be described as the development of an understanding of the problem. The information generated during these understanding phases must be stored such that it can be retrieved later for the solution of other subproblems. The design schema ensures that successive episodes are organized so information generated can be stored in a coherent representation of the developing solution.

The utilization of memory is influenced by its organization and by the effectiveness of the abstract cues provided by the schema. Experience enables concepts to be linked on the basis of the utility of considering the concepts together. This usefulness can be defined in terms of concepts that frequently occur in the same context (e.g., linked lists and efficient insertion and deletion of items at random places within the list) or that are alternative solution techniques to similar problems (e.g., a symbol table may be represented as a hash table or as a static tree table).

When a computer science concept is learned, that concept is associated with the context in which it is learned. For example, one might first learn about a particular data structure in the context of a certain problem. Later, in another problem that would be appropriate for this type of data structure, one might fail to apply this new concept, because the current context might not encourage its retrieval. Eventually, through experience with the concept in many other contexts, it becomes linked to more abstract conditions for its use. Further, as a person's design schema develops such that it can manage the complexity of alternate solutions, this concept would become connected to the concepts of other data structures that would be considered in similar contexts. Thus, memory organization is altered, reflecting the designer's developing schema and previous experiences.

The major control processes of the design schema are summarized as a set of very abstract production rules in Fig. 8.1. Each rule encapsulates a complex subprocess that an expert may use while generating a software design. The rules are an attempt to capture the global control processes only; many aspects of the design schema are not addressed at all. In particular, no reference is made to the processes that generate alternative solutions or critique designs, or to the memory coordination functions that the schema performs. Moreover, the rules only refer to the generation of a design; they do not encompass its comprehension.

The goal of software design is to break down a problem into a set of subprocesses that accomplish the task. After the initial decomposition, there may be multiple subproblems to be solved. The designer must have a way of selecting a problem to work on from the currently unsolved subproblems. The selection rule (Rule 1) provides a coherent way of determining what problem to tackle next. The rules assume that the list of unsolved subproblems are stored on an agenda. The selection rule results in one of them being marked as a current subproblem. The other rules are applied to this problem.

The usual order in which a designer attempts subproblem solution is top-down, breadth-first. The design schema causes each element of the current iteration to be expanded to the next level of detail. This expansion continues until a new representation of the complete solution is developed at the next level of detail. Solving the problem top-down, breadth-first ensures that all the information about the current state of the design at one level of abstraction will be available to the next iteration.

One reason for this strategy is that the elements of a developing design can interact with each other. Although one of the heuristics that guides the decomposition process is the attempt to define subproblems that do not interact or interact only weakly, this is not always possible. Further refinement of one element may require knowledge of decisions that will be made in developing a not-yet-considered element.

A designer may choose to deviate from this order. These deviations are dictated by individual differences in design style, in the amount of knowledge that the designer may have concerning the problem, or in differences in the solution model. The solution model with its various constituents may enable a designer to recognize that a solution relevant to the current problem is known.

DESIGN SCHEMA RULES: SELECTION RULE
DESIGN SCHEMA RULE 1:
    IF   (no current subproblem exists)
              AND (any unsolved subproblems on agenda)
    THEN   (select highest priority subproblem or, if multiple subproblems at
              highest priority, select next subproblem in breadth-first order
              at highest priority and make it new current subproblem)

DESIGN SCHEMA RULES: SOLUTION MODEL DERIVATION PROCESS
DESIGN SCHEMA RULE 2:
    IF   (p is current subproblem)
              AND (solution model for p does not exist)
    THEN   (set goal to create solution model for p)
DESIGN SCHEMA RULE 3:
    IF   (goal to create solution model for p)
              AND (p is not well understood)
    THEN   (retrieve information relevant to p and refine understanding of p)
              AND (add new subproblem p' to agenda)
              AND (make p' current subproblem)
DESIGN SCHEMA RULE 4:
    IF   (goal to create solution model for p)
              AND (p is understood as "trivial")
    THEN   (assert that p is solved)
              AND (delete p as current subproblem)
DESIGN SCHEMA RULE 5:
    IF   (goal to create solution model for p)
              AND (p is understood as "complex")
    THEN   (define solution model for p)

DESIGN SCHEMA RULES: SOLUTION RETRIEVAL PROCESS
DESIGN SCHEMA RULE 6:
    IF   (solution model for p exists)
    THEN   (search memory for potential solutions which match critical fea-
              tures of solution model for p)
DESIGN SCHEMA RULE 7:
    IF   (potential solution s to problem p is found)
    THEN   (evaluate applicability of s)
DESIGN SCHEMA RULE 8:
    IF   (potential solution s to problem p is highly applicable)
    THEN   (assert that p is solved)
              AND (delete p as current subproblem)
DESIGN SCHEMA RULE 9:
    IF   (potential solution s to problem p is moderately applicable)
    THEN   (add to agenda new subproblem p' created from solution model
              for p augmented by s)
              AND (make p' current subproblem)

FIG. 8.1.   A production system representation of the design schema control processes.

DESIGN SCHEMA RULE 10:
   IF   (potential solution s is weakly applicable)
   THEN (reject potential solution s)

DESIGN SCHEMA RULES: REFINE SOLUTION MODEL DECOMPOSITION
DESIGN SCHEMA RULE 11:
   IF   (no potential solution to problem p is found)
   THEN (expand solution model for p into well-defined subproblems using
            understanding and evaluation processes as needed)
            AND (add each new subproblem generated to agenda)

FIG. 8.1. (*Continued*)

This solution then can be adapted to the current situation. Also, the representation of each element of the solution model may enable a designer to estimate their relative difficulties or to identify potential interactions that impact further development of the design. The realization that one or more constituents have known solutions, are critical for success, present special difficulties, etc. can cause the designer to deviate from a top-down, breadth-first expansion of the overall design by assigning a higher priority to a particular constituent.

Once a subproblem has been selected, the designer attempts to derive a solution model for it (Rule 2). Recall that the solution model is an abstract simplified description of elements of the subproblem's solution. This solution model is the basis for all succeeding work on this problem. Rules 2 through 5 describe the processes that may result in the generation of the solution model for the current subproblem. If the current subproblem is perceived to be complex, the designer must first undertake to reformulate it before a solution model can be generated. Rule 3 represents the process by which information relevant to the subproblem is considered, and a new more understandable problem is produced. Once it is precisely formulated, a solution model is generated if the problem requires further decomposition (Rule 5). If the problem, once understood, is sufficiently simple, it is marked as solved and is not further considered (Rule 4).

The next set of rules (Rules 6 through 10) encompass the processes by which a designer attempts to retrieve from memory a previously constructed solution to all or part of the current subproblem. First, the solution model for this problem is used as a retrieval cue to access potential solutions in memory (Rule 6). These solutions are then evaluated for their usefulness in the current context (Rule 7). The rules give a simplified characterization of the results of this evaluation process. The solution is either accepted as is (Rule 8), modified to fit the current situation (Rule 9), or rejected (Rule 10).

If no usable solution to the current subproblem is found, the solution model is refined into a collection of well-defined subproblems (Rule 11). This refinement process takes into account data flow, functional analysis, aesthetic, practical, and other criteria, and implementation considerations. Each new subproblem thus generated is added to the agenda. The set of rules is applied to the subproblems on the agenda until all problems are considered to be solved.

The theory just presented describes a mechanism by which experts are able to integrate and structure their high-level knowledge of software design. Although experts in the field should manifest mature design schemata, we would not expect beginning designers to show evidence in their behavior of this complex organization. Therefore, many differences we might observe between experts and novices can be attributed to differences in the state of development of their design schemata.

A COMPARISON OF EXPERT AND NOVICE DESIGN PROCESSES

The processes involved in designing software are learned through experience. To examine their development, we collected thinking-aloud protocols from people at various skill levels. This set of protocols forms a rich data base of evidence about the problem-solving processes used in software design. There are, of course, many similarities in the way experts and novices approach this process; subjects at different levels used many of the same global processes. Differences as a function of expertise fall into two major categories: the processes used to decompose the problem and solve individual subproblems, and the representation and utilization of relevant knowledge. In this section, the similarities and differences among subjects are discussed and related to the theoretical ideas proposed earlier.

Subjects and Materials

Four of the subjects were experienced designers. They include a professor of electrical engineering (S35), two graduate students in computer science (S2 and S5), both of whom had worked as programmers and designers for several years, and a professional systems analyst with over 10 years experience (S3).

The five novices were undergraduate students recruited from an assembly language programming class. They had all taken from four to eight computer science courses; most had had part-time programming jobs. Whereas these subjects are moderately experienced programmers, they have little experience with software design per se. We selected two subjects from this group (S17 and S19) and examined their thinking-aloud protocols in detail. Both these subjects had taken a course that specifically taught software design.

We also collected a protocol from a subject with no software design experience (S25, whom we call a prenovice). This subject has taken several programming courses and has written programs in the course of the research in which she is involved. Her experience differs from the novices in two ways: her formal training has dealt solely with the practical aspects of programming, and therefore she has little knowledge of the theoretical constructs of computer science; and,

PAGE-KEYED INDEXING SYSTEM

BACKGROUND. A book publisher requires a system to produce a page-keyed index. This system will accept as input the source text of a book and produce as output a list of specified index terms and the page numbers on which each index term appears. This system is to operate in a batch mode.

DESIGN TASK. You are to design a system to produce a page-keyed index. The source file for each book to be indexed is an ASCII file residing on disk. Page numbers will be indicated on a line in the form /*NNNN, where /* are marker characters used to identify the occurrence of page numbers and NNNN is the page number.

The page number will appear after a block of text that comprises the body of the page. Normally, a page contains enough information to fill an 8½ × 11 inch page. Words are delimited by the following characters: space, period, comma, semicolon, colon, carriage-return, question mark, quote, double quote, exclamation point, and line-feed. Words at the end of a line may be hyphenated and continued on the following line, but words will not be continued across page boundaries.

A term file, containing a list of terms to be indexed, will be read from a card reader. The term file contains one term per line, where a term is 1 to 5 words long.

The system should read the source file and term file and find all occurrences of each term to be indexed. The output should contain the index terms listed alphabetically with the page numbers following each term in alphabetical order.

FIG. 8.2.   The text of the page-keyed indexer problem.

all her programming experience has been statistical programming in FORTRAN.

The particular problem given to the subjects is to design a page-keyed indexing system. The problem specifications are shown in Fig. 8.2. This problem was chosen because it is of moderate difficulty and understandable to individuals with a wide range of knowledge of software design, but does not require knowledge of highly specialized techniques that would be outside the competence of some expert subjects; that is, a reasonable design could be constructed for this task using only the techniques taught in upper-division undergraduate courses in computer science or those contained in standard textbooks on computer science algorithms. A variety of approaches, however, could be taken to design such a system.

The protocols of a subset of the subjects were analyzed in detail, whereas others were examined more cursorily to find corroborating evidence. The method by which this analysis was carried out and the results obtained can be found in Atwood and Jeffries (1980). The discussion following is based primarily on the detailed analysis, but examples have been chosen freely from all the protocols.

Similarities Across Expertise Levels

On a first reading of these protocols, one is struck by the variations in the design solutions as much within expertise levels as across them. Both the design style of the individual subject and the set of subproblems he or she chose to attack make each solution very different from any of the others. More careful consideration, however, brings up many similarities, both within experience groups and across all the subjects.

Almost all the subjects approached the problem with the same global control strategy: Decompose the problem into subproblems. They began with an initial sketchy parse of the problem, which we have called the solution model. Some subjects were quite explicit about their solution models, whereas for others it was necessary to infer the underlying model. Whenever a subject made a quick, smooth transition from one element of the solution to the next, without any overt consideration of alternatives and without reference to external memory, we assumed that the solution model underlay this decision.

The solution models for the indexer problem are surprisingly similar for both experts and novices. In general, subjects decided to read in the terms, build some sort of data structure to contain them, compare the terms to the text, associate the page numbers with each term, and output the terms and page numbers. We do not assume that this would be true for all software design problems. The indexer problem was chosen to be "straightforward"; for such a problem, expertise is needed not for the initial solution model but for the expansion of this model into a well-defined set of subproblems and the further refinement of those subproblems. Our results are therefore potentially limited to similar straightforward problems. In tasks for which the determination of a solution model is itself a difficult task, quite different problem-solving methods may be used. Once the initial solution model was derived, the subjects attempted to expand this iteratively. No subject went directly from the solution model to a complete solution. They broke the problem into subproblems and refined the solution through several levels.

As a group, the novices explored a set of subproblems similar to those examined by the experts. The initial decomposition led to equivalent constituents, and, in further iterations, the novices as a group developed subproblems that were still comparable to the experts. The experts tended to examine more subproblems and frequently found different solutions. Even for idiosyncratic aspects of the problem, however (e.g., how to treat hyphenated words, terms that cross page boundaries), the novices were as likely as the experts to incorporate a particular element into the solution.

Although the novices applied the same general problem-solving methods as did the experts, their solutions were neither as correct nor as complete. Furthermore, the novices were not able to apply the more efficient problem-solving processes that the experts used. The novices were lacking in skills in two areas:

processes for solving subproblems, and ways of representing knowledge effectively.

Subproblem Solution Processes

Decomposition.   When these subjects, both experts and novices, perceived a particular problem to be complex, they decomposed it into a collection of more manageable subproblems. The experts, of course, were more effective than the novices at doing this. They showed some stylistic differences in when and how they used the decomposition process, but its use is pervasive in all four expert protocols.

S2's protocol is an almost perfect example of solution by repeated decomposition. He is a proponent of design by stepwise refinement; in this protocol, he rigidly adheres to such a strategy. His initial decomposition is a listing of the major steps to be accomplished, little more than a precise reformulation of his solution model. On the next iteration, he adds a control structure to this collection of modules. Successive passes decompose these modules into sets of submodules until he is satisfied that he has reached the level of primitive operations.

S3 also iteratively decomposes the problem in a top-down, breadth-first, beginning-to-end manner. Her style and the design she eventually produces are similar to that of S2, except that her protocol is interspersed with digressions that relate to subproblems at other levels and at other positions in the problem. S3 also attempts fewer iterations than S2, bringing the problem to a slightly higher level of detail in two passes as S2 did in five or six. In fact, at the end of the protocol, she realizes that the second iteration is so much more detailed than the first that it taxes her ability to comprehend the solution. She then incorporates a sketchy third iteration at a "higher" level than the previous one.

After articulating his problem model, S5 notes that in order to know how to read the term file into a data structure, he needs to know more about how the matcher works. He then proceeds to work out the design of the matcher and its associated data structures. This places him directly in the middle of the decomposition tree, working simultaneously on two distinct branches. After ascertaining how the match process would operate, he proceeds to flesh out the design, proceeding from here in a top-down, breadth-first, beginning-to-end manner.

The core of S35's solution is an algorithm he retrieves that defines the term data structure and the matcher. Using this as a base, he builds the design in a top-down, breadth-first manner, although he does not expand it beginning to end. The reason for this is that he defines the problem in terms of data structures derived from his original functional analysis of the problem decomposition. Occasional deviations from this breadth-first order occur when he attempts to define low-level primitive actions that are the building blocks of his design.

All these experts demonstrate the existence of a polished design schema and a sophisticated ability to use the decomposition method to expand their designs.

Differences across experts were in part dictated by disparate design styles but to a great extent were due to differences in their knowledge of and ability to retrieve a relevant solution plan.

The novices, on the other hand, were much less effective in their use of the iterative decomposition method. They seem to lack the more subtle aspects of the design schema. A well-developed schema should guide the designer toward the production of a "good" design, as opposed to one that accomplishes the task "by hook or by crook." This means that considerations of efficiency, aesthetics, etc. should influence the manner in which design elements are expanded. There is no evidence of this in the novices. Furthermore, the schema should include procedures that enable designers to make resource decisions about the order in which to expand the modules (e.g., most difficult first, or a module that uses a data structure might be designed before the one that produces it). In the novices that we have examined in detail, we see no deviations from the default breadth-first, beginning-to-end consideration of modules.

The best of the novices was S19. He is the only novice that iterates the problem through more than two levels of decomposition. However, beyond the first level, he is unable to recursively apply some of the same decomposition strategies he used earlier. S19 gets particularly bogged down in his "compare" routine, rewriting it several times without complete success. On each attempt, he simply tries to generate a solution through brute force by writing down the necessary steps. There is no hint of having generated a model for this process nor of any attempt to further decompose it.

S17 was able to decompose the indexer problem and to generate an adequate initial pass at a solution. He then attempted to expand his solution (mostly at the urging of the experimenter). However, he makes no attempt to further decompose his chosen modules. Each subsequent iteration simply repeats the previous solution, adding on new "facts" as he discovers them. For example, at one point he considers the possibility that a term straddles pages. He changes his design to accommodate this, but he does so by augmenting existing elements, not by decomposing them into submodules. This sort of behavior indicates that S17 is unable to recursively apply the design schema.

Another of the novices writes down a solution in terms of steps, instead of modules. The distinction between steps and modules is necessarily a fuzzy one. However, a set of steps differs from a modular decomposition in that steps have no hierarchical structure, steps of very different levels of detail may occur together, and steps have only a primitive control structure. In the second iteration of his design, this novice merely produces a similar set of steps, more specifically tied to the architecture of a particular computer. He appears to understand that a problem should be broken down but has not developed a design approach that decomposes into subproblems.

Although the novices have not incorporated the more subtle aspects of the design schema into their behavior, they can apply the basic principles. The prenovice, S25, however, has not developed even a rudimentary design schema. First, S25's protocol is qualitatively different from those of the computer science majors. They produced designs that, although differing in many details from those of the experts, were at least marginally acceptable solutions to the problem. S25 did not produce a design. She generated a mixture of FORTRAN code and comments that together could be taken as a partial solution to the task of writing a program to solve the indexer problem. Moreover, she got quite bogged down in the selection of data structures for the text and terms and in the implementation of procedures to compare items in these structures. Because of these difficulties, she eventually abandoned the task without generating a complete solution.

S25 made no attempt to decompose the problem; she did not seem to be using any kind of an overall model to guide her solution. She let the problem description and the portion of the "program" already written direct her expansion of a solution. Information did not seem to accumulate over the solution attempt; she attacked the same subproblem repeatedly but often made no progress beyond the initial attempt. She did seem to understand that input, process, and output components were needed, but this was not sufficient to produce a correct initial decomposition of the problem.

We take this continuum of more effective use of the decomposition method with increasing experience as strong evidence for both the reality and the usefulness of the design schema. Another aspect of expertise that is apparent in these protocols is the ability of the experts to generate and evaluate alternative solutions to a subproblem.

Evaluation of Alternatives. When the experts are trying to determine whether a particular plan is actually a good solution to a subproblem, they state alternative solutions and select among them. S3, for example, explicitly mentions that the page numbers could be stored in an array or a linked list. She does some calculations of the relative storage requirements of each and chooses the linked list because it is more efficient. S35 spends some time considering two ways of implementing his term data structure; one is time efficient, and the other is storage efficient. He concludes that, without knowledge of the actual computer system to be used, he does not have enough information to decide which is better. He chooses to leave both as alternatives.

The novices seldom consider more than one possible solution to any subproblem. From the marginal utility of some of the solutions they do retrieve, it seems that they are hard pressed to find even one solution to many subproblems. For example, at one point, S19 says "This might be the only way I can think of to be able to do this. It's going to be awful expensive," and elsewhere, "It's inefficient and expensive, but it's easy." He seems to have some ability to critique his solutions but is at a loss to correct the deficiencies he finds.

In the few cases in which the novices choose among alternatives, they make simple dichotomous decisions (do X or not X). Their decision is invariably made on the basis of programming convenience. For example, S19 notices that a term could straddle a page. He spends some time deciding whether or not to permit this and decides that it is easier not to allow it, although this solution is unlikely to be realistic in terms of indexing a textbook.

Retrieval of Known Solutions. One of the features of the decomposition technique is that it enables the designer to convert a problem into a set of simpler subproblems, eventually reaching the point where all the subproblems have known solutions. Although the novices attempt to employ decomposition, we see no evidence that they do so in order to arrive at a set of known solutions. The experts, in contrast, seem to have a large repertory of solutions and of methods for decomposing a problem. The clearest examples of this are when some of the expert subjects were able to recall and apply a single solution to the major problem tasks. S35 and S5 both attempted this.

S35, after reading the specifications, immediately states "Well, the obvious answer to this is to use the technique of Aho and Corasick, which appeared in CACM (Aho & Corasick, 1975)." This article describes an algorithm for searching text for embedded strings. He says: "basically what you do is you read the term file, and you create a finite state machine from it. And then you apply this finite state machine to the text." S35 then spends the next 2 hours expanding this solution into a complete design, incorporating the idiosyncrasies of this problem (e.g., that the page number is not known until the end of the page) into this general algorithm. It is apparent that his understanding of the algorithm strongly influences the expanding design and many of the design decisions.

After his initial parsing of the problem, S5 notes that the match process is critical for an efficient and successful solution. This reminds him of a published algorithm (Boyer & Moore, 1977) that may be applicable to this situation: "Now my immediate inclination is to, about three CACMs ago, this particular problem was discussed." The algorithm he refers to is similar to the one recalled by S35.

S5's memory of this algorithm is somewhat sketchy, though, and he is unsure of how it interacts with the rest of the design. He works through the match process and its associated data structure in some detail. The resulting algorithm is similar to, but not identical with, the published algorithm. In a very real sense, he constructs an original solution that incorporates many of the features that he recalls from the Boyer and Moore algorithm. From there, he proceeds iteratively through refinements of the design as a whole.

Our other two experts, S2 and S3, did not retrieve a single solution to the major tasks, but they frequently solved subproblems by incorporating plans that they had used before. For example, S2 uses a linked list to store the page numbers. He notes that the insertion procedure is somewhat tricky to implement; he would prefer to refer to one of his earlier programs, rather than spend the time to work out the details again. S3, when considering the problem that hyphens can serve two distinct functions in the text (as part of a word or to divide a word at a line boundary), mentions that she knows of a similar case that was solved by requiring that distinct characters be used in each case.

The experts not only retrieve solution plans to all or part of the problem, but they are able to modify those solutions to fit the current situation. S35's design was a modification of a well-understood plan. S5 only retrieved the skeleton of a plan; he spent most of his time augmenting and altering this plan to fit the actual problem.

The novices show no evidence that they are trying to adapt previously learned solutions to any part of this problem. No novice ever made a statement like "this is just like X" or "I did something similar when Y." They do retrieve solutions, but only at the lowest levels. For example, S17 decided that he would flag the first empty position for each term in his page-number array. This is a solution to the problem of locating the current end of the page-number list, but it is far from the best one. S17 makes no attempt to alter this solution so that it accomplishes this in a more efficient manner. It is not clear whether this is due to his inability to realize the inefficiencies in this solution, or whether he simply does not know what modifications to make.

Knowledge Representation

Access to Background Knowledge.   The experts demonstrated an impressive ability to retrieve and apply relevant information in the course of solving this problem. The appropriate facts are utilized just when they are needed; important items are seldom forgotten. Moreover, they devote little time to the consideration of extraneous information. In contrast, the novices' lack of an adequate knowledge organization for solving this problem is apparent throughout their protocols. They frequently fail to correctly apply knowledge that is needed to solve the problem, and the information that they generate in the course of solving the problem is often not available to them when it is most needed. We attribute this, in part, to the inadequacy of the organizing functions provided by their immature design schemata.

The novices' failure to apply relevant knowledge can be seen in their selection of a data structure for the terms and page numbers. Each term can potentially have a very large number of page references associated with it, but the typical entry will have only a few references. The selected data structure should allow for the occasional term with an extreme number of references without having to reserve large amounts of storage for every term. A linked list is a data structure that allows these properties. Our experts used a linked list to hold the page numbers associated with each term. The course from which the novices were recruited had recently covered linked lists. In addition, most, if not all, of them had been exposed to this concept in other courses. Thus, we are confident that the subjects were familiar with the construct. In spite of this, none used such a list to hold the page numbers. They all stored page numbers in an immense array.

Several subjects mentioned that such an arrangement was inefficient, but none were led to change it.

The construction of a linked list is a technique with which these subjects are familiar. However, their understanding of when that technique is applicable does not extend to the current situation. Understanding of the conditions under which some piece of knowledge is applicable is one way in which knowledge about a domain becomes integrated. For this information to be useful, it cannot exist as a set of isolated facts but must be related to other knowledge. For example, linked lists would be interrelated with information such as additional types of data structures and methods of gaining storage efficiency in a program. The experts have achieved this integration of concepts, although it is still undergoing development in the novices.

Episodic Retrieval.   The design schema mediates retrieval of information within a problem-solving effort as well as retrieval of relevant background knowledge. The experts, with their more mature design schemata, were better able to accumulate useful information during the course of the solution attempt and to apply it at the relevant time. The clearest example of this is S3's handling of the issue of hyphens in the problem.

Early in the protocol, S3 notices that the text may contain hyphens and that this complicates the comparison process. At this point, S3 only notes this "as being a problem when you come around to comparing." This issue is not considered for long portions of the protocol, but it emerges whenever a module that is related to the compare operation or accessing the text is considered. S3 never mentions hyphens when she is expanding the "read terms" module, but it is one of the first things mentioned when the "construct index" module is taken up.

In contrast, the novices are not only less able to generate relevant information, but the information that they do generate is not stored in an easily retrievable form. S19 provides an illustration. Early in his solution, he notes that a term may straddle a page. He decides that this possibility complicates the design unnecessarily and legislates that it will not happen. He even writes down this assumption. Sometime later he again notices that this problem could occur. He treats this as an entirely new discovery; no mention is made of his earlier treatment of the topic. In fact, during this second episode, he decides to allow terms to straddle page boundaries but uses the ending page number instead of the starting page number as the reference. This too is written down, but neither then nor later does he notice that it contradicts his earlier assumption.

Another example is that S17 mistakenly assumes that terms will be single words, rather than phrases. In the middle of the problem, while rereading the specifications for some other purpose, he notices the error and comments on corrections that must be made to allow for multiword terms. However, none are incorporated into his next iteration of the problem, which only deals with single-word terms. At the end of the session, he notices once more that terms are phrases and that his design must be modified to account for that fact.

This failure to recall information over the course of a single solution attempt is probably the result of two handicaps under which the novices must operate. First, the solution to these problems consumes such a large portion of their resources that they are unable to monitor memory for other potentially relevant information. Experts can avoid overloading themselves by utilization of the design schema. Second, their memory representation of the problem is not organized in such a way as to facilitate the retrieval of previously generated information.

Understanding of Concepts. The novices fail to have an adequate understanding of many of the basic concepts of computer science. These undergraduates are generally familiar with only one machine (the CDC6400) and two or three programming languages. Much of their understanding of the basic concepts is tied to their experience with one or two exemplars of that concept and reflects the idiosyncrasies of that experience. These mistaken assumptions frequently lead to inefficient designs and occasionally to outright errors.

Several examples of incomplete or incorrect understanding of concepts can be found in the protocols of S17 and S19. S17, in particular, repeatedly attempts to incorporate constructs into his design that he is aware of but does not fully understand. He tells the experimenter that the book text should be stored as a "binary tree" [i.e., he intends to read in the book text and sort it into alphabetic order (presumably by word)]. A binary tree is an efficient structure for repeatedly searching ordered collections of items. It allows one to find an arbitrary item in the set with substantially less searching than a sequential search requires, in much the same way that one looks up an entry in a dictionary or a phone book. However, all the information as to which word follows another, which are necessary to isolate phrases from the text, is lost. S17 has apparently learned some of the conditions under which a binary tree should be used, but he clearly does not understand the concept well enough to reject it in this obviously unsuitable situation.

Contrast this with the solution of S5. He is quite concerned with efficient storage of the terms and the text. He spends over an hour working out appropriate data structures and how they will be searched, as opposed to the minute or two spent by S17. S5's solution is to store the text as a string, and, for very much the reasons mentioned previously, to store the terms in a binary tree. These decisions are exactly opposite to those arrived at by S17.

S19's protocol shows that he does not completely understand the difference between computer words and English words. On the computer that he is familiar with, a computer word will contain an English word of up to 10 characters, so for many practical purposes, the distinction is not needed. In his term data structure, he allocates five (computer) words for each term, one for each (English) word. Whereas this might not be the most effective way to store the terms, it might work for some data sets, at least on the CDC6400. His misunderstanding of the difference gets him into trouble, however, when he tries to read the text. He initially tries to read it a line at a time but abandons this because he cannot determine how many words are on a line. He then decides to read the text a word at a time. His assumption that an English word is a natural unit for input (it is not; it takes a substantial amount of computation to determine the word's boundaries) is due to his confusion between the two types of words.

S3, on the other hand, not only understands the difference between the two concepts but is also aware that the overlapping terminology is confusing. When she is allocating list pointers, she comments "the pointers themselves are actually in a vector of NT units, or words, well, computer words, I guess, . . . (that's certainly a misused word)." Thus, she is sensitive to the distinction between the concepts as well as the confusibility in terminology.

Yet another example is S17's confusion over what a flag is and when to use one. A flag is a variable that can take on two values, usually "true" and "false." It is used to indicate the status of some condition that changes within the program. S17 has some understanding of the use of flags, as he intends to "set a flag back and forth" to signal the end of the text file. Although this is not an error, it is not a particularly good use for a flag, as the end of the text file will only be reached once, and a simple test for the condition would be more suitable.

Later on in the design, he needs a way to indicate which terms have been found on the current page before the page number is available. Although his solution incorporates the idea of setting a flag, he calls it a "count." This misuse of terminology confuses him later on, when he mistakes this "count" for a count of the number of times each term occurs in the entire text.

Understanding of Implications.   In addition to their conceptual failures, the novices are often unable to extract all the implications of a piece of knowledge. In particular, they are frequently unable to derive the implications of the interactions between a task and a computer implementation of that task. This is exemplified by the differences in the way the experts and novices dealt with the subproblem that compares the text and terms.

This subproblem is the heart of this design, because the efficiency of this routine directly impacts the overall efficiency of the program. All the experts treated the matcher as a difficult problem. They concerned themselves with many aspects of it: whether comparing should be done character by character or word by word; how to organize the data to minimize the number of comparisons that are unsuccessful; what constitutes a correct match. The novices, for the most part, simply stated the subproblem and made no further effort to decompose it. They seemed to treat it as too simple to require further consideration. The experience most of the novices have with compare procedures is with those that deal with comparing numbers. For such cases, the procedure is quite straightforward. Questions about how much to compare at once and how to decide if a match has occurred never arise. The novices did not retrieve information about factors that must be considered in a character string compare, because they simply did not understand the implications of the way a computer compares data.

The novice protocols indicate that novices have mastered the jargon of the field; their comments are peppered with technical computer science terms. More careful examination, however, shows that these terms do not have the same meaning for the novices as they do for the expert. This implies that in some sense, design decisions that are described by the same words are not the "same" for people of different experience levels. In addition, as the earlier examples show, these misunderstandings and failures to deduce relevant implications frequently lead to the novices astray. They confuse similar concepts or apply a concept when it is inappropriate or do not take into account pertinent considerations. In actual designs these subtle errors could be disastrous, as they probably would not be noticed until the program was written. If the problem were serious enough that a major change to the design was required, large amounts of effort would have been wasted.

DISCUSSION

The decomposition process is central to the successful derivation of a software design. It serves to break a problem down into manageable and minimally interacting components. Thus, the task is reduced to one of solving several simpler subproblems. For experts, the decomposition and subproblem selection processes of the design schema dictate the global organization of their design behavior. They first break the problem into its major constituents, thus forming a solution model. During each iteration, subproblems from the previous cycle are further decomposed, most frequently leading to a top-down, breadth-first expansion of the solution. The iterative process continues until a solution is identified for each subproblem.

The data show a range of development in the utilization of the decomposition process. At least four distinct levels can be distinguished. The first level is exemplified by the prenovice, S25, who attempted to code the major steps of the solution directly in FORTRAN. A novice designer at the next level derives a solution model and converts it into a series of steps. Novices who broke the problem into steps were usually able to iterate over the steps at least once, producing a more detailed sequence of steps.

The more advanced novices are able to break the problem into meaningful subproblems, using their solution model as a basis. S17 is able to carry out this first level decomposition, but he is unable to recursively apply this strategy. S19 is able to recursively decompose the problem for the first few levels, but eventually he becomes so mired in details that the strategy breaks down.

The experts manifest the fourth level of development of the decomposition processes. They exhibit all three major components of the strategy: (1) They break the problem into manageable, minimally interacting parts; (2) they understand a problem before breaking it into subproblems; and (3) they retrieve a known solution, if one exists. S2 and S3 depended almost completely on the first two of these, whereas S5 and S35 were able to retrieve a known solution to a significant portion of the problem.

Experts devote a great deal of effort to understanding a problem before attempting to break it into subproblems. They clarify constraints on the problem, derive their implications, explore potential interactions, and relate this information to real-world knowledge about the task. The novices, on the other hand, show little inclination to explore aspects of a subproblem before proposing a solution. This has serious consequences for both the correctness and efficiency of their designs.

Expert designers employ a set of processes that attempt to find a known solution to a given subproblem. Critical features of the solution model are used to search for potentially applicable algorithms. Successful retrieval requires the designer to have knowledge of relevant solutions and their applicability conditions, to be able to retrieve the solution in a possibly novel context, and to adapt the solution to the particular context of the design problem. The experts show themselves to be skilled at retrieving algorithms for use in their designs. Novices show no evidence of recognizing the applicability of information in a novel situation that they had unquestionably learned previously. The novices' schemata are deficient in the processes that control the retrieval of information for integration into their designs.

The experts differed in their ability to recall high-level solutions to the problem, specifically, for the matcher and its associated data structures. S35 retrieved an algorithm from the literature and built his solution around it. S5 retrieved a skeletal solution to the same subproblems. However, he chose to work out this solution in some detail before proceeding with the remainder of the design. S2 and S3 did not retrieve information about possible solutions to these subproblems. Instead, they used the default decomposition processes to iteratively refine the problem. Both, however, recalled numerous low-level algorithms that they incorporated into their designs.

The objective of the decomposition process is to factor a problem into weakly interacting subproblems. However, subproblems can interact, and the individual solutions must be integrated. This can impose serious coordination demands upon the problem solver (Simon, 1973). The experts used two components of the design schema to solve this coordination dilemma. First, experts expand subproblems systematically, typically top-down, breadth-first. Second, they are able to store detailed and well-integrated representations of previous problem-solving activities and retrieve them when they become relevant.

Novices have difficulty coordinating their activities because of ineffective retrieval strategies. Because they do not recognize the implications of potential interactions, novices are often unable to correctly interface subproblems. They also fail to retrieve and incorporate information acquired in the classroom and are unable to integrate information generated during earlier parts of the solution attempt with later efforts. Thus, they do not generate a consistent and well-integrated solution to the problem.

The variations in performance, both within and between levels of expertise, demonstrate the complexities of learning the design schema. Basically, the schema is learned through actual experience in doing software designs; textbook knowledge is not sufficient. The experts' years of experience enable the procedures of the schema to become automatic, freeing the designer to focus more on the details of the specific problem. As the more sophisticated processes of the schema develop, the designer is able to deal more successfully with complex problems.

The differences in the ability to use the decomposition process demonstrate that the schema develops in stages. The levels along this continuum seem to correspond to incremental improvements in a designer's understanding and control of the decomposition process. Novices first understand that the problem has to be broken down into smaller parts, although they do not have a good understanding of the nature of those parts. Next, they add the idea that the breakdown should occur iteratively; that is, they should go through several cycles of breaking things down. At the next level, they acquire the ability to do the decomposition in terms of meaningful subproblems, and, finally, to recursively apply this strategy. The mature design schema would include at least the following additional processes: refinement of understanding, retrieval of known solutions, generation of alternatives, and critical analysis of solution components.

The processes people use to solve complex problems in their field of expertise are important to the understanding of the development of that skill. In software design, these processes appear to be specialized versions of more general methods, which are highly organized and automatic. Although these processes superficially resemble the default methods, they are so strongly tailored to the specific domain that they should be considered distinct methods in their own right. For any sufficiently complex and well-learned skill, these kinds of organizational structures would seem to be necessary. A crucial question, which remains to be addressed, is what types of skills lend themselves to the development of such structures.

ACKNOWLEDGMENTS

This research was supported by the Office of Naval Research, Personnel and Training Research Programs, Contract No. N00014-78-C-0165, NR157-414. Computer time was provided by the SUMEX-AIM Computing Facility at the Stanford University School of Medicine, which is supported by grant RR-00785 from the National Institutes of Health.

We wish to thank Dr. James Voss for his instructive comments on an earlier version of this chapter.

REFERENCES

Aho, A. V., & Corasick, M. J. Efficient string matching: An aid to bibliographic search. *Communications of the ACM*, 1975, *18*, 333–340.

Atwood, M. E., & Jeffries, R. *Studies in plan construction I: Analysis of an extended protocol* (Technical Report SAI-80-028-DEN). Englewood, Colo.: Science Applications, Inc., March 1980.

Balzer, R. M. *A global view of automatic programming.* In Third International Joint Conference on Artificial Intelligence: Advance Papers of the Conference. Menlo Park, Calif.: Stanford Research Institute, 1973, 494–499.

Balzer, R. M., Goldman, N., & Wile, D. *Informality in program specifications.* In Fifth International Joint Conference on Artificial Intelligence, Cambridge, Mass., August 1977.

Barstow, D. R. *A knowledge-based system for automatic program construction.* In Fifth International Joint Conference on Artificial Intelligence: Advance Papers of the Conference, Cambridge, Mass., August 1977.

Barstow, D. R. An experiment in knowledge-based automatic programming. *Artificial Intelligence*, 1979, *12*, 73–119.

Bhaskar, R. & Simon, H. A. Problem solving in semantically rich domains: An example from engineering thermodynamics. *Cognitive Science*, 1977, *1*, 193–215.

Biermann, A. W. Approaches to automatic programming. In M. Rubinoff & M. C. Yovits (Eds.), *Advances in computers* (Vol. 15). London: Academic Press, 1976.

Boehm, B. W. Software design and structuring. In E. Horowitz (Ed.), *Practical strategies for developing large software systems.* Reading, Mass.: Addison–Wesley, 1975.

Boyer, R. S., & Moore, J. S. A fast string searching algorithm. *Communications of the ACM*, 1977, *20*, 762–772.

Green, C. *A summary of the PSI program synthesis system.* In Fifth International Joint Conference on Artificial Intelligence. Cambridge, Mass., August, 1977.

Hayes–Roth, B., & Hayes–Roth, F. A cognitive model of planning. *Cognitive Science*, 1979, *3*, 275–310.

Heidorn, C. E. Automatic programming through natural language dialogue: A survey. *IBM Journal of Research and Development*, 1976, *20*, 302–313.

Jackson, M. A. *Principles of program design.* New York: Academic Press, 1975.

Larkin, J. H., *Problem solving in physics* (Technical Report). Berkeley, Calif.: University of California, Department of Physics, July 1977.

Levin, S. L. *Problem selection in software design* (Technical Report No. 93). Irvine, Calif.: University of California, Department of Information and Computer Science, November 1976.

Long, W. J. *A program writer* (Technical Report No. MIT/LCS/TR-187). Cambridge, Mass.: Massachusetts Institute of Technology, Laboratory for Computer Science, November 1977.

Mark, W. S. *The reformulation model of expertise* (Technical Report No. MIT/LCS/TR-172). Cambridge, Mass.: Massachusetts Institute of Technology, Laboratory for Computer Science, December, 1976.

Myers, G. J. *Software reliability: Principles and practices.* New York: Wiley, 1975.

Sacerdoti, E. D. *A structure for plans and behavior* (Technical Note 109). Menlo Park, Calif.: Stanford Research Institute, August 1975.

Simon, H. A. Experiments with a heuristic compiler. *Journal of the ACM*, 1963, *10*, 493–506.

Simon, H. A. The heuristic compiler. In H. A. Simon & L. Siklossy (Eds.), *Representation and meaning: Experiments with information processing systems.* Englewood Cliffs, N.J.: Prentice–Hall, 1972.

Simon, H. A. The structure of ill-structured problems. *Artificial Intelligence,* 1973, *4,* 181–201.

Sussman, G. J. *Electrical design: A problem for artificial intelligence research.* Proceedings of the International Joint Conference on Artificial Intelligence, Cambridge, Mass., 1977, 894–900. '

Warnier, J. D. *Logical construction of programs.* Leiden, Netherlands: Stenpert Kroese, 1974.

Yourdon, E., & Constantine, L. L. *Structured design.* New York: Yourdon, 1975.

9 Mental Models of Physical Mechanisms and Their Acquisition

Johan de Kleer and John Seely Brown
XEROX PARC
Cognitive and Instructional Sciences
3333 Coyote Hill Road
Palo Alto, California 94304

INTRODUCTION

In the past, many research projects have aimed at a better understanding of how one learns a language, a set of procedures, a large corpus of facts, nonsense syllables, etc. In this chapter, we focus on a new domain—one that shares very few properties with any of the previous. The domain is that of mechanistic devices, including physical machines, electronic and hydraulic systems, and even hybrids such as electro–mechanical systems. Our top-level goals are: (1) to investigate what it means for a person to understand a complex system, in particular, the mental models that experts form of how a system functions given the system's constituents and their interconnections; and (2) to discover principles that orient the acquisition of the capability to construct these models.

It is no surprise that these two goals are interrelated. In fact, it is nearly impossible to investigate the properties of the acquisition process without first having a clear notion of exactly what must be learned. Thus, we see that the first goal is a prerequisite for the second. What is surprising is that the second goal is intimately tied to the first, in that the properties that make these mental models learnable or that facilitate their development turn out to be essential characteristics of a highly robust mental model in the first place. In fact, each of the principles we discuss for guiding the learning process are equally well motivated as principles for guaranteeing the robustness of the mental model. As we shall see, the duality of these principles is not accidental. This means that our chapter can be read from two quite different perspectives. The first concerns what constitutes mental models of mechanistic systems and what characteristics enhance their utility for problem solving by an expert. The second concerns how these characteristics impact the acquisition of skills for constructing mental models.

285

Before we begin a technical discussion of these issues, we need to provide an overview of the kind of mental models we are discussing here, the processes underlying their construction, and the kind of learning principles that we are after.

The kind of mental models of a mechanistic system that we are interested in are generated, metaphorically speaking, by running a qualitative simulation in the mind's eye. We call the result of such simulation "envisionment." One of the most important properties of envisionment is its ability to manifest a system's causality, which not only makes it extremely useful for constructing causal models of how and why the system functions, but also makes the envisionment sufficiently self-evident that it, also, can be "run" efficiently in the mind's eye; that is, envisionments have the property that each new state change is *directly* caused by a prior event. Hence determining the next state involves very simple reasoning (de Kleer, 1979).

We can portray the basic entities involved in constructing mental models in a diagram, such as the one below:

MENTAL MODEL

DEVICE STRUCTURE = P1 => | ENVISIONMENT = P2 => CAUSAL ATTRIBUTION |

P1 denotes the process of examining the device's structure and from that constructing an envisionment of its behavior. P2 denotes the process of examining the resulting envisionment—both its form and its execution—and from that deriving a causal attributive description. The mental model is a combination of an envisionment and its causal attribution. But it is not a fixed entity because the attribution process (P2) can either be run to completion producing a complete description or can be allocated limited resources producing a partial description. For the purposes of this chapter, the details of the two processes are of secondary interest. Instead, our attention is focused primarily on discovering a set of principles of critiquing candidate mental models.

Briefly, it is the task of the learning system to provide an adequate process for generating an envisionment from a structural description of a device knowledge of what the device is supposed to do. Learning how to generate adequate envisionments is exceedingly complex, and we do not have a complete description of the learning process at this point in our research. However, the learning task falls naturally into two phases. It is the responsibility of the first to critique the given envisionment and isolate any parts not conforming to the behavior of the physical device or not meeting certain principles. By striving to meet these principles, an *esthetic* for the learning process is provided, thus setting the stage for the learning system to improve its current envisionment, even if it is already accurate and consistent. It is the responsibility of the second phase to critique the model construction process to isolate responsibility for the critiqued envisionment.

THE MOTIVATION FOR DEFINING SOME ESTHETIC PRINCIPLES

The purpose of defining a set of esthetic principles for critiquing simulation models—even those that are already consistent—is to provide a gradient or direction of progress for the learning process to improve its current model of the system. But toward what end?; that is, what are the properties of an ideal envisionment, and why are these properties important? The answer lies in the essential properties of an expert's models, those properties that maximize his ability to use the model to answer unanticipated questions or predict the consequences of novel situations.

Our approach to discovering these properties has not been to probe the models of an expert directly but rather to hypothesize what such a model might be, criticize it according to principles abstracted from our experience with its implementation, and then characterize the essential properties of the model that maximize its robustness (Brown, Collins, & Harris, 1977).

THE NO-FUNCTION-IN-STRUCTURE PRINCIPLE

We assume that a given system consists of a set of components, each of whose behaviors are satisfactorily modeled by a set of rules, and expect our simulation or envisionment to explain how the system's overall behavior is caused by the behavior of its constituents and their interactions. The preceding process is potentially recursive in that models can be embedded in models. Said differently, the behavior of a system's component can be characterized by a set of rules at one level of detail, and at another level be viewed as a system whose behavior is, itself, derivable from still lower-level components. Our concern is not the choice of appropriate level of modeling but rather, at a given level of detail, to examine the problem of constructing a qualitative simulation that is maximally robust. This robustness is achieved by ensuring that the system's simulation model does not presuppose the very mechanism it is trying to describe. We do this by having it satisfy a constraint called the ''no-function-in-structure'' principle. This principle states that the rules for specifying the behavior of any constituent part of the overall system can in no way refer, even implicitly, to how the overall system functions.

Violating the no-function-in-structure principle also limits one's ability to use the simulation in predicting how the system might function, given a modified or faulted component. Because a slightly modified component can sometimes radically alter the underlying mechanism of the overall system, those rules that specified a component's behaviors by implicitly presupposing this mechanism may no longer be valid. The predictive aspects of the simulation in such a case are highly questionable (Brown and Burton, 1975).

Fully satisfying this principle ensures that the behaviors of each of the system's parts can be represented and understood in a context-free manner, independent of the overall system. Failing to adhere to this principle leads to an explanation of how the system functions predicated on some aspect of how it functions. This recursion is not always bad; often, on first explaining a system, it is best to violate this principle, providing an explanation that establishes a framework on which to hang more satisfactory mental models.

THE WEAK CAUSALITY PRINCIPLE

Whereas the main purpose of the no-function-in-structure principle is to establish a criterion by which to evaluate hypothetical models, there are other principles that facilitate the learning process. The weak causality principle is the most important of this class. It states that every event must have a direct cause, meaning that the reasoning process involved in determining the next state change is local and does not use any indirect arguments in determining what the next state must be. An envisionment that satisfies this principle has the useful property that one can precisely identify which aspect of the envisionment is responsible for any piece of behavior that is inconsistent with the observed device. In other words, a learning system following this principle can discover where to assign credit or blame in the current model.

Duality of Purpose

Seen from the perspective of learning, the weak causality principle facilitates the assignment of credit. It is interesting to note that this same principle has quite a different role when seen from the perspective of performance—that is, performing the problem solving needed to construct the envisionment. From this perspective, a model that satisfies this principle enables the set of next possible states to be determined without requiring elaborate reasoning. Constraining the weak causality principle to require that the next state is also uniquely determined has a major impact on the efficiency of constructing the envisionment as well as facilitating the ease of using it. Later in the chapter we expand this strong causality principle.

The duality also holds for the no-function-in-structure principle. The latter provides a direction for improvement when used in a learning context, and it provides a guarantee of robustness when used in a problem-solving context.

METHODOLOGY

Our approach has been to study a class of devices that on the one hand are intuitively understood by nearly everyone but on the other hand are sufficiently complex to raise many problematic issues—some of which were unanticipated by us. The device we have chosen is a simple doorbell or electro-mechanical buzzer. It is sufficiently complex to stress any current theory of causal mechanisms including our own. Finding an internally consistent qualitative simulation of the buzzer that also satisfies both the causality principle and the no-function-in-structure principle turns out to be surprisingly difficult. Similarly, because the buzzer is a common household device, the reader can judge the subtleties involved in finding a principled simulation and appreciate how that simulation can be used to answer a wide variety of questions. Granted that the need for defining a set of principles constraining the representation of a system might have been more convincing had we chosen a more complex paradigmatic example, the chance of readers following and even anticipating the various pitfalls that unfold as we explore a sequence of potential models would have been radically reduced. Again, let us stress that, like any single device however complex, the buzzer itself is of no fundamental importance.

TECHNICAL ISSUES

What form should such a representation take, and what should we expect to be able to do with it? As with much of this chapter, let us proceed by example. Pictured here is a diagram of the buzzer. Its functioning seems to be easily

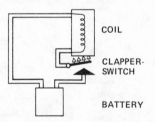

FIG. 9.1. Buzzer.

described by a small set of rules basically asserting: *The clapper switch of the buzzer closes, which causes the coil to conduct a current, thereby generating an electromagnetic field, which in turn pulls the clapper arm away from the switch contact, thereby opening the switch, which shuts off the magnetic field allowing the clapper arm to return to its closed position, which then starts the whole process over again.* Indeed, we could easily create a set of formal rules that would produce this ad hoc description, but does that description produce a useful understanding?

This question can be answered using the following definition of mental model robustness: A model is robust with respect to its device structure, if the questions that can be asked about the device structure can be answered correctly. The device structure implicitly defines the terms of a descriptive language, and questions using those terms concern the ramifications of changing the device structure or its component attributes. Our ad hoc description of how the buzzer is supposed to buzz does not provide an understanding that can address such possible questions.

For example, listed here are some typical questions that one might expect a person who has a thorough, qualitative understanding of the buzzer's mechanism to be able to answer without recourse to analytic models of its components, nor to differential equations, etc:

1. What happens if we reverse the leads of a battery (i.e., change the polarity of the battery in the circuit)?

2. What happens if we switch the leads of the coil?

3. What happens if we remove the battery from the circuit?

4. What happens if we short the switch contact?

5. What happens if we make the switch arm lighter (or even weightless)? For example, what happens qualitatively to the frequency of the vibrator or the size of the gap when such a change is made?

6. What happens if we place a light-weight permanent magnet on the clapper arm? Does the frequency of the buzzer change? Does it matter which way the battery is hooked up?

7. What happens if we put two clapper switches in series (or parallel)? If one buzzes with a lower frequency than the other when subjected to the same magnetic field, then what happens when they are placed in series?

Attempting to answer questions like the preceding—some of which are admittedly quite hard—demonstrates the surprising richness of inferences that can follow from a totally qualitative understanding of the underlying mechanisms of the buzzer. Similarly, the inadequacies of the previous description of how the buzzer functions become quite obvious. To answer these and other unanticipated questions just from a representation of how the buzzer works places quite a burden on that representation and the processes that interpret it. But apart from the failure of that description to answer such questions, there is a principled objection: A great deal of that description already presupposes how the buzzer works.

For example, the statement, "the clapper switch closes causing the coil to conduct a current" presupposes a source of current or battery in the circuit. Furthermore, it presupposes that the switch, coil, and battery are all arranged in a very particular way, and that when the switch closes it necessarily passes current. Switches in general do not pass current; they only pass current if they are connected to batteries and wires in particular configurations. Although it may be true for this buzzer that the switch passes current, we can only say so because we already understand how it works.

The desired level of understanding is this: Given a description of how the switch operates in all possible circuits, use that along with similar descriptions of the other parts of the buzzer to explain how and why the switch passes current as it closes. In general, the problem is how to connect the functioning of the device (i.e., its buzzing) with the structure of the device (i.e., the buzzer) without presupposing how the device functions.

Our distinction between structure and function is crucial, even in any formal analysis of the buzzer. For example, the coil could be modeled by $V = L(di/dt)$—a model valid for any electromagnet—and such models could be combined into differential equations and solved in standard ways. But for the engineer to assert a priori that the voltage V across the coil necessarily obeys some particular function, $f(t)$, would render his analysis suspect, because he would be using the solution in order to find it. Without an appropriate distinction between structure and function, an analysis can be uninformative. We assert that a meaningful analysis based on either quantitative or qualitative component models must not allow any of the solution (i.e., function) into the description (i.e., structure) of its pieces.

In the following sections, we present a series of successively more adequate simulation models. Each of these models is of interest in its own right in that each illustrates a problematic issue in constructing or critiquing possible envisionments.

A SIMPLE QUALITATIVE MODEL FOR THE BUZZER

The fundamental question we want to address is, given that the behaviors of components (magnets, batteries, coils, etc.) are understood generally and sufficiently, how do the understandings of the behaviors of the individual components combine to explain the behavior (buzzing) of the composite device (buzzer) constructed from these components? The following is an extremely simple model for describing how the buzzer functions. The purpose in presenting this model first is to introduce our techniques for formalizing qualitative models, illustrate the difficulty modeling even a simple device, and demonstrate that a formal qualitative model that does not obey certain principles is not necessarily very useful.

The two critical components of the buzzer are the coil, which produces a magnetic field, and the clapper switch, which moves in this field. The clapper switch is either closed, connecting the battery and the coil, or open, disconnecting them. The coil is either on, causing a magnetic field that attracts the clapper switch, or off, causing no field. The behaviors of the two components can be formalized as:

SWITCH : OPEN: battery and coil are disconnected.
CLOSED: battery and coil are connected.

COIL : ON: magnetic field is pulling at switch.

OFF: no magnetic field is pulling at switch.

Each component of the buzzer is indicated and its possible states are distinguished. For each such state, a description of its behavior in that state is included.

This model is incomplete because it does not indicate how the magnetic field of the coil can change the state of the switch, nor how the battery can change the state of the coil. We need to somehow associate pulling at the switch with its being open, and the battery-to-coil connection with the coil's being on. One possibility is to extend the description of the behaviors:

SWITCH : OPEN: battery and coil are disconnected,

magnetic field is pulling at switch.

CLOSED: battery and coil are connected,

no magnetic field is pulling at switch.

COIL : ON: magnetic field is pulling at switch,

battery and coil are connected.

OFF: no magnetic field is pulling at switch,

battery and coil are disconnected.

The rationale behind this model is that if the switch is open, the magnetic field must be pulling at it, because the field is what opens it. Similarly, if the coil is on, the battery must be connected to it, because otherwise the coil couldn't produce a magnetic field.

In order to understand this model's implications, consider a particular situation in which the switch is closed:

SWITCH : CLOSED: battery and coil are connected,

no magnetic field is pulling at switch.

According to the preceding model, the coil can now be neither on nor off. If the coil is off:

COIL : OFF: no magnetic field is pulling at switch,

battery and coil are disconnected.

The coil rule "battery and coil are disconnected" contradicts switch rule "battery and coil are connected." Further examination shows that every other possible component state is similarly contradictory. The model is completely inconsistent and thus of little use for understanding the operation of the buzzer.

A TIME MODEL OF THE BUZZER

The difficulties of the previous models cannot be removed by simply changing the descriptions; any model for the buzzer of the previous form will be inadequate, because the form has failed to consider time and causality. For instance "battery and coil are disconnected" does not necessarily contradict "battery and coil are connected," if these two hold at different times. By modifying the form to distinguish definitional from consequential behaviors, a qualitative notion of time can be introduced into the buzzer model. The symbol "$->$" is used to indicate consequential behavior.

SWITCH : OPEN: battery and coil are disconnected,
$->$ no magnetic field is pulling at switch.
CLOSED: battery and coil are connected,
$->$ magnetic field is pulling at switch.
COIL : ON: magnetic field is pulling at switch,
$->$ battery and coil are disconnected.
OFF: no magnetic field is pulling at switch,
-> battery and coil are connected.

The rationale for this switch model is that if the switch is open, the magnetic field will soon be cut off, because the battery is disconnected. Similarly, if the coil is on, the battery will soon be disconnected, because the magnetic field opens the switch. Because this model has an explicit notion of time, it is possible to simulate the behavior of the buzzer model over time. One way of describing the result is to arrange in tabular format the states of the components at successive time increments (we discuss this process in more detail in the next section):

t	SWITCH	COIL	BATTERY	->BATTERY	COIL	->COIL
0	CLOSED	ON	connected	disconnected	pulling	pulling
1	OPEN	ON	disconnected	disconnected	pulling	not pulling
2	OPEN	OFF	disconnected	connected	not pulling	not pulling
3	CLOSED	OFF	connected	connected	not pulling	pulling
4	CLOSED	ON	connected	disconnected	pulling	pulling
5						

The boxes indicate which states changed from the previous time increment. In the initial state ($t = 0$), the coil being on results in the battery being disconnected; therefore, the switch must change state from closed to open. In the next state ($t = 1$), the fact that the switch is open results in the coil not pulling; therefore, the coil must change state from on to off.

Although this model is internally consistent and capable of explaining the phenomenon (the vibration), it does not represent a very robust understanding of the buzzer. First, the model for the coil inherently assumes its connection to a battery and a switch, and, furthermore, it assumes that the battery-switch connection allows the battery to be disconnected from the coil whenever the magnetic field is pulling at the switch. This particular model for the coil has the entire functioning of the buzzer embedded within it and thus is inadequate for any device except this particular buzzer. It violates the no-function-in-structure principle. Second, the successor state is determined indirectly. For example, the consequence of the coil's being on is the battery's disconnection, and the only consistent state for the switch, in this case, is open. This indirect determination of state makes it impossible to determine credit or blame. The weak causality principle has been violated.

A CAUSAL MODEL FOR THE BUZZER

The difficulties of the previous buzzer models force us to expand the syntax to conditionalize the consequences and to make a component's consequences affect only the component itself. This change addresses both the no-function-in-structure principle and the weak causality principle. Because the model for a component is now less dependent on its surrounding context, more robust models for the components can be constructed. The conditional makes it possible to identify precisely why a component changes state, making it is easy to assign credit or blame.

The rule for a state consists of a definitional part (e.g., the battery is disconnected), and a conditional that makes a test (e.g., if the coil is not pulling) to determine whether some consequence applies (e.g., the switch will become closed). The general form for a component model is:

<component> : <state1>: (<definitional-part>)*, (if <test>,
          <consequence>)*
          <state2>: (<definitional-part>)*, (if <test>,
          <consequence>)*

"(...)*" indicates that "..." may occur an arbitrary number times. The <definitional-part> can be used in two ways. The first concerns its use as a criterion for determining whether the component is in a given state, and the second concerns its use as an imperative. Given that the component is declared to be in a particular state (criterion), then statements made in the <definitional-part> are asserted to be true (imperative) about the component's behavior. These assertions can then be examined by an inferential process to determine their ramifications. In simple cases, these ramifications can be determined by examining the tests of the current state of every component model.

The models for the buzzer parts are:

SWITCH : OPEN:
          battery is disconnected,
          if coil is not pulling, switch will become CLOSED.
      CLOSED:
          battery is connected,
          if coil is pulling, switch will become OPEN.
COIL : ON:
          coil is pulling,
          if battery is disconnected, coil will become OFF.

OFF:
　coil is not pulling,
　if battery is connected, coil will become ON.

In order to combine these descriptions of the behaviors of the individual parts to determine the behavior of the overall buzzer, we set out to construct a simulation. Starting with some arbitrary[1] initial state for each of the components (i.e., a cross product or composite state), their definitional parts are asserted, and then each test is examined to determine the consequences of those assertions being true. From these consequences, the next state is determined. The discovery of each next state can be considered as a time increment. The time elapsed between increments is variable, because increments refer to interesting events rather than the passage of some fixed unit of time. The determination of the next composite state can be very complex. The consequences of the prior composite state may indicate that multiple components will change state in the next time interval. In the actual physical system, it may be critical that one component change state before another, but in a qualitative simulation, the time scales for each of the models are not inherently comparable, because they don't utilize a uniform time metric. The exact ordering of the transitions cannot be directly determined without considering the overall purpose of the device and other nonlocal properties that require complex inferencing schemes. A second complication stems from the qualitative nature of the inputs and other internal parameters. In this case, it might be ambiguous whether some threshold in the test was passed, resulting in various components optionally changing state. Such a situation can force the consideration of parallel envisionments.[2]

The transition table is:

t	SWITCH	COIL	BATTERY	COIL
0	CLOSED	ON	connected	pulling
1	OPEN	ON	disconnected	pulling
2	OPEN	OFF	disconnected	not pulling
3	CLOSED	OFF	connected	not pulling
4	CLOSED	ON	connected	pulling
5				

In the initial state (t = 0), the coil's being on causes the switch to change state from closed to open. If the switch is open, the battery is disconnected by defini-

---

[1]For more complex devices, this choice cannot be arbitrary, because some of the composite device states may be either contradictory or inaccessible—requiring several initial states. A composite state is contradictory if the definitional parts of two of its component states make contradictory assertions.

[2]However, many of these difficulties can be avoided by detecting and eliminating self-contradictory device states and invoking other deductive machinery. It is the responsibility of the simulation process P1 to identify the ambiguities, but it is also the responsibility of P1 to prune as many of the resulting envisionments as possible based on local considerations.

tion. In the next state (t = 1), the battery's disconnection causes the coil to change state from on to off. If the coil is off, it is not pulling by definition. The construction continues. The simulation can also be represented as a state transition diagram.

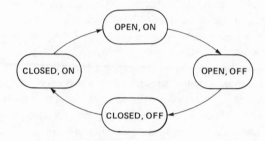

FIG. 9.2.   State-transition diagram for the buzzer.

The preceding table can also be used to construct a series of snapshots of the buzzer functioning over time (see Fig. 9.3).

NO-FUNCTION-IN-STRUCTURE AND THE LOCALITY PRINCIPLES

The buzzer model, although it explains the vibration, has so much of the knowledge of how the buzzer works embedded in the models of the individual components that it provides little insight into how the buzzer, as an interacting collection of components, functions. Implicit within each of the models is that it is connected to other constituent components comprising a buzzer. The models name other components and their internal states directly, thereby presuming that they are part of a buzzer. That the components are physically connected by wires and magnetic fields is often ignored. For example, the model for the switch assumes its connection to a battery and that when it opens it will prevent current from flowing and disconnect the battery from the coil. The model for the coil assumes that it is not the current flowing through it but the fact that some battery is connected to something, which enables the magnetic field to exist. Thus, much of the essential functionality of the overall buzzer has been embedded within its constituent parts. There is little chance that these same models would be useful for understanding a buzzer that was constructed even slightly differently. For example, a buzzer having two clappers hooked in series or parallel is sufficiently different for these models to be of little use.[3]

---

[3]Notice that in this case, contradictory states exist: If one clapper is open and the other is closed, the rules make contradictory assertions about whether the battery is connected. Or if that were resolved by having better switch models, the next state of the coil is ambiguous.

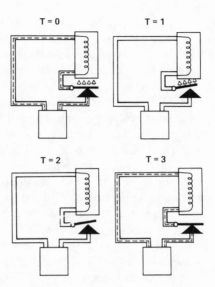

FIG. 9.3.   The functioning of the buzzer.

Syntactic restrictions can be placed on the models of the individual components to ensure that they reference *local* quantities. Such locality restrictions help to avoid gross violations of the no-function-in-structure principle. The first locality principle demands that there is no reference to other components in rule consequences. The previous models' rules met that principle. A similar locality principle can be used to restrict the definitional aspect of component rules. But if a locality principle were also enforced on the tests of component rules, there would be no way for models of different components to ever interact; thus, there is no way to avoid some nonlocality. To extend the locality principle to all three parts of a rule forces the introduction of connections as entities independent of the component models.

CONNECTIONS AND DEVICE TOPOLOGY

In order to avoid nonlocality in the component models, we need to draw a distinction between the models for components and the method by which these models communicate. We introduce *connection* as a simple stateless model that is primarily a placeholder for information. Although we make the internal state of a component inaccessible to other components and connections, models for components and connections communicate by sharing information. For example, both the model for a specific wire (e.g., wire 2) and its adjacent part (e.g., coil) will know the current flowing from the wire into the coil. The simplest model for a wire is one that consists of the knowledge of the current through it, and it shares this information with the components on either end of the wire. The only information that is shared by connections are *attributes* that are related to the actual physics by which components interact (e.g., voltage, current, pressure, force, flow, etc.) The no-function-in-structure principle also applies to connections. For example, it requires every wire in the buzzer to be modeled in the same way, and also every attribute of the same type (e.g., force) to be treated in the same way (e.g., obey Newton's laws). The component–connection distinction allows us to model the effect of the coil on the clapper switch: The coil being on (state of a component) causes a strong magnetic flux (attribute of a connection) that causes the clapper switch to open (state of a component).

Formally, it can often be arbitrary as to which parts of the buzzer are components and which are connections. All the buzzer models presented so far implicitly assume wires and magnetic fields to be connections. This is not necessary; we could have modeled a wire as a component having certain properties, but then we would have had to introduce an end-of-wire connection to attach the wire component to the switch component. The determination of which parts should be modeled as connections and which as components can be quite subtle, because a connection assumes that the model describing its behavior is extremely simple. For example, it would have been, in principle, impossible to model the switch as a connection because a switch has internal state. If we had decided the switch was a connection, we would never be able to construct an adequate model for the buzzer.

The device topology of a physical device consists of a description of the components of the device and their connections.

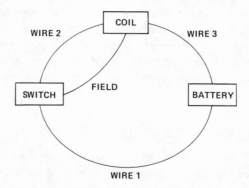

FIG. 9.4.   Device topology of the buzzer.

Although a specific model for a specific component is permitted to know about the current in a specific wire, the class wide or prototype is not. Therefore, the prototype model can only express its potential connection to some wire. It refers to information that it might possibly share with connections as variables. When the prototype model is used in a specific device, these variables need to be replaced with device-specific quantities, because that is the only way two component models can communicate.

A prototype model for the switch is:

Information terminals: i1, i2, f1
SWITCH : OPEN:
        i1 $<-$ 0, i2 $<-$ 0
        if f1 = 0, SWITCH will become CLOSED.
   CLOSED:
        i1 $<-$ 1, i2 $<-$ 1
        if f1 = 1, SWITCH will become OPEN.

A variable such as "i1" is intended to indicate the value of some attribute (e.g., a current of one ampere) that can then be communicated among models. Unlike component states that do not change until acted upon by some other model, variable values are direct results of components being in particular states and thus are only considered valid as long as the components that caused them do not change state. If a variable value is changed by some model, it may not be changed again until the component that originally caused the variable value changes state.[4] The semantics of "a $<-$ b" is a[t+1] = b[t] for each time t in which the rule is valid. Or informally, a's value gets b's value. In the previous model, b is a constant, and the effect of "a $<-$ b" is to set a's value to that constant. For example, as long as the switch is open, the rule "i1 $<-$ 0" applies, thus i1 is set to zero immediately after the switch becomes open and cannot change until after the switch ceases to be open. The actual amount of time elapsed moving from t to t+1 is arbitrary—it can be infinitesimally small or extremely large. Our convention is that time t+1 refers to the next interesting event after time t, thus the time elapsed moving from t to t+1 has no relation to the time elapsed moving from t+1 to t+2.

A prototype model for the coil is:

Information terminals: i1, i2, f1
COIL : ON:
        f1 $<-$ 1
        if i1 = 0, coil will become OFF
        if i2 = 0, coil will become OFF.
   OFF:
        f1 $<-$ 0
        if i1 = 1, coil will become ON
        if i2 = 1, coil will become ON.

An overly simplistic prototype model for the battery is:

Information terminals: i1, i2
BATTERY : i1 $<->$ i2.

---

[4]If this is violated, for example, if one component changes the current to one ampere and another to two, the model for the composite device is inconsistent.

"a $<->$ b" is a short-hand for "a $->$ b and a $<-$ b." In other words, propagate changes in whatever direction the behavior of the device dictates.

We now have a well-defined, precise way of moving from a device topology to a set of device-specific models that does not violate the no-function-in-structure principle. For each node in the device topology where a connection attaches to a component, a new unique quantity must be invented; then for each component and connection, a copy of its prototype is made with the information terminals replaced with the appropriate circuit-specific quantities. This process ensures that the component models are local, because the only quantities a model can reference are those that are associated with the connections that are adjacent to it in the device topology. Thus, many of the violations of the no-function-in-structure principle are avoided.

One possible set of specific models for the buzzer are:

SWITCH : OPEN:

   I1 $<-$ 0, I2 $<-$ 0

   if F1 = 0, switch will become CLOSED.

  CLOSED:

   I1 $<-$ 1, I2 $<-$ 1

   if F1 = 1, switch will become OPEN.

COIL : ON:

   F1 $<-$ 1

   if I2 = 0, coil will become OFF

   if I3 = 0, coil will become OFF.

  OFF:

   F1 $<-$ 0

   if I2 = 1, coil will become ON

   if I3 = 1, coil will become ON.

BATTERY: I1 $<->$ I3.

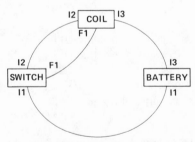

FIG. 9.5.   Model for buzzer.

We arbitrarily chose names for the circuit quantities I1, I2 over QUANTITY1, QUANTITY2 purely for expository reasons. The models for all three parts are completely symmetric, and it does not matter which way these components are placed in the buzzer. The simulation constructed using the previous models is:

t	SWITCH	I2	COIL	F1
0	CLOSED	1	ON	1
1	[OPEN]	1	ON	1
2	OPEN	[0]	ON	1
3	OPEN	0	[OFF]	1
4	OPEN	0	OFF	[0]
5	[CLOSED]	0	OFF	0
6	CLOSED	[1]	OFF	0
7	CLOSED	1	[ON]	0
8	CLOSED	1	ON	[1]
9				

The models used for the wires are not really adequate for more complex circuits, and a better model would have been one in which the wire was modeled as having two ends where the currents in the two ends were related by i1 $< - >$ i2. In such cases, the connections would be viewed more as conduits that have two ends with laws determining the transmission of information through the conduits. For the buzzer, this would only have obscured the point we were trying to illustrate.

A MYTHICAL TIME MODEL

The previous model has a serious problem with time. Doing the analysis to construct the entire table we see the problem:

t	SWITCH	I2	COIL	F1	I1	I3
0	CLOSED	1	ON	1	1	1
1	[OPEN]	1	ON	1	1	1
2	OPEN	[0]	ON	1	[0]	1

There are potential difficulties in the last two rows of the table. The current on one side of the coil I2 is 0, whereas the current on the other side of the coil I3 is still 1, because it takes one more time increment until I3 becomes 0. First, this raises the question whether the coil should really change state—although 12 = 0 is evidence for changing the coil's states from on to off, I3 = 1 is evidence for immediately changing the coil's back to on. Second, it violates Kirchoff's Current Law that requires the current flowing into a component to be equal to the current flowing out of it. We need to distinguish between the time taken for a component to change state and the instantaneous propagation of information in the connections or components that do not change state. For example, it is a myth that the flow of current in the wires happens instantaneously. We call such instantaneousness "mythical time," because no time elapses from the point of view of the state transitions, and the only reason it is important to retain some notion of time, albeit mythical, in the connections is to establish a causal relationship among the changes in attribute values (in this case current).[5] If all possible mythical time increments are considered before considering the next real time increment, the difficulties are resolved. Mythical time is indicated by hyphens in the transition table.

t	SWITCH	I2	COIL	F1	I1	I3
0	CLOSED	1	ON	1	1	1
1	OPEN	1	ON	1	1	1
1-1	OPEN	0	ON	1	0	1
1-2	OPEN	0	ON	1	0	0
2	OPEN	0	OFF	1	0	0
2-1	OPEN	0	OFF	0	0	0
3	CLOSED	0	OFF	0	0	0
3-1	CLOSED	1	OFF	0	1	0
3-2	CLOSED	1	OFF	0	1	1
4	CLOSED	1	ON	0	1	1
4-1	CLOSED	1	ON	1	1	1
5	...					

The information in the preceding table can be represented in an expanded state transition diagram. First, every change in a value or state is represented by a node (indicated by a boxed entry in the table). Second, edges are drawn from each state or value back to the states and values that caused them (these can be determined by examining the component rule that computed the new value or state). Arrowheads are placed pointing toward the new value or state. Third, the nodes are grouped together in larger nodes according to elapsed time increments. The resultant diagram is Fig. 9.6.

The behavior of the buzzer can now be regenerated by just tracing along the edges in the direction of the arrowheads.

A REPRESENTATION FOR CAUSAL ATTRIBUTION

Rieger and Grinberg (1977) have developed a system for representing cause-effect knowledge about physical mechanisms. A significant contribution of their work is an epistemology for the functionality of a physical mechanism. For example, their representation distinguishes between a state change and a tendency to produce a state change and allows a tendency to cause a state–change but not vice versa. However, the state of an object may enable a tendency to exist that causes a state change. This same effect is manifested in our models: The only way one part can affect another is through connections.

---

[5]The notion of attributes will become more important when the stuff flowing in the conduits is modeled in more detail, in that the stuff can have multiple attributes (e.g., voltage and current).

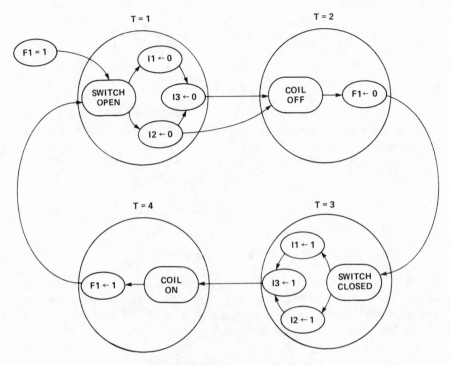

FIG. 9.6. Causation in the buzzer.

The prior analysis of the buzzer can be used to construct a crude representation similar to Rieger's. Events are represented by nodes of which there are only two types: (1) state changes, which represent a change in a component state; and (2) tendencies, which represent attributes of the connections being forced to some value. There are four types of links that represent the causal relationships between these two types of events.

The first link is **enablement:**

FIG. 9.7. Enablement.

The tendency T is a direct result of some component changing to a particular state SC, because the component being in that state SC is what enables tendency T to exist. For example, if the switch changes to the open state, the tendency of the current is toward zero.

The second link is **cause:**

FIG. 9.8.   Cause.

The tendency T is forcing the particular component to change state. For example, if the magnetic field starts the tendency of pulling, the switch will change state from closed to open (SC).

The third type of link is **propagate:**

FIG. 9.9.   Propagate.

The laws for connections derive T2 from T1, thus propagating values through the device topology. For example, if the current through the switch is zero, the current through the battery also becomes zero.

The final type of link is **antagonism:**

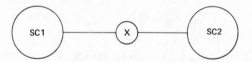

FIG. 9.10.   Antagonism.

Both state changes SC1 and SC2 cannot hold simultaneously and are therefore termed antagonistic. For example, the switch state open is antagonistic to the switch state closed.

A representation for the functioning of the buzzer represented in this epistemology is shown in Fig. 9.11.

This representation is easily constructed from Fig. 9.6 that was obtained from the transition table. The topology of Fig. 9.11 is isomorphic to that of Fig. 9.6, except for the addition of antagonism links. The edges of Fig. 9.6 are represented by the appropriate functional link type. Every edge that represents an attribute value being successfully tested for a state transition is represented by a cause link. Every edge where a definitional rule is used is represented by an enablement link. Every edge where a connection law is used to derive a new attribute value from an old one is represented by a propagate link. Note that this representation for function cannot be constructed from the transition table alone. To identify the origin of the changes in the table and their respective type requires referring back to the particular component rules that produced the change.

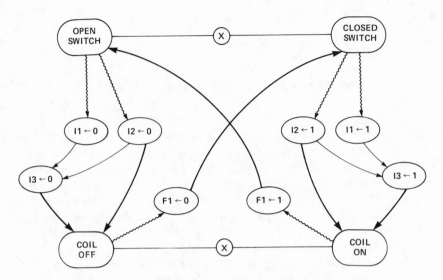

FIG. 9.11. Causal attribution of buzzer.

In order to determine the behavior of the buzzer over time, one can just step through the links in Fig. 9.11 reading the sequence of values at successive time increments.

CAUSALITY PRINCIPLES AND ENVISIONMENT

The representation of function meets one of the desiderata we were originally seeking for mental models but could not get: The next state (necessarily unique) of the composite device is directly and solely determined by the tests of component rules on the previous composite state. This desiderata subsumes the weak causality principle, which is important because it ensures that the simulation can be done efficiently and that every component state change be caused by the previous composite state. Because the causes for these state changes are identifiable, they can be used in identifying reasons for faulty and correct predictions, and thus the principle plays a fundamental role in learning.

This desiderata is partially met in the models, because state transitions can only be made by consequences of component rules, but this restriction only meets the weak causality principle. It does not guarantee the strong causality principle of unique successor state is met, because for example, a composite state may have multiple successor composite states. Furthermore, a great deal of deduction may be required to determine which states to eliminate. Thus, we see the simulation process (P1) responsible for constructing envisionments in clear perspective: Because its result does not necessarily obey the strong causality principle, a subsequent analysis (P2) is required to construct a representation that does obey the strong causality principle.[6]

A CRITIQUE OF THE RIEGER AND GRINBERG'S APPROACH

The goal of Rieger and Grinberg's research is to study how humans might represent cause–effect knowledge about physical mechanisms. We do not question their epistemology, nor that their representation for function is valuable, but rather we question whether a representation of function alone plays a major role in understanding physical mechanisms. Although their representation is intuitively appealing, it is mainly so because of its similarity to superficial characteristics of human explanation. They did not consider how the representation of structure could be constructed from the device itself.

What distinguishes our position from Rieger and Grinberg's on a theory of mechanism is our concern for a representation of the physical device itself, and more importantly, a theory of mechanism that deals with the relationship between the physical device (its structure) and the overall causal behavior manifested by that device (its function). A representation for either the structure or the function alone is by itself insufficient. No matter how each is represented, the important issue is the relationship between the two.

A theory of mechanism that is only concerned with functionality cannot address many of the questions we expect such a theory to answer. For example, the simple question, "What happens if the clapper switch is removed?" cannot be answered at all, because that question is asking what change in functionality results if the structure is altered. For their theory to have utility, Rieger and Grinberg have had to confuse their epistemology of functionality with some primitives that are inherently structural. For example, in their representation of the buzzer, two states "Open Switch" and "Closed Switch" need to be related by a link that states that both cannot hold true simultaneously. This link, like every other in their theory, needs to be added explicitly. If their theory included an adequate notion of structure, this would be unnecessary, because both of these states refer to the same clapper switch, and a single part can only be in one state at one time.

Although Rieger and Grinberg's notion of simulation may seem similar to ours, their's is used for an entirely different purpose. Their representation of the

---

[6]The buzzer is really too simple to illustrate the utility and difficulty of the analysis process P2. An examination of the component models reveals that the composite buzzer model will obey the strong causality principle completely. This can be seen by the fact that the topology of Fig. 9.11 is isomorphic to the topology of the rules. However, consider the case where the buzzer had two clappers. Here, there is some ambiguity as to which opens first, and this must be resolved in the representation of function.

functionality is specifically designed to apply for various inputs. What they call simulation is a reasoning process within that representation to determine the response of the device, given a particular stimulus. Stimuli not included in the original representation cannot be dealt with. Our use of simulation is as a step in a reasoning process on the representation of the structure to determine its functionality. This representation of structure is derived by a straightforward process utilizing a set of models valid for all devices in some class. As a consequence, Rieger and Grinberg's representation cannot be used to simulate devices that are even minutely different in structure, whereas ours can be used for any of a broad class of devices.

Another way to examine the distinction between the two theories is to ask what questions each can answer about a device. Rieger and Grinberg's representation can answer questions about the behavior resulting from some external stimulus, or about the consequences of removing or changing a causal link. However, it cannot answer questions about the consequences of some component being removed or faulted, or about behavior at some extreme section of its operating range. It is not surprising that the ability to answer these questions is necessary for designing or troubleshooting. What is more important is that it is necessary for adequately coping with malfunctions in devices. Having such a robust understanding of the buzzer requires the ability to determine the change in function that results from a change in structure.

DELETION PRINCIPLE

Our model for the buzzer still suffers a number of difficulties, and the remaining sections of the chapter sketch out some of these problems and what can be done about them.

Although the model conforms to the locality principles, it still has some of its function embedded in its structure. The model violates the deletion principle: models should not predict that a machine still functions when a vital part is removed. Application of this principle checks whether the functionality of some part is implicitly embedded in the structure of other parts. The models for the buzzer predict that it will continue to function even when the battery is replaced by a short circuit, because the model for a clapper switch assumes it is connected to a battery. Removing this assumption gives the following model for the clapper switch:

Information terminals: i1, i2, f1
SWITCH : OPEN:
    i1 <− 0, i2 <− 0
    if f1 = 0, switch will become CLOSED.
CLOSED:
    i1 <−> i2
    if f1 = 1, switch will become OPEN.

Unfortunately, the models now make no predictions at all, because after the switch changes from state open to closed, no rules derive a value for the currents, and thus the coil fails to change state from off to on. The problem here is that the models used for the connecting wires fail to refer to voltage. Using the hydraulic metaphor, current is the amount of material that is flowing, and voltage is the pressure on that material causing it to flow. The battery is the supplier of the necessary voltage in the buzzer. Because the models take neither voltages nor the battery, into account, it is not surprising that they are inadequate to characterize the behavior of the buzzer.

DISCONTINUITY

Another problem with the models is that they fail to characterize what actually occurs during the state transition. As the coil changes state from on to off, the current through the coil must change from 1 to 0. For a current to change from 1 to 0, it must be .5 sometime during the change. It could conceivably change from 1 to .5 to 10 to .5 to -100 to 0. A physical quantity cannot change abruptly and must vary continuously (i.e., if we make the time increments small enough, the changes in current must become arbitrarily small). However, as far as these models are concerned, the current changes discontinuously from 0 to 1. Because the models fail to characterize what happens during a state transition, they cannot completely describe how a transition is caused. It is incorrect to say that a transition can be caused by some attribute being at a particular value. For example, the rule

if $I = 0$, then coil will become OFF

is false. If no current is flowing through the coil, it is not the case that the coil will *become off*, rather it must have been off for current to be absent. This is not a situation where mythical or real time is at issue. The previous models used mythical time to model the transition, but that is an incorrect analysis of the actual physics. A transition is not caused by an attribute having some value but by some attribute changing value. Furthermore, the state transition is caused when the value crosses some threshold. For example, in the case of the coil, if the current drops from 1 to something slightly less than 1, the transition will probably not occur. But certainly, when the current almost reaches 0, the coil must have changed state. This may suggest that a coil should have three states: on, off, and between, but the transitions would still be discontinuous.

THE ROLE OF MOMENTUM IN QUALITATIVE REASONING

In order to model the behavior during transitions, the models will have to distinguish between the value of an attribute and the changing of an attribute. Space precludes us from presenting the set of resultant models, but some surprising consequences arise. In order to maintain internal consistency, we have to consider the notion of momentum. This should not be too surprising, because the buzzer could not possibly function if it did not have momentum, and each of the models discussed so far has implicitly assumed it. Consider what happens just as the magnetic field becomes strong enough to begin to lift up the clapper switch. The circuit will begin to open, less current will flow, and the magnetic field will begin to decrease. Because the magnetic field was just strong enough to begin to lift the clapper switch, this decrease will weaken the field enough so that it can lift the clapper switch no further. Therefore, the clapper switch will remain stuck at a position that just begins to open the circuit and the buzzer will fail to function.

The real buzzer functions because the attraction of the magnetic field acts on the mass of the switch, accelerating it. By the time the switch begins to open, this acceleration has built up a velocity in the switch. Although when the field dies, the acceleration due to gravity (or a restoring tendency in the clapper arm) pulls the switch back to its resting position, it will take some time before this acceleration even cancels out the velocity built up in the switch by the momentary magnetic field. Thus, even after the field dies, the switch will continue to open. The buzzer buzzes but only because the switch possesses momentum. In the original diagram Fig. 9.3, time increment t = 2 actually described a very complex event of the switch continuing to move toward the magnet, momentarily holding still and then beginning to fall back to its resting position. Having a distinction between the value of an attribute and a change in an attribute enables the new models to deal explicitly with momentum, because the essential point of momentum is that forces often act on changes in attribute values (their derivatives), not on the values themselves. This is especially important, because derivatives are usually only associated with quantitative or analytic analysis, and thus are not often thought to be relevant to the common sense understanding of mechanistic devices.

REFERENCES

Brown, J. S., & Burton, R. Multiple Representations of Knowledge for Tutorial Reasoning. In D. Bobrow & A. Collins (Eds.), *Representation and understanding*. New York: Academic Press, 1975.

Brown, J. S., Collins, A., & Harris, G. *Artificial intelligence and learning strategies* (B. B. N. Report 3634, I.C.A.I. Report 6. Cambridge: B. B. N., 1977. (Also in *Learning Strategies*. New York: Academic Press, 1978.)

de Kleer, J. "Causal and Teleological Reasoning in Circuit Recognition. *Artificial Intelligence Laboratory* (TR-529). Cambridge: M. I. T., 1979.

Rieger, C., & Grinberg, M. The Declarative Representation and Procedural Simulation of Causality in Physical Mechanisms. *Proceedings of the Fifth International Joint Conference on Artificial Intelligence*. 250-255, 1977.

10
Enriching Formal Knowledge: A Model for Learning to Solve Textbook Physics Problems

Jill H. Larkin
Carnegie-Mellon University

INTRODUCTION

In this chapter, I consider how individuals acquire skill in the task of solving problems in formal domains, domains involving a considerable amount of rich semantic knowledge but characterized by a set of principles logically sufficient to solve problems in the domain. Formal domains are different from toy domains (block worlds, puzzles, etc.) in that the number of such principles is large and the amount of additional knowledge needed to apply them skillfully is considerable. Examples of formal domains include mathematics, applied mathematics, most of what are called "hard sciences," as well as sophisticated games (e.g., chess, go). Formal domains are only a subset of what have been called semantically rich domains (Bhaskar & Simon, 1977). For example, biology, psychology, and English literature are not formal domains, because it is extremely hard to formulate an unambiguous set of principles sufficient to solve problems in these domains. Formal domains are interesting first because their apparent superficial structure provides a starting point for hypothesizing about the organization of knowledge in the domain. In addition, formal domains are educationally important, increasingly so as technology becomes more advanced. How then is skill acquired in solving problems in formal domains?

Individuals who have become skillful in such tasks usually report a relatively small amount of time spent studying textual materials or listening to lectures, but a much larger amount of time spent practicing solving problems. In this chapter, I first characterize the nature of the minimal, primitive knowledge a learner might acquire from study of a typical textbook. Then I propose mechanisms by which practice might enhance skill in applying this primitive knowledge skill to solve problems. The main features of this mechanism are then exemplified in a computer-implemented model that acquires skill in solving physics problems, and I discuss the similarities of the model's performance to that of human solvers with varying amounts of experience in physics.

LEARNING IN FORMAL DOMAINS

This section first considers two formal domains, physics and geometry, and characterizes the kind of knowledge that is present in textbooks in these disciplines. It then outlines the components of a knowledge system that could make use of the kind of information that is given in a textbook to solve related problems. Finally, I suggest how this knowledge might be enriched through practice to allow more rapid and skillful solution of problems.

Figure 10.1 shows the drawing provided for the following problem from a widely used high school geometry text (Jurgenson, Donnelly, Maier, & Rising, 1975).

> Given: *ZT* bisects *RS; RZ* is congruent to *SZ*
> Prove: △*RTZ* is congruent to △*STZ*

A skillful solution to this problem involves noticing that, according to the definition of bisect, *RT* is congruent to *ST*, and therefore the three sides of triangle *RTZ* are congruent to the sides of triangle *STZ*, implying that the triangles are congruent. Consider a learner attacking the preceding problem after

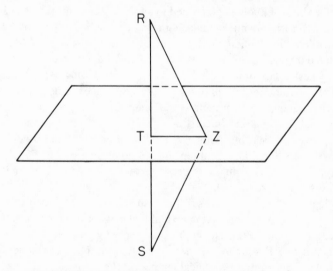

FIG. 10.1.   Drawing for a geometry problem.

studying the text that precedes it. What information does he have? The following two postulates are stated in the chapter containing this problem:

SSS If three sides of one triangle are congruent to the corresponding parts of another triangle, the triangles are congruent.

SAS If two sides and the included angle of one triangle are congruent to the corresponding parts of another triangle, the triangles are congruent.

Both are explained by brief statements that if a triangle is built with three sticks (two sticks and a specified included angle), then "only one kind of triangle is possible." Earlier there is some information of how to interpret corresponding parts.

Thus, the information available in the textbook includes general statements of principles (here postulates), together with information about how to interpret the terms used in these statements. There is no information about the conditions under which one postulate might be more useful than another.

A student who had just read the associated text solved the preceding problem in the following way. After apparently taking as his top goal proving the triangles congruent, he tried the most recently introduced postulate, *SAS*. When this didn't work, he tried *SSS*, but only after lengthy search through earlier chapters and ultimately help from the experimenter did he recall the definition of bisects so as to find the needed third pair of equal sides.

In summary, a geometry text presents the "principles" (postulates, definitions, theorems) that are logically sufficient to solve the associated problems. However, there is little information about how to search for a useful principle, or how to determine whether a principle is actually applicable. Thus, a novice solver must rely on very general search strategies (looking at the most recently introduced principle; working backwards from the desired conclusions).

The following physics problem is typical of many found in elementary mechanics.

Problem 1 A block of mass *m* moves from rest down a plane of length *l*. If the coefficient of friction between block and plane is μ, what is the block's speed as it reaches the bottom of the plane?

Figure 10.2 shows a sketch that might be made by a skillful solver constructing the solution given in Table 10.1. What knowledge might a student have for solving a mechanics problems like the preceding immediately after studying a typical textbook? For example, in a section presenting Newton's second law,

$$F = ma,$$

a widely used university-level textbook (Halliday & Resnick, 1966) provides a careful operational definition of mass *m* and force *F*, relating them to accelera-

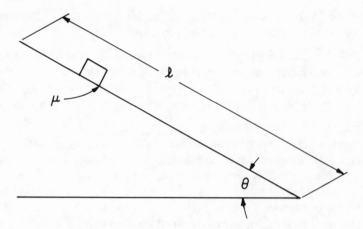

FIG. 10.2.   Sketch for a sample physics problem.

tion a, and then shows that from these definitions follow the relation $F = ma$. The major condition for this relation to be true, that the acceleration be measured relative to an inertial reference frame, appears two sections earlier in an unmarked paragraph about Newton's first law. There is some information about how to interpret this principle, specifically that "F is the (vector) sum of all the forces acting on the body, m is the mass of the body, and a is its (vector) acceleration."

On the basis of information like that described previously, students typically solve a problem like the preceding as shown in Table 10.2.

TABLE 10.1
Skilled Solution to a Physics Problem

The motion of the block is accounted for by the gravitational force,

$F_g^{ll} = mg \sin \theta$ directed downward along the plane,

and the frictional force

$f = \mu\, mg \cos \theta$ directed upward along the plane.

The block's acceleration a is then related to the (signed) sum of these forces by

$F = ma$,

or

$mg \sin \theta - \mu\, mg \cos \theta = ma$.

Knowing the acceleration a, it is then possible to find the block's final speed v from the relations

$l = (\tfrac{1}{2})at^2$

and

$v = at$.

TABLE 10.2
Typical Novice Solution to a Physics Problem

To find the desired final speed v requires a principle with v in it, say

$v = v_o + 2at.$

But both a and t are unknown, so that seems hopeless. Try instead

$v^2 - v_o^2 = 2ax.$

In that equation v_0 is zero and x is known, so it remains to find a. Therefore try

$F = ma.$

In that equation m is given, and only F is unknown, therefore use

$F = \Sigma F\text{'s}$

which in this case means

$F = F_g^{ll} - f$

where F_g^{ll} and f can be found from

$F_g^{ll} = mg \sin \theta$
$f = \mu N$
$N = mg \cos \theta$

With a variety of substitutions, a correct expression for speed,

$v = \sqrt{2(g \sin \theta - \mu \cos \theta)},$

can be found.

In summary, like the geometry text, the physics text presents the principles needed to solve the problems together with information about how to interpret the general symbols in the principle. However, it does not present information about how to search for useful principles. Thus, the novice solver relies on whatever general search strategies he has. The example preceding illustrates what has repeatedly been observed in novice solvers, a use of means–ends analysis using the algebraic form of the principles. The first equation must contain the desired quantity, and (usually) no more than one unknown quantity. Subsequent equations are cued by the new "desired" quantities that were unknown in the preceding equation (Larkin, McDermott, Simon, & Simon, 1980a; Larkin, McDermott, Simon, & Simon, 1980b; Luger, 1979; Simon & Simon, 1978).

In the following paragraphs, I generalize the observations made about the geometry and physics examples, summarizing the kind of knowledge that is available in textbooks, and the kind of general knowledge a solver must have available to use this knowledge in working problems.

Textbooks provide knowledge of the principles of the domain stated in very generally applicable form. If the principle is stated in mathematical form, the symbols used are general symbols standing for a large class of possible entities for which the principle is true. If the principle is stated verbally, then many of the words have the same characteristic, for example, "Two triangles are congruent if their corresponding sides are congruent" or "Inertial mass equals gravitational mass."

If a system has just knowledge of principles, its first difficulty when confronted with a specific problem is simply to access from memory a possible principle to use. Perhaps this accounts for the common phenomena of the diligent student who studies the text but then is totally unable even to start work on a problem. In order to solve problems using textbook knowledge, a solver must have some general information for locating potentially useful principles. Examples of such general search strategies include looking for principles recently stated in the text and looking for principles involving the goal of the problem (e.g., if the goal in a geometry problem is to prove triangles congruent, then look at principles stating that triangles are congruent; or in physics, if the goal is to find a speed, then look at principles involving speed). The common feature of all these strategies is that they are domain independent—a learner can use them in any of the formal domains he encounters. What we have then is something that looks rather like GPS (Ernst & Newell, 1969)—it includes some powerful domain-specific principles, plus a general means–ends mechanism for selecting among them. I focus here on one strategy, means–ends analysis, although I suspect that in realistic learning situations, the others mentioned earlier also have substantial importance.

In addition to the general statements of principles, textbooks do include some information of the conditions under which the principle is applicable, and this knowledge too is in a very general abstract form. For example, a physics text states "For an isolated system involving no dissipative processes, macroscopic energy is conserved." The conditions (isolated system, no dissipative processes) are not features immediately evident in any typical physics problem that might, for example, involve colliding billiard balls, or a wagon rolling down a hill. Although the conditions do apply to each of these situations, properly interpreted, the connections are not obvious. What is needed are some ways of ascertaining whether the conditions of a principle are satisfied. For example, to apply conservation of macroscopic energy, there needs to be a means of ascertaining whether dissipative processes occur, and of identifying an isolated system. The mechanisms for testing conditions of applicability are complex, and I certainly don't understand them very well. However, I later argue that an appreciable amount of the solution time required by inexperienced human solvers is involved in condition testing.

After a principle has been located and found to be applicable, it must still be interpreted in the current context. For example, the innocuous-looking principle,

$$F = ma,$$

in physics must be interpreted by knowing that F is a symbol for the vector sum of all the forces on a system due to its interactions with all other systems.

Generally, each symbol in a principle has attached to it a meaning that must be interpreted in the local context. Usually, these meanings also interact; that is, they must be interpreted coherently throughout the principle. Unlike the search knowledge, this interpretation knowledge is specific to the problem domain involved.

Suppose a primitive knowledge system has some general search strategy (say means–ends analysis), and abilities to test whether the conditions of a principle are satisfied. In addition, it has received from a textbook general statements of principles together with information for interpreting in specific contexts the symbols in the principles. What are the characteristics of the problem-solving performance of this system?

First, the order in which principles are accessed is controlled by the general search strategy, rather than by any domain-specific knowledge. This implies inefficiencies in principle selection and frequent backtracking before a useful set of principles is found. Second, because the principles are accessed in general form and knowledge for interpreting symbols is separate, there will be considerable time spent in interpreting each principle. Third, because conditions for applicability are stored separately, there will be considerable time spent prior to the application of the principle in determining whether it is applicable. To an expert in the domain, this performance will seem slow and cumbersome and also blind and "unintuitive," because no domain-specific knowledge is used in deciding what to do.

Any learning mechanism one proposes should satisfy two criteria. First, it should allow learning through practice. I cannot recall a single expert in a formal domain ever saying that this expertise was acquired through extensive review and study of text, or even through listening to or watching others. Almost universally, experts report the extensive importance of practice. Second, the learning mechanism must operate without a lot of conscious control, because almost all learners do get better through practice, and few can describe a conscious process through which this growth was accomplished.

I propose the following simple mechanism and will argue that it accounts for much (but by no means all) of how knowledge is enriched through practice. If, in solving a problem, the solver manages to apply a principle to generate new information, it stores both the sequence of actions taken to get the information and the conditions that made this action possible. Then if the same conditions arise in a subsequent problem, the analogous information is generated automatically, without any need for condition testing, interpretation, or search (beyond the recognition of a familiar information pattern).

After the learning mechanism described previously has operated for a long time on many problems, a lot of very specific but very powerful pieces of knowledge are accumulated, and the workings of the system change profoundly. A principle is now not applied through explicit search and condition testing, followed by statement and interpretation of a general principle. Instead, ordinarily the solver recognizes a specific pattern of information that allows application of a principle to generate a specific new piece of information, and this is done in a single step. In other words, a knowledge of a single principle has been replaced or enriched by a bundle of knowledge about how the principle is applied in a variety of specific circumstances.

For example, in the geometry problem considered earlier, the general *SSS* principle might be enriched by knowledge that allows recognition of a pair of triangles that satisfies that principle, because a pair of corresponding sides is formed by a bisected segment.

What kind of problem-solving behavior characterizes this more sophisticated problem-solving system? First, the order in which principles are selected for application is determined by domain-specific knowledge about what new information can be developed from the current information available in the problem. This bottom-up principle selection is what we have called elsewhere a knowledge-development strategy (Larkin, McDermott, Simon, & Simon, 1980a, Larkin, McDermott, Simon, & Simon, 1980b, Simon & Simon, 1978). Second, the system spends essentially no time either checking conditions or interpreting principles, because the knowledge required to do this in most special cases has been stored and now executes automatically. For example, such a system solving the physics problem earlier would immediately note the pattern of an object of known mass m on plane inclined at a known angle θ and conclude that the gravitational force component is $mg \sin \theta$.

A MODEL FOR PROBLEM SOLVING IN PHYSICS

This section describes a computer-implemented model, called ABLE, that learns by enriching its formal knowledge of mechanics principles. The barely ABLE model has the kind of primitive knowledge outlined in the preceding section, together with the primitive mechanism for learning from experience suggested there. In the process of solving many problems, ABLE acquires specific knowledge for applying principles, knowledge that changes substantially both its characteristic order of selecting principles for application and the time required for applying these principles.

Architecture

ABLE is a *production system,* a type of model commonly used for psychological simulation (Newell, 1973, Newell & Simon, 1972). Like most simple production systems, this model encodes permanent knowledge in a collection of condition-action pairs called productions. The condition parts of the productions are continually matched against the contents of a small and constantly changing working memory. When the condition part of a production is satisfied by these contents, the model executes the associated action, which ordinarily includes adding or deleting elements in working memory. Thus, the contents of working memory are changed, creating a situation where new productions can act. The result is a model that is flexibly responsive to the current situation because the productions essentially sit in parallel, each waiting for its condition to be satisfied.

Production systems have the following major virtues: (1) They involve plausible and parsimonious assumptions about the human information-processing system. All permanent knowledge is encoded homogeneously without a priori distinctions between (for example) declarative or procedural knowledge. (2) Their architecture makes modeling learning easy. All knowledge is encoded in relatively independent productions, and adding knowledge just means adding productions. Thus, knowledge can grow through small increments. (3) Productions can be written so that each corresponds to a bit of knowledge that makes psychological sense. Thus, they are fairly transparent representations of verbal theories.

The Primitive Model

The model, before learning has occurred, is called *barely* ABLE to distinguish the *more* ABLE model that results after substantial learning. The barely ABLE model has stored a list of the principles appearing in Table 10.3. These principles can be used to solve a problem like that stated earlier by two different methods. The "force" method uses force and kinematics principles, as illustrated in the solutions presented in Tables 10.1 and 10.2. The "work" method uses force principles to find the force on a moving body and then work principles to relate its initial and final speeds to the distance it travels.

These principles are actually not used by ABLE in the algebraic form given in Table 10.3. ABLE stores them simply as a list of symbols for the quantities involved (e.g., (Fma) for $F = ma$. The reason is that ABLE does not actually perform algebra but merely manipulates lists of equations, combining and substituting for quantities as if they were equations. Thus, for example, ABLE might combine principles K1 and K2 to obtain a relation $(v \, v_0 \, a \, x)$. The workings of ABLE are described in more detail elsewhere (Larkin, McDermott, Simon, & Simon, 1980b).

To access its physics principles, the primitive barely ABLE model uses the general algebraic means–ends strategy described earlier. Thus, the problem solution in Table 10.2 is one of those produced by barely ABLE.

In its current form, ABLE does not do condition testing, because the principles it knows about are applicable to all the problems it encounters. What it should do is access for a tentatively selected principle (e.g., K1 in Table 10.3) its associated conditions (motion of a particle along a straight path with constant acceleration). This condition should then be matched against the problem situation by means of productions that can recognize a straight path and conditions under which acceleration ought to be constant (here because only constant forces, friction, and gravity act on the block).

TABLE 10.3
Physics Principles Used by ABLE

Forces

$F1\ F\ =\ ma$
$F2\ F\ =\ \Sigma\ F\text{'s}$
$F3\ f\ =\ \mu N$
$F4\ N\ =\ mg\ \cos\ \theta$
$F5\ F_g{}^{ll}\ =\ mg\ \sin\ \theta$

a is the acceleration of a particle of mass m acted on my a total force F that is equal to the sum, ΣF's, of individual forces on the particle. f, N, and $F_g{}^{ll}$ are the frictional, normal, and gravitational component forces acting on a particle of mass m resting on a plane inclined at an angle θ with the horizontal, where μ is the coefficient of friction between particle and plane.

Work

$W1\ \Delta K\ =\ (1/2)mv^2\ -\ (1/2)mv_0{}^2$
$W2\ W\ =\ \Delta K$
$W3\ W\ =\ F\ \cdot\ x$

ΔK is the change in the kinetic energy of a particle with initial speed v_0 and final speed v. ΔK is equal to the work done on the particle during that interval, which is also equal to the distance x traveled times the total force component in that direction.

Kinematics

$K1\ v\ =\ v_0\ +\ at$
$K2\ x\ =\ v_0t\ +\ (1/2)at^2$
$K3\ v^2\ =\ v_0{}^2\ +\ 2ax$
$K4\ v\ =\ (v_0\ +\ v)/2$
$K5\ x\ =\ vt$

v is the average speed of a particle moving with constant acceleration. Other symbols are as defined earlier.

The knowledge for interpretation in ABLE is largely the ability to match algebraic symbols in the problem statement with identical symbols appearing in a principle. Thus, if v_0 appears in a principle, and (v_0 known) or ($v_0 = 0$) appears in the problem representation, ABLE marks the v_0 in the principle as known. However, one set of symbols, the right side of principle

F2 F = ΣF's,

requires special knowledge for interpretation. This indefinite summation means that, for a particular object, all forces on the object are to be found and summed (as vectors). Thus, ABLE has knowledge enabling it to search a problem situation for all objects that might exert forces on an object of interest. Specifically, it locates all objects in contact with it and includes the gravitational force due to the earth.

In addition, barely ABLE has knowledge for "solving" the "equations" (lists of symbols) that result from the interpreted principles. Specifically, it checks to determine whether all but one of the symbols is known in the problem context, and, if so, marks the remaining quantity as also known.

The primitive barely ABLE model described previously solves problems in a manner that has several characteristic features. First, the order in which principles are selected for use reflects the means–ends strategy; the first principles selected are ones containing the desired quantity; there is then a sequence of principles each containing a quantity desired, because it remained unbound when the preceding equation was interpreted; finally the last equations selected involve known quantities, except for the single quantity to be found.

Second, even with its currently restricted set of principles, the barely ABLE model does select principles that are not useful and must discard them and choose others (i.e., engage in backtracking).

Third, an appreciable fraction of the "time" (number of productions executed) spent by barely ABLE is involved in interpreting equations in the current context (i.e., in deciding whether the variables appearing in the principle are known or desired, or whether in this context they are simply unbound). Specifically, the application of one principle typically requires one means–ends production accessing the principles, two to four productions that interpret the symbols in the principle, and about five productions to "solve" the resulting "equation" (to determine that all but one symbol is known and therefore the remaining symbol can be considered as known). In a typical problem, this interpretation of principles accounts for about one half of the productions executed.

The Learning Mechanism

The barely ABLE model "learns" in the following way. Whenever it successfully applies a principle to generate some new information (i.e., to combine the values of some already-known quantities to make a new quantity known), it then stores the sequence of actions it took together with the ingredients that made this action possible.

Specifically, it stores the known quantities it substituted into the principle as the condition side of a new production and places the new known quantity that was found as the action side of the production. For example, in the primitive solution in Table 10.2, the first production built would be a production saying that if a particle of known mass is lying on plane inclined at a known angle, then the gravitational component F_g'' is also known.

This learning mechanism is implemented in the following way. In the working memory are elements representing each of the quantities appearing in a principle that has been stated, and with each is an indication of whether the quantity is known, desired, or simply "unbound" to any information in the problem. A group of productions then acts to collect all the quantities marked as known and to determine whether only one quantity in the principle remains unknown or unbound. If this is the case, then the barely ABLE model "solves" the equation by stating that the remaining quantity is known. At the same time, it builds a new production with a left-hand side including the quantities it has determined are known, and a right-hand side asserting that the remaining quantity is also known. The production is general only in that it can refer to any object.

Thus, for example, if barely ABLE solved the equation $v = v_0 + at$ for the quantity a, then it would also build a production stating:

IF   the quantities v, v_0, and t, all refering to the same object, are known,

THEN assert that the acceleration a is also known for that object.

Notice that these principle–application productions are both very specific and very powerful. The production described previously will not help if the acceleration is known but the initial velocity is not. However, in the specific situation in which it works, this single production, in one step, recognizes the utility of a principle and applies it to generate new information without any need for separate interpretation of a generally stated principle.

The More Sophisticated System

The primitive barely ABLE model "practices" by producing solutions to a variety of problems and concurrently building productions that match specific situations to which various principles apply. Through this process, the model becomes more ABLE in the following ways:

1. The solution paths, the order in which principles are selected for application, are profoundly different. When there are a large number of specific, powerful productions, these productions dominate the behavior of the system. Thus, the first principles accessed in a problem situation are those cued by a characteristic pattern of known quantities. The new known quantity can then cue other specific productions, resulting in the production of further new quantities. For the simple problems considered here, this process ultimately terminates in the generation of the desired quantity, thus solving the problem. The solution in Table 10.1 shows a solution path produced by the more ABLE model.

2. Every principle applied by the more ABLE model does produce a new piece of information, and, in the kind of restricted problems considered here, this strategy almost completely avoids backtracking.

3. The more ABLE model spends essentially no time interpreting principles, because the principle–application productions have this process built in to them. Thus, in one step, a situation where new knowledge can be developed is recognized, and a principle (in specific form) is applied to develop that knowledge.

A Further Learning Mechanism

Although the preceding learning mechanism is the only one implemented in ABLE, it is clear from the work of human solvers that a second mechanism is operating.

The solutions paths produced by the more ABLE model are quick and stable, with little backtracking. Thus, a sequence of principle–application productions always executes in the same way for a particular type of problem. This seems to me to be an ideal situation for the operation of a collapsing mechanism of the kind described by Neves and Anderson (1980). If one production executes after another and the output of the first is used in the input of the second, then a new production is built that collapses the two. The result would be increasing use not of individual principle–application productions but of productions that apply two or more principles at once.

Summary of the Model

The ABLE model exists in basically two forms. The barely ABLE model has knowledge of the principles in Table 10.3, knowledge of how to interpret the symbols in these principles, and a primitive domain-independent method (algebraic means–ends analysis) for searching these principles. Thus, it has exactly the kind of knowledge I argued earlier might be used initially to apply the formal knowledge in textbooks.

The more ABLE model has, for each principle, an enriched cluster of knowledge that enables it to recognize specific situations to which the principle might usefully be applied and, automatically in a brief step, to interpret the principle in that context and generate the new information. This more ABLE model developed automatically from the barely ABLE model through the action of the learning mechanism described, as the model worked a sequence of mechanics problems.

HUMAN SOLVERS

On the basis of the ABLE model that learns, I want to hypothesize that at least some key features of expert problem solutions will correspond to the solutions of the experienced more ABLE model, and that beginners' solutions will look either like those of the barely ABLE model or like those of some hybrid models called the slightly ABLE models. To assess this hypothesis, I first match the order of the principles selected and used by ABLE with the order employed by human solvers with varying degrees of skill. Then I informally compare the times required by the human and model solvers to perform various parts of a problem solution.

Methodology

The beginners were students at the University of California, Berkeley, who had completed about 8 weeks of their first university-level physics course. Thus these students had recent instruction and practice in the principles of kinematics forces, work, and energy that were required to solve the problems presented i the experiment. The experienced subjects were all professors or advance

graduate students in physics at Berkeley, who had recently taught an u
graduate course involving the material relevant to the problems in the exp
ment. The work of one expert subject on Problem 1 was lost due to tape failu

The two problems discussed here (including the one described earlier) i
volved relating the motion of one object to its interaction with other objects
They could be solved either with kinematics and force principles or with work
and energy principles.

Subjects solved one practice problem, followed by five problems of which
those considered here were the first and fourth. They worked individually and
were asked to read the problem aloud and then to "talk aloud as much as possible
while solving the problem as you normally would." If a subject was silent for
more than about 10 seconds, the experimenter intervened by saying, "Can you
say what you're thinking?" Otherwise the experimenter remained almost entirely
silent, and virtually all subjects talked continuously.

Order of Principle Application

The typed transcripts of the verbal protocols were coded by first constructing a
list of all the quantitative relations stated. The lists were then edited to remove
statements of values (e.g., $x = 3$ meters), immediate repetitions of principles,
and algebraic manipulations. In addition, we removed from a few novice protocols sequences of principles repeated once or more in what appeared clearly to
be a check of previous work. Finally, if two or more principles were required to
generate the relation stated by the subject, these principles were written separately. For example, if in solving the problem given earlier, a subject stated

The frictional force is mu m g cosine theta,
This was coded as the application of two principles:

$$N = mg \cos \theta$$
$$f = \mu N.$$

The result is, for each subject, a sequence of physical principles applied in
solving the problem.

The model compared with the work of the expert subjects is the more ABLE
model; that is the original model after it had solved the two problems and so had
acquired the enriched knowledge needed to solve them efficiently. ABLE does
acquire, in solving a problem once, the ability to produce for that problem a
solution using just enriched knowledge. However, its performance on new problems depends on its having solved many problems and acquired a rich cluster of
knowledge for each principle.

As described in the discussion of Table 10.3, there are two methods for
solving the kind of problems considered. The more ABLE model can use either
method, depending on the order in which it considers the principles selected by
its productions (force principles first, or work–energy principles first). The more

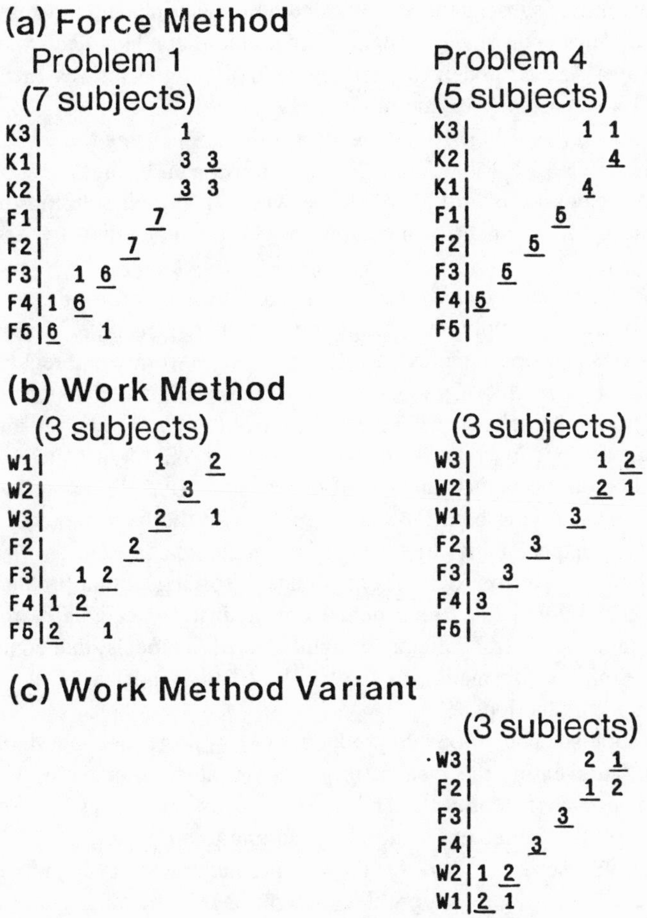

(a) Force Method

Problem 1
(7 subjects)

```
K3|            1
K1|               3 3
K2|               3 3
F1|           7
F2|         7
F3|   1 6
F4|1 6
F5|6     1
```

Problem 4
(5 subjects)

```
K3|            1 1
K2|                 4
K1|            4
F1|         5
F2|       5
F3|   5
F4|5
F5|
```

(b) Work Method

(3 subjects)

```
W1|        1    2
W2|           3
W3|         2    1
F2|       2
F3|   1 2
F4|1 2
F5|2    1
```

(3 subjects)

```
W3|            1 2
W2|              2 1
W1|         3
F2|       3
F3|   3
F4|3
F5|
```

(c) Work Method Variant

(3 subjects)

```
·W3|           2 1
F2|            1 2
F3|         3
F4|       3
W2|1 2
W1|2 1
```

FIG. 10.3. Expert solution paths.

ABLE model was run with both selection priorities. In addition, a minor change in the selection priorities among work principles produces a variant of the work method.

Figure 10.3 shows the solution paths (the order of principles applied) for the expert subjects and for the more ABLE model. The physics principles are indicated on the vertical axis by the labels given in Table 10.3. The horizontal axis represents the sequence in which the principles are applied. The numbers in the body of the graph indicate the number of subjects using the corresponding principle in that sequence. For example, in Fig. 3a, six subjects applied principle F5 first, whereas one subject applied it as the third principle. Underlining indicates the solution path of the more ABLE model. In Fig. 10.3 and elsewhere, the principle labels are ordered so that a top-to-bottom sequence is a selection order consistent with the barely ABLE model (i.e., the first principle contains the desired quantities; subsequent principles contain quantities unknown in previous principles). Thus, a downward-sloping path on these graphs reflects work similar to the barely ABLE model, whereas upward-sloping paths (as in Fig. 10.3) relfect work consistent with the more ABLE model.

Parts (a) and (b) of Fig. 10.3 show data for subjects using the force and work solution methods (see Table 10.3). Part (c) shows data from three subjects who used for Problem 4 the work method, but who began their solutions by finding kinetic energy K from the known final speed v, rather than by first finding forces.

For the expert subjects, a consistently good fit is given by the more ABLE model. If one omits simply interchanging two principles (e.g., K2 and K3 in Fig. 3a) out of 123 principles applied, a total of 13 do not follow the sequence of the more ABLE model. Six of these aberrations consist of interchanging $F_g'' = mg \sin \theta$ (F3) with the pair $N = mg \cos \theta$, $f = \mu N$ (F4, F5). The remainder are a brief sequence done in a means–ends order (W1 W2 W3 for one subject using the work method on Problem 1) and use of the unusual principles K3 and K4 by one subject each in solving both Problem 1 and 4 with the force method.

One would expect many beginners to have acquired some enriched knowledge through their already considerable experience in solving similar problems. Thus, the novice solution paths are matched not against the original barely ABLE model but against several variants, "slightly" ABLE models, that contain all the original primitive information in the barely ABLE model as well as selected sophisticated productions.

These sophisticated automatic productions state principles, but mark them as "suspect," preventing the system from making later use of them. This feature corresponds to novice subjects tendency not to use principles that seem to be evoked early in the problem solution by automatic processes.

Generally, a subject's work for the two problems was sufficiently consistent that productions acting in one problem did not have to be modified or deleted to account for work in the other; the only exceptions are discussed at length in the following.

Figure 10.4 and 10.5 show the solution paths (order of principles selected) of the novice solvers and of several slightly ABLE models. The format is the same as that used for expert subject in Fig. 10.3, with principles indicated by labels from Table 10.3.

Figure 10.4 shows solution paths for those subjects using the force method (Table 10.3). Subjects 1, 4, 8, and 10 for Problem 1 and subjects 1, 2, and 4 for Problem 4 show the most common pattern—a few bits of automatic knowledge are used, followed by a sequence that follows the barely ABLE model. Subjects 2 and 5 also use a few bits of automatic knowledge, with a different search order, or without principles reevoked at the end in respond to the means–ends strategy. Subject 6 on Problem 4 matches the barely ABLE model almost exactly.

Figure 10.5 shows data for subjects using the work method. Subjects 9 and 11 on Problem 1, and 5 and 9 on problem 4 are matched against the barely ABLE

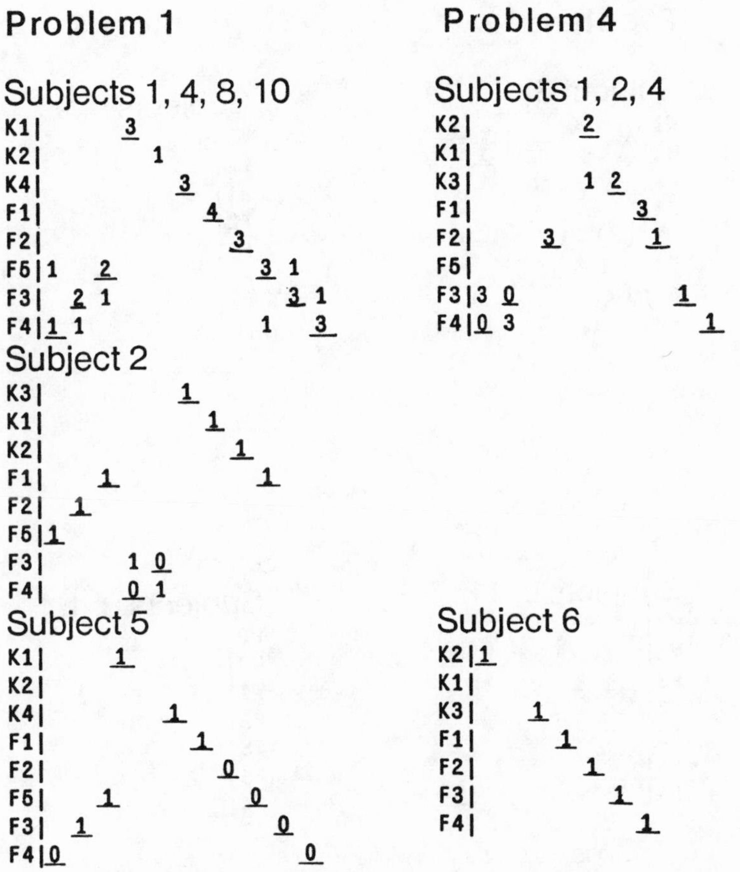

Problem 1

Subjects 1, 4, 8, 10
```
K1|      3
K2|        1
K4|         3
F1|          4
F2|           3
F5|1   2          3 1
F3|  2 1           3 1
F4|1 1           1   3
```

Subject 2
```
K3|        1
K1|          1
K2|           1
F1|   1       1
F2| 1
F5|1
F3|       1 0
F4|       0 1
```

Subject 5
```
K1|     1
K2|
K4|         1
F1|          1
F2|           0
F5|   1        0
F3| 1          0
F4|0           0
```

Problem 4

Subjects 1, 2, 4
```
K2|       2
K1|
K3|      1 2
F1|          3
F2|   3       1
F5|
F3|3 0            1
F4|0 3             1
```

Subject 6
```
K2|1
K1|
K3|   1
F1|     1
F2|       1
F3|         1
F4|          1
```

FIG. 10.4. Novice solution paths using force method.

model, and subject 3 against the full more ABLE model. Subjects 8 and 10 are matched against a slightly ABLE hybrid, with automatic knowledge for principles F2, F3, and F4.

Figures 10.4 and 10.5 show the novice subjects' work on 17 out of the total of 22 problems worked (two for each of 11 subjects). Of the remaining six solutions, two are completely consistent with a slightly ABLE model that uses a variant of the work method involving summing works rather than summing forces. The final three solutions involve extensive errors and are not reported here. However, when the barely ABLE model was given a list of the incorrect principles used in each of these solutions, the solution paths it produced were very close to those produced by the novice solver.

Compared with the expert subjects, novice solvers show considerably more variability. The solution paths of both experts and novices show three variants in search order. In addition, the novice solutions are matched against slightly ABLE

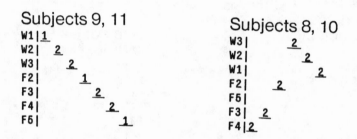

FIG. 10.5.   Novice solution paths using work method.

model variants that contain some productions for applying selected principles automatically in specific situations. These principles are applied first, and then, if necessary, the general barely ABLE model takes over to complete the solution.

Using these model variants, however, provides a fairly good account of novice work. Excluding interchanges of principles and the three idiosyncratic solutions, a total of five out of 97 principles applied by the novice subjects are not accounted for by the models. In addition, the models predict seven principles not actually stated by the subjects.

As indicated by the often downward slopes of the graphs and discussed earlier and elsewhere (Larkin, McDermott, Simon, & Simon, 1980b; Simon & Simon, 1978), these subjects tend to use a means–ends backwards-working strategy, captured here by the basic strategy built into the barely ABLE model. However, especially at the beginning, many subjects used a few principles low on the vertical axis, corresponding to the acting of the few automatic productions part of their slightly ABLE model.

Thus, the ABLE model provides a reasonably good account of the order in which principles are selected and used by human solvers with varying degrees of skill. Furthermore, once the models matching novice performance have been constructed, one can use them to analyze in more detail the nature of novice knowledge and its difference from the more competent knowledge of the more ABLE model.

Working Times

In addition to predicting different orders of principle selection, the ABLE model predicts that novices should spend far more time than experts both in applying individual principles (because each principle must be individually interpreted) and in work not associated with any individual principle (work involving search for a possibly applicable principle and testing whether that principle applies in the particular problem situation). How then do expert and novice solvers spend their time?

The data comes from the same protocols discussed earlier. The transcripts were marked to indicate 5-second intervals. The protocols were then coded into sequential episodes, each episode being a period of time during which the same kind of work was done. The kinds of work considered were the following:

Reading: Reading the problem; the words in the protocol are essentially those appearing in the problem text.

Principle application: Effort associated with a specific physics principle. These episodes include stating the principle, finding values for its variables, executing any associated arithmetic and algebra. Their order corresponds to the order of principle application discussed earlier.

Digressions: Any comment totally unconnected with the problem solution (e.g., "I'm hungry," "The tape recorder is ticking)."

Condition testing and search: This category includes all comments that are relevant to the problem but that are independent of any particular principle. Examples include, "Sounds like kinematics with a random force on m," "I'm wondering what an energy approach would do here." Thus, this category includes both search for possible principles and testing of conditions for applicability.

The times spent by expert and novice solvers in applying individual principles are very different. The minimum amount of time required is about 5 or 10 seconds, and experts use more than this time relatively rarely. Three quarters of the principles applied by experts require 10 seconds or less for access and application. In contrast, for the novice subjects, about half the time spent applying principles is spent on principles requiring 40 sec. or more.

Novice subjects also require much more time for condition testing and search, an average of 210 sec. for each problem, whereas the expert subjects averaged under 50 seconds per problem.

In summary, novice solvers require more time both to apply individual principles and to select principles to apply. The application of principles includes not only the direct interpretation of algebraic symbols modeled in ABLE but also more sophisticated interpretation, such as applying trigonometric and algebraic relations so as to obtain from a principle in standard form a particular equation applicable to the problem at hand.

Failure to Learn

ABLE's simple learning mechanism produces changes in the behavior of the model that is quite consistent with the order of principle selection for more- and less-skilled human solvers, and at least qualitatively consistent with the times such solvers require for various aspects of their work. I turn now to consider in more detail the nature of the principle knowledge of the novice solver.

The most striking feature of this knowledge is that only for one principle are substantive errors consistently made. Figure 10.6 summarizes the pieces of knowledge contained in the various slightly ABLE models that were matched against the novice solutions as described earlier. Along the left column are labels of physical principles from Table 10.3; across the top are subjects indicated by number. Three *'s indicate knowledge in automatic form (i.e., a corresponding automatic production acted, and the information produced was used in subsequent work). Two *'s indicate knowledge that existed tentatively in automatic form (i.e., an automatic production acted, but the results were subsequently ignored and then reproduced using explicit knowledge). One * indicates knowledge used in explicit form. The X's indicate principles that were either applied incorrectly or applied differently in the two problems. A blank indicates that there was no opportunity for this principle to be applied, and so no information available.

In general, novice knowledge includes extensive explicit knowledge. However, the vector addition of forces, $F = \Sigma F$'s, and labeled $F2$ in Fig. 10.6, causes great difficulty for many individuals. Let us then look more closely at this principle and the difficulties it causes. The vector addition of forces states that the total force on a system is equal to the sum of the forces on it due to all individual objects with which it interacts. This principle is quite different from principles that correspond to well-defined equations, written as a whole from memory and then connected to the information in the problem. Writing this principle requires study of the problem to determine how many individual entities there are. For example, solving the problem discussed here requires studying the moving object, noting that two forces act on it (that due to gravity and that due to

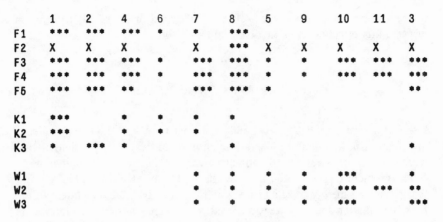

	1	2	4	6	7	8	5	9	10	11	3
F1	•••	•••	•••	•	•	•••					
F2	X	X	X		X	•••	X	X	X	X	X
F3	•••	•••	•••	•	•••	•••	•	•	•••	•••	•••
F4	•••	•••	•••	•	•••	•••	•	•	•••	•••	•••
F5	•••	•••	••		•••	•••	•				••
K1	•••		•	•	•	•					
K2	•••		•	•	•						
K3	•	•••	•			•					•
W1					•	•	•	•	•••		•
W2					•	•	•	•	•••	•••	••
W3					•	•	•	•	•••		•••

FIG. 10.6.   Knowledge in slightly ABLE models.

friction), and then summing these two forces to obtain the total force. This process is not captured by any stored equation.

As suggested by the preceding comments, modeling knowledge for applying the vector addition of forces principle has some complexities. In the barely ABLE model, an ordinary principle typically has one or two associated productions that recognize when one of the quantities in the principle is desired and then states the corresponding principle as an equation. The vector addition of forces has associated with it one production that recognizes when either a total or an individual force is a desired quantity, three productions that examine the problem for interactions that might give rise to forces, and four productions that collect these interactions and write the appropriate instance of the vector addition of forces, for example $F = F_g + f$.

Learning, or acquiring automatic productions, for the vector addition of forces is also difficult for ABLE. For example, suppose ABLE works first a problem involving just a frictional force. It then builds automatic knowledge that if ever again it wants to find a total force and already knows a frictional force, then the total force is just equal to the frictional force. Such a production causes no trouble if ABLE also has automatic knowledge letting it find a total force from other combinations of forces. The reason is that ABLE applies to the most specific applicable production (Larkin, McDermott, Simon, & Simon, 1980b; McDermott & Forgy, 1978). However, if it has only a one-force vector addition of forces in automatic form, this production can act erroneously even when two or more forces do exist. Thus, ABLE is very subject to what we call "limited-force" bugs in applying the vector addition of forces. If it has only a partial set of automatic productions, the specific production for a situation may not exist, and another automatic production, matching a subset of the existing forces, may act, yielding an equation with some forces missing. Thus, ABLE is particularly vulnerable to omitting forces in applying the vector addition of forces. The novice subjects are prone to precisely the same kind of errors. Of 15 errors in applying this principle, nine involve omitting a force.

THE REALITY OF THE MODEL

ABLE is a simple model that certainly does not reflect all the complexities of how human knowledge is enriched through practice in solving problems. However, I think it does capture important features, in particular the following.

The problem representation used by the ABLE model is exceedingly primitive, consisting merely of sets of known or desired algebraic quantities. I think this representation does capture to a considerable degree the dominant representation used by novice solvers. They seem almost totally absorbed in finding the answer by means of writing and relating various algebraic equations. In contrast, although still very primitive, the problem representation used by the more ABLE model is considerably less algebraic. Equations are not stated, but instead new pieces of information (known quantities) are simply generated from old. This feature of the model reflects experts' ability to look over a problem and "know" that he can find all the energy and momenta of various particles.

I do not, however, think that this ability to generate information automatically in a bottom-up knowledge-development fashion captures everything important in expertise. In particular, when solving more difficult problems, experts clearly do many more clever things, such as planning or using alternate problem representations. However, I think that these more sophisticated abilities operate effectively only on the basis of the kind of automatic knowledge development that I have described here. For example, in planning a problem solution, an expert may tentatively decide to use momentum arguments. He is then capable of "seeing" all the momenta in the problem and automatically knowing what information can and cannot be found. He can then readily discard or pursue this approach with almost certain knowledge of whether or not it will be effective. Without this ability to generate automatically information, planning would be a cumbersome process, perhaps indistinguishable from simply working out a trial approach.

I also think that this automatic generation of knowledge is by no means restricted to knowledge of quantities. Experts automatically generate a great deal of qualitative knowledge about the problem, for example, how relatively large or small various quantities are or whether certain quantities can be neglected.

In learning, ABLE finds difficulty in acquiring accurate, usable knowledge about the vector addition of forces. I think this difficulty is indicative of a general learning problem among human students of physics. Physics has many so-called "fundamental" principles that state in simple form broadly applicable knowledge. However, this generally means that interpretation of the symbols in any particular situation is very difficult. This it the case with the vector addition of forces considered here. The symbols "ΣF's" are a drastic shorthand for the process of finding all entities that might exert forces and figuring out what those forces are. Similarly, the fundamental principle of conservation of energy requires being able to recognize many very different kinds of energy (kinetic, potential, rotational, microscopic, etc.) and to relate them appropriately.

In general, the principles that are called fundamental, because they are so widely applicable to very different situations, are exactly the principles that students find difficult to learn because they will have to learn to interpret the symbols in so many different situations. This difficulty is probably aggravated by the fact that these principles, with their cryptic general symbols, look like any ordinary equation with symbols to be interpreted merely by simple knowledge of what each symbol means.

SUMMARY

I have presented ABLE, a simple computer-implemented model that learns by enriching its knowledge of abstract principles, as it works a succession of problems. Specifically, whenever a principle is successfully applied, the learning mechanism acts to store in ABLE's memory a production with a condition indicating the situation to which the principle was applied, and an action that adds to the problem representation knowledge that can be generated by that principle.

Thus initially, the barely ABLE model searches for principles by means of a general weak domain-independent strategy (means–ends analysis) and retrieves principles in general form that must then be interpreted in the particular context of the problem. As the model becomes more ABLE through practice, its behavior becomes dominated by the specific information it has learned, and new information is automatically added on the basis of recognized patterns of information already present in the problem.

This simple model that learns provides a very good account of the order of which physics principles are selected for application by solvers of more and less skill. It is also qualitatively consistent with the fact that novice solvers spend an extensive amount of time applying each principle, especially those that require extensive interpretation, whereas expert solvers rarely spend more than a minimal amount of time in applying a principle. In addition, I have hypothesized, although not included in the ABLE model, that novice solvers access along with a principle some general statements of the conditions for applicability, and they explicitly match these against the current problem representation. In contrast, expert solvers assess these conditions automatically as part of the condition sides of their specific productions. These statements are consistent with the fact that novice subjects spend far more time trying to assess whether a particular principle is applicable than do expert solvers. Most importantly, the model encounters difficulty in learning the same fundamental principle that human novices consistently misuse.

REFERENCES

Bhaskar, R., & Simon, H. A. Problem solving in semantically rich domains: An example from engineering thermodynamics. *Cognitive Science*, 1977, 1, 193–215.

Ernst, G. W., & Newell, A. *GPS: A case study in general problem solving.* New York: Academic Press, 1969.

Halliday, D., & Resnick, R. *Physics, second edition.* New York: John Wiley & Sons, 1966.

Jurgensen, R. C., Donnelly, A. J., Maier, J. E., & Rising, G. R. *Geometry.* Boston: Houghton Mifflin, 1975.

Larkin, J. H., McDermott, J., Simon, D. P., & Simon, H. A. Expert and novice performance in solving physics problems. *Science*, June, 1980, 208, 1335–1342. (a)

Larkin, J. H., McDermott, J., Simon, D. P., & Simon, H. A. Models of competence in solving physics problems. *Cognitive Science*, 1980, in press. (b)

Luger, G. F. *A Comparison of Human and Automatic Problem Solving in Two Areas of Mechanics* (Technical Report), Department of Artificial Intelligence, University of Edinburgh, 1979.

McDermott, J., & Forgy, C. Production-system conflict resolution strategies. In Waterman, D., & Hayes–Roth, F. (Eds.), *Pattern-directed inference systems*, New York: Academic Press, 1978.

Neves, D. M., & Anderson, J. R. Becoming an expert at cognitive skill. In Anderson, J. R. (Ed.), *Cognitive skills and their acquisition*, Hillsdale, N.J.: Lawrence Erlbaum Associates, 1980.

Newell, A. Production systems: Models of control structures. In Chase, W. G. (Ed.), *Visual information processing*, New York: Academic Press, 1973.

Newell, A., & Simon, H. A. *Human Problem Solving.* New York: Prentice-Hall, Inc., 1972.

Simon, D. P., & Simon, H. A. Individual differences in solving physics problems. In Siegler, R. (Ed.), *Children's thinking: What develops?*, Hillsdale, N.J.: Lawrence Erlbaum Associates, 1978.

11 Analogical Processes in Learning

David E. Rumelhart & Donald A. Norman
University of California, San Diego

INTRODUCTION

One of the more lamentable results of the information-processing revolution within psychology over the past twenty years has been the replacement of the term *learning* by the term *memory*. Whereas it is sometimes difficult to distinguish the learning experiments of twenty years ago from today's memory experiments, it is increasingly clear that remembering is only one kind of learning. As long as our theories of knowledge representation were simple, this substitution caused no problem. If knowledge is essentially declarative and unstructured, new learning can be carried out by simply *adding* new facts to the data base. Over the past several years, however, we have been led to a significantly more complex representational theory. In particular, we have come to see knowledge as embedded in schemata that we see as largely composed to specialized bits of procedural knowledge (Bobrow & Norman, 1975; Rumelhart, in press; Rumelhart & Ortony, 1977). In a recent paper (Rumelhart & Norman, 1978), we began a logical analysis of what learning must amount to in the context of a schema-based representational system. According to our analysis, the adoption of the schema as the basic unit of knowledge representation has implicit in it three qualitatively different kinds of learning.

1. *Accretion*—the encoding of new information in terms of existing schemata. In our view, new information is interpreted in terms of relevant preexisting schemata, and some trace of this interpretation process remains after the processing is complete. This trace can serve as the basis for a later reconstruction of the original input. Thus, processing information changes the system, giving it the ability to answer questions it could not have previously answered.

335

The system has thereby learned something new. This is presumably the most common and least profound sort of learning. Note that no new schemata are involved in this sort of learning. An organism that learned only in this way could never gain any new schemata; all learning would be in terms of instantiations of already existing schemata.

2. *Tuning or schema evolution*—the slow modification and refinement of a schema as a function of the application of the schema. Schema evolution is presumably a central mechanism in the development of expertise. With experience, an existing schema can be slowly modified to conform better and better to the sorts of situations to which it is to apply.

3. *Restructuring or schema creation*—the process whereby new schemata are created. This kind of learning, which we have called *restructuring,* or more recently simply *structuring,* involves the creation of new schemata that, through tuning, can themselves become highly refined and distinct concepts.

Our models of memory are thus models of learning by accretion. Many such models exist. It is substantially more difficult to create models of learning of the other two types. Therefore, we have begun to focus our attention on the processes of schema creation and schema evolution. In this chapter, we report some of the theoretical and empirical approaches we have taken to the study of schema creation. We begin with a discussion of knowledge representation and show why we believe learning to be central and why we believe analogy is such an important mechanism of learning. Then we describe a simple model of how new schemata might be formed by analogy. Finally, we describe an empirical situation in which we think we find evidence for such learning and show how our model might generate the results we have observed.

SOME CHARACTERISTICS OF THE HUMAN KNOWLEDGE REPRESENTATION SYSTEM

Because the issue of knowledge representation has played a central role in our thinking about learning, it is useful to begin our discussion with a few observations on some of the important characteristics of knowledge representation. It is, of course, a cliche that it is impossible to evaluate a representational system apart from the process that operates on it. Consequently, in modeling any cognitive process, there is always the problem of deciding how to partition that part of the knowledge system that is "process" from that part that is "data." Depending on the relative amounts of the system allocated to "process" and to "data," we have what Winograd (1975) has called "procedural" or "declarative" representational systems. Some authors have emphasized the "data," trying to have as few special-purpose procedures as possible; such a system is called *declarative.* Others have emphasized the processes involved and have largely embedded the knowledge of the system within these processes. These systems are generally called *procedural*. The issues involved in choosing one or the other of these strategies has been described by Winograd as the "declarative-procedural controversy." In his paper on this topic, Winograd (1975) offered a useful analysis of the topic. We summarize the issues briefly now.

On the one hand, there are facts. It is often quite convenient to conceptualize the contents of memory as a set of facts and to imagine retrieval from memory to be the application of general, content-free retrieval processes. With this view, reasoning can be conceptualized as the production of inferences based on these facts. Of course, a representational system such as this requires rules of inference separate from these "facts," but these rules are conceptualized as very general and in no way tied to the specific content of the fact to which they apply. Here, the best analogy is between the axioms and theorems of a mathematical system on the one hand (the facts) and the rules of inference of that system on the other (the processes). Once the rules of inference are specified, the axioms can be changed at will and the system will still continue to produce correct inferences.

On the other hand, there are operations. It is often convenient to construct special-purpose procedures that have special knowledge of the various contingencies of use built into them. All systems must have some operations. Procedurally based systems consist primarily of such special operators.

In his comparison of these two representation types, Winograd notes four basic characteristics on which the two kinds of representational systems typically differ.

1. Flexibility. Within a declarative system, the same fact can be used whenever it is relevant. Once a fact is added to the data base, it is available for use by any of the inference rules. In a procedural system, with knowledge contextually embedded, relevant information may be known but not available. Because it is stored implicitly, as part of a procedure, independent access to the knowledge is impossible. In a declarative system, on the other hand, knowledge does not have to be specified differently for each context in which it may be needed.

2. Learnability. It is easy to add new information to a declarative system. A new statement (or axiom) or even an entirely new domain of knowledge can be added to the data base and new inferences automatically become possible *without* the addition of any new rules of inference. In procedural representations, the procedures are generally handcrafted by the theorist and it is difficult to see how new procedures could be evolved. Moreover, because what is general and what is specific about procedural representations are not often easily separated, there is little or no transfer from one domain to another. In short, the process whereby new knowledge is added to procedurally based systems is enormously more difficult than adding new knowledge to declarative systems.

3. Accessibility. Knowledge separated out in the form of a set of discrete statements is relatively easy to find and express as isolated entities. Knowledge stored in a more procedural, context-dependent fashion is impossible to separate from the contexts in which it is employed. Knowledge that is relatively easy to express is taken to be stored declaratively, whereas knowledge that is known only tacitly is taken to be procedural.

4. Efficiency. Procedural representation systems have the advantage of *efficiency*. With *general* inference rules, care must be taken to "handle" even the most obscure cases. With procedural representations, however, specific aspects of the problem domain can be taken directly into account in the procedures. It is therefore possible to employ heuristics that might fail in general but work in specific cases. This allows for the very direct solution of problems for which the system is best tuned, but perhaps no solutions at all for problems outside that domain. In practice, the ability to "get away with" limited but efficient solutions makes it much easier to specify a knowledge system that works at all.

In many ways it seems that humans have more of the characteristics attributed to procedural systems than those attributed to declarative ones. Our ability to reason and otherwise use our knowledge appears to depend strongly on the *context* in which the knowledge is required. Most of the reasoning we do apparently *does not* involve the application of general-purpose reasoning skills. Rather, it seems that most of our reasoning ability is tied to particular bodies of knowledge.

Perhaps the classical case of using *knowledge how* (procedural knowledge) to produce *knowledge that* (factual knowledge) occurs in the domain of grammatical judgments. The knowledge that we have about language seems to be largely embedded in the procedures involved in the production and comprehension of linguistic utterances. This is evidenced by the relative ease with which we perform these tasks when compared with our ability to explicate the knowledge involved in them. Semantic knowledge would appear to be the same. Whereas we can quickly interpret sentences, it is only with the most painstaking effort that we can produce definitions of terms with any generality.

Perceptual knowledge is even more plausibly viewed as knowledge how. Whereas we all know a dog when we see one, it is very difficult to sort out exactly what we look for in making our judgment. We know how to tell a dog without knowing how we know it. Similarly, we know how to perform many skills (e.g., playing tennis), but it is rather difficult to access the *facts* on which this knowledge is based. Thus, it seems useful to imagine knowledge such as this to be in the form of procedures or programs for doing these activities. The knowledge that we have is implicit—somehow tied up in the operations in which we actually use that knowledge.

One nice demonstration of this comes from the work of Wason and Johnson-Laird (1972) and some more recent replications and extensions of their work

If vowel, then odd on back.   If total > $30.00, then sign back.

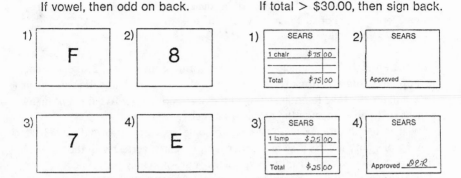

FIG. 11.1.   Stimuli for the two conditions of D'Andrade's reasoning experiment.
The left panel shows the stimuli for label factory condition. The right panel shows
the stimuli for Sears store condition.

carried out by Roy D'Andrade.[1] Subjects in D'Andrade's experiments were
given one of two formally equivalent problems to solve. Half of the subjects were
given the task illustrated in the left portion of Fig. 11.1. Subjects were shown the
four cards illustrated in the figure and told the following:

> All labels made at Pica's Custom Label Factory have a letter printed on one side
> and a number printed on the other side. As part of your job as a label checker at
> Pica's Custom Label Factory, you have the job of making sure that all labels with a
> vowel printed on one side have an odd number printed on the other side. Which of
> the labels . . . would you have to turn over to make sure the label was printed
> correctly?

Only 13% of the subjects correctly indicated that cards 2 and 4 (the cards marked
with an 8 and an E, respectively) must be checked. Card 4 must, of course, be
checked because it may have an even number on the back. Card 2 must also be
checked because it might have a vowel on the back and thus violate the rule. No
other cards must be checked.

It has been argued that this is a case of our interpreting the simple conditional
as a biconditional. In any case, results like these are often taken to illustrate the
weakness of the human reasoning system. However, the results of the second
part of D'Andrade's experiment point up the fallacy in this conclusion. The right
panel of Fig. 11.1 illustrates the stimuli for these subjects. Subjects were told the
following:

> As part of your job as an assistant at Sears, you have the job of checking sales
> receipts to make sure that any sale of over $30.00 has been approved by the section

---

[1]Roy D'Andrade has kindly given us access to the data from his as yet unpublished experiment.

manager. (This is a rule of the store.) The amount of the sale is written on the front of the form. Which of the forms . . . would you have to turn over to make sure the sales clerks had followed the regulation?

In this case nearly 70% indicated the correct forms, forms 1 and 2, the $75 and the unsigned forms. Formally, these two problems are identical. Yet, when phrased in terms of the familiar setting of the Sears store, over five times as many subjects were able to solve the problem correctly.

What is the difference here? Why do people appear not to understand the meaning of *if* in the first case and understand it nearly perfectly in the second? This is exactly the kind of effect expected if our knowledge is embedded in a relatively inaccessible procedural format rather than as general rules of inference. The first case of the label factory represents a relatively unfamiliar case in which we cannot rely on specific knowledge and must, therefore, rely on general reasoning processes. The second case more nearly approximates our "real-life" problem-solving situations. Once we can "understand" the situation, the conceptual constraints of our specific knowledge can be brought into play, and the problem readily solved. It is as if our knowledge representation already contains all the reasoning mechanisms ordinarily required.

Thus, it would appear that the context dependencies inherent in the more procedural representational systems are also present in the human reasoning system. Similar results can be observed by watching a person attempt to learn a new body of knowledge. When we attempt to teach a child a new domain, we do not, in general, present it as an abstract piece of knowledge. Rather, we carefully instruct the child using the knowledge already tacitly available to "get across" the concept in question.

Consider, for example, how we teach children the concept of a fraction. Most curricula use the pie analogy. One-half corresponds to one piece of a pie that has been cut down the middle. One-fourth corresponds to one piece of a pie cut into four equal pieces, etc. Here, the teacher is taking advantage of the child's spatial intuitions to teach the abstract notions of a fraction. This analogy is very useful; upon learning it, the reasoning and problem-solving strategies implicit in his knowledge of pies, operations that can be performed on them, etc., can be carried over into this abstract domain. The child can see that two-quarters make a half, that if you have a whole and take away one-quarter, you have three-quarters remaining, etc. The child needn't know *how* he knows this. These inferences are simply implicit in the analogy.

However, as with all analogies, the analogy is not perfect. Sometimes operations are required in the target domain (in this case with fractions) that are difficult or unnatural within the domain of the analogical source. Thus, whereas addition and subtraction of fractions is natural within the pie analogy, multiplication and division of fractions is unnatural and difficult to conceptualize. How do you take one piece of pie times another or, worse yet, how do you divide one piece of pie *into* another.

Fractions are sometimes taught through a different analogy. Once a child has learned multiplication and division, fractions can be understood as operations. A fraction is a *compound operation*. A fraction is merely a multiplication and a divide. Thus, one-half of a number is that number multiplied by one and divided by two. Similarly, three-fourths of a number is that number multiplied by three and divided by four, and so on. Those taught by the *operation* method find the multiplication and division of fractions a very natural extension of their conceptualizations. One can, of course, readily do a "multiply and divide" of a fraction and produce a new fraction. These children, however, often find addition and subtraction of fractions very difficult. How do you add one multiply and divide to another?

Thus, depending on which of the two systems of analogies are tapped by the curriculum in question, the sorts of difficulties a child will have are predictable. If a child is taught through the pie analogy, he or she finds the addition and subtraction of fractions relatively natural. These are operations carried rather directly from the original pie domain. Multiplication and division of fractions, on the other hand, are often very difficult for these children.

Here again, it appears, that knowledge of fractions is best *not* thought of as a list of facts but rather as a set of procedures we have learned. Moreover, these procedures are apparently *not* created *de novo* but are generated through a systematic mapping of prior, often only implicitly known, knowledge. Curriculum developers are always on the lookout for the perfect analogy. The perfect analogy is one in which the learner is already able to reason within the source domain with ease and in which all of and only the operations of the target domain are represented in the source domain. Needless to say, such domains are rare. Two kinds of diagnostic problems often arise. First, learners will have great difficulty in learning operations not implicit in the original source domain. This is illustrated by the previous example. Secondly, learners will often carry features of the source domain incorrectly into the target domain. We discuss an example of this later. Both of these examples are useful to the analyst for it is through these kinds of errors that we can find evidence of the analogical nature of the learning.

As yet another example of *using knowledge how to derive knowledge that*, consider the task of remembering the number of windows in your house. Most people report systematically "going through" the rooms in their house and "counting the windows." Clearly, in these cases, the knowledge of our windows is *implicit* in another body of knowledge. We can, however, derive this implict knowledge by using our ability to imagine the rooms of our house systematically. Note, we *know how* to imagine the rooms of our house and make use of that ability to *know that* we have so and so many windows in our house.[2]

---

[2]Note this example has occasionally been used to demonstrate the *visual* characteristic of our knowledge. It would seem to illustrate better how much of what we "know" is embedded in what we can "do."

To push this view perhaps harder than it ought to be pushed, it may well be that we "know" the alphabet by virtue of our knowing *how* to recite it. Although this may seem silly at first glance, it is certainly plausible that we "know" the identity of the letter before the letter before *k* by virtue of our ability to recite the alphabet.

The human system does differ from existing procedural systems in one important way, however. The human system is notoriously adaptive. We are capable of applying knowledge learned in one domain to another; we are capable of readily learning new concepts and modifying old ones. Mimicking this flexibility has been the major problem for the procedural representational systems. It has proved rather difficult to build moderately general self-modifying procedures.

For the past several years, we have been involved in the development of a representational system that combines the important aspects of the procedural and declarative structures in somewhat different ways (Norman, Rumelhart, & LNR, 1975; Rumelhart & Norman, 1973). In our representational system, dubbed the *Active Semantic Network,* we have combined the declarative advantages of *semantic networks* with the procedural convenience of LISP-like languages. We developed a representational system in which a LISP-like interpreter operates directly on semantic networks (rather than lists) to perform its operations. In this system, procedures are encoded as configurations of links in a semantic network. Whenever we treat a piece of network as a procedure, we employ a general interpreter that produces various outputs and modifications of the network. During these times, the fact that the procedures are themselves encoded in the network is irrelevant. These procedures could equally well be entirely external to the data base. However, because the procedures *are* encoded in the data base, they can, on occasion, be interrogated by other procedures. This allows procedures to be modified, retrieved, compared, deleted, and otherwise operated on as only declarative data normally can be.

Although this conception has been a part of our representational system for some time, in practice (like most LISP structures) pieces of semantic net have either always been treated as data or always been treated as procedures. The one exception to that was the work of Scragg (1975) who proposed a system that "looked through" a set of procedure definitions in order to answer hypothetical questions about what might happen if certain of those procedures were carried out.

In our recent work, we have leaned more and more heavily on the procedural view of our data structures, and the fact that they can also be viewed as semantic networks has been less and less important. We have argued that *schemata* (Rumelhart & Norman, 1978; Rumelhart & Ortony, 1977) are procedures that scan the input for information relevant to whether aspects of the input could represent instances of the concept represented by the schema. In doing this, the internal structure of the schema is irrelevant. The important question has been *the operation* of the schema, not its internal structure.

The internal structure of the knowledge representation is important when old knowledge must be applied to domains beyond that which it was originally designed to represent, when new knowledge must be assimilated, and when pieces of knowledge must be compared. In short, it is under these conditions that the purely procedural perspective is inadequate and the knowledge must be viewed declaratively. We believe that the most common way in which people apply knowledge learned in one domain to another one is through analogical reasoning. We believe that the border between the procedural perspective and the declarative perspective can be usefully spanned by developing a mechanism for specifying new procedures based on the structure of old ones.

NEW SCHEMATA BY ANALOGY WITH OLD

We thus propose a representational system in which *all the data* can be viewed as either data or process. Such a system captures many facts about human knowledge in a natural way. We propose that all knowledge is properly considered as *knowledge how* but that the system can sometimes interrogate this *knowledge how* to produce *knowledge that*. The means whereby this knowledge is extended is, we believe, best viewed as an analogic process similar in form to that proposed by Moore and Newell (1973). Just as new concepts in MERLIN are defined as old ones with certain specified differences, one can define new schemata as systematic modifications on old ones.

The basic scheme whereby this may be done can be illustrated in terms of some very simple examples. Imagine that our knowledge of how to draw a square were embedded in the following simple turtle geometry program for drawing a square:

define square(:x)
   loop(4,&(forward(:x),right(90))).

This procedure would be represented within our Active Semantic Networks as shown in Fig. 11.2. In this representation, terminal nodes represent either constants or variables whereas nonterminal nodes represent subprocedure names. Each branch on a tree represents an argument of a procedure. The leftmost branch represents the first argument; the rightmost one, the last argument. Intermediate branches represent intermediate arguments. It is useful to observe that along with the conceptually important concepts of there being four sides and that the angles are 90 degrees there are a number of "technical" aspects of the procedure needed in order to make it actually work out and be properly interpreted by the interpreter. In particular, there is LOOP that counts out the number of sides, and there is the & that combines FORWARD and RIGHT into a single argument for LOOP.

This program successfully draws squares, and for most purposes the fact that it has the particular internal representation that it does makes no difference. It represents a kind of "knowledge how." Now consider what a similar sort of program to draw a pentagon might be like.

SQUARE

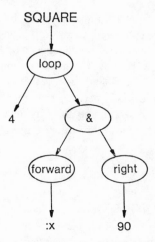

FIG. 11.2.   The Active Semantic Network representation of SQUARE, a procedure for drawing squares. Terminal nodes represent either constants or variables. Nonterminals written in ovals are subprocedure names. Arcs represent the arguments of the subprocedures.

define pentagon(:x)
  loop(5,&(forward(:x),right(72))).

Figure 11.3 shows the network representation of this procedure. A comparison of Fig. 11.2 and 11.3 shows the similarity of structures of these two procedures. Note that all the basic bookkeeping and technical aspects of the two procedures are identical. They differ only in the fundamental ways pentagons and squares differ, that is, in terms of the number of sides (five instead of four) and of the angels through which the turtle must turn in order to draw the figure (72 instead of 90 degrees). It should be clear that this new procedure, the pentagon procedure, could readily be made by copying the structure of the square procedure and replacing the constant 4 by the constant 5 and the constant 90 by the constant 72. We see this as the fundamental process of learning by analogy, taking one schema and creating another one identical to it except in specified ways.

We have implemented this process within our computer simulation program with a program we call IS-LIKE. The statement

   pentagon is-like "square" with 5 for 4 and 72 for 90.

causes the program pentagon to be created. It is important that all the handcrafted aspects of SQUARE are automatically brought into the structure of PENTAGON without any need for special knowledge of what these structures are. Of course, the same procedure could readily be applied to generate an OCTAGON or any other regular polygon we might wish. In fact, the statement

   regular-polygon is-like "square" with :n for 4 and ratio (360 to :n) for 90.

PENTAGON

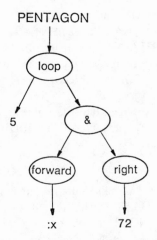

FIG. 11.3. Active Semantic Network representation of PENTAGON, a procedure for drawing pentagons.

will generate the structure illustrated in Fig. 11.4 that will draw any regular polygon. In general, the "is-like" program can generate any new procedure in which every occurrence of a particular constant or variable is replaced by another constant, another variable, or a subnetwork or in which every occurrence of a particular subprocedure is replaced by another. This last point is illustrated in the following discussion.

REGULAR-POLYGON

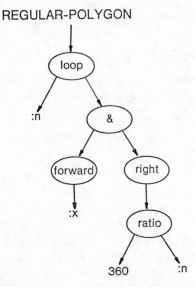

FIG. 11.4. Network representation for REGULAR-POLYGON, a procedure for drawing a regular polygon.

Note that the PENTAGON and the SQUARE procedures are completely distinct; changes made in SQUARE after PENTAGON has been generated will not be transferred to PENTAGON. However, the lineage of PENTAGON remains in the incidental aspects of the way it draws its pentagon. In particular, both SQUARE and PENTAGON construct their respective figures in a clockwise fashion, turning right at every corner. If it were important, we could readily create a LEFT-SQUARE that generates its figure in the opposite direction by replacing the occurrences of the subprocedure RIGHT with the subprocedure LEFT. Thus, the statement

left-square is-like "square" with "left" for "right."

will create a procedure that draws its figure in a counterclockwise direction. The network representation for LEFT-SQUARE is identical to SQUARE except that the nonterminal node for RIGHT is replaced by one for LEFT.

There are additional aspects of this scheme of creating new schemata through analogy to old ones that require a somewhat richer domain to illustrate. Thus, consider the domain of kinship relations. Imagine a system in which the basic kinship relations are stored in a network like the one illustrated in Fig. 11.5. It is possible to represent all the possible kinship relations of English in terms of the five basic relations illustrated in the figure—namely, "child," "parent," "spouse," "male," and "female." The figure is supposed to represent the fact that "Mary" is the daughter of "Alice," that "Maggie" is the grandmother of "Mary," and that "Alice" and "Henry" are married.

Now consider, as an example, the following procedural definition of a function that produces as its result the set of all parents of individual :x:

define parent(:x)
  return nodeset with "child" to :x.

This function merely returns, as a result, the set of nodes that have a pointer labeled "child" to node :x. The network representation of this procedure is given in Fig. 11.6. One could then define "child" by analogy with "parent,"

child(:x) is-like "parent" with "parent" for "child."

The appropriate definition of "child" is then constructed by creating a new function that is a copy of the old, except that for every occurrence of "child" in the original, the term "parent" is put in its place. This would produce a function that would return the set of nodes accessible through the pointer "parent." In the framework illustrated in Fig. 11.5, this would be a correct procedure for producing the set of children for some individual :x. Now the procedure NODESET is defined so that if the variable :x is filled by a set of nodes rather than by a node for a single individual, it will generate a set that contains all the nodes that can reach any of the nodes in question through the named pointer (e.g., "parent" or "child"). Thus, the function FEMALE defined by analogy with PARENT as

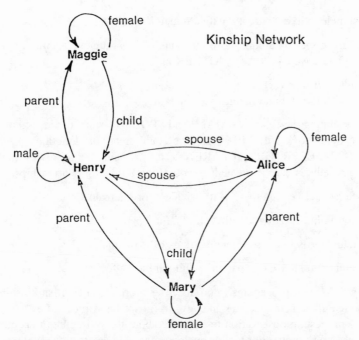

Kinship Network

FIG. 11.5.   An example of a piece of a network encoding knowledge about kinship relations. The network consists of a set of nodes representing people and a set of arcs representing the basic relationships among people. Only three different arc types are required to represent the kin relations and two to represent the sex of the individuals. These are CHILD, PARENT, SPOUSE and MALE and FEMALE, respectively. Special procedures can then be defined to operate on such a network to determine the kinship relation that holds among any two individuals in such a network.

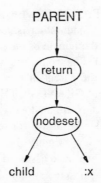

FIG. 11.6.   Network representation for PARENT. The function NODESET takes two arguments, an arc name (in this case, "child") and a set of individuals (in this case, the variable :x). It then returns as a result the set of nodes in the data base that have the specified arc pointing to any of the set :x.

female is-like "parent" with "female" for "child."

will return a set containing those elements of its argument set that represent a female. Thus, we can define MOTHER as

define mother(:*x*)
    return female parent :x.

Then, assuming the functions MALE and SPOUSE (which could, of course, be defined by analogy with FEMALE), we could create the functions, FATHER, SON, DAUGHTER, GRANDPARENT, etc., by using the following analogies. These procedures can be created by noting the following relationships:

father is like "mother" with "male" for "female."

son is like "father" with "child" for "parent."

daughter is like "son" with "female" for "male."

grandparent is like "parent" with parent(:x) for :x.

With a little care, procedures to produce the entire set of English kinship terms can be readily constructed, by analogy, from two basis procedures.

One interesting observation to be made about the procedures thus created is that there are a number of possible analogies that will create procedures that carry out the same task, but, depending on the particular analogies used, different ways of computing the same things will be employed. For example, we could say that

grandmother is-like "mother" with "grandparent" for "parent."

or we could say

grandmother is-like "mother" with parent(:x) for :x.

These two ways of defining GRANDMOTHER correspond to two conceptions of a grandmother, one in which grandmother is conceived of as the female of the grandparents as the mother is the female of the parents and another in which she can be conceived as one who differs from a mother by being the parent not of the individual in question but of the parent of that individual. The network representations of these two different GRANDMOTHER procedures is shown in Fig. 11.7. It may well be that not only are analogies important in the initial teaching of a concept, but they may also be useful for teaching alternate conceptualizations. It may well be that this is a primary role of metaphor.

In all our examples so far, we have assumed that the relevant dimensions of modification were already known to the system. In general, of course, we do not know the relevant dimensions of comparison. It is to point out the relevant dimensions that four-term analogical relations are important. Consider the following four-term analogy:

grandfather is-to "grandmother" as "father" to "mother."

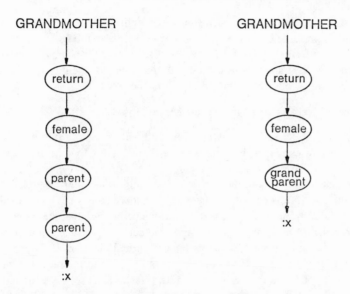

FIG. 11.7. Network representations for two different versions of the GRANDMOTHER procedure. Both procedures produce the same results; they simply do it in different ways.

This statement will cause a new GRANDFATHER procedure to be created in the following way: first the structures for FATHER and MOTHER are compared and their differences are found. In this case, they differ only in that where MOTHER uses the procedure FEMALE, FATHER uses the procedure MALE. This set of differences can then be applied, through the IS-LIKE mechanism, to GRANDMOTHER, finally creating FATHER. Note that this procedure will work whichever of the conceptualizations of GRANDMOTHER had been chosen.

In general, this process of matching pairs of procedures to find their differences is very similar to the matching processes in MERLIN and, like MERLIN, is generally not deterministic. Depending on exactly how the differences between pairs of procedures are characterized, many different mapping functions can be found. Each of these mapping functions represent a way of characterizing the difference between a pair of procedures. If, like this example, the original procedures are rather close together, the process of extracting differences will be relatively straightforward. In other cases, for example the differences between MOTHER and SQUARE, the differences will be relatively complex, and an analogy probably cannot usefully be drawn between them.

Of course, the examples discussed here are not intended to represent the particular knowledge about squares, parents, or grandparents that people actually have. Rather, they are intended as mere demonstrations of the sorts of processes that can be employed to create new schemata from old ones. Once created, the new schemata no longer depend on the schemata from which they were spawned but are full-fledged procedures in their own right with all the features of procedurally represented knowledge. Nevertheless, a number of schemata, all spawned in different ways from the same schema, will share a good deal of common structure, and it is possible to compare pairs of them to find the pattern of modifications required to get from one to the other.

Analogical Extensions of Lexical Meanings

We believe that the sort of processes just outlined play an important role in our learning of new concepts. It seems especially interesting to consider some of the analogies that can be drawn among the meanings of various classes of verbs. It appears that often, as with the analogy involving "son" and "daughter," relatively simple differences occur among verbs that are consistent with the idea that procedural definition could be given to various verbs such that these verbs, when encountered in a text, would determine whether the facts (or some part of the facts) being communicated by the verbs were already known. If not, they would create a memory representation of the relevant facts and inferences. One of the verbs we defined was the verb "move" (intransitive sense). We suggested that *move* could be defined roughly as follows:

>   *define move(:x,from :y to :z)*
>   means change(from loc(:x,:y), to loc(:x,:z)).

Similarly, we defined the verb "get" to be roughly

>   *define get(:x,:y,from :z)*
>   means change(from possed-by(:y,:z) to possed-by(:y,:x)).

It can be seen that "get" can easily be constructed from "move" by the analogy:

>   get is-like "move" with "possed-by" for "loc" :x for :z, :y for :x and :z
>   for :y.

Jackendoff (1975) produced a rather interesting set of examples illustrating large sets of verbs whose meanings are related in just the same relatively simple sorts of ways as the familial relations. Thus, for example, Jackendoff argued that the verb "keep" in the positional sense (e.g., Bill kept the book on the desk.) and in the possessional sense (e.g., Bill kept the book.) differ in much the same ways we suggested for "move" and "get." Jackendoff showed that a rather large array of verbs and verb meanings could be related to one another by relatively simple analogical relationships.

ANALOGICAL PROCESSES IN LEARNING A TEXT EDITOR

For several years now, we have, with several of our colleagues, carried out a series of studies aimed at understanding what we have called "complex learn-

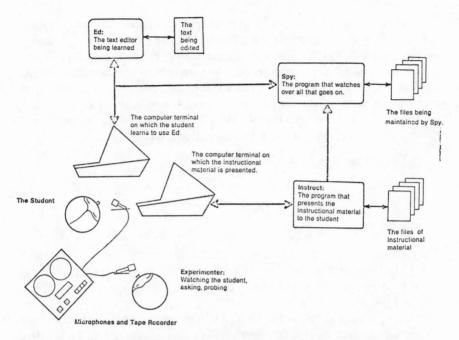

FIG. 11.8.   Basic experimental situation for observing students learning Ed. The student sat in a booth before two computer terminals. One terminal was used to give commands to Ed and carry out the text editing task. The other terminal was used to instruct the students on the editor and was controlled by INSTRUCT, an interactive program for teaching. All interaction with either Ed or INSTRUCT was monitored and recorded by another program SPY. An experimenter sat in the booth with the student and occasionally asked questions. All conversation was tape-recorded.

ing'' (Bott, 1978; Norman, 1975; Norman, 1978; Norman, 1980; Norman & Gentner, 1978; Gentner, & Stevens, 1976). We sought to study topics that required several hours rather than several minutes or several weeks to learn. We studied a variety of different topics. Ultimately, we focused most of our attention on observing people while learning to use a text editor.

The particular text editor available in our laboratory is the *Ed* text editor available under the UNIX operating system. In our experimental situation, we asked students to learn how to use the text editor by actually using it, referring to an instructional manual for guidance. In the examples that follow, we were using a very simple manual that we wrote. The basic experimental situation is shown in Fig. 11.8. The student sat in the booth, typing material to Ed on a computer terminal. The instruction manual was displayed to the student a paragraph at a time on a second terminal. All keystrokes, along with their interstroke intervals, were recorded by the computer. In addition, an observer sat in the room with the student and occasionally asked questions or asked the student to think aloud during portions of the learning period. Each session was tape-recorded.

An experimental situation such as this generates an enormous quantity of data. We have analyzed numerous segments of the learning protocol. In this chapter, we focus on a typical example that illustrates how the sorts of analogical processes discussed in the previous section show up in such learning situations. At the start, the Ed screen was always blank except for a *cursor*. The student began by reading a basic introduction to text editing on the instruction terminal. Then, an attempt was made to teach the specific commands used by Ed. Students were given the following instruction on the instruction terminal:

> You are going to learn how to print the text on the screen.
>
> Type
>
> 3p
>
> Type the key marked RETURN

Most students typed this sequence without difficulty, and the message illustrated in Fig. 11.9 appeared on the screen. The first line on the screen is the command typed by the student (3p). The second line is the resulting output from Ed, and the third line is the cursor.

We might imagine that as a result of this experience the student would create an internal representation of the event similar to that shown in Fig. 11.10. Here we have a little procedure for printing text line three—pressing the keys 3 and p causes line 3 to be printed on the screen.

The next part of the instruction manual was built on the following statement:

> Now try printing the fifth line.

Clearly, this statement requires that the student learn by analogy. We can imagine that this command would be interpreted by the student as

> print-text-5 is-like "print-text-3" with 3 for 5.

This procedure would, of course, work and produce a procedure exactly like that of Fig. 11.10 except for the 5 replacing the 3 in the figure. Presumably, the student could also have made the inference from this experience that

> print-text is-like "print-text-3" with :x for 3.

This would produce the general program for printing any line of text illustrated in Fig. 11.11.

Somewhat later in the session, students were taught to understand the "delete" command. The text of the beginning of the lesson on "delete" from the instruction manual for Ed is given below:

> Suppose we want to get rid of extra lines in the buffer. This is done by the delete command "d." Except that "d" deletes lines instead of printing them, its action is similar to that of "p."

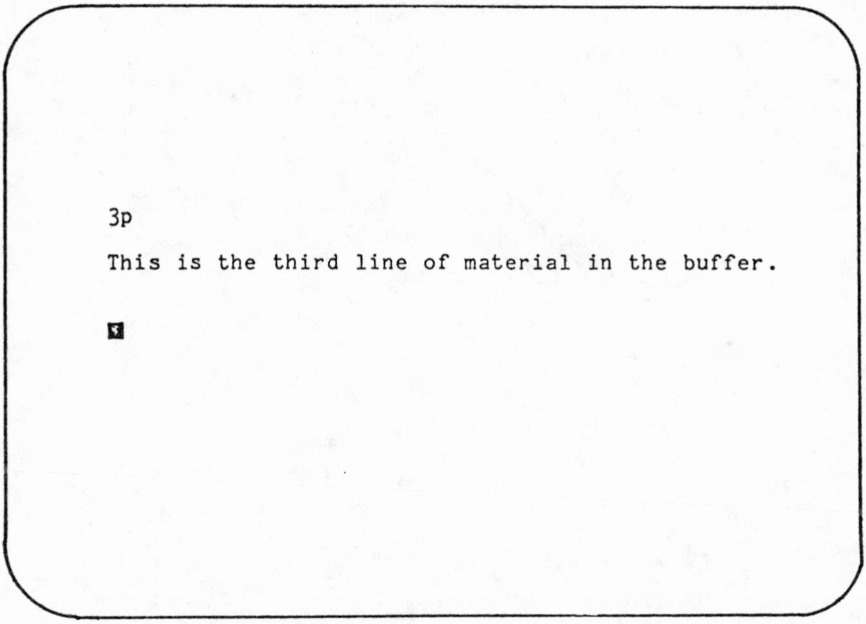

```
3p

This is the third line of material in the buffer.

▮
```

FIG. 11.9.   The contents of the terminal screen following a command to type the third line of the text.

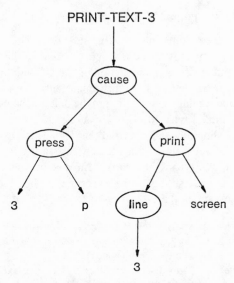

FIG. 11.10.   Representation of a procedure PRINT-TEXT-3 that we suppose may have been created as a result of the instruction to print out the third line of the text.

PRINT-TEXT

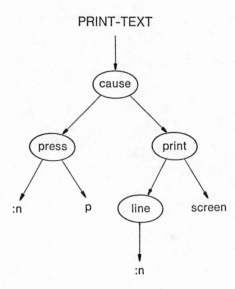

FIG. 11.11.   Network representation of a procedure for printing out any line of a text.

This text is an invitation to build a structure for ''delete'' by analogy with that for print. According to the model we have been discussing, we might imagine that the student would interpret this as follows:

delete-text is-like ''print-text'' with ''d'' for ''p and ''delete'' for ''print.''

This would lead to the structure illustrated in Fig. 11.12. There is some evidence that our students actually constructed a schema similar to this for delete.

In one example, after receiving instruction on the deleting lines from a buffer, a student was asked to delete line 4. At this time, the screen contained a number of lines of text, including line 4. According to the delete schema illustrated in the figure, the student should type 4d. This was done. However, the schema also predicted that line 4 should be deleted from this screen. It was not. After typing ''4d'' and seeing nothing happen, the student sat staring at the screen of the terminal and then looking back and forth from the instruction manual to the screen. The experimenter, sitting in the experimental booth with the student, asked the student to explain the problem:

Experimenter: What did you just do?
Student: I deleted line 4, at least I was thinking I was deleting line 4.
Experimenter: What did you expect to happen?
Student: I expected line 4 to disappear, either that or the text to be reprinted without line 4 in it.
Experimenter: Uh-huh, but that didn't happen.
Student: It didn't happen.

A common response of students was to assume that somehow or other Ed didn't "notice" the command, so they typed "4d" once more. This action invoked the delete command a second time, thereby eliminating in the buffer the new line 4, which used to be line 5.

Although this analysis fits rather neatly into the model we have been describing, the situation is really more complex and points to additional constraints on how students will create analogies. The error committed by the students was in part a result of their incomplete conceptualization of the various parts of the computer system. They reasoned that the screen was a sort of window on the computers knowledge, so if a line was deleted from the computers memory, it should no longer be visible on the screen. These same inferences did not occur when the very same instruction manual and editor were used on a hard copy terminal. Here the student's model of the relationship between the paper and the computer's knowledge were very different. They found it easy to see the paper as a medium on which the computer typed commanded messages. They knew the computer could not physically erase a line previously printed and thus interpreted the description of the delete command differently. The difference in the kinds of mental models that students bring to the situation clearly plays a critical role in the kinds of analogies students will employ. It is a far more important role than that of the formal instruction received.

This was only one of the many problems that our students had in attempting to understand the operation of the text editor. We found that although students made many errors in learning to use the editor, their errors were *not* random. Rather,

DELETE-TEXT

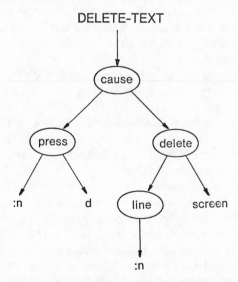

FIG. 11.12.   Network representation of procedure DELETE-TEXT that is derived by analogy from the general PRINT-TEXT procedure.

they almost always were responding in terms of a plausible interpretation of what they were told. They created models and made plausible inferences by analogy with situations they already understood. We found that before we could really teach them to understand the operation of the text editor, in general, and the delete process, in particular, a rather different approach was required.

To make Ed understandable, we needed to give the students analogical frameworks more appropriate than the ones they naturally used. The difficulty, however, was that our students knew nothing of computers, so either our model was going to be incomplete or we were going to have to spend considerable time giving them a complete model. We discovered an interesting solution to this dilemma: Give many different conceptual models, each one simple, each making a different point.

We developed three distinct models that, together, seemed to offer a reasonable account for the various aspects of a text editor. We developed the "secretary" model, the "card file" model and the "tape recorder" model. The secretarial model explains some aspects of Ed, especially the overall format of intermixing commands and textual material. The difficulty with this model, however, was that our students expected Ed to be as intelligent and understanding as a real secretary would be. Hence, if they gave the *append* command, they then fell prey to what we have called *the append-mode trap*. When they finished appending test, they would issue a command and expect Ed to carry it out. Instead, Ed would treat the command as another line of text and simply add it to the file. But, because Ed often received commands and follows them without giving any visible reaction, the students were sometimes unaware of what happened. Presumably, a real secretary is able to distinguish between the text being taken in dictation and the interspersed comments about the format of the letter, etc. Ed takes everything literally and has to be told explicitly to suspend dictation and register a command, etc.

Therefore, the secretarial model has some virtues and some difficulties. The tape recorder model helps students understand the append-mode trap. Think of Ed as a tape recorder and the append command as equivalent to recording on the tape recorder. Once a tape recorder has been put into record mode, it faithfully records every sound that reaches its microphones. The only way to stop the recording is to perform the explicit action that terminates the record mode (usually by pushing the lever marked "stop").

The tape recorder model has the virtue of explaining about the append-mode trap, but it is deficient in explaining the delete command. The filing card model offers a good analogy for understanding the line-oriented structure of the recorders kept by Ed. Thus, the renumbering of lines that takes place after a delete or append command is completed is easy to interpret, given the model of the removal or addition of cards in the file. Clearly, the filing card model by itself does not explain why the deleted line is not removed from the text the student sees on the screen, but it does provide the proper conceptual framework. An appropriate interpretation of the situation is that the contents of the file cards are not visible to the user of Ed. Those are Ed's private files. If you want to know what is in the files, you must ask to see them with a "print" command.

The need for three separate models is reminiscent of the case of teaching fractions. None of the "pure" models are perfect. Each has its own advantages and disadvantages. Apparently, what happens as we become expert in a domain is that we become better and better at choosing the appropriate model for the situation at hand. The success of such models in teaching are, we believe, an essential clue to the normal learning process. Students appear to create their own models if not given any such guidance. A major pedagogical issue here is that a student's own creations are often surprisingly good at providing an explanation of what has been happening. Thus, neither student nor instructor realizes how bad the model is, and it is not until the model leads to some major difficulty that the hint of trouble develops.

CONCLUSIONS

We have adopted the view that much of our knowledge exists embedded in specialized procedures that are employed in the interpretation events in our environment. We call these packets *schemata*. One problem with such a view is that it is difficult to see how such procedures can be built up through experience. How can we create new schemata? We have proposed that complex new procedures can be readily created by modeling them on existing schemata and modifying them slightly. We believe that the typical course of such a learning process consists of an initial creation of a new schema by modeling it on an existing schema. This new schema, however, is not perfect. It may occasionally mispredict events and otherwise be inadequate. We then believe that the newly acquired schema undergoes a process of refinement that we have dubbed *tuning*. We have not addressed the tuning problem in this chapter. Instead we have focused on this process of modeling one schema on another. We believe that this modeling process is properly called *learning by analogy*.

We find examples of learning and teaching by analogy to be absolutely ubiquitous. It appears that the usual learning sequence proceeds as follows: Whenever one encounters a new situation, he or she seeks to interpret it in terms of existing schemata. If one succeeds, he or she understands the situation and no new schemata need be created. Occasionally, however, there are no existing schemata that can offer a satisfactory account of a situation. In this case, we assume that the next best schemata are found. Presumably, because no completely applicable schemata existed, the schemata used to interpret the input had regions of mismatch with the input situation. In some cases, essential features of the interpreting schemata might not be present with other features in their place. Presumably, such a situation serves as a trigger for the creation of a new schema. The schema applied inappropriately to the current situation can thus serve as the source domain and thus as a model from which to generate the new schema. The ways in which the inappropriate schema is inappropriate give an initial set of differences by which the new schema is different from the old. Importantly, those characteristics of the new schema that are not contradicted by the new situation are assumed to be carried over into the new domain, even though they are not specifically apparent in the initial learning situation. It is through such carrying-over that the analogical process is both powerful and prone to error. Carrying over existing features of existing schemata allows us to make inferences about the new situation without explicit knowledge of the new situation. It allows us to learn a good deal very quickly. It also can lead to error. If the analogy is a good one, most of the inferences we make will be appropriate. On the other hand, some of them will be incorrect. It is these incorrect inferences that can allow us, as analysts, to see the features of the source schemata in a subject's performance on a new domain.

There are, we believe, a number of instructional implications of the view of learning we have been developing. In particular, it suggests that the appropriate way to teach a domain is to provide the student with a conceptual model that has the following properties:

1. It should be based on a domain with which the student is very knowledge-able and in which the student can reason readily.
2. The target domain and the source domain should differ by a minimum number of specifiable dimensions.
3. Operations that are natural within the target domain should also be natural within the source domain.
4. Operations inappropriate within the target domain should also be inappro-priate within the source domain.

Typically, no single model will suffice for any reasonably complex subject matter. In such cases, a set of models, each with their specifiable domains of applicability, are often useful. Ultimately, several schemata may be created for any given domain, each with their own, built-in, context dependencies determin-ing when each one is applicable. Each of these schemata can be considered alternate conceptualizations of the target domain.

ACKNOWLEDGMENT

Preparation of this chapter was supported by the Office of Naval Research under Contract N00014-79-C-0323.

REFERENCES

Bobrow, D. G., & Norman, D. A. Some principles of memory schemata. In D. G. Bobrow & A. M. Collins (Eds.), *Representation and understanding: Studies in cognitive science*. New York: Academic Press, 1975.

Bott, R. A. *A study of complex learning, theory and methodologies*. Unpublished doctoral dissertation, University of California, San Diego, 1978.

Jackendoff, R. A system of semantic primitives. In R. Schank & B. L. Nash-Webber (Eds.), *Papers from the conference on theoretical issues in natural language processing (TINLAP-1)*, Cambridge, Mass.: June 1975.

Moore, J., & Newell, A. How can MERLIN understand? In L. W. Gregg (Ed.), *Knowledge and cognition*. Potomac, Md.: Lawrence Erlbaum Associates, 1973.

Norman, D. A. Learning and teaching. In P. M. A. Rabbitt & S. Dornic (Eds.), *Attention and performance V*. Proceedings of the Fifth Symposium on Attention and Performance, Stockholm, Sweden. London: Academic Press, 1975.

Norman, D. A. Notes toward a theory of complex learning. In A. M. Lesgold, J. W. Pellegrino, S. Fokkema, & R. Glaser (Eds.), *Cognitive psychology and instruction*. New York: Plenum Pub., 1978.

Norman, D. A. Teaching, learning, and the representation of knowledge. In R. E. Snow, P. A. Frederico, & W. E. Montague (Eds.), *Aptitude, learning, and instruction* (Vol. 2): *Cognitive process analyses of learning and problem solving*. Hillsdale, N.J.: Lawrence Erlbaum Associates, 1980.

Norman, D. A., & Gentner, D. R. Human learning and performance. *Naval Research Reviews, 1978, 31*(9), 9–19.

Norman, D. A., Gentner, D. R., & Stevens, A. L. Comments on learning: Schemata and memory representation. In D. Klahr (Ed.), *Cognition and instruction*. Hillsdale, N.J.: Lawrence Erlbaum Associates, 1976.

Norman, D. A., Rumelhart, D. E., & the LNR Research Group. *Explorations in cognition*. San Francisco: Freeman, 1975.

Rumelhart, D. E. Schemata: The building blocks of cognition. In R. Spiro. B. Bruce, & W. Brewer (Eds.), *Theoretical issues in reading comprehension*. Hillsdale, N.J.: Lawrence Erlbaum Associates, in press.

Rumelhart, D. E., & Levin, J. A. A language comprehension system. In D. A. Norman, D. E. Rumelhart, & The LNR Research Group, *Explorations in cognition*. San Francisco: Freeman, 1975.

Rumelhart, D. E., & Norman, D. A. Active semantic networks as a model of human memory. *Proceedings of the Third International Joint Conference on Artificial Intellegence*. Stanford, Calif., 1973.

Rumelhart, D. E., & Norman, D. A. Accretion, tuning and restructuring: Three modes of learning. In J. W. Cotton & R. Klatzky (Eds.), *Semantic factors in cognition*. Hillsdale, N.J.: Lawrence Erlbaum Associates, 1978.

Rumelhart, D. E., & Ortony, A. The representation of knowledge in memory. In R. C. Anderson, R. J. Spiro, & W. E. Montague (Eds.), *Schooling and the acquisition of knowledge*. Hillsdale, N.J.: Lawrence Erlbaum Associates, 1977.

Scragg, G. W. Answering questions about processes. In D. A. Norman, D. E. Rumelhart, & The LNR Research Group, *Explorations in cognition*. San Francisco: Freeman, 1975.

Wason, P., & Johnson-Laird, P. N. *Psychology of reasoning: Structure and content*. Cambridge: Harvard University Press, 1972.

Winograd, T. Frame representations and the declarative-procedural controversy. In D. G. Bobrow & A. M. Collins (Eds.), *Representation and understanding: Studies in cognitive science*. New York: Academic Press, 1975.

12

The Central Role of Learning in Cognition

Pat Langley and Herbert A. Simon
Department of Psychology
Carnegie-Mellon University

INTRODUCTION

If we compare the past 2 decades of research in cognition, increasingly carried out within an information-processing framework, with the previous 2 decades, mainly Behavioristic and Hullian, we note a remarkable decline in the attention paid to learning. Maze learning experiments with rats, operant conditioning of pigeons, human rote-verbal learning experiments, and experiments in classical conditioning dominate the pages of the Journal of Experimental Psychology during that earlier period. In the later period, the focus on learning is replaced by a concern with performance, from the simplest reaction-time tasks to the most complex tasks of solving problems, recalling information from memory and understanding language.

Within the past 3 to 5 years, two developments have conspired to bring about an accelerating revival of research on learning processes as distinguished from performance processes. First, the study of performance has progressed to the point where we now have a good understanding of the cognitive skills that are required (at both novice and expert levels) in a considerable range of difficult cognitive tasks. This repertory of analyzed performance programs instructs us about the final products of the learning process, the targets at which learning must aim.

Second, new ideas have emerged about the nature and organization of learning processes. Perhaps the most important of these ideas is the *adaptive production system,* first demonstrated by Waterman (1970) in a dissertation describing a poker-playing system that was capable of improving its game.

Is there reason to think that the revival of learning research is more than a passing fad? Why has psychology exhibited such fascination with the phenomena of learning? Historically, there appear to have been two principal reasons for this preoccupation: one theoretical, the other practical. Psychology has only recently lost its close bonds with philosophy. A central question of epistemology is how we come to know the external world. Translated into psychological terms, this becomes a question of how we perceive and how we learn. One has only to go back to John Locke to see the common ancestry of the two disciplines, and it is still quite visible in William James' *Principles*.

On the applied side, education has always been one of the principal domains of practical use for psychological knowledge. Educational institutions, although they are demonstrably successful in imparting skills and knowledge, have had to proceed (as nineteenth century medicine did) by rule of thumb, and without any deep understanding of the learning processes they seek to nurture. If a genuine theory existed of how people learn, it would hold out great promise of marked improvements in educational practices.

The Search for Invariants

The reasons just stated for psychology's interest in learning are as valid today as they ever were. But another reason, as important as these two, can be added. The goal of cognitive psychology is to understand the workings of the human mind. The mind is an adaptive system whose biological function is to enable the organism to behave effectively and, hence, to survive in a complex, changing, and often unpredictable environment. Adaptation takes place on several different time scales. On the shortest time scale, each problem that the environment presents to the organism challenges its adaptive capacity; that is to say, problem solving and other performance skills are the most immediate adaptive mechanisms. On the longest time scale, the biological evolution of the genotype is the adaptive mechanism. Between the rapid processes of problem solving and the slow processes of evolution lie learning processes that gradually bring about improvements in the organism's performance programs on an intermediate time scale.

A difficult problem arises for psychology, because knowledge and strategies are not fixed but are modifiable through learning. Science searches for laws, for invariant regularities of behavior. In the presence of learning mechanisms, knowledge and strategies are not invariants of the mind but are highly malleable. Hence, the description of performance programs, however useful and essential that may be for psychology, will not achieve the goal of describing the human mind in an invariant way. A theory of learning may supply the desired invariants. John Stuart Mill (1950) put the matter this way:

> In other words, mankind have not one universal character, but there exist universal laws of the formation of character. And since it is by these laws, combined with the facts of each particular case, that the whole of the phenomena of human action and feeling are produced, it is on these that every rational attempt to construct the science of human nature in the concrete and for practical purposes must proceed [p. 319].

The Search for Generality

During the past quarter century, the history of research in human cognition has closely paralleled the trends in artificial intelligence research. This is not surprising, because psychology has adopted information processing as its central paradigm. Most of the chapters presented in this volume make use of computer simulation as a technique for describing learning mechanisms in a fully operational way and for exploring their performance in complex task environments.

During the decade of the mid 50s to mid 60s there was, in artificial intelligence, a striving toward generality—toward programs capable of performing in a wide range of task environments. The General Problem Solver (Newell, Shaw, & Simon, 1960a) and EPAM (Feigenbaum, 1961) were characteristic products of that decade. In these programs, processes like means–ends analysis and recognition by means of discrimination nets were identified as possible invariants of human cognition.

In this same decade, there was considerable activity directed at developing learning programs, also employing very general mechanisms. Most of this kind of learning research was invested with a "clean slate" viewpoint. It preferred to begin with a system processing no initial knowledge and only very general learning mechanisms, hence to rely on learning as the source of all the system's final intelligence. The research on Perceptrons and other self-organizing networks was typical of this point of view (Rosenblatt, 1958). The results of the research were ultimately rather disappointing, and this line of inquiry has tended to die out.

During the decade from the mid 60s to mid 70s, attention in AI turned to professional-level performance in complex task domains. It was discovered, or rediscovered, that expert performance requires knowledge—large amounts of it—as well as wit. Taking a "knowledge-engineering" point of view, researchers built expert systems (e.g., DENDRAL (Feigenbaum, Buchanan, & Lederberg, 1971), INTERNIST (Pople, 1977), MYCIN (Shortliffe, 1976) in a number of task domains, each system limited strictly to a single domain and each resting solidly on a large data base.

Here was the contingent, learning-dependent character of human behavior exhibited in its starkest form. But even in the specialized expert programs, the general mechanisms, the invariants that had been discovered in the first decade, survived, for the large knowledge bases possessed by these programs had to be searched in intelligent fashion. Mechanisms like means–ends analysis and discrimination nets served in the expert programs as principal components of the control structure that guided search through the data bases.

Nevertheless, the proliferation of task-specialized programs during the second decade produced a certain amount of malaise. It seemed to imply that cognitive psychology was almost indistinguishable from an enormous encyclopedia of human knowledge and human skills, and hence was totally contingent on the change and growth of knowledge and its selective allocation to specialized human crania. That the knowledge-based systems required some common core of control structure was only a partial comfort and went only a part of the distance toward providing general, invariant, and parsimonious psychological principles.

Scope of this Chapter

The search for generality and invariance, together with the opportunity provided by the discovery of adaptive production systems, provides the background for the present decade's renewed interest in research on learning, and specifically for the chapters that have been presented in this volume. In a description of the learning process, we look for a new set of invariants to be adjoined to those of the first decade—invariants that will characterize human cognition even when that cognition applies itself to the almost limitless range of specialized tasks that humans are capable of learning to perform.

In this final chapter, it is not our intention to provide a detailed critique of the excellent chapters that have been presented in this volume (nor was that part of our bargain with the chairman), but rather to assess their common conceptual background—the *Zeitgeist* that we have just been describing. In order to do this, we need to say something about the characteristics that a scientific explanation should possess and to make some hypotheses about the multiplicity of learning mechanisms we should expect to find in a system as complex as the human cognitive system. These considerations lead us to ask whether there exist general principles of learning and whether these principles are fully invariant. Our conclusion that they are not leads us, finally, to the topic of learning to learn.

CHARACTERISTICS OF A GOOD EXPLANATION

In addition to stating an invariance, there are at least four additional criteria that a scientific explanation should satisfy: (1) it should explain a variety of phenomena; (2) it should be more basic than the phenomena it explains; (3) it should be simpler than those phenomena; and (4) it should be free of ad hoc components. In the following sections we discuss each of these criteria in turn, along with their implications for theories of learning.

Scope of Explanation

An explanation should summarize and predict data, empirical generalizations, or lower-level laws. The more of these it explains, the better; also, the more diverse the phenomena it explains, the better. A theory that explains only a single empirical law holds no advantage over the law itself.

The classical example of an explanation of broad scope is the law of universal gravitation, which provides a unified explanation for Kepler's laws of the planetary movements, Galileo's law of falling bodies, and the phenomenon of the ocean tides. We would presumably be satisfied with a little less generality than that in a learning theory, but we would be less happy with a system that, while purporting to produce learning about some specific task, itself used knowledge that was obviously specific to the task in question.

For example, we know that the first language a person learns is determined by the language he hears as a child. Thus, a theory of first language acquisition should account for the learning of Finnish and Hopi, as well as for the learning of English. Although an adaptive production system that could learn any Indo–European language would be impressive, we would be even more impressed by one that could learn Finno–Ugric tongues as well.

The proceduralization and composition processes discussed in this volume by Neves and Anderson and by Lewis are good examples of explanations of wide scope. These mechanisms are applicable to any domain in which behavior can be described as a production system (not a small set). Moreover, the composition process alone can account for four diverse phenomena: the speeding up of behavior, acquiring the ability to search in parallel, the loss of intermediate results, and Einstellung. In addition, Anderson has noted (personal communication) that, because composition leads to a reduction in memory load, it can enable behavior that had been impossible earlier because of short-term memory limitations.

Thus, learning mechanisms can be far more general than the knowledge or skills that are learned with their aid in any particular domain. In the chapters of this volume, essentially the same mechanisms show up repeatedly in such domains as geometry, physics, and programming. Learning theories are generally superior to theories of task performance on the criterion of scope of explanation and promise us some of the generality we were in danger of losing with the elaboration of specific individual theories for individual task domains.

Depth of Explanation

A good explanation should be more basic than the phenomena it explains and should not contain important aspects of those phenomena. We regard the law of gravitation as deep, because it derives the orbits of the planets from postulates about how their mutual attractions produce their accelerations—a distinctly non-trivial connection. At the other extreme, explaining a flower's odor by hypothesizing that its atoms have that odor would not be regarded as basic. (It would not even be true, but if true, still not a genuine explanation.) Nor would we accept an explanation of perceptual phenomena that postulated a homunculus inside the head to interpret the information presented by the retina.

A theory of rote memory that simply postulated that stimulus material was stored verbatim in long-term memory would be regarded as providing an exceedingly shallow explanation of learning—if, indeed, we were willing to regard it as an explanation at all. Moreover, such a theory would not predict any of the empirical phenomena of learning other than the simple fact that memory exists, and information can sometimes be transfered to it.

On the other hand, a learning mechanism that took natural language statements as its inputs and produced procedures as its outputs could lay claim to being a relatively deep explanation of the sources of the skills represented by the procedures. (Whether it would be an empirically *valid* explanation of particular phenomena is a separate question.) Although the physics and geometry programs that have been discussed in this volume do not start with natural language, they do convert information from declarative to procedural mode and hence qualify as reasonably deep theories.

One common cause of shallowness in explanations is that too much knowledge (e.g., subject-matter knowledge) is built into them. Fortunately, such built-in knowledge may be detected quite easily by testing a model in different domains. If a theory that purports to explain the learning of language assumes a particular fixed word order, its shallowness is readily exposed by giving it the task of explaining learning in a language that uses a different word order. This suggests that, usually, shallow explanations will fare poorly on the scope criterion; conversely, narrowness of scope is a signal that domain-dependent knowledge may have been built into a system.

More subtle homunculi may hide in the representation of data that the learning theory assumes is available. Some theories, though incorporating learning mechanisms that are apparently general, may produce learning only if a particular representational scheme is used. Because a very large part of human learning, at least in school subjects, begins with oral or written natural-language input, learning theories that do not accept such input have, to that extent, somewhat less depth than we might wish and also need to be tested for scope.

Shallowness of an explanation may be revealed by the fact that it is too facile—that it describes as simple phenomena that can be shown empirically to be complex. Most adaptive production system models learn too quickly because their transformations are too powerful. In this respect, the mechanisms for generalization, discrimination, and strengthening incorporated by Anderson in the ACT system are more satisfactory, for they require interaction with environmental stimuli over long periods to produce an effective performance system.

In comparison with performance systems, all learning systems introduce at least one more step of indirection between environmental stimuli and successful task performance. Most learning systems inject several such intervening steps. Hence, learning theories meet the depth criterion to a greater degree than do performance theories.

Simplicity of Explanation

Although an explanation need not be simpler than every lower-level law it explains, it should be simpler than the collection of these laws taken together. An adaptive production system for explaining some kind of learning that created fewer new productions than the number of productions it contained would not be regarded as a very helpful explanation of the learning.

Simplicity refers to the explanation itself, not the derivation that takes us along the entire path from explanation to empirical phenomena. Hence, an explanation may be simple, yet deep.

Most adaptive production systems score rather well on the criterion of simplicity. One frequently used strategy in such systems has been called "learning by doing" (Anderson, Greeno, Kline, & Neves, this volume; Anzai & Simon, 1979). Weak general methods are used to perform a task (e.g., solve the Tower of Hanoi puzzle, prove a theorem in geometry). The solution then provides information to the mechanisms for creating new productions that enables them to build more powerful solution procedures, which are usually specific to the task domain. Both the weak general problem-solving methods and the adaptive productions are nearly task independent and relatively simple.

Freedom from Ad Hockery

An explanatory mechanism will often consist of a number of (possibly interacting) components. Whereas not all of the components may be essential for explaining any specific phenomenon, the explanation cannot be regarded as parsimonious unless most components are needed for explaining most of the phenomena. Special-case or ad hoc components should be avoided.

Freedom from ad hockery tends to go with scope of explanation. Conceptually at least, none of the learning theories presented in this volume incorporate ad hoc components, for all are, in principle, capable of being extended to task domains beyond those for which they were specifically designed and would use the same mechanisms in those new task domains.

Summary: Criteria of Explanation

Our survey of the criteria that might be used to evaluate theories of human cognition shows that on all scores, except possibly for simplicity, it is usually easier for learning theories to meet these criteria than performance theories. Human learning programs are more likely to be invariant over time then are performance programs, to apply to wide ranges of tasks instead of to special task domains, to be deep, and to be free from ad hoc mechanisms. Hence, there seems to be a sound basis for the current return to learning as a (if not *the*) central preoccupation of cognitive psychology.

LEARNING IN COMPLEX SYSTEMS

Learning is any process that modifies a system so as to improve, more or less irreversibly, its subsequent performance of the same task or of tasks drawn from the same population. For example, if a person solves the Tower of Hanoi problem twice in a row, requiring less time and/or fewer moves the second time, we would attribute the change to learning. We would also say that learning is taking

place if solution times decrease as a person solves a sequence of different algebraic equations, or if a person proving the second of two theorems proves it more
rapidly than another person who hasn't proved the first.

In understanding a new task, a person stores away information that may show
up as learning in a subsequent situation. After the four-disk Tower of Hanoi
problem has been understood (even if not solved), it does not take as long to
understand the five-disk problem. Here understanding, per se, is not learning,
but the process of understanding may result also in learning. Similarly, although
problem solving is not learning, it may leave behind a learned residuum (e.g., the
problem solution may be remembered and used to help solve another problem).

If a system has many components as the human cognitive system has, there
may be many ways in which it can be modified, each constituting a different
form of learning. Hence, it is more realistic to speak of a theory of learning
mechanisms than a theory of learning. The human performance systems in which
we are interested make use of large knowledge bases and sophisticated strategies,
some of which are specific to particular task domains (e.g., strategies for shifting
gears in an automobile), whereas others are relatively general (e.g., means–ends
analysis and other problem-solving strategies).

Learning may involve modification of any component of the information
processing system, including:

1. Additions to or reorganization of its knowledge base: an associative node-
   link memory organized in schemata.
2. Augmentation of the recognition mechanism, or index, for the knowledge
   base: a discrimination net (EPAM net).
3. Augmentation of search strategies: organized as production systems.
4. Modification of evaluation functions stored in memory and used to guide
   search.
5. (Apparent) augmentation of short-term memory capacity by storing new
   chunks in long-term memory.
6. Augmentation of lexical, syntactic, and semantic knowledge in language-
   processing systems.
7. Enrichment of the representations of information (ways of organizing information) in memory.

Internally, all these changes can take the form of additions to, or alterations
in, data structures or production systems.

The Knowledge Base

The most direct kind of learning is the accumulation of a knowledge base,
declarative in form, which might be acquired, for example, by processing input
in natural language or in the form of list structures. In the chapters of this
volume, several learning processes, including the encoding stage of the learning

described by Neves and Anderson and the remarkable use of mnemonics reported p14 l by Chase and Ericsson, have special relevance for this aspect of learning.

Efforts at modeling the acquisition of knowledge and the use of knowledge in enhancing subsequent performance go back to the beginnings of artificial intelligence and cognitive simulation. The Logic Theorist (LT; Newell & Simon, 1956), the earliest theorem-proving program that used heuristic search, was able to store in memory the theorems it proved and to use them as premises in proving new theorems.

Storing knowledge in usable form is more than rote memory. It requires conversion of the knowledge to a form of data representation that makes the newly stored knowledge available to the problem-solver's processes. In LT, this was accomplished by storing theorems as list structures (alias node-link structures, or schemata), so that axioms and theorems served as inputs to the search processes and were produced again, in exactly the same form, as outputs. With this kind of homogeneity of memory, search programs have a recursive structure. Search processes operate on expressions to produce new expressions, or chunks are combined into new chunks having the same form and the same capabilities for combination.

Recognition Mechanisms

Studies of the skill of chessmasters, and particularly of their prodigious abilities to recognize familiar patterns of pieces, have demonstrated the important role of recognition abilities in expert performance and the vast amount of learning necessary for acquiring these recognition skills. Models of these learning processes date back to the early years of cognitive simulation. The EPAM program postulated mechanisms for growing discrimination nets, employing sequences of feature tests to recognize patterns presented repeatedly as stimuli. Concept attainment programs were constructed by Winston and others that responded to appropriate stimuli by building up trees of tests enabling them to discriminate among familiar classes of objects.

Studies of the differences in method between experts and novices, of which the volume's chapter by Polson, Atwood, Jeffries, and Turner is an excellent example, almost uniformly attest to the importance of recognition in expert performance. Their most expert subject instantly recognized the solution, known to him from the professional literature, of the key subproblem of the complex software design problem they presented to their subjects.

There was little explicit mention of recognition processes in the learning models reported in this volume, but a deeper analysis of the structure of production systems shows that such processes are invariably embedded in them. The condition side of a production is in fact a set of tests that recognizes a situation as appropriate for the execution of that production. Moreover, if the production system is at all large, it is much too time-consuming to search productions sequentially for their applicability. Instead, there are built into such systems automatic processes for "indexing" the productions—(i.e., constructing a hierarchic organization of the tests, so that they can be searched in "twenty-questions" fashion instead of sequentially).

In research on learning, not much attention has yet been given to the nature of the elementary tests or features that are used to build up recognition nets. Certainly the sources of origins of such features are not addressed in any of the chapters that have been presented here—they are simply taken for granted in the conditions that are incorporated in the productions. For example, in the geometry programs, it is assumed that the simulated subject can recognize a triangle or a line segment. All the systems that have been described possess, at the outset, the ability to discriminate among strings of alphabetic characters. Hence, characterization of the elementary features that can be discriminated and explanation of how these features combine into the tests that appear on the condition sides of productions need to be placed on the agenda for research.

Strategies

The central focus of most of the chapters presented in the volume has been upon the learning of problem-solving strategies for specific task domains. It is here that the machinery of adaptive production systems shows itself to best advantage.

As with the acquisition of knowledge bases and recognition capabilities, the acquisition of strategies has a history that predates the current prominence of production systems. At the heart of the General Problem Solver (GPS) is a so-called "table of connections." This table associates with each of the differences between present situation and goal situation that GPS can detect one or more actions that might be relevant for eliminating or reducing that difference. A number of schemes were proposed, but never completely tested, for acquiring the table of connections through learning (Eavarone & Ernst, 1970; Newell, 1963; Newell, Shaw, & Simon, 1960b). Today, we would recognize the differences and actions in the table of connections as the condition and action parts, respectively, of productions.

But real impetus for learning schemes of this kind came with the explicit introduction of production systems and Waterman's initial design of an adaptive production system for learning to play poker (Waterman, 1970). To this were added various ideas for the source of the information the adaptive productions would employ: Neves' (1978) notion, for example, of learning from worked-out textbook examples and Anzai and Simon's (1979) notion of "learning by doing."

In the present volume, systems for learning strategies are proposed in the chapters by Neves and Anderson, by Anderson, Greeno, Kline, and Neves, by Hayes-Roth, Klahr, and Mostow, and by Rumelhart and Norman. The first two of these chapters use explicitly the machinery of adaptive production systems. The volume's chapters demonstrate a high level of activity and considerable success in developing mechanisms for the acquisition of new strategies.

Evaluation Functions

When problem solving is carried out by heuristic search, evaluation functions of some kind are needed to assess the promise of different branches of the search tree, hence to control the continuation of the search. As early as 1959, Arthur Samuel, in his research on checkers programs, showed that a modifiable evaluation function could be a powerful learning mechanism for improving a system's performance. Samuel used weighted linear functions of elementary features to evaluate positions reached in the look-ahead search. On the basis of its playing success or failure, it could change the weights in these functions or even eliminate some of the less useful features and introduce new ones from a predetermined list. This simple learning procedure enabled his program to progress in a few hours' play from novice status to state-championship level.

None of the chapters that have been presented discusses learning by the modification of evaluation functions. Perhaps one reason for this is that the task domains under study—at least geometry and elementary physics—do not call for extensive heuristic search with the construction of large search trees. However, in the chapter by Anderson, Greeno, Kline, and Neves, processes of generalization, discrimination, and strengthening of associations make use of statistical information about success and failure to tune search. Hence, the statistics that are computed may be viewed as implicit evaluation functions.

Chunking: STM

If, as is generally believed, the capacity of STM is limited to a very small number of chunks—perhaps only three or four—then an enlargement of chunk size can increase the informational content of each chunk and consequently ease the restrictions on processing imposed by the STM limits. But enlargement of chunk size entails an elaboration of the discrimination net that indexes information held in long-term memory, for the larger chunks will be more specialized, hence more numerous. Hence, the learning of discriminations should, as John Anderson observed, serve to relieve somewhat the STM bottleneck.

Two chapters here address the chunk-size question. Newell and Rosenbloom try to show how the observed data on gradual and continuing improvement of skills with practice can be explained as a consequence of chunk acquisition. Chase and Ericsson, in interpreting the performance of their mnemonist, propose that the use of schemata already available in LTM as "placeholders" for newly presented information may make it possible to transfer that information very rapidly to LTM and hence to avoid the congestion of STM.

The work of Shiffrin and Dumais, exploring the effects of a variety of variables on the development of automatism in performance, casts additional light on the chunking phenomena, as well as on the process of composition studied by Lewis in previous works, and in this volume by Neves and Anderson.

Language

None of the chapters in the volume has addressed directly the question of how humans acquire language, and particularly their first language. This topic, a central one for both cognitive and developmental psychology, has also been the focus of earlier research. Some years ago, Uhr built a system that was capable of acquiring a simple syntax, and about a decade ago, Siklóssy (1972) built the ZBIE system, which, when presented with a symbolic representation of a simple scene together with a sentence describing that scene, was able to extract syntactic information about natural language from the pairing. Several other language-learning schemes of a similar kind, and of gradually increasing power, have followed.

In these language-learning schemes, it is assumed that the simulated subject is already able to store perceptual information, for example, to store simple structures involving two or three objects and relations among them. Learning language means (at least) acquiring the ability to map appropriate language strings on these perceptual structures, not simply by rote, but in such a way that new combinations of objects and relations can now be described in words. Thus, having learned "bat hits ball," "boy drinks milk," and "man throws brick," such a system should be able to handle "boy throws ball" when presented with the corresponding percept.

Because it has already been accomplished at a simple level, it is clear that relatively simple formalisms are capable of supporting schemes for learning syntax—that is, for learning to map language structures onto perceptual structures, and vice versa. Developing such schemes of progressively greater power should be high on the agenda for research on learning.

Representations

Another centrally important aspect of learning that has been only lightly represented in this volume is the learning of effective representations for handling problems in different task domains. Two of the chapters did, however, have relevance for this topic. The data obtained by Chase and Ericsson provide clear evidence of the stages of development of the schemata their subject used as part of his mnemonic system. The data provide a rather remarkable picture of the gradual growth of a pattern of list structures in long-term memory. The chapter by Rumelhart and Norman gives us a theoretical view of how new schemata can be obtained by borrowing and modification of analogous structures already in memory.

Not many existing systems model the acquisition of new schemes of representation. Perhaps the clearest example is the UNDERSTAND program (Hayes & Simon, 1974), which, given a natural language description of a simple problem or puzzle, creates a representation of the problem space and operators that enables a GPS to go to work on the problem. Given a description of the Tower of

Hanoi problem, for example, UNDERSTAND creates symbolic entities that denote *pegs* and *disks* and a list structure that describes the arrangement of the disks on the pegs. It then constructs a legal move operator that is capable of modifying the list structure by moving disks from one peg to another.

In the case of the Tower of Hanoi, UNDERSTAND represents a single problem. However, the same mechanism can be used to represent a whole class of problems from a domain. Provided with information about *theorems* and *proof steps,* it could construct a simple set of schemata for representing the domain of geometry.

Novak, in his ISAAC program, showed how a set of schemata stored in LTM could be used to guide a system in its understanding of physics (statics) problems. A program like UNDERSTAND (or, more accurately, a more powerful version of it) could be used to create the sorts of schemata that ISAAC employs.

Hence, we would add to our list of items for the agenda of research on learning the study of how representations can be generated from descriptions of tasks in natural language.

ARE THERE GENERAL PRINCIPLES OF LEARNING?

Whatever part of the information-processing system is adaptively modified by learning, certain basic principles define the conditions under which learning can take place and describe some of the concomitant phenomena. Six of the most prominent and central of these are:

1. *Knowledge of results.* The learning mechanism must be able to detect improvement or degradation of the performance system.[1] In the psychological literature, knowledge of results, a cognitive mechanism, is often confounded with reward, a motivational mechanism. The term *reinforcement* embraces both elements. This volume has been primarily concerned with the cognitive aspects of learning and has ignored the motivational (without denying in any way their great importance in human learning).

2. *Generation of alternatives.* The learning mechanism must be able to try alternative behaviors, hence must be able to generate them in some manner unless they are provided by a teacher. One of the best ways to learn is to make mistakes, but errors can produce learning only if new behaviors are then attempted.

3. *Causal attribution.* Learning in a complex system can be efficient only to the extent that good or bad performance can be attributed accurately to specific

---

[1]In some concept attainment and pattern recognition tasks, knowledge of results may be supplied by internal criteria of "goodness" of the pattern description, hence may not require feedback from external sources.

you can debug by replacing parts trying tests etc

No

components of the system. The system can learn from its mistakes only if it can discover the source of its error.

4. *Hindsight.* Knowledge of results *follows* performance. Hence efficient learning will reexamine and reevaluate past performance in terms of subsequent knowledge of results and causal attribution. (The values of hindsight are known to most A students and to few C students.)

5. *Learning from instruction.* A teacher can provide knowledge of results, information to be stored, a sequence of problems or examples, causal attribution, algorithms, and so on, with large effects on what is learned and how fast.

6. *Automatization.* Continued practice of skills that have been learned will cause continuing improvement in speed and accuracy of performance.

The hallmark of theorizing-by-simulating, well illustrated by the chapters of this volume, is that principles of learning are not stated explicitly in classical fashion but are embedded in programs that actually learn. To see what general principles are exemplified by the programs, we must examine and compare program structures and discover the communalities among them.

Knowledge of results, for example, is implicit in any scheme for learning by doing. In such a scheme, problems are first solved by weak methods often involving much trial and error. Once a correct solution path has been discovered (or provided directly by a teacher), knowledge of this path provides the information that an adaptive production system can use to create new productions that will henceforth permit the same or similar problems to be solved more efficiently. Such uses of knowledge of results are illustrated by the programs described by Neves and Anderson, by Anderson, Greeno, Kline, and Neves, by Hayes-Roth, Klahr, and Mostow, and by Larkin. A minimal knowledge of results (illustrated, for example, by LT) is knowledge of the correct answer; for the answer can be added to memory as a starting point for new searches.

a number equation or procedure ?

?

Likewise, all the learning programs described in the volume are capable of *generating alternatives,* primarily in the course of their problem-solving searches. Schemes using analogy, such as the one sketched by Rumelhart and Norman, must have capabilities for modifying schemata that are already available to fit them to new situations.

Brown and de Kleer develop a formal scheme for *causal attribution* that permits complex systems to be analyzed in terms of functional components and their interrelations. In the adaptive production systems, causal attribution is usually implicit. When a new production, $C \rightarrow A$, is constructed by appending an action, A, to the conditions, C (the latter describing the change it produced in some symbolic structure), this conjunction amounts to a tacit assumption that the action was the causal agent for the change.

Hindsight is illustrated by all the programs (e.g., Neves & Anderson, Larkin) that learn by doing or learn from examples. The knowledge of results produced

N either don't resolve old problems do they (with new techniques

by actually working a problem provides the information necessary for acquiring better methods of solution.

The chapter by Hayes-Roth, Klahr, and Mostow explores some of the possibilities of *learning from instruction*—in this case, learning by taking advice. The advantage of instruction, of course, is that a benign environment (the instructor) can provide precisely the information that will facilitate the acquisition of the next increment of skill. In the adaptive production systems, learning from instruction is implicit in the order in which problems are presented to the system. Although this fact is not explicitly demonstrated in the chapters, any such system will learn rapidly or slowly, depending on that order.

IS LEARNING REALLY INVARIANT?

In an earlier section, we asked whether the learning process is one of the invariant components of the human information-processing system. Nothing we have said about learning demonstrates such invariance, and indeed, there is considerable empirical evidence that learning processes can change over time (Harlow, 1949). These *learning to learn* phenomena challenge our thesis that laws of learning can serve as the central invariant core of psychological theory. To assess how gravely the thesis is damaged, it will be helpful to get a clearer picture of the mechanisms that might underlie learning to learn.

We discuss two possible explanations of learning-to-learn phenomena. As the first possibility already alluded to in our discussions of the knowledge base and of chunking, the accumulation of new concepts in memory may speed up the learning process even when the basic learning mechanisms remain unchanged. As the second possibility, we examine some of the ways in which the learning mechanisms could themselves evolve. In both cases, although we draw, for our examples, upon artificial intelligence programs that are primarily concerned with discovery, we see that these programs have much in common with the theories of learning we have been considering. Discovery—acquiring knowledge by putting questions to Nature—is simply the limiting case of learning—acquiring knowledge from all the sources that are available.

Defining New Concepts

Within the past few years, two artificial intelligence systems have been constructed, AM and BACON, that discover new laws and concepts. The two systems handle quite different classes of problems. AM, given an initial stock of mathematical concepts, strives to invent interesting new concepts and to make conjectures about the relations among concepts. BACON (we are concerned here with the version known as BACON.3), given a body of empirical data, strives to find invariant relations among the variables contained in the data set. In spite of this difference in goals, both systems define new concepts in order to represent information parsimoniously, and both use these newly defined concepts recursively in their subsequent discoveries. Thus, by applying the same discovery heuristics again and again, AM and BACON.3 can generate a potentially endless procession of laws and higher-level concepts.

The AM Program.   Three sets of "givens" are provided to AM (Lenat, 1977): a set of criteria for judging how "interesting" a concept or conjecture is, a set of heuristics to guide the search for interesting concepts and conjectures, and a core of basic knowledge about some domain of mathematics. The first two of these three classes of "givens" are part of the structure of AM; the third is particular to each task domain.

A few examples will illustrate their flavor. A concept is interesting if it is closely related to other concepts that have already been found to be interesting. It is interesting if examples that satisfy it can be found, but such examples are not too easily found. A conjecture is interesting if it has strong consequences. The search heuristics suggest generalizing a concept when it is too hard to find examples, but specializing it when it is too easy. Limiting cases of concepts deserve special attention.

There are several hundred such criteria and search heuristics in AM. The system operates by best-first search through the space of concepts and conjectures, using the interest criteria to guide the search and the search heuristics to generate new alternatives.

When AM was provided with the basic ideas of set theory (the concept of set, union and intersection of sets, and so on), it generated, in the course of a couple of hours of computer time, the concepts of the integers, of the operations of addition, subtraction, multiplication, and division on the integers, of factors of an integer, of prime numbers, and many others. It conjectured that any integer can be represented uniquely as a product of powers of primes (the so-called Fundamental Theorem of Arithmetic), and that any even integer can be represented as a sum of two primes (Goldbach's conjecture).

None of this was new to mathematics, but all of it was new to AM—the program had no access to the relevant mathematical literature. Nor was it given any indication of its targets—of what concepts to search for. It operated entirely on the basis of a forward search, guided in the manner that has already been described.

What is of particular interest for our discussion here is that each step AM takes—each new concept or conjecture it reaches—makes still other concepts and conjectures attainable that were not so before. In this sense, AM can be said to "learn to learn." A little later, we will mention a proposed extension to AM that would reduce still further its invariant core in relation to those of its components that are subject to modification.

The BACON.3 Program. The way in which BACON.3 (Langley, 1979) extracts laws from data can be illustrated with an actual example of its work: the (re)discovery of Kepler's Third Law of planetary motion. The law states that the period of revolution of a planet about the sun varies as the 3/2 power of its distance from the sun. In this case, BACON.3 is provided with two independent variables—the *orbiting body* and the *central body,* and two dependent terms— the mean *distance d* between the two objects and the *period p* of revolution. At the outset, the program gathers data about the planets' orbits about the sun: the *central body* is the *sun,* whereas the *orbiting body* takes on values like *Mercury, Venus, Earth,* and so forth.

BACON.3 examines its data to see whether either of the variables, p or d, varies monotonically (directly or inversely) with the other. In the present case, d increases as p increases. Cued by this regularity, BACON.3 computes d/p to see if it is constant. It is not but does vary monotonically with d, motivating BACON.3 to consider the new ratio d^2/p and finally d^3/p^2.

Because this last term has a constant value whenever the *central body* is the *sun,* BACON.3 formulates an hypothesis to this effect. At this point, the program makes another series of observations in which the *central body* is *Jupiter,* and the orbiting bodies are that planet's satellites. However, instead of retracing its earlier path, BACON.3 simply recalculates the values of the terms d/p, d^2/p, and d^3/p^2. The last of these is again constant, though with a different constant than in the earlier situation.

Thus, the system arrives at an equivalent law for Jupiter much more rapidly than it did for the sun. It can do this because it applies its discovery heuristics to higher-level terms it had defined earlier. Although BACON.3's learning rules did not change, they *appeared* to become more efficient because they already had a useful representation to operate on. Perhaps all learning-to-learn phenomena can be explained through similar recursive mechanisms.

Learning to Learn

An alternative to the previous approach assumes that the learning process actually changes over time. Then the learning-to-learn mechanisms would replace the learning processes as the ultimate cognitive invariant. However, this scheme introduces another layer to the basic architecture, a complexity one would like to avoid. And inevitably, someone would soon suggest that even the learning-to-learn process is not *really* invariant and would propose yet another layer.

Fortunately, there is a third approach that bypasses this infinite regress of learning processes. Assume that the system starts with a few weak but general learning mechanisms, but with an important difference. These heuristics can be used to learn in the standard sense, but they can also be applied to one another. Thus, a heuristic for creating discriminant rules might act upon a generalization heuristic to create a more powerful domain-specific generalization heuristic. In this scheme, the learning heuristics are *identical with* the learning-to-learn heuristics, because they can act upon each other and upon themselves.

This perspective suggests an explanation for the common distinction between conscious and automatic learning. A number of chapters in this volume have explained automatization through a composition process in which condition-action rules are combined. If one assumes that all learning is initially slow and deliberate but that it is possible to learn to learn, then one can imagine the composition process leading to faster and more automatic versions of these learning techniques. Thus, automatic learning occurs when the learning heuristics in use have been sufficiently practiced, whereas conscious learning occurs when less familiar learning rules are used.

Lenat and Harris (1977) have proposed an extension to the AM system that would let it modify its own learning heuristics. AM represented its learning heuristics in one form and the concepts resulting from those heuristics in a different form. The new system would represent both concepts and heuristics in the same format. This would allow heuristics to apply to each other (and to themselves) as easily as to nonheuristic concepts. Such an approach should allow learning to learn to occur without postulating a separate set of mechanisms for that purpose.

A RESEARCH STRATEGY

We have proposed two alternate explanations of learning to learn phenomena, but we have made no claims as to which (if either) is correct. Whatever may be the mechanism for learning to learn, *assuming learning is invariant* is a useful research strategy for the immediate future. If learning is invariant and learning to learn is an artifact resulting from concept formation, then this strategy needs no justification. But even if learning to learn is a reality and the learning mechanisms evolve, they must do so at a much slower rate than do performance procedures. Because the learning-to-learn mechanism must take information about the learning of standard procedures as its data, normal learning must be repeated a large number of times before the learning process can modify itself by observing the outcomes.

Hence, we can expect learning to be invariant in the short run, and laws of learning to be close approximations to the cognitive invariants we are seeking. Because physics has taught us many times that approximate laws may be very useful, and because the laws that appear to be best confirmed are often only approximate, it should cause no great concern to find ourselves in the same plight. Learning theory does indeed have a central role to play in formulating parsimonious, nearly invariant laws of cognition.

ACKNOWLEDGMENTS

This research was supported by Research Grant MH-07722 from the National Institute of Mental Health and Grants SPI-7914852 and IST-7918266 from the National Science Foundation.

REFERENCES

Anzai, Y., & Simon, H. A. The theory of learning by doing. *Psychological Review*, 1979, *86*(2), 124–140.

Eavarone, D. S., & Ernst, G. W. A program that discovers good difference orderings and tables of connections for GPS. *Proceedings of the 1970 IEEE Systems Science and Cybernetics Conference*, N.Y.: IEER, 1970, 226–33.

Feigenbaum, E. A. The simulation of verbal learning behavior. *Proceedings of the Western Joint Computer Conference*, 1961, 121–132.

Feigenbaum, E. A., Buchanan, B. G., & Lederberg, J. On generality and problem solving: A case study using the DENDRAL program. *Machine Intelligence 6*. Edinburgh: Edinburgh University Press, 1971.

Harlow, H. F. The formation of learning sets. *Psychological Review*, 1949, *56*, 51–65.

Hayes, J. R., & Simon, H. A. Understanding written problem instructions. In L. W. Gregg (Ed.), *Knowledge and cognition*. Potomac, MD: Lawrence Erlbaum Associates, 1974.

Langley, P. Rediscovering physics with BACON.3. *Proceedings of the Sixth International Joint Conference on Artificial Intelligence*, 1979, 505–507.

Lenat, D. B. Automated theory formation in mathematics. *Proceedings of the Fifth International Joint Conference on Artificial Intelligence*, 1977, 833–842.

Lenat, D. B., & Harris, G. Designing a rule system that searches for scientific discoveries. In *Proceedings of the Workshop on Pattern-Directed Inference Systems, SIGART Newsletter*, 1977, 63.

Mill, J. S. A system of logic. Reprinted in E. Nagel (Ed.), *John Stuart Mill's philosophy of scientific method*. New York: Hafner Publishing Co., 1950.

Neves, D. M. A computer program that learns algebraic procedures by examining examples and working problems in a textbook. *Proceedings of the Second National Conference of the Canadian Society for Computational Studies of Intelligence*, 1978, 191–195.

Newell, A. Learning, generality, and problem solving. *Proceedings of the IFIP Congress, 62*. Amsterdam: North-Holland Publishing Company, 1963, 407–12.

Newell, A., Shaw, J. C., & Simon, H. A. Report on a general problem-solving program for a computer. *Information Processing: Proceedings of the International Conference on Information Processing*. Paris: UNESCO, 1960, 256–64. a.

Newell, A., Shaw, J. C., & Simon, H. A. A variety of intelligent learning in a general problem solver. In M. C. Yovits & S. Cameron (Eds.), *Self-organizing systems: Proceedings of an interdisciplinary conference*. New York: Pergamon Press, 1960. b.

Newell, A., & Simon, H. A. The logic theory machine: A complex information processing system. *IRE Transactions on Information Theory*, 1956, *IT-2*(3), 61–79.

Pople, H. The formation of composite hypotheses in diagnostic problem solving. *Proceedings of the Fifth International Joint Conference on Artificial Intelligence*, 1977, 1030–37.

Rosenblatt, F. The perceptron: A probabilistic model for information storage and organization in the brain. *Psychological Review*, 1958, *65*, 386–407.

Samuel, A. L. Some studies in machine learning using the game of checkers. *IBM Journal of Research and Development*, 1959, *3*, 210–29.

Shortliffe, E. *Computer-based medical consultations: MYCIN*. New York: Elsevier, 1976.

Siklóssy, L. Natural language learning by computer. In H. A. Simon & L. Siklossy (Eds.), *Representation and meaning*. Englewood Cliffs, N.J.: Prentice-Hall, 1972.

Waterman, D. Generalization learning techniques for automating the learning of heuristics. *Artificial Intelligence*, 1970, *1*, 121–70.

Author Index

Numbers in *italics* indicate pages with complete bibliographic information.

A

Aho, A. V., 274, *282*
Allen, J., 237, *253*
Anderson, J. R., 4, 10, 11, 12, 25, *53, 54,* 61, 62, 65, *83,* 161, 163, *187,* 191, 224, 225, *229,* 323, *334*
Anzai, Y., 367, 370, *379*
Atkinson, R. C., 112, *139*
Atwood, M. E., 175, *188,* 269, *282*

B

Bachelder, B. L., 141, *187*
Baddeley, A. D., 157, 176, 187, *187*
Balzer, R., 236, 238, *253,* 258, *282*
Baron, J., 2, *54*
Barr, A., 235, *253*
Barstow, D. R., 238, *253,* 258, *282*
Beasley, C. M., 62, 65, *83,* 191, 224, *229*
Bennett, J., 235, *253*
Bernard, J. E., 87, 89, *110*
Bhaskar, R., 260, *282,* 311, *334*
Biermann, A. W., 257, 258, *282*
Blaha, J., 79, *83*
Bobrow, D. G., 163, 186, *189,* 207, *229,* 335, *359*
Boehm, B. W., 257, *282*

Book, W. F., 220, *229*
Bott, R. A., 351, *359*
Bower, G. H., 50, *53,* 142, 160, 163, *187*
Boyer, R. S., 274, *282*
Bransford, J. D., 163, *189*
Briggs, G. E., 79, *83*
Broadbent, D. A., 159, *187*
Broadbent, D. E., 118, *139*
Brown, J. S., 141, *188,* 287, *309*
Bryan, W. L., 142, *188*
Buchanan, B. G., 363, *379*
Budiansky, J., 112, *140*
Bundy, A., 86, *110*
Burge, J., 235, 236, *253*
Burr, B., 4, 8, 9, 25, *53*
Burton, R., 287, *309*

C

Caharack, G., 111, 118, 119, 123, 128, *139*
Calfee, R. C., 2, *53*
Card, S. K., 3, 4, 8, 9, 12, 25, *53*
Carry, L. R., 87, 89, *110*
Chaiklin, S., 191, 193, *229*
Charness, N., 157, 177, *188*
Chase, W. G., 50, *53,* 142, 159, 163, 177, *188,* 228, *229*

Subject Index

A

Active semantic nets, 342–357
Advice taking, 231–253, 375
  operationalization, 237–243
  representation of advice, 235–237
Algebra, 85–110
  combined operations, 96–106
  novice-expert contrasts, 88–98, 106–110
Analogy, 200–203, 222, 264, 335–358
  in learning a text editor, 350–357
  learning new schemata by analogy with old,
    343–358
  See also Subsumption
Automaticity
  composition and proceduralization, 78–82
  controlled vs. automatic processing, 111–139
  definition of automatism, 115–125
  development, 125–138

B,C,D

Backward inferences. *See* Working backwards
Capacity limitations. *See* Automaticity
Causal models. *See* Mental models
Chunking
  power law, 40–51
  See also Composition
Combined operation, 96–106
Composition, 67–71, 217–218, 225–226, 235–
  237, 323

combined operations, 102–104
  See also Chunking
Controlled processing. *See* Automaticity
Declarative representations, 60–65, 200–205,
  214–217, 232, 335–343, 368–369
  See also Active semantic nets; Semantic nets
Digit span. *See* Memory span
Discrimination, 224–225
Discrimination nets, 164–168, 369–370

E,F,G

Einstellung, 72–73
Expert behavior. *See* Novice-expert contrasts
Explanation (scientific), 364–367
Forward inferences. *See* Working forward
Generalization, 222–223
Geometry, 57–84, 191–229, 312–313
  proof generation, 192–200
  reason-giving, 58–59

H,I,J,K

Historical view of learning, 361–367
Intermediate memory, 168–186
Interpretive application of knowledge, 63–65,
  203–205, 215–217
  See also Operationalization